Macro Social Theory

Frank W. Elwell
With a forward by Davis D. Joyce

Elwell, Frank W.
Macro Social Theory | Frank W. Elwell
with a foreword by Davis D. Joyce

Books by Frank W. Elwell

Technique and Control: Jacques Ellul's Sociology (2025)

Macro Social Theory (2014/2025)

Karl Marx: A Reference Guide to His Life and Works with Brian Andrews & Kenneth E. Hicks (2021)

Sociocultural Systems: Principles of Structure and Change (2013)

Macro Social Theory (2010) previously published as Macrosociology: The Study of Sociocultural Systems (2009)

Macrosociology: Four Modern Theorists (2006)

A Commentary on Malthus' 1798 Essay on Population as Social Theory (2001)

Industrializing America: Understanding Contemporary Society through Classical Sociological Analysis (1999)

The Evolution of the Future (1991)

For Students of Sociology

I believe that what may be called classic social analysis is a definable and usable set of traditions; that its essential feature is the concern with historical social structures; and that its problems are of direct relevance to urgent public issues and insistent human troubles. □I also believe that there are now great obstacles in the way of this tradition's continuing--both within the social sciences and in their academic and political settings--but that nevertheless the qualities of mind that constitute it are becoming a common denominator of our general cultural life and that, however vaguely and in however a confusing variety of disguises, they are coming to be felt as a need.

--C. Wright Mills, 1959

Table of Contents

Acknowledgements

I thank several people who have helped me directly with this revised edition. This includes Drs. Davis Joyce and Jeff Gentry who continued to provide moral support through the first edition as well as the third. I also need to thank my colleagues at Rogers State University, especially Christi Mackey, Brian Andrews, Lorie O'Malley, Mary Millikin, and Rebekah Chamberlain (who helped me through a knotty formatting problem). In addition, Zion Solomon provided questions and comments throughout the process of revision and provided some copyediting as well. Finally, I thank my family—Hazel and the girls—for allowing me the time and focus to work on this edition. I thank all who had a hand in this book, though I take full responsibility.

Foreword

As a historian, my favorite approach was always historiography, defined as the study of historians and their interpretations of history. I am reminded of this approach by Frank W. Elwell's work here, for he focuses on telling us about the work of a number of different important sociological theorists, past and present. One, more specific, example of the similarity is in my work on the radical activist historian Howard Zinn, and Elwell's chapter on "John Bellamy Foster's Ecological-Marxism." Here the relationship is not just one of approach, but also content–Foster and Zinn must have been reading each other's books. Elwell is also deeply sensitive to the contribution the social sciences might make, should make, beyond the academic world; he speaks of providing people "with the tools necessary to achieve a more just and egalitarian world."

One thing I learned in trying to take the historiographical approach with students was that the individual approach worked best, that students might be more likely to get interested if I was talking about Howard Zinn himself, including a bit about him personally, rather than just plunging directly into his theories/interpretations. Perhaps that is part of why this work by Elwell has such a chance of being well received by students. But it's more than that: Elwell writes well, in a style that should be accessible/comprehensible to serious students and the interested general reader as well. The relationship between history and sociology is interesting in a broader way, as well. Especially macrosociology, defined here as "the study of large-scale social patterns." Elwell continues: "Closely related to history and anthropology, it focuses upon total societies and their constituent parts, such as economic and political structures, family and religious institutions, and how these institutions interrelate with one another and with the whole." Sounds a lot like history to me–especially since the "new social history" of the 1960s and after transformed the discipline to be more inclusive than its traditional political/diplomatic/economic focus. One of the outstanding radical historians of the 60s, Stoughton Lynd, went so far as to say that history and sociology "are not concerned with different objects; they are different ways of looking at the same object." Says Elwell: "A related concern of the field [i. e., macrosociology] is how sociocultural systems maintain themselves, and how they change over time." Change over time–a central concern of historians.

I like that Elwell's approach seems to have multi-disciplinary/ interdisciplinary implications. He notes that Immanuel Wallerstein went so far as to call for a "unidisciplinary" approach involving all the social sciences, erasing the traditional specializations of economics, political science, sociology, anthropology, and history.

Another area I've worked in as a historian is environmental history–the study of the human relationship with the environment, their use (and abuse) of natural resources, etc. Especially Elwell's treatment of Gerhard Lenski's "ecological-evolutionary theory" resonated with me here. (It is also noted that Lenski considered history a foundation of his sociology.)

It occurred to me in reading Elwell's excellent overview of the theories of Karl Marx that one thing it might help students do is get over the tendency to react in a predictable knee-jerk negative way to things they really know little to nothing about–such as Marx, and socialism.

I could carry on at great length. But I won't. What you need to do is get started reading Elwell. His chapter on "Neal Postman's Technological Determinism" was revelatory to me since I went in, I confess, not knowing about Postman at all. But I understood it, enjoyed it, and learned from it. So, I suggest, can you. New technology, Postman insists, is making history. But he is not necessarily positive about all technological developments. Indeed, he seems to suggest that the printed medium is superior to television, for example. And he's right. This book is better than anything you can see on TV!

Dr. Davis D. Joyce

Davis D. Joyce is Professor Emeritus of History at East Central University in Ada, Oklahoma, and is author of Howard Zinn: A Radical American Vision, and numerous books on Oklahoma and United States History.

Introduction to the Third Edition

I am pleased to present the third edition of "Macro Social Theory," an endeavor that not only builds upon the strengths of the original work but also incorporates two new chapters dedicated to additional explorations of the rationalization process first described by Max Weber. The first addition is a chapter on the influential sociologist, C. Wright Mills. By introducing Mills into the discourse, this edition brings forth fresh perspectives and insightful ideas that enrich the sociological landscape. The second addition is more unconventional, Roderick Seidenberg was an architect and a keen social observer who wrote in the mid-twentieth century about the increasing dominance of rational social organization over the thoughts and actions of individuals, mirroring Weber's rationalization theory and positing its continuance into the indefinite future.

The primary goal of this edition is to provide students and readers with easy access to the ideas of the founding figures in sociology, while also integrating contemporary expressions of that theory to reflect the ever-evolving nature of our society. In shaping this edition, I have taken into consideration the invaluable feedback received from students and professionals who found the original text to be a valuable resource.

Furthermore, the book has been rewritten to ensure a seamless and comprehensive reading experience, emphasizing the common themes of macro social theory. My aim is to make the complex theories and concepts of macro social theory more approachable, engaging, and relevant to the sociological landscape of today. By weaving together the foundational principles of sociology with the contemporary expressions of social theory, I provide readers with a holistic understanding of both the historical and current sociological frameworks.

I am grateful to the publisher of the original work for granting permission to offer this edition in a relatively inexpensive format. My intention is to make this knowledge accessible to students and anyone interested in gaining deeper insights into how professional sociologists perceive modern society and the trajectory of social evolution. I firmly believe that macro social theory, when properly cast and understood, holds great relevance for comprehending our social world and the direction of sociocultural change. This is more a labor of love than of commerce or even of professional prestige.

The ancient Chinese curse of "May you live in interesting times" seems to be our lot. There are several interrelated threads running through our timeline that began intensifying in the mid-nineteenth century: the rise of capitalism, intensifying technological innovation, organizational enlargement and centralization, rationalization, polarization, rise of fascism, nuclear proliferation, decline of primary groups, and environmental destruction. It is no wonder that apocalyptic dystopian literature has become a major genre in the modern era. Macro Sociology is focused on describing this social-evolutionary trajectory, as well as devising strategies to create a better future for all.

I sincerely hope that this revised edition serves as a valuable tool for students, scholars, and individuals who are curious about the intricate workings of our social world. May it inspire critical thinking, encourage lively discussions, and foster a deeper understanding of the dynamics that shape our societies.

Thank you for embarking on this journey of exploration and discovery with me.

Frank W. Elwell | April 2025

Introduction: The Classical View of Sociocultural Systems

Though limited, the diversity in human social life is noteworthy. Societies range from simple hunting and gathering groups with little division of labor, simple technology, and a handful of people to overly complex hyper-industrial societies with thousands of specialized jobs, sophisticated technology relying upon advanced physics, chemistry, and biology, and millions of people. Economic systems range from communal to socialistic to capitalistic, political systems from totalitarian to representative democracy to pure democracy. Variety also exists in marriage forms, sex roles, occupational specializations, cultural values, beliefs, and norms. However, upon reflection, the common characteristics among human societies are also worthy of note. All rely on technology to manipulate their environments for food and other necessities. All have some form of distribution systems to allocate goods and services (though these vary in the degree of inequality of this distribution), and all have forms of marriage and family, religious belief and ritual, ideologies and values.

Another noteworthy feature of social life is how societies exhibit stability and change. Why are societies similar in certain broad respects? Why do they differ in important ways? Why do some change with great magnitude and speed while others change so little and so slowly? What accounts for the differences in these social phenomena? Furthermore, how do these social phenomena affect human behavior and thought? These are the central focus of this book; they are the central questions of sociology.

Sociology studies human social life—the regular patterns of human behavior and thought. Our primary focus is on behavior and thought that is common among people by virtue of their membership within a group or a particular sociocultural system. The field of sociology can be broadly split into two categories. Microsociology focuses on small-scale social groups and processes. This field is focused on such phenomena as face-to-face interaction (say classroom behavior), children's socialization, or a particular group's influence on the political behavior of its membership. As seen from our introductory texts, microsociology increasingly dominates the field of sociology. The field increasingly emphasizes micro because it resonates with Americans, who tend to be very much oriented to the individual.

Consequently, they find microsociology much easier to grasp and apply daily, and we need students. Macrosociology, however, is the study of large-scale social patterns. Closely related to history and anthropology, it focuses on whole societies and their constituent parts, such as economic and political structures, family and religious institutions, and how they interrelate with one another and the whole. A related concern of the field is how sociocultural systems maintain themselves and how they change over time. The micro/macro distinction is present in all the social sciences of economics, anthropology, sociology, political science, and history. A sociologist within the macro level of analysis may have far more in common with an anthropologist working within that tradition than with her fellow sociologists working within the micro tradition. Immanuel Wallerstein believes that micro/macro is the only distinction within the social sciences that has use and relevance.

This book is exclusively concerned with macro social theory. It is devoted to systematically examining the significant similarities and differences among societies, the nature of sociocultural change, and stability. It is intended to introduce students to the classical social theory of T. Robert Malthus, Karl Marx, Emile Durkheim, and Max Weber, and the modern expressions of these perspectives. It does this through two mechanisms. First, it provides an overview and critique of sociology's four major classical theoretical traditions. Rather than discussing these theories as history, the book will focus on elements of the perspectives that have proved most helpful in understanding sociocultural systems. Then, the book will provide an overview and critique of the perspective and analyses of three contemporary social scientists writing within each of these traditions. The book's overarching goal is to provide students with an in-depth understanding of classical sociological traditions and their usefulness in understanding contemporary societies. By studying contemporary social scientists such as Lenski, Foster, Nisbet, and Elias, students will appreciate the breadth and depth of social theory and its usefulness in understanding contemporary and historical sociocultural systems.

The inclusion of Marx, Durkheim, and Weber follows the standard sociological treatment of the influence of these titans on modern social thought. This book will break new ground by claiming Malthus as a founder of one of four classical macro theories, that of social evolution. The evolutionary perspective fell out of favor in the social sciences in the first half of the nineteenth century but is currently experiencing a revival. Many credit Spencer as the founder of the perspective—placing him just under the big three of Marx, Durkheim, and Weber in the sociological pantheon. As demonstrated in Part 4 of this book, this place of honor belongs to Malthus.

Each classical theorist is a founder of a distinct macro theoretical tradition. These traditions can be distinguished in the modern era by the prime determinant of sociocultural stability and change in their theoretical systems. For Malthus, that prime determinant was population and production; for Marx, it was capitalism; for Durkheim, the division of labor and anomie; and for Weber, bureaucracy, and the rationalization process. The contemporary theorists covered represent different directions or emphases taken within each tradition. Writing in the tradition of Marx, we will look at the social theory of Harry Braverman, who focuses on work in modern capitalist societies. Furthermore, John Bellamy Foster applies Marx's ecology to the contemporary world and examines capitalism's role in American imperialism.

Durkheim's is the most ignored of sociological traditions today. While many sociologists give him lip service as one of the discipline's founders and structural-functional theory, very few now write in this tradition—though the few that do amply illustrate its power. The first modern sociologist within the Durkheimian tradition dealt with in this book is Stjepan Mestrovic, a sociologist who claims Durkheim is central to understanding our modern world. We then turn to the sociology of Robert K. Merton, a representative of the older structural-functionalist tradition. We will examine the social theory of Robert Nisbet, who shares Durkheim's concerns about the erosion of intermediate institutions that provide a cushioning effect between individuals and the state. Finally, we look at the work of Neil Postman, a Communications theorist, and social critic who aptly illustrates the power of many of Durkheim's insights in understanding modern sociocultural systems.

We then turn to the Weberian tradition. The modern sociologists used to illustrate the power and scope of this classical tradition are C. Wright Mills, writing of centralization, bureaucracy, and power in American society. Norbert Elias writes extensively about the rise of the state and the civilizing process (a variant of rationalization). Finally, George Ritzer writes of modern-day rationalization, bureaucratization, and disenchantment.

Finally, writing in the tradition of Malthus is Ester Boserup, an economist who looked at prehistoric and contemporary agricultural societies relying heavily upon Malthusian theory. Gerhard Lenski was the first modern sociologist to advocate and systematically apply an ecological-evolutionary perspective, and Stephen Sanderson, whose contemporary writings are firmly within this tradition.

The social scientists who illustrate the different perspectives were not chosen because they are all great theorists (though some are). Instead, they were chosen because they explicitly apply many elements of classical theory, aiding students in understanding and appreciating that theory and sociocultural systems themselves. Braverman, Wallerstein, and Foster do Marx better than Marx does Marx. One can get the richness of Weber's perspective across to students by examining his influence on such exciting contemporary figures as Mills, Elias, and Ritzer. By examining the theory of Mestrovic, Merton, and Nisbet, one can make Durkheim's theories about the division of labor and anomie evident and relevant in today's world. One can demonstrate that the sociological perspective is indispensable in understanding the social world by examining classical theory as updated and used by contemporaries.

II

The exclusive emphasis on macro social theory is significant because it is central to the social science disciplines but often needs to be given more than cursory and incomplete treatment in modern texts. Macro social theory—a comprehensive worldview of sociocultural system stability and change—provides structure and guidance in understanding world events. The promise of such understanding is the initial draw for many sociology students. Unfortunately, classical theorists are often treated as historical artifacts rather than useful guides in understanding sociocultural systems; modern macro theorists are not usually given significant textbook treatment. This book will provide a vehicle for students to reintegrate macro-social theory into the social science discipline.

Thomas Kuhn (1962] 1996), a physicist, introduced social scientists to the concept of paradigm in his book, *The Structure of Scientific Revolutions*. Kuhn's prominent use of the term was to denote the shared metaphysical view of practitioners within a particular field of science towards the subject matter of their field, a worldview, if one will, of science. In his book, Kuhn asserted that science does not advance by the slow accumulation of knowledge within a given paradigm; instead, science advances by paradigmatic revolution. Kuhn's model begins with a dominant paradigm in a field. Observers and scientists practice "normal science" under this reigning paradigm, Kuhn believes, often interpreting their observations in ways consistent with this dominant worldview. Normal science is a period of the slow accumulation of knowledge. In these periods, scientists work within the reigning paradigm, often making modifications and expansions to the paradigm to accommodate new observations and data. However, during this period of normal science, anomalies, or observations that do not easily fit into the paradigm, inevitably accumulate. Eventually, so many of these anomalies build up that a "crisis" is reached in the science; some scientists begin critiquing and attacking the reigning paradigm, and some begin to cast around for a new paradigm that can explain known facts and patterns. At this point, somebody looks at the field differently; they formulate a new paradigm that can explain all that the first paradigm explained and the anomalies that it could not. This new paradigm then begins to compete for the allegiance of scientists in the field. The proponents of the new paradigm are often attacked and ridiculed—sometimes expelled from the ranks of scientists.

Nevertheless, if the new paradigm makes more sense of reality over time, it gains supporters, and the new paradigm becomes dominant in the field. The stage is then set for the process to repeat itself. Kuhn gives several examples: Copernicus and the sun-centered universe, Newton and physics, Lister and antiseptics, Darwin and Evolution, and Einstein and relativity.

An interesting theory for the sociology of science, but perhaps of more lasting influence, was the concept of the paradigm itself. Unfortunately, Kuhn gives many definitions of the term in his work, but George Ritzer (1975, p. 7) gives a more precise definition: "[A paradigm is a] fundamental image of the subject matter within a science. It serves to define what should be studied, what questions should be asked, how they should be asked, and what rules should be followed in interpreting the answers obtained. The paradigm is the broadest unit of consensus within a science and serves to differentiate one scientific community (or subcommunity) from another. It subsumes, defines, and interrelates the exemplars, theories, and methods and instruments that exist within it."

A paradigm is essentially a set of assumptions about how the world works; in sociology, what characteristics and relationships are essential or central in understanding the sociocultural world? Such common assumptions, concepts, and perspective aid in understanding and organizing what is known in a field. They form an intellectual roadmap that gives researchers conceptual categories, points to relationships that are likely to exist (or expected) and informs practitioners of what to look for and what we are likely (probably) to find. We often bring this framework to our observation and professional readings, allowing us to fit new facts into our framework (thereby "understanding") or, if necessary, extend or modify this framework as the data dictates.

Shortly after Kuhn introduced the concept of paradigm, a debate started over its applicability to sociology. For example, George Ritzer looked at the sociology field and claimed it was a multiple-paradigm science, with three paradigms struggling for dominance. The three paradigms within sociology perceived by Ritzer were the "social facts" of functionalism and conflict theory. "Social definition" includes action theory, symbolic interaction, and phenomenology. Furthermore, the "social behavior" paradigm comprises behavioral sociology and exchange theory. (While these are not relevant to this discussion, it is interesting to note that the "social facts paradigm" is decidedly macro level, while the other two "paradigms" are mainly at the micro level of analysis.) This book is based on quite a different premise. There is a single unified paradigm within macro sociology. Wallerstein (1974, p. 11) carries this argument further and argues for a "unidisciplinary approach" among all social sciences, erasing the traditional specializations of economics, political science, sociology, anthropology, and history. Each of these disciplines takes a piece of sociocultural systems and specializes in studying the past, culture, market, or society. Wallerstein believes such specializations stand in the way of genuinely understanding sociocultural systems.

This sociological worldview begins with the assumption that society is a system and that distinct parts affect one another and the system as a whole. The various parts of a social system comprise distinct categories of variables. Ideas, ideologies, values, and norms are widely conceived as impacting human behavior and are often classified as cultural variables. Social structural variables include groups, institutions, and characteristics such as size, resources, and leadership. These variables impact human behavior, attitudes, and opinions in combination with cultural variables and are independent of these variables. A final characteristic of sociocultural systems is material; the environment, both physical and social, characteristics of a population such as size, age, and sex composition, and the technology and practices by which a population manipulates its environment to secure needed food, clothing, shelter, and other necessities. The sociological paradigm considers these characteristics of sociocultural systems—material, structural, and cultural—central to understanding human behavior and culture. Macro theories within sociology, many of which will be explored in this book, are from this dominant paradigm. They differ mainly in the weight they give to different classes of variables. They share the same canon (Marx, Durkheim, and Weber are all in the first tier), organizations, and journals. Alternative paradigms to the macro-sociological would include the biological, psychological-behavioral, and in anthropology, the post-modern.

One of the more exciting facets of Kuhn's advancement of science through paradigm conflict is that it introduces the irrational into the scientific process. According to this view, it is not the case that science is an ivory tower of pure thought, rationality, and reason. It is decidedly not the case that social scientists—or "real" scientists, for that matter—look at all the theories available in a field and choose the one with the most empirical evidence in its favor. As humans, social factors must enter into their choices. Consider (tongue in cheek) the following: A psychologist who becomes a Freudian may do so because of faulty toilet training. Alternatively, she may have given her allegiance to Freudian theory because it was the first theory she encountered in her field, and a favorite teacher was expounding upon it. Another alternative, she (the psychologist) may have bought into Freud because she needs a father figure and Freud fits the bill or because sexual desires have tormented her all her life, and Freud frequently speaks to those desires. If one is into conditioning, she may have become a Freudian because she had an excellent experience answering an essay question on Freud. Finally, she may have become a Freudian because all her friends became Freudians, or it may have been the only perspective taught at her university.

New paradigms, as Kuhn wrote, are often met with hostility and scorn. People schooled and productive within the old paradigm have emotional, professional, and sometimes fiscal attachments to the old; often, these attachments prevent them from accepting new ways of seeing. While this may be true for paradigmatic conflict within the sciences, it is also apparent in the conflict between theories within a single paradigm. These social factors may be even more pronounced in the social sciences since clashes between theories can rarely be settled empirically. In addition, conflicts between social theories are compounded by the fact that the subject matter we deal with is social life. Many theoretical issues are directly related to widespread political and economic ideologies.

Part 5 of this book will emphasize the common ground upon which macro social theory in sociology stands rather than the conflict and the differences between the theories. Many of these differences have been grossly exaggerated to make a point. They are more a product of the critic's imagination and biased reading than a fundamental difference between theories. Sometimes the role of summarizing another's work and our critique of that work are of conflicting interest. It is in the critic's interest to downgrade the theory of one (say, "he does not give enough weight to population factors in explaining inequality") in order to highlight our contribution ("I give far more weight to population in my theory"). Many summaries and critiques of both classical and contemporary theorists too often gloss over the finer points of a social theorist and then critique them for failing to recognize these points.

For this reason, this book engages in a far more extensive summary than most and closely footnotes interpretations of the theorists to original texts. All the theorists in this volume claim that material, structural, and cultural factors are central to understanding human behavior; again, the differences are in the weight and the emphasis they assign to these factors. The theories are far more compatible with one another than most sociologists acknowledge.

The shoddiness of many secondary sources is striking. Once errors, misinterpretations, or outright misrepresentations get into the literature, they are rarely challenged or corrected in subsequent treatments. When doing a book on Malthus' social theory, I was especially appalled with the treatment of his 1798 *Essay* found in the literature. With rare exceptions, reviewers had only read misleading secondary sources about the *Essay* rather than the work itself. Alternatively, if they had read the original *Essay*, the secondary literature would have completely biased them against it and completely mangled his thought. There are also critiques of many of the theories covered in this volume that seriously misrepresent the theory.

In the Preface to his book, *Evolutionism in Cultural Anthropology*, Robert Carneiro (2003, p. xiii) states that he has a "passion for quotation" that stems from a strong desire for accuracy. His mentor, Leslie White, taught him that he should directly quote the theorist's writings rather than alleging what a particular theorist had said. In the case of the classical theorists covered in this volume, except for Malthus, I have had to rely heavily on secondary sources—I do not read German or French—but quote heavily from translations of their work. The secondary sources I have relied upon are among the best, they quote the theorist in question extensively, and I have used many of these quotes in their original contexts to support the characterizations of classical theory.

The contemporary theories summarized in this volume are directly from the sources. While copyright laws rightfully prohibit extensive quotations from recent works, characterizations of the theories are supported with citations to the work and page numbers where the idea is expressed. The actual words of these contemporary theorists are the data; it is necessary to anchor the exposition closely to this data. To repeat what I wrote in the Preface of *Macrosociology: Four*

Modern Theorists as it applies equally to this work: "In writing this book I did not think it my task to heavily critique these theorists. There is often a conflict of interest between exposition and criticism when dealing with social theory. To shine in the role of the critic, authors oftentimes set up straw men, avoiding the subtleties and caveats of the theorist under examination to score cheap points or add their personal twists to the theory. My role here is different. As famed historian Leopold von Ranke put it, our job as historians is to present history '*wie es eigentlich gewesen ist*' (as it actually was). While this goal may be unattainable in most areas of history, it is a realistic goal in intellectual history. The goal, therefore, is to present and document each theory as accurately, as comprehensively, and in as straightforward a manner as possible, '*wie es eigentlich gewessen ist*'" (Elwell, 2006, p. xv). While summarizing a theorist's life work in 30 pages or so means that much is lost in the translation, it does serve as a valuable introduction to the theorist and, with the broad selection offered here, a useful introduction to macro social theory. However, nothing can replace reading the original works.

III

Sociology began as a discipline in 19th-century Europe, mainly reacting to the capitalist, democratic, and industrial revolutions. Many then became acutely aware that their traditional society was crumbling. They were primarily concerned with where society was going. We will examine each of the four traditional theories attempts to explain how societies originate, maintain themselves over time, and change. These theories do not attempt to explain all of social reality. They attempt to encompass sociocultural systems' most critical features and how they relate to one another and the whole. If one attempted to account for all of social reality, the resulting theory would be long, tedious, and as confusing as social reality itself. The best social theories describe the essential features of social reality using the fewest possible statements and assumptions.

Contrary to popular belief, theories are not devised to torment students; instead, they aim to aid students in understanding the social world. A good theory should contribute to your understanding and serve as a framework to organize the diverse data you encounter. A theory should serve as a guide that is especially helpful when you begin the study of a new social area; it should tell you what to look for, how variables relate to one another, and what you are likely to find. Theory is essential in scientific enterprise. Our understanding of human societies can only be advanced through continually advancing and testing theory; it is the core of sociological enterprise.

Sociology is the scientific study of human social life. Natural and social science is a system of perspectives and beliefs. These perspectives and beliefs are continually being tested against empirical reality, gradually weeding out the irrational, untrue, and mythical features, moving toward a social theory that better reflects reality. Science is not a perfectly rational system. It cannot be. It is a human construction of reality and, as such, must be imperfect. No scientific theory is absolute; none will ever arrive at "truth." All sciences are tentative interpretations of reality; there should be doubt and continual checking of empirical reality to discipline theory to interpret better and explain reality. C. Wright Mills said that "the purpose of empirical inquiry is to settle disagreements and doubts about facts, and thus to make arguments more fruitful by basing all sides more substantively. Facts discipline reason; but reason is the advance guard in any field of learning" (Mills, [1959] 1976, p. 205). Norbert Elias elaborates further. Science, he claims, is distinguished from nonscientific thought by its connection to the physical world. Because of this connection, and because this accumulated body of knowledge is continually checked and replicated by others, science provides the avenue to filter out the "fanciful" and mistaken and arrive at ideas, concepts, and theories that more closely approach physical reality and the relationships between objects in this physical reality. In making this claim, Elias hopes to avoid the philosophical arguments regarding what is real and what is not and focus instead upon a theory of science that, like all theory, can be verified and replicated "by observation, and if necessary revised." For example, he writes,

At one time, people imagined that the moon was a goddess. Today we have a more adequate, more realistic idea of the moon. Tomorrow it may be discovered that there are still elements of fantasy in our present idea of the moon, and people may develop a conception of the moon, the solar system and the whole universe still closer to reality than ours. The comparative which qualifies this assertion is important; it can be used to steer ideas between the two towering, unmoving philosophical cliffs of nominalism and positivism, to keep the current of the long-term development of knowledge and thought. We are describing the direction of this current in calling special attention to the decrease in the fanciful elements and increase in the realistic elements in our thinking, as characteristics of the scientificization of our ways of thinking and acquiring knowledge ([1970] 1978, 23-24).

Moreover, the perspectives presented here, the four paradigms, are of the same cloth—all part of the increasing scientific way "of thinking and acquiring knowledge" about the sociocultural world. Contrary to the arguments of many, the macro perspectives presented here are not mutually contradictory but are compatible with one another. "The cultural history of Western Civilization for the period illuminated by written records can be considered from many aspects. It can be conceived under the guise of a steady economic progression, diversified by catastrophic collapses to lower levels. Such a point of view emphasizes technology and economic organization. Alternatively, history can be conceived as a series of oscillations between worldliness and otherworldliness, or as a theatre or contest between greed and virtue, or between truth and error. Such points of view emphasize religion, morality, and contemplative habits eliciting generalizations of thought. Each mode of consideration is a sort of searchlight elucidating some of the facts and retreating the remainder into an omitted background" (Whitehead [1931] 1963, 43). Like the parable of the blind men and the elephant, each of the various theories focuses on the part of a complex social reality; arguments for the exclusivity of any one view are specious.

> Udana 68-69: The Parable of the Blind Men and the Elephant: Several disciples went to the Buddha and said, "Sir, there are living here in Savitha many wandering hermits and scholars who indulge in constant dispute, some saying that the world is infinite and eternal and others that it is finite and not eternal, some saying that the soul dies with the body and others that it lives on forever, and so forth. What, Sir, would you say concerning them?"
>
> The Buddha answered, "Once upon a time, a certain raja called to his servant and said, 'Come, good fellow, go and gather together in one place all the men of Savitha who were born blind... and show them an elephant.' 'Very good, sire,' replied the servant, and he did as he was told. He said to the blind men assembled there, 'Here is an elephant,' and to one man, he presented the head of the elephant, to another, its ears, a tusk, to another, the trunk, the foot, back, tail, and a tuft of the tail, saying to each one that that was the elephant.
>
> "When the blind men had felt the elephant, the raja went to each of them and said, 'Well, blind man, have you seen the elephant? Tell me, what sort of thing is an elephant?
>
> "Thereupon, the men presented with the head answered, 'Sire, an elephant is like a pot.' Moreover, the men who had observed the ear replied, 'An elephant is like a winnowing basket.' Those who had been presented with a tusk said it was a plowshare. Those who knew only the trunk said it was a plow; others said the body was a grainery; the foot, a pillar; the back, a mortar; the tail, a pestle—the tuft of the tail, a brush.

"Then they began to quarrel, shouting, 'Yes, it is!' 'No, it is not!' 'An elephant is not that!' 'Yes, it's like that!' and so on, till they came to blows over the matter. "Brethren, the raja was delighted with the scene." Just so are these preachers and scholars holding various views blind and unseeing. In their ignorance they are by nature quarrelsome, wrangling, and disputatious, each maintaining reality is thus and thus."

Then the Exalted One rendered this meaning by uttering this verse of uplift:
O how they cling and wrangle, some who claim
For preacher and monk, the honored name!
For, quarreling, each to his view, they cling.
Such folk see only one side of a thing.
(Wang, 1995).

The book's final chapter will present a theoretical synthesis that will draw upon elements of many of the theories presented, which have stood the test of time and empirical study. Such an exposition is also designed to encourage you to develop unique and explicit social theory drawing upon this rich tradition. This exercise will help you to both understand and navigate the modern world.

Part 1: Domestic and International Capitalism

Throughout history, certain intellectuals have emerged as beacons of profound social analysis, challenging the prevailing narratives of their time and offering alternative perspectives that shape our understanding of society. Karl Marx stands tall among these luminaries, and his revolutionary ideas resonate with scholars and thinkers today. This introductory essay delves into Macro Social Theory, explicitly focusing on the work of four significant theorists—Karl Marx, Immanuel Wallerstein, Harry Braverman, and John Bellamy Foster. While these thinkers emerge in a distinct era and context, their theories exhibit profound commonalities with Marx's foundational ideas. By exploring these connections, we unravel the enduring relevance of Marx's work and its impact on contemporary macrosocial theory.

At the heart of Marx's contributions lies the framework of historical materialism, which asserts that society's economic organization shapes its political, cultural, and social structures. Marx argued that capitalist societies are characterized by class struggle, where the owners of the means of production (bourgeoisie) exploit the laboring class (proletariat) to accumulate wealth. This exploitation, Marx contended, gives rise to inherent contradictions within the capitalist system, eventually leading to its demise.

Immanuel Wallerstein's world-systems theory, developed in the late 20th century, shares fundamental connections with Marx's ideas. Wallerstein's theory posits that the global capitalist system is organized into a core, periphery, and semi-periphery, with the core nations exploiting and dominating the periphery. Like Marx, Wallerstein acknowledges the centrality of economic factors in shaping social relations and power dynamics. He highlights how the capitalist world system perpetuates inequality, dependency, and imperialism, ultimately echoing Marx's concern for class struggle and the structural contradictions within capitalism.

In the mid-20th century, Harry Braverman's influential work on labor process theory further underscores the commonalities with Marx's analysis. Braverman examined how capitalist production systematically alienates workers from the products of their labor, transforming their creative activities into monotonous, repetitive tasks under the control of capital. This alienation, as Marx argues, results from the extraction of surplus value by the capitalist class. Braverman's work highlights the enduring relevance of Marx's critique of the capitalist mode of production and its dehumanizing effects on workers.

In recent times, John Bellamy Foster has emerged as a prominent figure within ecological Marxism, intertwining Marx's analysis of capitalism with environmental concerns. Foster emphasizes the inherent contradictions between capitalism's ceaseless pursuit of profit and the planet's ecological limits. Echoing Marx's understanding of capitalism's drive for expansion and exploitation, Foster contends that capitalist modes of production jeopardize ecological sustainability, reinforcing the notion that the capitalist system contains inherent contradictions that threaten social and ecological well-being.

By examining the work of Immanuel Wallerstein, Harry Braverman, and John Bellamy Foster alongside Karl Marx's foundational theories, we witness the enduring influence of Marx's ideas on contemporary macrosocial theory. These scholars, each situated in different historical contexts, build upon Marx's analysis of capitalism, class struggle, and social contradictions, applying his core concepts to novel arenas and expanding their relevance to new societal challenges. Their shared emphasis on economic factors, class dynamics, and the critique of capitalist modes of production attests to the enduring significance of Marx's contributions and his continued relevance for understanding the complexities of modern society. As we delve deeper into the theories of these remarkable thinkers, we gain a richer appreciation of the legacy of Marx and the ongoing dialogue he initiated within macrosocial theory.

Chapter 1: The Sociology of Karl Marx

Karl Marx (1818-1883) is a complex theorist. A good deal of the problem is that he has become a significant historical figure. As such, he has inspired social movements and individual revolutionaries--some of whom have been faithful to his work, while many more have misused his name and writings. In the not-too-distant past, the professor teaching Marx had to deal with the Cold War and anti-Communist attitudes that students would bring to class. Not only would these students have many misconceptions of Marx's thought and theory--equating it with the Communist Parties of the old Soviet Union and other totalitarian societies-- but many would also be actively hostile to learning anything about it. Since the end of the Cold War, students have usually not been active anti-Communists. However, they still tend to equate Marx with Communism, thus assuming that his thoughts have been thoroughly rejected and relegated to the dustbin of history.

In this chapter, we will not deal with the issue of historical Communism. Marx died well before the revolution in Russia. While he inspired many revolutionaries, he bears little responsibility for the totalitarian regime that emerged (to explain the Soviet government, look to the Czarist regimes). Marx is not Stalin.

A related problem with writing about Marx is his multiple roles during his lifetime. Marx was a socialist prophet pol, political organizer, and social theorist. As a prophet, he forecasted the eventual revolution of the working class, the destruction of capitalism, and the establishment of a stateless, socialist society. Many of his political followers admire him deeply, considering his thought an exemplary expression of humanism and compassion for his fellow human beings. Some have characterized him as the "last of the Old Testament prophets." As a prophet, he expressed a deep conviction that humankind would someday create a paradise where we would live in brotherhood, sharing our talents and wealth. Not only did he believe in the possibility of such a utopia, he considered it inevitable. His belief, of course, bears striking similarities to the Christian belief in establishing an earthly paradise (though absent the Second Coming). In his book *Jailbird*, Kurt Vonnegut has Starbuck—his main character—hauled up before the House Un-American Activities Committee. Asked how he could be a Marxist in America, the character replies: "Why? Because of the Sermon on the Mount, sir." In this fictional account Vonnegut quoted Powers Hapgood, a 20th-century labor leader, to answer a similar question.

As a political organizer (and propagandist), Marx wrote to inspire men and women to take immediate action rather than think. "The philosophers have only interpreted the world in various ways; the point is to change it" (Marx [1945] 1976, p. 571). While he wove his prediction and calls to action into his analyses of capitalist society, the revolution, and its socialist aftermath are the most speculative parts of his theoretical structure--prophesized more in hope and faith than in rigorous analysis. Even if we reject his vision of an inevitable and workable socialist society, Marx's analysis of capitalism still has much value and use.

This chapter will focus exclusively on Marx as a social theorist. As a theorist, his writings have enormously impacted all social sciences. His most significant contribution is *establishing a conflict model of social systems.* Rather than conceiving society based on consensus, Marx's theory posits the domination of a powerful class over a subordinate class. However, this domination is never long uncontested. The fundamental antagonism of the classes that produce class struggle transforms sociocultural systems. "The history of all hitherto existing societies is the history of class struggles" (Marx and Engels [1848] 1954, 1). The engine of sociocultural change, according to Marx, is class struggle. Social conflict is at the core of the historical process.

A second significant contribution is that Marx locates *the origin of social power in the ownership or control of the forces of production* (also referred to as the *means of production*). Marx contended that the production of economic goods- what is produced, how it is produced, and how it is exchanged- profoundly affects the rest of society. For Marx, the entire sociocultural system is based on how men and women relate to one another in their continuous struggle to secure needed resources from nature.

A third contribution to the social sciences lies in Marx's *analysis of capitalism and its effects on workers, capitalists, and entire sociocultural systems.* Capitalism as a historical entity was an emerging and rapidly evolving economic system, and Marx brilliantly grasped its origin, structure, and workings. He then predicted with an astonishing degree of accuracy its immediate evolutionary path. Each of these contributions goes beyond the narrow confines of formal Marxist theory. One need not accept Marx's theories whole cloth to integrate his insights into a coherent worldview. Much of his thought is essential in understanding sociocultural systems and, thus, human behavior.

Social Theory

Humanity's food, shelter, housing, and energy needs are central to understanding the sociocultural system. "The first historical act is," Marx writes, "the production of material life itself. This is indeed a historical act, a fundamental condition of all of history" (1964, 60). Unless men and women successfully fulfill this act, there would be no other. All social life depends upon fulfilling this quest for sufficiency in eating and drinking, habitation, and clothing. The necessity of production is as accurate today as it was in prehistory. Do not be fooled. Marx is telling us we are as dependent upon nature as ever. The quest to meet basic needs was man's primary goal then and remains central when we attempt to analyze the complexities of modern life. However, men and women are perpetually dissatisfied animals. Our struggle against nature does not cease when we gratify these primary needs. The production of new needs evolves (secondary needs) when means are found to satisfy our primary needs. Marx argued that men and women form societies to satisfy these primary and secondary needs. The first of these societies, communal in nature, were based on a minimal division of labor. These classless societies in which men hunted and women and children gathered vegetables, tubers, and grains were egalitarian. With the domestication of plants and animals, the division of labor begins to emerge in human societies. The division of labor, or increasing specialization of roles and crafts, eventually gives people differential access to resources, skills, and interests. This division eventually led to the formation of antagonistic classes, the prime actors in human history. From then on, humans engage in antagonistic cooperation to meet their primary and secondary needs. "By thus acting on the external world and changing it, he at the same time changes his own nature" (Marx [1867] 1915, p. 198).

All social institutions depend on the economic base, and a thorough analysis of sociocultural systems will always reveal this underlying economic arrangement. How a society is organized to meet material needs will profoundly affect all other social structures, including government, family, education, and religious institutions. "Legal relations as well as the form of the state are to be grasped neither from themselves nor from the so-called development of the human mind, but have their roots in the material conditions of life. [...] The anatomy of civil society is to be sought in political economy" (Marx & Engels, 1962, p. 362). [The "so-called general development of the human mind" is a reference to August Comte's evolutionary theory, which centered upon the evolution of ideas.

The means of production is the most potent factor influencing the rest of the social system. Marx regarded society as a structurally integrated system, like all the great macro social theorists. The various parts of the social system--such as legal codes, education, art, and religion--could only be understood with reference to the various parts and the whole.

Means and Relations of Production

The *means of production* are the technology and work patterns men and women use to exploit their environment to meet their needs. These means of production are expressed in relationships between members of society. The *relations of production* are the social relations people enter through their participation in economic life. They are socially patterned, independent of the wills and purposes of the individuals involved.

While industrialism is a particular means of production, capitalism represents a particular relation of production. How much independence does Marx accord the two factors? Marvin Harris notes that Marx's concepts of the "means of production" and the "relations of production" have long been debated. Are the concepts separable, and if so, which has primacy? The orthodox view, he reports, is that Marx merged the two into the "economic foundation of society" (Harris, 1998, pp. 187-188). Harris, however, disagrees with this interpretation and insists that Marx considered the two separate forces. Moreover, Marx is clear on this distinction in his writings:

> In the production process, human beings work not only upon nature but also upon one another. They produce only by working together in a specified manner and reciprocally exchanging their activities. In order to produce, they enter into definite connections and relations to one another, and only within these social connections and relations does their influence upon nature operate – i.e., does production take place.
>
> *These social relations between the producers, and the conditions under which they exchange their activities and share in the total act of production, will naturally vary according to the character of the means of production.* With the discovery of a new instrument of warfare, the firearm, the whole internal organization of the army was necessarily altered, the relations within which individuals compose an army and can work as an army were transformed, and the relation of different armies to another was likewise changed.

We thus see that the social relations within which individuals produce, the social relations of production, are altered, transformed, with the change and development of the material means of production, of the forces of production. The relations of production in their totality constitute what is called the social relations, society, and, moreover, a society at a definite stage of historical development, a society with peculiar, distinctive characteristics. Ancient society, feudal society, bourgeois (or capitalist) society, are such totalities of relations of production, each of which denotes a particular stage of development in the history of mankind.

Capital also is a social relation of production. It is a bourgeois relation of production, a relation of production of bourgeois society. *The means of subsistence, the instruments of labor, the raw materials, of which capital consists – have they not been produced and accumulated under given social conditions, within definite special relations? Are they not employed for new production, under given special conditions, within definite social relations? And does not just the definite social character stamp the products which serve for new production as capital?* (Marx [1891] 1902, p. 35).

That the two forces are separate is a critical point. Unless the forces and relations of production are held as separate forces, the effects of capitalism and industrialism will easily be confounded. As we will see, Stephen Sanderson insists on merging the two forces—the forces and relations of production—into a single economic infrastructural variable. The merging of these two forces is an error and leads to great confusion.

Following Harris's interpretation, Marx gave center stage to the means of production. Nevertheless, while Marx gave primacy to the means of production, he never conceived it as a simple case of the means of production determining the relations. Instead, there is an ongoing and continuous interplay between technology and the relations of production throughout social evolution. The close interactions of the means and the relations of production are especially apparent in Marx's analysis of the transition between economic systems. This interaction is critical to Marx because his prediction of the inevitability of socialism was predicated on the full development of industrialism under capitalism. The lack of industrial development is why the Soviet Union was not widely hailed as fulfilling Marx's prediction. The rise of capitalism precedes the Industrial Revolution by at least a century. It should be noted that the rise of capitalism and the Industrial Revolution are historical processes and not single events. We treat them as such only as a matter of convenience, and neither has a clearly defined "natural" starting point or endpoint. Many argue that the industrial revolution continues to this day and that capitalism continues to evolve along with industrial development.

At first, capital production was closer to feudal society's handicrafts than industrial methods. The structure of the capitalist system, with its drive toward profit and expansion, stimulates technological development, the factory system, and a more detailed division of labor. In turn, this industrial development has affected the continuing development of capitalism itself. "Social relations are closely bound up with productive forces. In acquiring new productive forces men change their mode of production; and in changing their mode of production, in changing the way of earning their living, they change all their social relations. The hand-mill gives you society with the feudal lord; the steam-mill, society with the industrial capitalist" (Marx [1847] 1920, p. 119). The means of production and the relations of production are intimately connected. However, they can and should be theoretically separated and examined for their separate and combined impact on the rest of the sociocultural system.

For Marx, the means and relations of production are the foundation of all sociocultural systems. Combined, they profoundly impact the rest of the system, strongly influencing all other aspects and thus affecting the very social character, values, beliefs, and ideologies of the members of that social system. Marx states:

> In the social production which men carry on as they enter into definite relations that are indispensable and independent of their will; these relations of production correspond to a definite stage of development of their material powers of production. The sum total of these relations of production constitutes the economic structure of society--the real foundation, on which rise legal and political superstructures and to which definite forms of social consciousness. The mode of production in material life determines the general character of the social, political and spiritual processes of life. It is not the consciousness of men that determines their existence, but, on the contrary, their social existence determines their consciousness (Marx [1859] 1904, pp. 11-12).

However, it is not the case that Marx explains all social life as a mere reflection of economic production, for it is a sociocultural system, and the various parts interact. Marx elaborates: "The political, legal, philosophical, literary, and artistic development rests on the economic. But they all react upon one another and upon the economic base. It is not the case that the economic situation is the sole active cause and that everything else is merely a passive effect. There is, rather, reciprocity within a field of economic necessity which in the last instance always asserts itself" (Marx & Engels, 1962, p. 304). Material conditions (the means of production and the human relations based on these means) are "ultimately determinant" in historical change. However, superstructural elements (political, legal, philosophy, ideologies, and religious beliefs) react upon this material base, often determining social change's direction, speed, and character.

Class

Men and women are born into societies in which their relation to the means of production has already been determined by birth. This relationship to the means of production gives rise to different class positions. Social mobility, though recognized by Marx, plays no role in his analysis. Just as a person cannot choose her parents, she has no choice regarding her social class. Once a person is ascribed a specific class by birth, once he becomes master or slave, feudal lord or serf, worker or capitalist, his behavior is prescribed for him. By being born into a specific class, his attitudes, beliefs, and behaviors are all "determined." The class role broadly defines the person. In his 1867 preface to the first German edition of *Capital,* Marx wrote: "But here individuals are dealt with only in so far as they are the personifications of economic categories, embodiments of particular class-relations and class-interests. My standpoint, from which the evolution of the economic formation of society is viewed as a process of natural history, can less than any other make the individual responsible for relations whose creature he socially remains, however much he may subjectively raise himself above them." Social classes have different class interests flowing from their position to the mode of production.

These class interests are primary determinants of attitudes, ideologies, political views, and behavior. In saying this, Marx does not deny the operation of other factors affecting human beliefs and behavior. Nevertheless, his theory is that an individual's objective class position, whether an individual is aware of their class interests or not, strongly influences human behavior.

"The history of all hitherto existing societies is the history of class struggles. Freeman and slave, patrician and plebeian, lord and serf, guild-master and journeyman, in a word, oppressor and oppressed, stood in constant opposition to one another, carried on an uninterrupted, now hidden, now open fight, a fight that each time ended, either in a revolutionary re-constitution of society at large, or in the common ruin of the contending classes" (Marx & Engels, [1848] 1954, p. 1). All social systems—save those of prehistory and the socialist utopias to come—are fundamentally divided between classes who clash in pursuing their interests. Every society has two classes of concern: the ruling and the oppressed. Relationships between people are shaped by their relative position regarding the forces of production and differing access to needed resources. The ruling class dominates the sociocultural system. "In every epoch, the ideas of the ruling class are the ruling ideas; that is, the class that is the ruling material power of society is at the same time the ruling intellectual power. The class having the means of material production also has control over the means of intellectual production, so that it also controls, general speaking, the ideas of those who lack the means of intellectual production. The ruling ideas are nothing more than the ideal expression of the dominant material relationships grasped as ideas, hence of the relationships which make the one class the ruling one and therefore the ideas of its domination" (Marx and Engels [1846] 1994, p. 129). In this connection, the business class rules American society, and their ideas and interests dominate society. We come to think naturally in their class categories: The point of human existence is accumulating possessions. The goal of the economic system is to grow. Progress is our most important product. The point of education is to promote economic development. The business of America is business. This dominance is not done through conspiracy but as a pervasive viewpoint enshrined in our institutions, norms, and values. Because the ruling class controls the means of production, the class can dominate (seemingly) non-economic institutions. Economic elites' viewpoint becomes the society's widely accepted view through influence (if not outright control) over crucial institutions such as the government, media, foundations, and higher education. This viewpoint, of course, emphasizes maintaining the status quo.

The oppressed class, consisting of those who do not control the means of production, usually internalizes these elite ideologies. However, under certain conditions, the oppressed class can generate and widely internalize ideologies that undermine the power of the dominant class. Marx terms these conditions "revolutionary," which we will turn to in the next section.

Evolution and Revolution

According to Marx, every economic system produces counterforces that, over time, lead to a new economic form. The process begins with the forces of production, technological development, or changes in the division of labor. Over time, these technological changes become so great that they can harness untapped resources to satisfy human needs. Consequently, it sometimes happens that "the social relations within which individuals produce, the social relations of production, are altered, transformed, with the change and development of the material means of production, of the forces of production. The relations of production in their totality constitute what is called social relations, society, and, moreover, a society at a definite stage of historic development, a society with peculiar, distinctive character. Ancient society, feudal society, bourgeois (or capitalist) society, are such totalities of relations of production, each of which denotes a particular stage of development in the history of mankind" (Marx [1891] 1902, p. 36).

In the feudal system, for example, the market and guild system emerged but were incompatible with the feudal way of life. The market created a full-time merchant class, and the guilds and towns created a new working class independent of the land. Consequently, a new class structure emerged, with wealth increasingly based on the new economic form. This merchant class created tensions with the old feudal institutions; the newly wealthy merchants wanted power and prestige to further their economic interests. The emerging bourgeoisie became revolutionary because their interests were thwarted; they expected to gain through a change in property relations. This revolutionary class began to view existing property relations (feudalism) as a "fetter" (a restraint or shackle) upon the further development of their interests (trade and the production of goods through the factory system).

New social relationships based upon the new forces of production began to develop within the old social order. The merchant class, which amassed great wealth, began challenging the hold of the classes that had dominated the feudal order. Conflict resulted, feudalism was replaced by capitalism, land ownership as the basis of wealth was replaced by trade, and eventually, the ownership of capital. "The economic structure of capitalist society has grown out of the economic structure of feudal society. The dissolution of the latter sets free elements of the former" (Marx [1867] 1915, p. 786).

The potential for class conflict is present in any society with a division of labor. The emergence of a self-conscious revolutionary class--a class that recognizes that its condition is due to the systematic domination and exploitation of the elite--depends on (a) the emergence of a critical mass of people within the exploited class; (b) a developed network of communication, organization; and (c) an ideology that identifies a common enemy as well as a program of action.

The Nature of Capitalism

As an economic system, ideal capitalism consists of four primary characteristics: 1) Private ownership of capital to produce goods and services in all potentially profitable markets; 2) Individuals striving to maximize profit; 3) Market competition between companies which assures high quality and the lowest market price; and 4) Government enforcement of economic contracts and allowing the private accumulation of capital (refraining from expropriating all through taxation). While there is a myth of government laissez-faire in economic matters, there have been close ties between government and capital from the beginning of the modern state and the capitalist economic system. According to Marx, the way to maximize profits is to produce and sell goods and services for more than it costs to manufacture and provide them. Moreover, Marx adds that the way to do that is by creating surplus value. "The essential difference between the various economic forms of society, between, for instance, a society based on slave labour, and one based on wage labour, lies only in the mode in which this surplus-labour is in each case extracted from the actual producer, the labourer [...] The rate of surplus-value is therefore an exact expression for the degree of exploitation of labour-power by capital, or of the labourer by the capitalist" (p. 241).

It begins with labor power, specifically the purchase and sale of labor power. The purchase of labor, according to Marx, is fraught with consequences for the entire sociocultural system. The value of all goods and services (all commodity value) is created by human labor. Capitalism is a system built around the drive to increase capital. To expand his capital, the capitalist invests it in the purchase of labor. He then attempts to get more value from this labor than he has invested. The more surplus he can expropriate from his workforce, the greater the profitability and the greater his capital.

According to Marx, all surplus value is created by human labor. Suppose, for example, a self-employed person making picture frames pays $10 for the material to make each frame and sells each for $20. Suppose further that she can comfortably make one frame in an hour, and she needs $40 a day to purchase the necessities of life (food, clothing, shelter) and to live a comfortable lifestyle. In such a scenario, she only needs to work 4 hours daily to make a living. This form of production is called simple commodities production.

Now, this same individual has decided to become a capitalist. She hires a man at $5 per hour. This man can also make one frame per hour. The material for each frame still costs $10; she sells each for $20. Minus the material and labor costs, her profit is now $5 per frame. This profit is possible only because there is a difference between the labor cost ($5 per hour) and the value added to the raw materials ($10). In this case, the worker adds $10 to the materials' value during his hour of work but is only paid $5 for his efforts. This surplus value of $5 per hour created by the worker is taken by the owner and is called profit.

Continuing the example, for the capitalist to live comfortably, she still needs at least $40 daily and must work her employee for at least 8 hours daily to get this profit. For the employee to live, he also needs $40 and must work the capitalist 8 hours a day. She had to work only 4 hours a day to make a living through simple commodities production, and he had to work 8 hours a day under capitalist production to do the same. *This difference in hours is because his labor now supports himself and the capitalist.*

Under capitalism, the capitalist has a great incentive to increase her profit. Assuming a constant demand for her picture frames, she can increase her profit in several ways. (While we assume a constant demand, this is never a safe assumption in the real world. In the never-ending quest to accumulate capital, such uncertainty is not profitable. Capitalist enterprises, therefore, attempt to control and stimulate demand through advertising and opening new markets for the goods produced.) However, assuming a constant demand she can hire more workers to make more picture frames. She can pay her workers less per hour while requiring them to make the same number of frames. She can get her workers to work faster or more efficiently by dividing and simplifying the tasks that go into making the frame. Alternatively, she can introduce tools and machinery to increase their output. Again, she is incentivized to take any or all these steps. The worker is incentivized to minimize energy expenditure and maximize rewards (or to minimize exploitation). Therein lies the conflict.

Exploitation and Alienation

It is through work that human beings realize the self. Through work, we become fully human. We differ from all other life on earth because we realize our imaginations in action on the external world. For humans, the work process is a unity of imagination and action. Marx writes:

> We are not now dealing with those primitive instinctive forms of labour that remind us of the mere animal. An immeasurable interval of time separates the state of things in which a man brings his labour-power to market for sale as a commodity, from that state in which human labour was still in its first instinctive stage. We pre-suppose labour in a form that stamps it as exclusively human. A spider conducts operations that resemble those of a weaver, and a bee puts to shame many an architect in the construction of her cells. But what distinguishes the worst architect from the best of bees is this, that the architect raises his structure in imagination before he erects it in reality. At the end of every labour-process, we get a result that already existed in the imagination of the labourer at its commencement. He not only effects a change of form in the material on which he works, but he also realizes a purpose of his own that gives the law to his modus operandi, and to which he must subordinate his will (p. 198).

Man is, primarily, "homo faber," man the maker. Capitalism, in its quest for greater profit, destroys this unity. It does this by breaking the labor process into more simplified tasks, removing control of the work process from the worker, and separating intellectual from manual labor. This process is aided by employing machinery—capital or "dead labour" that has been converted into an "automaton."

> Every kind of capitalist production, in so far as it is not only a labour-process, but also a process of creating surplus-value, has this in common, that it is not the workman that employs the instruments of labour, but the instruments of labour that employ the workman. But it is only in the factory system that this inversion for the first time acquires technical and palpable reality. By means of its conversion into an automaton, the instrument of labour confronts the labourer, during the labour process, in the shape of capital, of dead labour, that dominates and pumps dry, living labour-power. The separation of the intellectual powers of production from the manual labour, and the conversion of those powers into the might of capital over labour, is, as we have already shown, finally completed by modern industry erected on the foundation of machinery. The special skill of each individual insignificant factory operative vanishes as an infinitesimal quantity before the science, the gigantic physical forces, and the mass of labour that are embodied in the factory mechanism and, together with that mechanism, constitute the power of the 'master' (p. 462).

Laborers become unskilled servants of the capitalist's machinery to create more surplus value. Rather than realize themselves, they become mere instruments of the capitalist in the production process.

Alienation is the social-psychological feeling of estrangement from work, our fellow human beings, and the self. Marx believes this alienation is rooted in the capitalist mode of production itself. Work becomes an enforced activity, done for the paycheck alone, a place where the individual must deny themselves, separating physical activity from mental life—not living as a whole human being. The worker becomes alienated from all aspects of labor, beginning with the product they produce. Marx writes: "The object produced by labor, its product, now stands opposed to it as an alien being, as a power independent of the producer [...] The more the worker expends himself in work the more powerful becomes the world of objects which he creates in face of himself, the poorer he becomes in his inner life, and the less he belongs to himself" (Marx, 1964b, p. 122). Not only is the individual alienated from the product he produces, but from the production process itself. Furthermore, humans are defined by their work. Workers do not own the tools, set the pace, or determine their actions on the job. Marx continues,

> However, alienation appears not merely in the result but also in the process of production, within productive activity itself [...] If the product of labor is alienation, production itself must be active alienation [...] The alienation of the object of labor merely summarizes the alienation in the work activity itself...This is the relationship of the worker to his own activity as something alien, not

belonging to him, activity as suffering (passivity), strength as powerlessness, creation as emasculation, the personal physical and mental energy of the worker, his personal life [...] as an activity which is directed against himself, independent of him and not belonging to him (pp. 124-125).

In addition to becoming alienated from the product and the production process, the individual becomes alienated from the self. "Work is external to the worker [...] It is not part of his nature; consequently, he does not fulfill himself in his work but denies himself [...] The worker therefore feels himself at home only during his leisure time, whereas at work he feels homeless" (p. 125). The more time the worker spends on the job, the poorer her inner mental life and the less human she becomes. Since humans are, more than anything else, creative beings who realize themselves through work, alienation from work leads to alienation from the self, fellow human beings, and finally, from life itself. "What is true of man's relationship to his work, to the product of his work and to himself, is also true of his relationship to other men [...] Each man is alienated from others [...] each of the others is likewise alienated from human life" (p. 129).

In creating surplus value and the degradation and alienation of labor, the capitalist is aided by science and technology. Capitalism and its drive to increase profit become associated with the advancement of science and the application of technology in creating new products and the production process.

> Modern industry rent the veil that concealed from men their own social process of production, and that turned the various, spontaneously divided branches of production into so many riddles, not only to outsiders, but even to the initiated. The principle which it pursued, of resolving each process into its constituent movements, without any regard to their possible execution by the hand of man, created the new modern science of technology. The varied, apparently unconnected, and petrified forms of the industrial processes now resolved themselves into so many conscious and systematic applications of natural science to the attainment of given useful effects (Marx [1867] 1915, p. 532).

Capitalism thus becomes committed to automation and technology to increase production and lower costs by replacing workers and simplifying the remaining work tasks.

The Dialectic

Marx maintained that capitalism carries the seeds of its destruction like all hitherto existing economic systems. The structure of the capitalist system itself has several internal contradictions, which become exacerbated with its continued development. Competition, the lifeblood of capitalism, implies winners and losers. Over time, competition causes the rise of monopoly capitalism, which seeks to control the market in terms of cost and quality (p. 836). Because of the dynamics of capitalism, society will be polarized into a few wealthy capitalists, a great mass of workers, and a reserve army of unemployed. Capitalists constantly need to exploit new markets, adopt ever more sophisticated technology, and employ a more detailed division of labor in a constant search to expand capital. To maximize profits, capitalists automate factories, send jobs overseas, and break jobs down into simple, unskilled components requiring little training or skills. Workers are forced to accept lower wages or become structurally unemployed.

> But if a surplus labouring population is a necessary product of accumulation or of the development of wealth on a capitalist basis, this surplus-population becomes, conversely, the lever of capitalistic accumulation, nay, a condition of existence of the capitalist mode of production. It forms a disposable industrial reserve army, that belongs to capital quite as absolutely as if the latter had bred it at its own cost. Independently of the limits of the actual increase of population, it creates, for the changing needs of the self-expansion of capital, a mass of human material always ready for exploitation (Marx [1867] 1915, p. 693).

Thus, millions will be pauperized by an economic system that views all labor as a cost and all costs to be controlled. "The more extensive, finally, the Lazarus-layers of the working class and the industrial reserve army, the greater is official pauperism. *This is the absolute general law of capitalist accumulation*" (p. 707, emphasis in the original). The poor become a surplus population that the existing production and distribution systems cannot adequately support. Nevertheless, Marx argued that they become surplus because of the laws of capitalism, not because of the laws of nature. (The "not because of the laws of nature" was a swipe at Malthus, who argued that the poor were a proportion of the population that existing production methods could not adequately support. He attributed this to the laws of nature, not to capitalism.)

With its continued development, the contradictions worsen, and the boom and bust cycles become more extreme. The lack of centralized planning under capitalism results in the overproduction of some goods and the underproduction of others, thus causing economic crises such as inflation and depression (p. 495).

> With the accumulation and the development of the productiveness of labour that accompanies it, the power of sudden expansion of capital grows also [...] The mass of social wealth, overflowing with the advance of accumulation and transformable into additional capital, thrusts itself frantically into old branches of production, whose market suddenly expands, or into newly formed branches [...] In all such cases, there must be the possibility of throwing great masses of men suddenly on the decisive points without injury to the scale of production in other spheres [...]

This increase is effected by the simple process that constantly 'sets free' a part of the labourers; by methods which lessen the number of labourers employed to the increased production. The whole form of the movement of modern industry depends, therefore, upon the constant transformation of a part of the labouring population into unemployed or half-employed hands (pp. 693-694).

Since capitalism is international in scale, the people of all nations become part of the capitalist world system, with an industrial center exploiting much of the world for raw materials, food, and labor. "A new and international division of labour, a division suited to the requirements of the chief centres of modern industry springs up and converts one part of the globe into a chiefly agricultural field of production, for supplying the other part which remains a chiefly industrial field" (p. 493).

Marx predicts that the capitalist class will fully develop productive forces as the system matures, filling every profitable niche. Marx argued that existing property relations (capital goods in the hands of private interests) would eventually restrain the further development of productive technology. Needed social goods and services will not be produced because there will be no profit for the capitalists who control the means of production. The masses will be increasingly impoverished amid exorbitant wealth for the few--and the unfulfilled potential to supply the many. The control of the state by the capitalists, with their organization, money, and power, leads to the passage of laws favoring their interests and blocking real structural change to address the crises (Marx, 1964, p. 78). The wrath of a growing number of workers will rise; the proletariat will become more progressive with a fundamental antagonism toward the owners of capitalism. Eventually, Marx says, these contradictions of capitalism will produce a revolutionary crisis.

> Along with the constantly diminishing number of the magnates of capital, who usurp and monopolize all advantages of this process of transformation, grows the mass of misery, oppression, slavery, degradation, exploitation; but with this too grows the revolt of the working-class, a class always increasing in numbers, and disciplined, united, organized by the very mechanism of the process of capitalist production itself. The monopoly of capital becomes a fetter upon the mode of production, which has sprung up and flourished along with, and under it. Centralization of the means of production and socialization of labor at last reach a point where they become incompatible with their capitalist integument [outer shell]. This integument is burst asunder. The knell of capitalist private property sounds. The expropriators are expropriated (pp. 836-37).

Prophecies of Revolution and Socialism

Capitalism will then produce a class of oppressed people (the proletariat or the workers) bent on destroying it. With the development of communication and spreading a counter ideology that identifies the existing corporate structure as the enemy, the workers will organize and revolt. This revolt will take control of the means of production for the good of all and mark the end of classes and the end of history as we know it. "The prehistory of human society will come to an end" (Marx, 1964, p, 53). A socialist system will be established where the means of production will be employed to provide for human happiness rather than profit.

Contrary to his calls for immediate revolutionary action in such political tracts as *The Communist Manifesto:* "The Communists disdain to conceal their views and aims. They openly declare that their ends can be attained only by the forcible overthrow of all existing social conditions. Let the ruling classes tremble at a Communistic revolution. The proletarians have nothing to lose but their chains. They have a world to win. WORKING MEN OF ALL COUNTRIES, UNITE!" (1848, pp. 32-33, emphasis in the original), Marx did not predict any imminent revolution in his academic works. His analysis of the rise of capitalism makes clear that any overthrow of capitalist society could only occur after capitalism fully develops the means of production (industrialism), therefore setting the material conditions for socialism. "No social order ever disappears before all the productive forces for which there is room in it have been developed; and new higher relations of production never appear before the material conditions of their existence have matured in the womb of the old society" (Marx, 1964, p. 52). Moreover, "The economic structure of capitalist society has grown out of the economic structure of feudal society. The dissolution of the latter sets free the elements of the former" (p. 133). As a historian and sociologist who studied capitalism extensively, Marx must have recognized that it was a relatively new economic system and that industrial production was beginning to intensify. As the quotes above make clear, Marx expected the transition to socialism to be a long-term evolutionary process.

It is only after the overthrow of capitalism and the long-term establishment of a socialist society, in which the proletariat cooperatively owns the forces of production, that society will attain a state of equality and authentic community.

> In a higher phase of communist society, after the enslaving subordination of the individual to the division of labor, and therewith also the antithesis between mental and physical labor, has vanished; after labor has become not only a means of life

but life's prime want; after the productive forces have also increased with the all-around development of the individual, and all the springs of cooperative wealth flow more abundantly—only then can the narrow horizon of bourgeois right be crossed in its entirety and society inscribe on its banners: From each according to his ability, to each according to his needs! (Marx, [1875] 2008, pp. 26-27).

All of which mirror the communal society of hunting and gathering societies in prehistory. Marx argues that such a communal society is possible because the distribution of goods and services within present-day society results from the mode of production itself.

For example, the capitalist mode of production rests on the fact that the material conditions of production are in the hands of nonworkers in the form of property in capital and land. At the same time, the masses are only owners of the personal condition of production, of labor power. If the elements of production are so distributed, then the present-day distribution of the means of consumption results automatically. If the material conditions of production are the cooperative property of the workers themselves, then it likewise results in a distribution of the means of consumption different from the present (pp. 27-28).

Marx's vision of life after socialism is incomplete. The detailed division of labor would be allowed but limited. Industrial technology will be harnessed to provide happiness rather than profit—though some capital would have to be reinvested into maintaining, expanding, and improving production technologies.

Marx's hopes and longings for a better world probably distorted his analyses. His analysis of the conditions of a capitalist society is compelling. His predictions of the ever more detailed division of labor, the alienation of work, the growth in the number of the proletariat and their gradual impoverishment, the replacement of workers by technology, and the growth of the "industrial reserve army" are incisive, particularly when considering capitalism on an international scale. His forecast that the capitalist class will become fewer in numbers but far wealthier and more powerful is prescient. However, given this class's wealth, power, authority, and the tools of repression, cooptation, and manipulation, his predictions of an eventual proletarian revolution are far less compelling. His vision of a socialist utopia, if not an absurdity, is at least an improbable outcome given his analysis of human needs and self-interests. Marx's hopes, dreams, and values have influenced his vision of a socialist utopia as the end of history. Still, there is much to commend in his theory of capitalism, and it is this theory that is his legacy for sociology.

Marx's Legacy

While Marx gets much of the credit and the blame for the communist revolution in Russia, it was very much counter to his theory of historical materialism. He asserted that 1) capitalism had to develop the means of production fully; 2) the new society had to mature within the womb of the old; 3) revolutionary consciousness would have to develop among the proletariat; 4) capitalism would undergo crises because of its internal contradictions, these crises becoming progressively more severe; 5) only then would the proletarian revolution occur, establishing socialism under the dictatorship of the proletariat; and 6) the socialist society would prepare man for the transition to Communism. Russia was a feudal society at best, with only a small working class; it was a revolution led by a vanguard party in a backward land; it was not in accordance with Marx's theory and did not fulfill his predictions. While he may well have inspired some of the revolutionaries, and they may have selectively borrowed from his writings to justify their actions, he bears little responsibility for their crimes.

Nor is Marx's legacy his analyses of the structure and dynamics of socialist or communist societies. His writings on these future societies are slim and consist of vague generalities. In the *German Ideology*, for example, Marx writes:

> [...] while in **communist** society, where nobody has one exclusive sphere of activity but each can become accomplished in any branch he wishes, society regulates the general production and thus makes it possible for me to do one thing today and another tomorrow, to hunt in the morning, fish in the afternoon, rear cattle in the evening, criticize after dinner, just as I have a mind, without ever becoming hunter, fisherman, shepherd or critic. This fixation of social activity, this consolidation of what we ourselves produce into an objective power above us, growing out of our control, thwarting our expectations, bringing to naught our calculations, is one of the chief factors in historical development up till now (p. 9).

How this vision accords with Marx's later economic analysis on the necessity of capital's development of productive forces as a foundation for socialism is problematic. The vision is more suitable for agrarian rather than industrial forces of production. The later assertion of a "dictatorship of the proletariat," which was supposed to aid in the transition to Communism, is also problematic; even contemporaries like the revolutionary anarchist Mikhail Bakunin recognized that such unchecked power would lead to abuse. In sum, his writings on socialism and Communism are neither extensive nor very convincing. There are far better advocates of socialism and descriptions of how it would work in an industrial setting.

Marx's true legacy, which is why he should be read and studied today, lies in his analysis of capitalist society. Marx developed the perspective of historical materialism that emphasizes how a society exploits its environment to provide the necessary resources for its population. In his masterful three-volume work, *Capital*, Marx described the origins, structure, and functions of capital circulation and growth in detail. Writing in the early stages of capital development, he grasped the essence of its political economy. He forecasted a future of intensifying technological innovation and mechanization, accelerated productivity, industrialization of agriculture resulting in environmental degradation, accelerated urbanization, centralization and enlargement of capitalist firms through credit and joint stock companies (corporations); economic cycles of hyper-activity and recession; a rising class of corporate managers; growing inequality between capitalists and workers; the growth of the working class; the continuation of a large surplus population ready to be employed in good economic times, and sloughed off during dire; the development of a capitalist world economy with a division of labor between nation states; the control of the state by capital interests; and ongoing class struggle between capitalists and the proletariat. Indeed, his analysis of the capitalist system's evolution in the one hundred forty years after his death is remarkable.

Finally, we come to his theory of crisis and proletarian revolution. This theory is intimately tied to the full development of capitalism. While he predicted periodic crises, he also thought that the proletariat would develop a revolutionary consciousness through them, and in some future crises, they would revolt. While the periodic economic crises are accurate, there is little evidence of the widespread development of revolutionary consciousness among the working class in advanced capitalist societies. This prediction was always dependent on class action; it was never to be automatic. The major flaw in his analysis is that he underestimated the capitalist's power to control social reality through money, the development of new communication and surveillance technologies, improved social technologies of propaganda and advertising, and the proliferation of creature comforts. Alternatively, the economic crises may not be severe enough to break through consumer complacency, and the revolution is yet to come.

Within contemporary academic sociology, the Marxian tradition is alive in world-systems analysis, a perspective developed by Immanuel Wallerstein (b. 1930) in the 1970s. According to Wallerstein, the modern nation-state exists within a broad economic, political, and legal framework, which he calls a world-system (for a more extended discussion of Wallerstein, see

Elwell 2006, 73-102). Just as individual behavior cannot be fully understood without reference to the society in which they are members, individual societies or nation-states cannot be understood without reference to the world systems in which they are embedded. Modern nation-states are all part of the world system of capitalism, and it is this world-system that Wallerstein seeks to understand.

Wallerstein believes that there are only three basic types of social systems. The first he terms "mini-systems" are the small, homogenous societies studied by anthropologists. Hunting and gathering, herding, and simple horticultural societies are self-contained economic units that produce all goods and services within the sociocultural system. The second type of social system encompasses multiple cultures, each contributing goods and services to the whole. Wallerstein terms these "world-systems," and they are of two types. The first, world-empires, has an economy based on extracting surplus goods and services from outlying districts. Much of this tribute goes to pay for the administrators who extract it and for the military to ensure continued domination; the rest goes to the political rulers at the head of the empire.

Unlike world empires, the capitalist world-system has no unified political system, nor is its dominance based on military power alone. However, like a world empire, the capitalist world system is based on extracting surplus from outlying districts to enrich those who rule at the center. From the start, Wallerstein argues capitalism has had a division of labor encompassing several nation-states. The capitalist world-system began in Europe in about 1500 and, under the spur of capital accumulation, expanded over the next few centuries to cover the entire globe. In this expansion, the capitalist world-system has absorbed small mini-systems, world empires, and competing world economies. The capitalist world economy was created by establishing long-distance trade in goods and linking production processes worldwide, allowing the significant accumulation of capital in Europe. However, these economic relationships were not created between regions in a political vacuum. The modern nation-state was created in Europe along with capitalism to serve and protect the interests. The establishment of a world economy based on a highly unequal division of labor between European states and the rest of the system was in the interests of early European capitalists. Also, in their interests was establishing strong European states with the political and military power to enforce this inequality.

For Wallerstein, the capitalist world economy is a mechanism of surplus appropriation that is both subtle and efficient. It relies upon the creation of surplus through constantly expanding productivity. It extracts this surplus for the benefit of the elite through profit creation. This extraction is far more efficient than the extraction by force of the surplus through tribute. It has the added advantage of softening and disguising the exploitative relationship. It becomes difficult for the victim to identify his exploiter or even the exploiter to recognize that he is expropriating surplus! All of it is left to—and defined by—market forces. Organizing and coalescing against such an enemy is challenging to revolt against in such situations.

The capitalist world system is based on a two-fold division of labor in which different classes and status groups are given differential access to resources within nation-states. The different nation-states are given differential access to goods and services on the world market. Both types of markets, both those within and those between nation-states, are very much distorted by power.

Wallerstein divides the capitalist world economy into core states, semi-peripheral, and peripheral areas. The peripheral areas are the least developed; the core exploits them for cheap labor, raw materials, and agricultural production. The semi-peripheral areas are intermediate, both exploited by the core and taking some role in exploiting the peripheral areas. Recently, they have been expanding their manufacturing activities, particularly in areas that are no longer very profitable. The core states are in geographically advantaged areas—i.e., Europe and North America. These core states promote capital accumulation internally through tax policy, government purchasing, sponsorship of research and development, financing infrastructure development (such as sewers, roads, and airports—all privately constructed), and maintaining social order to minimize the class struggle. Core states also promote capital accumulation in the world economy itself. For historical reasons, these states have the political, economic, and military power to enforce unequal exchange rates between the core and the periphery. This power allows core states to dump unsafe goods in peripheral nations and pay lower prices for raw materials than in a free market. It is power that allows the core to exploit the periphery for cheap labor, lax environmental, consumer, and worker safety laws, erect trade barriers and quotas to their advantage, and establish and enforce patents. The core's economic, political, and military power allows significant capital to be accumulated into the hands of a few. This capitalist world-system produces and maintains gross economic and political inequalities within and between nations.

As with capitalism within nation-states, Wallerstein argues, this power is contested; it is the subject of struggle; there are internal contradictions that, over time, cause political and economic instability and social unrest. Eventually, a worldwide crisis will be reached, and the system will necessarily collapse, opening the way for revolutionary change. It should be the goal of social scientists to comprehend these developments and translate and disseminate our understandings into facts and concepts for a broad audience. Through this work, we can provide people with the tools necessary to achieve a more just and egalitarian world.

We will now turn to a more extensive treatment of two other theorists who rely heavily upon Marx for understanding contemporary sociocultural systems. The first, Harry Braverman, focuses on the American working class; the second, John Bellamy Foster, writes extensively on the growing environmental crisis. As will be seen, Marx is alive and well and still has much to offer.

Chapter 2: Harry Braverman's Marxist Analysis

Harry Braverman (1920-1976) is a follower of Karl Marx. While other modern theorists covered in this book have been strongly influenced by the sociological theory of the nineteenth century, the nature and strength of this influence differ from Braverman's. While many theorists work from the tradition of a single theorist, most combine this with their insights and those from other theorists to arrive at a distinctive analytical perspective. Braverman, however, is much closer to Marx's theory. His overall theory is taken directly from Karl Marx. His problem--a study of the objective conditions of the working class--is identical to the task Marx set for himself in the first volume of *Capital*. The value of Braverman's work is not in extending Marx's analyses or combining Marx's insights with others. Instead, the value of the work is that it applies Marx's analyses to American society in the latter half of the 20th century and renders Marx's analyses genuinely accessible to a modern audience. It is a successful work on both counts.

Braverman ([1974] 1998) begins his analysis by pointing to a contradiction in the literature on work. There is a widespread belief and assertion that current occupations are more demanding regarding technical skills, educational levels, and training. So entrenched is this belief that it is rarely questioned or examined. However, even some of the same people making these assertions report widespread dissatisfaction with work--the hours, the pace, the lack of meaningful participation, low morale, high absenteeism, and early retirement (p. 3). He points out that these two views are contradictory, though there is little attempt in the literature to reconcile these differences. This contradiction is surprising in that work, Marx (and thus Braverman) asserts, is central to the human animal, and it is through work that men and women realize their very humanity.

The Free Labor Market

Capitalism begins with labor power, specifically purchasing and selling labor power. According to Braverman (and thus Marx), this labor purchasing is fraught with consequences for the entire sociocultural system. The value of all goods and services (all commodity value) is created by human labor. Capitalism is a system built around the drive to increase capital. To expand his capital, the capitalist invests some in the purchase of labor. He then attempts to get more value from this labor than he has invested. The more surplus he can expropriate from his workforce, the greater the profitability and the greater his capital.

Three conditions must be met for widespread labor power purchase and sale (pp. 35-36). First, workers need to be separated from the means of production; they can gain access to livelihood only by selling their labor power to others. Historically, the peasantry was one of the pools for such newly created labor power. Various land reforms and technological innovations moved many of these peasants off the land, thus denying them access to other ways of living. To survive, these people had to turn to the new industrial mode of production. This process is still occurring in advanced industrial societies, but since it is nearing completion, it is much more apparent in industrializing societies.

A related pool for such newly created labor power was self-employed. In the early part of the nineteenth century, Braverman reports, perhaps four-fifths of the U.S. population was self-employed (many of these would be farmers, but the category would also include small shop owners, carpenters, and independent professionals). By 1870, he reported that the self-employed accounted for about one-third of the labor force. By 1940, only one-fifth, and by 1970, only about one-tenth (p. 36). (This figure still holds at about 10 percent today.)

Once created, there are ongoing streams that replenish the pool of labor for the market. These sources would include population growth and immigration from non-industrial societies (neither of which Braverman addresses). Moreover, changes in the structure of occupations within the sociocultural system also replenish the pool. Occupational structure changes often occur with technological change. Such changes involve the decline of some types of occupations, such as agriculture and manufacturing, and the rise of others, such as service or clerical workers--though these do not always fall and rise in tandem.

The second factor needed to create a market for the sale and purchase of labor power lies in freeing workers from legal constraints, such as serfdom or slavery, allowing them to enter such arrangements. This factor is intimately associated with the first. While liberating the individual from legal constraints on her freedom, liberation also involves separating the individual from her means of livelihood. Most enter the labor market with nothing to exchange except their physical labor.

The third factor required for creating an overall labor market is establishing an economic system where individuals strive to increase their capital or investment. To do this, capitalists must employ human labor to create value in commodities. Capitalism began to emerge in fourteenth-century Europe as the feudal system declined.

While the buying and selling of labor power existed in Europe and other parts of the world since antiquity, it was not a significant factor in the production process until the rise of capitalism (36). Early capitalism, however, relied upon traditional production processes--such as the exchange of the surplus products of peasants or the commodities produced through the skill of artisans--rather than on an industrial mode of production. So, it was only with the rise of industrial capitalism in the latter half of the eighteenth century that a large labor market became numerically significant.

With the establishment of a labor market, the worker enters employment because there are few other options to make a living. The capitalist enters the relationship to make a profit.

> Thus, the labor process is set in motion, which, while it is a general process of creating useful values, has now also explicitly become a process for expanding capital and creating profit. From this point on, it becomes foolhardy to view the labor process purely from a technical standpoint, as a mere mode of labor. It has become, in addition, a process of accumulation of capital. Moreover, it is the latter aspect that dominates the mind and activities of the capitalist, into whose hands the control over the labor process has passed (pp. 36-37).

Braverman's entire analysis is based on this point. The working life of the vast majority in capitalist societies is dominated and shaped by the needs and interests of the capitalist class. Primary among these interests is to expand capital to maximize profit.

The Problem of Management

The "problem of management" begins when workers are gathered in significant numbers and employed by a single capitalist (p. 41). While early industrial capitalism employs traditional skills and crafts workers, even independent artisans require coordination regarding supplies, scheduling, assignments, records, payrolls, sales, and accounting. Also, with the gradual rise of more complex production and assembly processes (Braverman's examples are shipbuilding and coach making), as well as those that were not based on traditional production techniques (such as sugar refining and distilling) the need for managerial coordination and control significantly increased (p. 41).

However, the capitalist management problem is much greater than the need to coordinate large numbers of workers. Other systems have coordinated large numbers of workers prior to the capitalist era. Braverman notes that the vast public works of Egypt, China, and other ancient and medieval societies were all produced by such labor (p. 44). The capitalist coordination problem is different, however, in that the capitalist works with "free" labor in a system of constantly expanding technology spurred on by a driving need to expand production and profitability.

The capitalist management problem is rooted in the buying and selling of labor. "It is, of course, understood that the useful effects or products of labor belong to the capitalist. However, what the worker sells, and what the capitalist buys, is not an agreed amount of labor, but the labor over an agreed period of time" (p. 37). Such labor represents a cost for each nonproductive hour. Workers have an interest in conserving their energy, and capitalists in expanding it. Therefore, there is a fundamental antagonism between worker and capitalist, between "those who manage and those who execute, those who bring to the factory their labor power, and those who undertake to extract from this labor power the maximum advantage for the capitalist" (p. 47). While early industrial capitalism used outright force and coercion to attain this maximum advantage, management must now exercise more subtle control methods (pp. 45-47). How do capitalists expand their capital through a "free" labor force? What are the foundations of monopoly capitalism?

Consistent with Karl Marx, Braverman asserts that it is through labor that value is created. According to Marx, the way to maximize profits is to produce and sell goods and services for more than it costs to manufacture and provide them. Moreover, Marx adds that the way to do that is by creating surplus value through human labor. The amount of human labor that an employer can get from a worker depends not only on her physical and mental capabilities but also on cultural norms and understandings, social and scientific technologies, as well as the beliefs and attitudes of the workers. Human beings are infinitely malleable; in this malleability, the capitalist finds the key to capital expansion (p. 38).

The fact that human beings can produce more than they consume, Braverman writes, is not anything special in and of itself. Even farm animals have this ability. Four factors determine the extent of the surplus all can produce: 1) the intensity of labor; 2) the technology utilized in the production process; 3) the definition of subsistence (whether it be living in a cardboard box eating cereals or the suburbs eating meat); and 4) the duration of the labor process. The capitalist can manipulate these factors to increase the surplus created by his labor force, and all of them can be manipulated to expand capital (pp. 38-39).

While capitalists buy human labor with infinite potential, it is also labor with a mind of its own. Being human, workers tend to have some interest in the intensity of the effort they are willing to make, the pace of work they are willing to sustain, and even the best way to perform a particular task. Capitalists have a strong interest in expanding capital and, therefore, maximizing the production of workers to control the labor process. This control presents a problem for workers because they become alienated from the production process. The need to maximize the production of alienated workers is a continuing management problem (pp. 39-40).

The Division of Labor

Braverman states that the earliest and perhaps most important principle of the capitalist mode of production was the manufacturing division of labor. The concept of the division of labor has a long history in economics and other social sciences. However, there needs to be more clarity around the term (pp. 50-51). The social division of labor, or the breakdown of social labor based on craft specialization, has existed in all known societies. Often based initially on age and sex roles, the social division of labor is an essential factor in determining the rate of technological development, the extent of stratification and inequality, and the degree of sociocultural solidarity and cohesion.

However, the manufacturing (or detailed) division of labor is a vastly different phenomenon. The manufacturing division of labor breaks the manufacturing of a product down into simple, discrete steps and then assigns each task to an individual worker. The detailed division of labor was first described by Adam Smith in *The Wealth of Nations* ([1776] 2000) in the manufacture of pins:

> The most significant improvement in the productive powers of labor, and the greater part of the skill, dexterity, and judgment with which it is anywhere directed, or applied, seem to have been the effects of the division of labor […] To take an example, therefore, the trade of the pin-maker; a workman not educated to this business, nor acquainted with the use of the machinery employed in it, could scarce, perhaps, with his utmost industry, make one pin in a day, and certainly could not make twenty. But in the way in which this business is now carried on, not only the whole work is a peculiar trade, but it is divided into a number of branches, of which the greater part are likewise peculiar trades. One man draws out the wire, another straightens it, a third cuts it, a fourth points it, a fifth grinds it at the top for receiving, the head; to make the head requires two or three distinct operations; to put it on is a peculiar business, to whiten the pins is another; it is even a trade by itself to put them into the paper; and the important business of making a pin is, in this manner,

divided into about eighteen distinct operations, which, in some factories, are all performed by distinct hands, though in others the same man will sometimes perform two or three of them (p. 1).

Smith points out that he had observed small factories of ten men engaged in the detailed division of labor, which could produce some 48,000 pins daily. This production would amount to some 4,800 pins for each worker. However, Smith estimates that if they had worked at fashioning the pins independently, each man performing all the steps himself, each would be hard pressed to produce twenty in a day. This performance is only a "two hundred and fortieth" part of what they can do when the work tasks are "properly" divided.

From this example, Smith concludes that such a detailed division of labor can cause a proportionate increase in productivity wherever it can be introduced. It has proceeded furthest in the most developed societies, "what is the work of one man in a rude state of society being generally that of several in an improved one" (p. 16). The increase in productivity caused by the detailed division of labor, Smith surmises, is due to three independent factors: 1) Increase of dexterity in performing a simple operation repeatedly; 2) Saving of time that is lost in passing from one type of work to another; and 3) Invention of machines to assist in these simple tasks. The more the manufacturing process can be broken up into simple, discreet tasks, the more these tasks are assigned to separate workers, and the greater the productivity.

The problem for the worker, Braverman points out, is not with breaking down a complex task into simple steps (p. 54). The breakdown of work into detailed tasks is something that the worker often does willingly to suit his own needs. Confronted with a need to produce twenty funnels, for example, a worker may first fashion a pattern, trace the pattern twenty times on sheet metal, cut all the tin, roll each into the proper shape, and then solder each of the seams. Rarely will the worker take the next step on their own; rarely will they voluntarily become a lifelong detail worker (pp. 54-55). Such a work role calls for the endless repetition of a simple task; human beings would only choose such a role if compelled.

However, the capitalist has no hesitancy in taking the second step by assigning specialized tasks to separate workers (p. 55). The fact that the resulting jobs are mind-numbing, devoid of variety, human initiative, and thought, and any skill save manual dexterity does not enter into the equation. Further, not only will assigning different workers to narrow, restricted roles in the production process increase labor force productivity, but it will also increase the capitalists' control over the labor process. No longer will the capitalist be at the mercy of the skilled craftsman's work rules and specialized knowledge. By dividing the work into such detail, the manager takes more direct control over the process and pace of work. Braverman states that the detailed division of labor is carried out in the name of profit, disregarding human needs and capabilities. It dismembers the individual worker and is a crime against the person and humanity (pp. 50-51).

While Adam Smith wrote of the technical advantages of the detailed division of labor in increasing productivity, Braverman reports that Charles Babbage (1832) pointed out the cost advantage of employing detail workers. The detail worker becomes "unskilled" labor by specializing in a single task. Workers come to the labor market without specific skills; following the laws of supply and demand, their labor is interchangeable with many others. Consequently, there is little incentive for the capitalist to offer more than the regional rate for such labor and little leverage that the unskilled laborer can use to increase their wage.

Following Adam Smith, ten skilled pin makers will produce only a fraction of the number of pins that can be produced by ten unskilled laborers when the work tasks are "properly divided." Following Babbage, the ten skilled workers must also be paid more. By breaking the labor task into simple steps, each of which can be mastered in hours, the capitalist need only hire unskilled workers (p. 57). The detailed division of labor, Braverman claims, underlies all relations between capitalists and labor. Under capitalism, labor power becomes a commodity to be sold on the market, and labor power is the only commodity workers can exchange for necessary goods and services. The detailed division of labor has reorganized this labor market according to the needs and interests of the purchasers of this labor power, not the sellers (p. 57). It significantly boosts productivity, lowers wages, and dramatically extends the capitalists' control over the pace and process of labor.

Even today, Braverman asserts, the process continues in areas far removed from manufacturing. Jobs are continually broken up into simple tasks. Exceptional skills, knowledge, and control are reserved for those few at the top of the hierarchy. Braverman goes as far as to call this the "general law of the capitalist division of labor." Its impact shapes our working lives and the character of the entire sociocultural system. This process polarizes capitalist society into a small, powerful elite at the top and a mass of unskilled labor at the bottom (pp. 57-58).

Taylorism

Many believe the "scientific management" movement initiated by Frederick Winslow Taylor at the end of the 19th century is ancient history. Modern management theorists—often located in personnel departments or academic departments of business, sociology, or psychology—like to contrast their new management theories with the old Taylorism. They claim that scientific management failed to consider the "human factor" in production. Calling themselves "human relations managers," such moderns style themselves as having overthrown the scientific management theory of the past and replaced it with a theory that leads to a kinder and gentler workplace, one much more friendly, flexible, and compassionate to the worker.

Braverman asserts that such an assessment does not do justice to the continuing influence of Taylor's ideas. Taylorism is not a separate school of management theory today because it has become the basic principle of work design. The successors to Taylor are to be found in "engineering and work design," not in personnel departments or the academy's management and social science divisions. It is the engineers who design the work tasks following Taylor's principles. At the same time, the softer side of management "have busied themselves with the selection, training, manipulation, pacification, and adjustment of 'manpower' to suit the work processes so organized" (p. 60).

"Scientific management" styled itself as applying science to designing the most efficient work process in each environment, but it was never an actual science. Instead, Taylorism views the workplace as a conflict between managers and workers, and it sees workers as obstinate and hostile to both work and the needs of management. The point of Taylorism is not to change these conditions, for they are taken as a given, as a natural part of the condition of capitalism and labor. Taylorism aims to adapt this workforce to the needs of capital production. Braverman concludes that, far from being a science, Taylorism is simply management "masquerading in the trappings of science" (p. 59). Its role is to provide the ideology and the techniques to control alienated labor while maximizing production (p. 62).

Taylor's goal was to create conditions that would get the optimum work from each laborer. He reasoned that the greatest obstacle to achieving this goal was the tendency of the men to loaf or "soldier." To counter this tendency, Taylor took the concept of managerial control to a new level. "His 'system' was simply a means for management to achieve control of the actual mode of performance of every labor activity, from the simplest to the most complicated. To this end, he pioneered a far greater revolution in the division of labor than any that had gone before" (p. 62).

Braverman notes two fundamental principles of Taylor's scientific management. By removing all skill from the worker, Taylor broke the labor process into as detailed a division of labor as was practical and economical. By separating the conception of a task from its execution, Taylor achieved managerial control of the production process's efficiency and pace (p. 78). Management would henceforth dictate every movement and action of the worker. Braverman refers to this as the "dehumanization" of the labor process because, as you will recall, it is the unity of conception of the task to be done and the consequent execution of that task that distinguishes human labor from its animal form. While this is often called the separation of manual and mental labor, Braverman points out that this is becoming somewhat of a misnomer. The separation now occurs with many mental tasks as well (p. 79).

Taylorism arose in the last decades of the 19th century when industrial labor was transformed from a skilled workforce based on craft and tradition to an increasingly unskilled labor force based on tending machines. "Its role was to render conscious and systematic, the formerly unconscious tendency of capitalist production" (p. 83). Taylor pushed the detailed division of labor to its fullest and created a large pool of unskilled, powerless, and low-paid workers suitable for these industrial tasks. Moreover, it systematically concentrated all technical knowledge and control in the hands of management. It is Taylorism, Braverman claims, that underlies modern management practices.

The Role of Manipulation

Braverman did not think much of the new management philosophies of his day, and he characterized these philosophies as changes in style rather than substance (pp. 26-27). Capitalist enterprises are increasingly turning to such management tools as the quality of work-life projects, flexibility in adjusting machines, job enrichment, cafeteria benefits, job swapping, pep rallies, and worker participation activities designed to give some choice within the limited parameters set by management. All these are mere window-dressing and all work within the current structure of management control over all aspects of the work processes. All aim to "habituate" the worker to employment on the terms of the capitalist enterprise (pp. 97-99). Braverman believes these "petty manipulations" are far more common in the new mass office occupations, where office structure and the physical layout currently allow more flexibility than the fixed machinery and detailed division of labor of factories (p. 25).

This is not to say that Braverman thinks manipulation is insignificant in habituating the worker to the capitalist labor force. In fact, he assigns manipulation a leading role in the process. However, he describes this manipulation as more integral to the capitalist system (pp. 103-104). Workers are driven into capitalist production through the utter destruction of alternative modes of employment like farming or traditional crafts. They are ensnared in a consumer lifestyle through the growth of marketing in which the consumption of goods becomes a way of life. They are seduced through labor contracts in which their unions accept less worker autonomy in return for limited job protection and higher wages for some. These manipulations have evolved as integral parts of the capitalist system.

However, Braverman asserts that this manipulation can only be partially successful. The hostility of the worker to the system is never completely eradicated. This hostility is expressed in the high absentee rates, the lack of worker loyalty to the organization, the unbounded cynicism of the workers toward their jobs, and their hostility to their managers. The apparent calm and tranquility of the workplace often break into open conflict whenever the capitalist class overreaches or pushes too hard in the regimentation and rationalization of the workplace.

Science and Technology

Back in 1867, Marx wrote of the systematic exploitation of science and technology to serve the interests of capital. However, Braverman points out that these assertions were more prophetic than descriptive (p. 107). Until the latter half of the 19th century, science was the preserve of amateurs, tinkers, philosophers, and men of wealth. While it played a role in the initial stages of the Industrial Revolution, it was not the leading role that was often ascribed to it by moderns. Mechanics and artisans who understood little of the science behind their inventions made many technological innovations (pp. 107-108).

In the latter decades of the 19th century, this began to change. Increasingly, capitalist enterprises began to recognize the utility of science in the production process and as a key towards capital accumulation (pp. 109-110). Braverman attributes this growing awareness to the rise of the electrical, steel, coal, and petroleum industries, which increasingly relied upon science in production. At the turn of the century, Germany was the leading country to employ the sciences in production. At this point, the growing monopolies in the U.S. began systematically developing the physical sciences to amass capital. The tremendous corporate research laboratories began at this time (p. 112). Stimulated by World War I and II and the defection of many German scientists, basic scientific research was increasingly performed at the behest of the capitalist class and through their government (p. 114).

The scientific-technical revolution that reinvigorated the industrial revolution at the turn of the 20th century was not due to any specific scientific discovery or single invention (pp. 114-115). While some have named succeeding ages--coal, oil, nuclear energy (and since Braverman, the computer and biological revolutions)—these developments do not mark the age. Instead, the age can only be understood as one in which science and technology have become an adjunct to capitalism, an age in which science and technology are systematically developed, shaped, and exploited to expand capital.

In the Pursuit of Profit

The heart of Marx's critique of capitalism beats in his analysis of the effect of the capitalist mode of production on the working class. Braverman carries on this tradition. Under capitalism, workers become a "labor force," another factor of production, another commodity to be purchased. Amassing capital is the overriding goal of the capitalist enterprise; the chief means lie in minimizing costs and maximizing productivity. To do this, the capitalist class has created jobs that use men and women inhumanely, separating their labor power from their critical faculties (p. 96). The fact that the process is repugnant to the workers is apparent from the high absentee rates, widespread job dissatisfaction, early retirements, and alienation. The critique's validity, however, does not rely on such indicators but on the objective conditions of the work itself. Real skill is replaced by manual dexterity, conception and thought are removed from execution, and control of action and pace is removed from the worker and placed in management.

Turning workers into commodities is continually being extended into more areas of the economy. Each succeeding generation must be acclimated to the new mode of work; each must be socialized to overcome the initial revulsion to the ever-more detailed division of labor and the consequent rending of human beings. This ever-widening process, Braverman claims, becomes a permanent feature of capitalist society (p. 96). Laborers are increasingly seen as machines that can readily adapt to most jobs' requirements. This view of man as a machine, Braverman says, has become more than a mere analogy. For the capitalist class, the laborer as a machine is how the class has used labor; it is how it has come to view humanity (p. 124).

Monopoly Capitalism

To this point, Braverman has detailed some of the internal shifts in the workshop. His focus has been on innovations such as the ever-finer division of labor, moving decision-making and controls away from the worker, and the increasing use of science and technology, all in a never-ending effort to increase productivity and profit. However, these shifts in the nature of work have consequences outside the workshop; they have also caused massive sociocultural changes (p. 178).

The first result of this intensification is the changed structure of the capitalist economic system. The era of competitive capitalism—firms owned by private individuals, families, or even partnerships intensely competing over markets—is over. While the myth of competitive capitalism lives on in our advertising, markets in advanced capitalist societies are increasingly controlled by large concentrations of capital in the form of corporations (p. 175). According to Braverman, the intensification of production is both a function of monopoly capitalism and a necessary condition for making monopoly capitalism possible (p. 176). Braverman points out that Marx predicted this development by describing capitalism's tendency to merge into larger and larger units. As a result of competition between firms, there are winners and losers. Over time, there are fewer and fewer winners, and they tend to be ever more significant (p. 179).

The corporation allows for the accumulation of vast amounts of capital, thus concentrating enormous wealth and social and political power into a single organization. These organizations dwarf individual wealth and power. Operating control of these organizations is no longer vested in the capitalist owner. Nor is control of the corporation vested in major shareholders. Instead, day-to-day control is given over to a specialized management team (p. 179). The top managers of the largest of these corporations, Braverman says, are drawn from the same capitalist class.

To belong to the capitalist class through ownership, all one needs to do is possess adequate wealth by inheritance. To belong to the capitalist class as a manager of a large corporation, however, one must exhibit a talent for organization, accumulation, and marketing. Most such talent, Braverman writes, comes from within the capitalist class. However, some with the requisite talent do rise from other social classes. In these cases, Braverman adds, "the ownership of capital later follows from the managerial positions, rather than the other way around" (p. 180). In this way, the interests of the capitalist class and managers rising from other classes become identical.

With the rise of the corporation and the executive arm of the capitalist class, business operations' scale and extent grew significantly. Over time, a few large firms dominate production in each market. Firms continue rationalizing their production lines to increase profitability further, constantly seeking more efficient production methods. As capitalist enterprises, corporations also look to increase their profitability through increasing sales. This expansion can be made by increasing their market share for the goods and services they produce or finding new markets they can exploit (p. 181).

At about the turn of the century, the food industry developed a national marketing structure that includes advertising, promotion, distribution, and sales (p. 182). This structure served as a pattern for other industries to follow. Marketing soon becomes a key to further massing capital and becomes second in importance only to production (p. 181). Braverman states that marketing dominates production in many industries, dictating product design and making all other divisions subordinate to its needs (p. 185).

As in all administrative control, the overall purpose of marketing, Braverman states, is to eliminate uncertainty and increase predictability. Markets are an area of great uncertainty, and marketing seeks to reduce this uncertainty by inducing or creating demand. While production and marketing become the first significant divisions of the corporations, with further growth, other management functions are soon parceled out. Finance, personnel, public relations, research and development, construction, legal, and training all become separate divisions, and these themselves become subdivided. As corporations continue to increase their sales, they seek greater profitability through the purchase of other corporations, integrating their operations vertically (from mining ore to marketing cars) or horizontally (merging formerly independent auto producers into a single corporate entity) (pp. 183-184).

As a result, administration becomes larger: managers, assistant managers, and supervisors are added, as well as additional staff positions (clerical and secretarial help) performing the actual duties of the various departments. "Management has become *administration, which is a labor process conducted for the purpose of control within the corporation,* and conducted moreover as a labor process exactly analogous to the process of production, although it produces no product other than the operation and coordination of the corporation" (p. 186, emphasis in the original). These new administrators are subjected to the same processes as the workers in production. The division of labor is subdivided to the point that many do simple tasks with little thought but excellent efficiency; control over operations and decision-making is placed at higher levels. In addition, innovative technologies are only now being introduced to make administration even more efficient and less labor-intensive. Braverman states that when examining such administrative structures, we should remember that we are looking at labor processes analogous to the labor relations in manufacturing. The same antagonisms exist between staff workers and upper managers, and the same tendency to maximize profit by controlling workers through dehumanizing tasks, deskilling workers, and devaluing human beings.

Commodification of Social Life

Braverman's analysis of the commodification of social life is an example of classic functional analysis. This functionalism should come as no surprise. Marx's theory and the theories of Malthus, Durkheim, and Weber all view society as a sociocultural system. A system's orientation naturally leads to a view of the various components of the system having reciprocal effects on one another, of change in one part of the system leading to changes in other parts of the system, and thus to overall system change.

The prime causal factor in Braverman's analysis is the growth of monopoly capitalism, the consequent intensification of production, the rise in marketing, and the search for new markets in a never-ending effort to increase profits. This need for profit, Braverman says, has transformed all of society into a "gigantic marketplace" (C. Wright Mills called this "the big bazaar"), "subordinating" the individual, family, and community to capitalist needs and dramatically changing the occupational structure as well (p. 188).

Braverman states that most production occurs within the family and community in an agrarian society. Farm families carried out domestic labor, such as growing food, building shelters, making clothing, and supplying services to their members or the wider local community (pp. 188-189). In the initial stages of industrial capitalism, this began to shift. However, as with most systems analysis, there is no simple explanation for the transition. When discussing systems, one must trace several interrelated factors, many of which are continuous processes rather than events with no clear beginning and ending (much like the Industrial Revolution itself).

According to Braverman, the process of the commodification or the creation of the universal market under monopoly capitalism includes the following: 1) Urbanization in which farm families are moved off the land, confining them in an environment where the traditional crafts and self-provisioning cannot be practiced; 2) Rising income levels of manufacturing jobs that make the purchase of such items from industry more affordable, thus making such home crafts uneconomical (except, Braverman adds, during periods of unemployment): 3) The mass production and concurrent cheapening of these manufactured goods, thus making home crafts even more uneconomical; 4) Social custom, advertising, and fashion that derogates "homemade" and attaches prestige to "store bought"; 5) The deterioration of skills to engage in home crafts; 6) Instilling in the population the desire for income and "independence," the latter being defined as the ability to purchase goods and services rather than the ability to craft them; 7) Expansion of capitalist production to incorporate all goods and services needed by the members of the society; and 8) The creation, invention and marketing of new goods and services, some of which become essential to living and participating in social life (pp. 190-195). Over time, Braverman says, the population no longer relies upon the informal social organization of family, neighbors, and community to provide goods or services. However, it must purchase these goods and services through the market. Moreover, being channeled through the market, Braverman sometimes adds a colorful phrase: they must "pay tribute to capital."

Such commodification has a dramatic impact on social life. Social life becomes "atomized" as families and friendship groups lose their functions as mutual aid communities and thus become more brittle and less permanent (p. 192). Furthermore, the process continues. As communities and families weaken, the market economy expands, providing new goods and services as commodities—day care for young and old, entertainment and amusements galore, security services, psychological counseling, and labor-saving devices for the home that free us further from domestic tasks. Moreover, this substitution of the market for human relations, according to Braverman, further weakens family life, thus changing the very character of social life itself (p. 192).

Monopoly capitalism has provided conveniences and comforts beyond measure. It has created an intricate and complex urban civilization with products and services, entertainment, and amusements, which no other economic system has ever equaled. However, Braverman adds, it could work better. It embraces much misery. The universal market created by monopoly capitalism has confined most of its subjects to dehumanized and degraded labor, and many others are excluded entirely. It has also destroyed our communities and families, laying waste to personal relationships and replacing them with cash-oriented relations in the market.

The Role of the State

Braverman, like Marx, views the state as an arm of the capitalist class. Long before the development of monopoly capitalism, the state, through such powers as taxation, regulation of trade, sale and rental of public lands, and the maintenance and use of armed forces, had used its powers to support and enrich the owners of capital. The state, Braverman adds, assures that the laws are written and enforced to preserve the conditions for the further amassing of capital and provide the necessary protection for the resulting unequal distribution of wealth and property.

The role of the state has dramatically expanded with monopoly capitalism. The state has become involved in four broad economic activities: First, monopoly capitalism is vulnerable to economic disruptions in inflation and depression. Widespread unemployment, declining productivity rates, and social and political unrest mark these periods. The government has, therefore, stepped up its role in regulating the economy to level out these cycles. Second, the aftermath of the two world wars and the Cold War have put many capitalist countries on a permanent wartime footing, significantly increasing military spending. Braverman claims these wars resulted from capitalist competition for foreign markets and resources. In addition, the capitalists' tendency to dominate non-industrialized countries also gives them an interest in policing the world. There is also great profit in supplying governments with the necessary war materials. Third, as more people who cannot compete in the labor market are cut loose from employment and community, the welfare arm of the state has grown. Such welfare assists people who temporarily lose their jobs in an ever-changing economy or people who do not have the capacity for labor, such as the elderly, children, the chronically poor, the disabled, and the mentally ill. Welfare is designed to ameliorate some of capitalism's worst abuses and relieve some of the insecurity in those who might otherwise seek to overthrow the social structure. Fourth and finally, urbanization and the increased pace of economic life have caused the growth of many government-provided services. The role of education has dramatically expanded. Other expansions have been in transportation, communication, and public health. Still, other government services, such as social work, prisons, and police, have expanded because of the antagonistic social life of the cities we have created (pp. 197-200).

Braverman further points out that while there has been a tremendous increase in government spending throughout the 20th century, employment in government has remained the same. Most government spending is through the market rather than for government employees (p. 200). Braverman cites figures indicating that government spending has gone from about 2 billion at the turn of the century to 149 billion in 1961, an increase of 75. During the same period, government employment (at all levels) only increased by a factor of 13, from 1 million to about 13 million.

U.S. Government employment, then and now, is concentrated as civilian employees of the Department of Defense at the federal level and education at the state and local levels. Most government spending goes to private firms that produce weapons systems, construct buildings and roads, or provide services; in Braverman's phrase, most government spending pays tribute to capital.

The Working Class

Many in the media and academe equate the working class with traditional blue-collar labor, that is, manual occupations in the goods-producing industries. The conventional wisdom is that this working class is a small and shrinking minority in modern societies and that we are rapidly moving into a "postindustrial" world. In this new world, almost everyone is becoming professional or at least "white collar," the average pay and working conditions of the remaining working class have made them part of the middle class and the bourgeoisie.

Supporters of such conventional wisdom point to the decline of manufacturing jobs and the rise of white-collar work in offices and the new service industries. When academicians write of white collar, they call forth images of managers, computer programmers, and accountants. When writing about the rise of service occupations, they call forth images of lawyers, physicians, and dietitians. The reality, according to Braverman, is far different.

As detailed in previous sections, there have been tremendous gains in productivity among manufacturing industries. The tasks of designing the product, laying out the production steps, coordinating the tasks, selecting the materials, scheduling the processes, calculating costs, and keeping records are all removed from the factory floor and placed in the office. By dividing the labor in such a detailed manner, the capitalist gains productivity, a less skilled and thus less costly workforce, and total control over the production process (p. 86). Applying more sophisticated technology to production leads to further gains in these areas. Overall, the gain in productivity means that the capitalist can now employ fewer workers to produce a specific output level.

However, this increase in labor productivity has been offset by a tremendous increase in production scale (you will recall that the scale of production makes such innovations economically feasible). Consequently, employment in production industries has not declined in absolute numbers but *in relative* size. Braverman gathers data demonstrating that workers in manufacturing, construction, and other goods-producing industries (excluding agriculture) grew from about 14 million in 1920 to slightly over 23 million in 1970. However, their proportion of the working population has declined from about 46 percent in 1920 to only 33 percent of the workforce in 1970 (pp. 163-164).

Two main types of employment tables need to concern us. The first just remarked upon divides workers in terms of their employment industry. This table looks at the number of employees by industry, including all occupations within these industries. So, for example, employment in "Manufacturing" would include not only the blue-collar production worker on the assembly line but also the service worker sweeping the shop, the executive who runs the personnel department, and the secretary typing and filing the executive's correspondence. The other type of employment table of interest looks at employment by occupational classification. The U.S. Census Bureau uses six broad classifications. "Managerial and professional specialty," "Technical, sales, and administrative support," "Service Occupations," "Precision production, craft, and repair," "Operators, fabricators, and laborers," and "Farming, forestry, and fishing." There are many subcategories under these categories.

The difference between employment in industries and occupations can be striking. In comparison, service industries employed some 37% of the 2001 workforce, but only 14% of all employed people worked in service occupations. These figures (and many more from the U.S. Census and other government sources), available at your local library and through the Internet, are instrumental in that they are records of change over time in industries and occupations.

If one equates working in production industries with the working class, the class will appear to be a small and shrinking minority. Braverman, however, defines the working class in much broader terms. The working class, he says, consists of those who come to the labor market with nothing to sell but their labor (p. 261). That labor is systematically exploited and degraded by the capitalist system. Businesses break skills down into simple tasks to grow profit, automate where economically feasible, and manipulate production speed. These processes do not just occur in manufacturing operations, Braverman adds, but throughout the capitalist economy.

While the first separation of conception and execution of tasks occurs between the factory and the office, the second separation occurs in the office itself. In the United States, the proportion of clerks and administrative assistants in the working population climbed from 2 percent in 1900 to 18 percent by 1970 (p. 204). While traditionally classified as "white collar," Braverman points out, the vast bulk of these jobs involve minimal skills and initiative and garner wages and benefits equivalent to manual occupations.

He reports that service workers rose from 1 million at the turn of the century to 9 million by the 1970 census. While a couple of occupations in this grouping require educational credentials and extensive on-the-job training (for example, police supervisors, detectives, and firefighters), most are low-skill, low-paying, and often temporary. Some examples of the types of jobs encompassed in the service classification are janitors, chambermaids, bussers, dishwashers, childcare workers, and the like. The skills required for most of these jobs are minimal. The pay, Braverman reports, is the worst average of all census job classifications. Braverman adds retail sales workers and cashiers to this group, people with the same skills and compensation as most service workers. In 1970, Braverman reported 3 million such workers (p. 253).

According to Braverman's figures, the percentage of the workforce engaged in essentially rote manual occupations, with little skill, educational requirements, autonomy, or decent compensation, has grown each decade since the turn of the century, going from 51 percent of the labor force to 69 percent in 1970 (p. 262). He arrives at these figures by adding the number of people working as Operatives and Laborers, Craftsmen, Clerical workers, and Service and Retail Sales workers for each census year from 1900 to 1970. It should be emphasized that these figures do not include agriculture, a significant occupation in 1900 (in terms of numbers). Braverman argues that while the compensation for such an occupation was uneven (though often low), the autonomy and skill were extremely high. Braverman admits that the methodology is crude. It is intended as a rough computation based on Census data gathered for other purposes and is therefore not ideal for this exercise. Some occupations will be included in his working-class estimate with compensation closer to a managerial scale and in which the occupation grants a degree of autonomy to the worker. However, other occupations will be excluded from his estimate, particularly in some of the technical fields that grant little autonomy or compensation.

The Industrial Reserve Army

In addition to the working class, many unskilled or outmoded skilled laborers have been excluded from full labor force participation through technological change or lack of suitable full-time jobs. This "industrial reserve army" consists of temporary and chronic unemployed, underemployed, sporadically employed, part-time, racial underclass members, and migrant laborers.

Braverman, citing Marx, asserts that this reserve army is a necessary part of the workings of capitalism. They are objects of exploitation for their unskilled labor and the marketing of inferior goods and services, and their existence keeps labor costs low. They are, in effect, the surplus population created by monopoly capitalism. Moreover, according to Marx and Braverman, their numbers will expand as capital grows (p. 267).

Official unemployment, Braverman reports, fluctuated between 4 to 5 million in the early 1970s. However, he says this is merely the beginning. Hidden unemployment, or those not reflected in official statistics because of how they are compiled, nearly doubles the official rate (pp. 269-270). For example, those who express the desire for a job are only counted if they have given up actively searching for one, and those who work part-time but prefer to work full-time. Many others would also include the underemployed or those who work at jobs that do not fully utilize their skills or education.

Another indication of the massing of the industrial reserve army, Braverman reports, is a steady decline in the labor force participation rates for the male population, from 89.6 in 1947 to 82.2 in 1971. The decline is found in every age category. While part of this decline is due to increased school attendance and retirement, this does not fully explain the decline. At least some of the decline, he asserts, reflects a portion of the population moving into the reserve army. The labor-force participation rates of women have been, of course, on the increase in recent times. However, Braverman notes that women are paid substantially less than men (p. 271).

Industries in the automation process throw off laborers whose only options are the labor-intensive service industries or other jobs unsuitable to modern technologies (whether for technological or economic reasons). Thus, the fastest growing occupations, Braverman reports, tend to be low skill (p. 264). Wages in these occupations are kept low by the existence and continual replenishment of the industrial reserve army (pp. 256-257). This reserve army, Braverman claims, is why advanced monopoly capital experiences the phenomenon of rising numbers of working poor, families who must have two wage earners to maintain a decent lifestyle, and individuals who must hold multiple jobs to make ends meet.

The Middle Levels

Braverman asserts that work in monopoly capitalist economies has become very polarized, with a few people having all the technical expertise and managerial control over an unskilled and uneducated workforce. As conception and execution are separated, increasingly technical expertise is concentrated in fewer hands. Braverman estimates that, at most, only 3 percent of the 1970 workforce consisted of such technical specialists as engineers, architects, drafting technicians, designers, natural scientists, and technicians (pp. 166-167). Braverman allows that many managers who are technical specialists have been excluded from this list. However, it is also true that a portion of those on the list includes those "whose jobs are confined to the repetition of simple activities that are rapidly learned and do not encompass any true conceptualization or planning functions" (pp. 166-167).

In addition to this 3 percent, Braverman acknowledges that many individuals are engaged in lower levels of management and professional specialties. He estimates that this middle level accounted for about 20 percent of occupational employment in 1970 (p. 279). However, Braverman points out these occupations should not be equated with the old middle class of independent entrepreneurs of an earlier capitalist era. Most wage earners are dependent upon corporations or the government for their employment. Unlike the old middle class, they are part of the exploitation system. Taking their character from both capitalist and worker, he says, they take part in the expropriation of surplus from the workers but have the same dependent characteristics as other workers, with only their labor to sell. The working class's sheer productivity and the resulting surplus's expropriation make the number of middle-level managers possible. Further, Braverman asserts that this group is prone to the same rationalization techniques as other labor as soon as enough mass is gathered to make a detailed division of labor and automation (pp. 281-282).

Braverman appears uneasy about the size of this middle stratum and its import for the Marxist analysis of capitalism. According to Karl Marx (and thus Braverman), as capitalism develops, the working class is supposed to become progressively deskilled, exploited, and more extensive as former capitalists and the middle stratum of self-employed small businesspeople are absorbed into its ranks. Eventually, most people within capitalist society become workers (95 percent is a figure often given), with just a few capitalists at the top. Then comes the revolution. Nevertheless, as Braverman points out, class is a dynamic process; it is constantly changing and often difficult to encapsulate into neat theories and formulas. Science does not require theory to explain all (pp. 282-283). Marxists are insistent that their brand of social science is genuinely scientific.

Because the U.S. economic system is dominated by capitalism, the entire sociocultural system is organized around an insatiable need to expand profits. This drive is behind the ever more detailed division of labor, the adoption of computers and other technologies to replace workers, the commodification of social life, the degradation of work and workers, and the polarization of the elite and masses. Despite emphasizing capital, Marx's theory is not a simple mono-causal theory.

Marx (and thus Braverman) maintains that societies are complex systems in which the various parts interact; social stability and change are the products of ongoing sociocultural interactions between capital, technology, science, cultural norms, ideologies, and values. More than this, they assert, sociocultural systems are part of historical processes and can only be understood within the context of their unique history (p. 15).

About Braverman

Harry Braverman was born in Brooklyn, New York, on December 9, 1920. His parents, Morris and Sarah, were Jewish Polish immigrants. His father was a shoe worker. Attending Brooklyn College for one year, Braverman was forced to withdraw for economic reasons and find employment (he was not to return to college until the early 1960s when he received a Bachelor of Arts degree from the New School for Social Research in 1963). During his single year of college as a young man, he first became exposed to Marx and socialism. Shortly after, he joined the Young People's Socialist League. At 16 (1937), Braverman found work at the Brooklyn Naval Yards as a coppersmith apprentice, where he worked until 1941. In a brief autobiographical sketch in *Labor and Monopoly Capitalism*, Braverman characterized his early working life:

> I began my working life by serving a four-year apprenticeship in the coppersmith's trade, and worked at this trade for a total of seven years [...] These seven years were spent in a naval shipyard, a type of industrial enterprise which, at that time, was probably the most complete product of two centuries of industrial revolution [...] The extremely limited nature of employment in my trade, and its rapid decline with the substitution of new processes and materials for the traditional modes of copper working, made it difficult for me to continue work as a coppersmith when I moved to other parts of the country or from job to job. But because the trade of working copper provided a foundation in the elements of a number of other crafts, I was always able to find employment in other trades, such as pipefitting, sheet-metal work, and layout, and I did work of these sorts for another seven years (p. 4).

In these trades, Braverman understood the impact of science-based technology on jobs. "I had the opportunity of seeing at first hand, during those years, not only the transformation of industrial processes but the manner in which these processes are reorganized; how the worker, systematically robbed of a craft heritage, is given little or nothing to take its place" (p. 5). Braverman was drafted toward the end of the war (either 1944 or 1945) and was "sent by the Army to Cheyenne, Wyoming, where as a sergeant he taught and supervised locomotive pipefitting" (Foster 1998, p. x). In either 1946 or 47 he moved to Youngstown Ohio with his wife, Miriam, to find work as a steelworker.

Fired from one company "at the instigation of the FBI," Braverman managed to find work at others (p. x).

From his early years in college, Braverman continued his commitment to socialist ideology and organizations devoted to establishing these ideals. He joined the Socialist Workers Party (SWP) and attended a six-month Marxist study course at their Trotsky School in the early 1950s. However, there were deep divisions in the SWP in the early 50s. In 1953, Braverman left (or was expelled from) the SWP and became a co-leader with Bert Cochran of a splinter group, the Socialist Union. He began co-editing and writing for their paper, the *American Socialist*, under his party name, Harry Frankel. While working and writing for this paper, he worked out many of the ideas expressed in *Labor and Monopoly Capitalism.*

When the *American Socialist* folded after some seven years, Braverman moved into book publishing, becoming an editor for Grove Press in 1960. "While at Grove, he edited and published *The Autobiography of Malcolm X* when that book was dropped by Random House, the publisher who had initially commissioned the project" (Livingston, 2000). He then became a vice president and general manager at Grove Press until leaving in 1967, "when the president of the company refused to publish a book by Bertrand Russell on American war crimes in Vietnam" (Livingston, 2000). Braverman then became the director of Monthly Review Press and worked there until his death from cancer on August 2, 1976, at 55.

While working in publishing, Braverman experienced the typical office processes and changes due to automation. "As an executive in publishing," he says

> I was able to see, and in fact design, some of the administrative processes involved in modern marketing, distributing, accounting, and book production routines, and this experience twice included the transition from conventional to computerized office systems. I would not pretend that this background is as extensive as that of many others who have worked for longer periods of time in larger organizations, but at least it does enable me to understand, in some detail and concreteness, the principles by which labor processes are organized in modern offices (Braverman [1974] 1996, p. 5).

Braverman began writing *Labor and Monopoly Capital* in his "spare time" at night and on weekends beginning in 1970 (p. 4). Initially published in 1974, it was well received, sold well, and is still in print. This popularity is remarkable for a Marxist critique of American capital and society. However, the book resonates with many Marxists and non-Marxists alike. "The unique background as a socialist intellectual who had been a worker and an activist within the productive core of world industry," John Bellamy Foster writes, "one who rose by dint of his political struggles and intellectual brilliance to executive positions within two important presses, gave Braverman unique qualifications to take on the difficult task of stripping the veil away from the capitalist labor process […] Based on this single treatise, Braverman is now renowned worldwide as one of the great social scientists of the twentieth century: a legendary figure who rose from the depths of production to combat 'the great god Capital,' armed only with what he had learned while working with his own two hands and through his struggles as an organic intellectual, a human embodiment of the unification of theory and practice (Foster 1998, p. xi). While most will not agree with Braverman on every count, *Labor and Monopoly Capital* will give many an appreciation for the devastating effects of the detailed division of labor on human life and the role of capitalism in spreading this division.

Chapter 3: John Bellamy Foster's Ecological-Marxism

According to John Bellamy Foster (b. 1953), as it has been received from our forebears, the great sociological tradition is developed almost entirely devoid of any concern for or foundation in nature. Marx, Durkheim, and Weber seemingly developed their theories "as if nature didn't matter" (Foster, 2000, p. 18). (As we will see, Malthus takes nature as the foundation of his social theory; consequently, the human-nature interface is of primary concern. However, Malthus is not accorded major status within mainstream sociology, and the character of his posited human-nature interface is little known among sociologists.) In the case of Marx, however, Foster contends that this notion is quite mistaken. What did Marx have to say about ecology? Moreover, why should we care? Foster's goal is not to reinterpret Marx considering present-day ecological thinking; such an exercise would be useless. Nor is an examination of Marx's social-ecological thought merely to underscore that the relationships between humans and nature were at the heart of Marx's analysis. While such underscoring may be valuable in more fully understanding Marx's thought and thus crucial for contemporary social scientists and historians, it would only hold relevance if it were confined to such a narrow purpose. Instead, the real value in examining Marx's social ecology is in bringing Marx to the serious attention of ecologists, who still need to appreciate the implications of Marxist theory for understanding the ecological crises of our time (19).

The Ecological Theory of Marx and Engels

According to Foster, the major problem with modern ecological thought is that it is too idealistic and spiritual (p. 20). By "idealistic," Foster means that causation is attributed to ideas and ideologies instead of material conditions. By "spiritual," he refers to the mystical and sacred stance taken toward nature by many ecologists. On the other hand, Marx and Engels rooted ecology in their materialism, assuming that the natural world is the foundation for all that exists. Physical reality "is independent of and prior to thought" (p. 2). The centrality of Nature in Marx's thought is clearly expressed in a passage from Marx's early writings, cited by Foster. "The universality of man manifests itself in practice in the universality which takes the whole of nature as his inorganic body, (1) as a direct means of life, and (2) as the matter, the object and tool of his activity. Nature is man's inorganic body nature as far as it is not the human body. Man lives from nature, i.e., nature is his body, and he must maintain a continuing dialogue with it if he is not to die. To say that man's physical and mental life is linked to nature simply means that nature is linked to itself, for man is a part of nature" (p. 72).

For Marx, physical human beings are a part of nature. Besides our bodies, nature forms the "inorganic body" that supplies the material means of life for humans (air, water, food, sun, and shelter) and the tools needed to access these material needs. Humans relate to nature through the production of goods and the reproduction of the species. Humans transform nature (the "inorganic body") into products for human use through production. The reproduction process ensures society's continuation and regulates the resources needed from the natural environment. These processes are, therefore, central to understanding how humans relate to the environment, that is, in understanding human ecology. "The first premise of all human existence and, therefore, of all history," Foster cites Marx and Engels,

> is that men must be in a position to live in order to be able to 'make history.' But life involves before everything else eating and drinking, housing, clothing, and various other things. The first historical act is thus the production of the means to satisfy these needs, the production of material life itself. And indeed this is an historical act, a fundamental condition of all history, which today, as thousands of years ago, must daily and hourly be fulfilled merely in order to sustain human life [...] *the production of life, both of one's own in labour and of fresh life in procreation*...appears as a twofold relation: on the one hand as a natural, on the other hand as a social relation [emphasis added] (p. 116).

The material conditions that make life and society possible and the means men and women use to manipulate the natural environment to obtain essential goods become the foundation of Marx's social theory. These means of relating to the natural world are through production and reproduction; the passage clarifies that natural or physical conditions and social conditions determine both. Regarding the production process, the natural aspects that govern environmental-societal relationships are physical tools and technologies; reproduction, too, is governed by physical relations between men and women. By "social" regarding production, Marx and Engels refer to social relationships between people as the division of labor that takes place in the organization of production processes, as well as how men and women relate to one another in the production of necessary goods and services. By "social" regarding reproduction, Marx and Engels refer to such social phenomena as mating patterns, marriage customs, and other social forms of regulating reproduction. The social relations of production and the consequent distribution of goods and services largely determine these social forms of reproduction. Foster clarifies that Marx and Engels vigorously rejected Malthus' claim that the population was governed by natural law, keeping the population level down to the available means of subsistence. The means of subsistence, they argued, was subject to vast improvement. Instead, a surplus population of the poor existed because the class controlling the forces of production had no interest in feeding people experiencing poverty. They had an interest in maintaining or even increasing their numbers. (See Foster 2000, pages 82-109, and pages 143-151 for a more extensive discussion of the relationships between the ideas of Malthus and Marx and Engels from a Marxist's point of view. However, Foster's discussion of Malthus goes overboard in his critique, and Malthus is far subtler than is characterized by either Marx and Engels or Foster. The Malthusian and Marxian positions on the relationships between production and population, as Marvin Harris (1968) argues forcibly, are not opposed.) For Marx and Engels, both the physical and social aspects of production and reproduction are central to understanding the relationship of humans to the natural world. However, their focus is predominantly on the social aspects of this relationship. The technologies used to exploit the environment are essential in understanding a society's relationship to the natural world. The purposes of technologies, the interests they serve, and the extent and growth of their use are central.

Marx and Engels argued that population size and growth were not subject to natural law as Malthus posited but determined by historical conditions. The ever-increasing polarization of wealth in capitalist societies (both within and between nations) is a primary cause of the growth of an extensive working class as well as an "industrial reserve army" of the surplus population (unemployed and underemployed) that lives in "a situation of relative impoverishment and degradation." This industrial reserve army is necessary for capital accumulation because it assures a chronic oversupply of workers on the labor market, thus keeping wages in check and allowing workers to be more fully exploited by capitalist enterprises. Marx formulates these relationships in his "absolute general law of capitalist accumulation." Under the rule of Capital, the greater the wealth, the more it becomes concentrated in the hands of a few; the more significant this concentration, the more extensive the mass of workers and surplus population, as well as their productivity.

Furthermore, the greater this concentration of wealth, the more intensive the exploitation of these masses. The large working class, the surplus population, and their exploitation and degradation are all necessary for the accumulation and growth of Capital (pp. 173-174). Further, it is not the relationship between population and food supply that determines whether a society is overpopulated; it is the relationship between population and employment (p. 109). Overpopulation in capitalist societies—defined as the part of the population that is denied full access to the means of subsistence—is caused by the rule of Capital itself (p. 141).

Marx and Engels are not sentimental about nature; they do not believe it should be preserved just for its own sake. According to Foster, "Their position—which became clearer as their writings evolved—was rather that of encouraging a sustainable relation between human beings and nature through the organization of production in ways that took into account the metabolic relation between human beings and the earth" (p. 138). This emphasis on sustainability is clear in Marx's definition of the labor process. Foster (p. 157) cites Marx's writing in *Capital*: "Labour is, first of all, a process between man and nature, a process by which man, through his own actions, mediates, regulates and controls the metabolism between himself and nature. He confronts the material of nature as a force of nature. He sets in motion the natural forces which belong to his own body, his arms, legs, head and hands, in order to appropriate the materials of nature in a form adapted to his own needs. Through this movement he acts upon external nature and changes it, and in this way he simultaneously changes his own nature" (Capital vol. 1, 283).

The alienation of labor so central to Marxian thought—the alienation of labor regarding the product, the production process, the self, and the community—is inseparable from human's alienation from nature (pp. 72-73). "Marx's notion of the alienation of nature," Foster writes, "which he saw arising out of human practical life, was no more abstract at its core than his notion of the alienation of labor. Both were grounded in his understanding of the political-economic thrust of capitalist society. The alienation of labor was a reflection of the fact that labor (power) had become reduced virtually to the status of a commodity, governed by the laws of supply and demand" (p. 73). The alienation of humans from nature was reflected in the fact that nature also became commodified, governed by simple economic laws of supply and demand as opposed to the more complex laws of nature and man.

The metabolic relationship between society and nature is very much a part of Marx's view of the sustainability of agriculture, which he arrived at through a close reading of the agricultural science of his day. Foster (2000, pp. 155-156) again cites Marx's writing in *Capital*:

> Capitalist production collects the population in great centres and causes the urban population to achieve an ever-growing preponderance. This has two results. On the one hand, it disturbs the metabolic interaction between man and the earth, i.e., it

prevents the return to the soil of its constituent elements consumed by man in the form of food and clothing; hence it hinders the operation of the eternal condition for the lasting fertility of the soil [...] But by destroying the circumstances surrounding that metabolism [...] it compels its systematic restoration as a regulative law of social production, and in a form adequate to the full development of the human race [...] all progress in capitalist agriculture is a progress in the art, not only of robbing the worker but of robbing the soil; all progress in increasing the fertility of the soil for a given time is a progress toward ruining the more long-lasting sources of that fertility [...] Capitalist production, therefore, only develops the technique and the degree of combination of the social process of production by simultaneously undermining the sources of all wealth—the soil and the worker (pp. 637-638).

Urbanization severed the relationship between the production and consumption of food, and the necessary recycling of waste to fertilize the soil was disrupted. Capitalism is an exploitive relationship; it exploits the worker as it exploits the natural world. As such, it cannot be sustained. "Large-scale industry and industrially pursued large-scale agriculture," Foster (2000, p. 155) cites Marx's writing in *Capital*, "have the same effect. If they are originally distinguished by the fact that the former lays waste and ruins labour-power and thus the natural power of man, whereas the latter does the same to the natural power of the soil, they link up in the later course of development, since the industrial system applied to agriculture also enervates the workers there, while industry and trade for their part provide agriculture with the means of exhausting the soil" (p. 638).

Under the rule of Capital, agricultural decisions are not based on long-term sustainability. Instead, capitalists make such decisions based on market prices, rents, and short-term profits (Foster, 2000, p. 164). Marx and Engels recognized capitalism's tremendous power in developing society's productive forces. "The bourgeoisie," they write in the *Communist Manifesto* (p. 10), "during its rule of scarce one hundred years, has created more massive and more colossal productive forces than have all preceding generations together. Subjection of nature's forces to man, machinery, application of chemistry to industry and agriculture, steam-navigation, railways, electric telegraphs, clearing of whole continents for cultivation, canalization of rivers, while population conjured out of the ground. What earlier century had even a presentiment that such productive forces slumbered in the lap of social labor?" (Foster, p. 138). However, Foster writes that Marx and Engels also recognized that this productive force was unleashed to serve the material interests of only one class. This material interest was served through the ever more extensive and intensive exploitation of nature and humankind (p. 139). In opposition to this exploitation—both of labor and nature—they advocated the social control of the forces of production to bring them under rational human control, exploit nature sustainably, and distribute the products of labor more equitably to all. Citing Capital, Volume 3, Foster quotes: "Freedom in this sphere [the realm of natural necessity] can consist only in this, that socialized man, the associated producers, govern the human metabolism with nature in a rational way, bringing it under their own collective control instead of being dominated by it as a blind power; accomplishing it with the least expenditure of energy and in conditions most worthy and appropriate for their human nature" (p. 159). Socialism, or the control of the productive forces of industry by the people themselves, employing these forces to satisfy the human needs of all within the social order rather than to expand the Capital of a few, is the prescribed solution to the tightening environmental crisis.

Since its inception, capitalism has continued to expand and intensify globally. Capitalism began in Europe in the 15th century, significantly fueled by the expropriation of the riches of the Americas, Africa, and parts of Asia. Again, Foster (p. 173) cites Marx's Capital: "The discovery of gold and silver in America, the extirpation, enslavement and entombment in mines of the indigenous population of that continent, the beginnings of the conquest and plunder of India, and the conversion of Africa into a preserve for the commercial hunting of blackskins, are all things which characterize the dawn of the era of capitalist production. These idyllic proceedings are the chief moments of primitive accumulation" (p. 915).

Using this plunder as initial Capital, the capitalists and the nation-states, under their influence, used military force and economic imperialism to create the capitalist world system. Capitalism became "a world system under its control that extracted wealth and raw materials for capitalist industry for the benefit of Europe, while destroying communal systems of property elsewhere" (Foster, p. 173). This view is, of course, highly consistent with Wallerstein and world-systems theory.

This alienation of the bulk of humanity from nature or the earth begins when a few claim land ownership. In feudal society, this takes the form of the nobility claiming the land as their exclusive property, granting access to the land (and thus livelihood) to rule the peasantry. The nobility enclosed their lands during the first phase of capitalism in Britain ("mercantilism" or capitalism based on the trade of raw materials, agricultural products, and some crafted luxury goods). They evicted the peasantry to convert their estates into grazing lands for sheep, an enterprise that— through the wool trade—more fully integrated the estates into the market economy than traditional feudal agriculture. This "enclosure movement," according to Marx, "drives the overwhelming majority of the population into the arms of industry and reduces its own workers to total misery" (Foster, 2000, p. 74).

According to Marx, it is in the cities where capitalism thoroughly exploits and abuses nature and workers. "Even the need for fresh air," he writes,

> ceases to be a need for the worker. Man reverts once more to living in a cave, but the cave is now polluted by the mephitic and pestilential breath of civilization. Moreover, the worker has no more than a precarious right to live in it, for it is for him an alien power that can be daily withdrawn and from which, should he fail to pay, he can be evicted at any time. He actually has to pay for this mortuary. A dwelling in the light, which Prometheus describes in Aeschylus as one of the great gifts through which he transformed savages into men, ceases to exist for the worker. Light, air, etc.—the simple animal cleanliness—ceases to be a need for man. Dirt—this pollution and putrefaction of man, the sewage (this word is to be understood in its literal sense) of civilization—becomes an element of life for him. Universal unnatural neglect, putrefied nature, becomes an element of life for him (p. 75).

The expansion of the market drove the peasantry off land. The search for new markets, investment opportunities, products, workers, resources, techniques, and technologies to expand Capital and to exclude other values and considerations—has led capitalism to thoroughly exploit and abuse workers and the environment. Nevertheless, Marx writes in *Capital, Vol. 3*, that this exploitation will pass, because it is unsustainable and morally wrong. "From the standpoint of a higher socio-economic formation [future socialist society], the private property of particular individuals in the earth will appear just as absurd as the private property of one man in other men. Even an entire society, a nation, or all simultaneously existing societies taken together, are not the owners of the earth. They are simply its possessor, its beneficiaries, and have to bequeath it in an improved state to succeeding generations as boni patres familias" [good heads of household] (p. 164). If nothing else has convinced the reader, the above passage alone should establish Marx's bona fides as a theorist who has thoroughly integrated ecology into his perspective.

Marxist Ecology

What does Marx bring to our understanding of modern ecology? What does a Marxian perspective add to the analysis of environmental problems? Foster contends that industrial technology and demographic factors are not the primary cause of the environmental destruction around us. While undoubtedly real, these material forces are rooted in the social relations of production—the institution of Capital and its ever-expanding drive for accumulation. Consequently, demographic and technological forces are not responsive to the individual's will; instead, they are responsive to the needs and interests of Capital. Moreover, the needs and interests of Capital are simple: the accumulation of more Capital or, more simply, profit (Foster, 1999, p. 12).

While all societies have affected their environments, some even collapsed because of their exploitation; societies were small, and the problems were localized. The worldwide expansion and intensification of the capitalist world system led to population growth in many core and peripheral nations—many of which are still expanding due to poverty (p. 107). Because capitalism is based on growth, there is a drive to expand and intensify markets, commodify all goods and services, create new "needs" and luxuries, and stimulate ever-greater consumption. Because of this drive, core nations have a tremendous consumption rate of raw materials and energy; within nation states—core or periphery—wealthy individuals and classes also have higher consumption rates (Foster, 2002, p. 9). With population and industrial expansion, Foster writes, "the scale of human economic processes began to rival the ecological cycles of the planet, opening up as never before the possibility of planet-wide ecological disaster" (Foster, 1999, p. 108). Under the rule of Capital, human societies have grown in both populations and the power of their technology. This growth has led to the ever more intensive mining of raw materials and energy from the earth and consequently to the accelerated pollution of the environment (Foster 2002, p. 10 & p. 44).

Growth is not inherent in industrial production, which consists of rational technologies and social practices to exploit the environment for human use. Instead, the commitment to economic growth stems from the nature of capitalism itself. Capitalism aims to maximize the rate of profit as quickly and efficiently as possible; it is a system of economic accumulation. A stationary capitalism rejecting economic growth and expansion is contradictory (p. 89, pp. 95-96). The men who control the economic institutions in society are inextricably committed to economic growth, and through their power and influence, it has become an unquestioned goal of social life. Through the institutions that dominate the organizational structures of societies—government, mass media, education—people worldwide have become convinced that unrestrained economic growth is both necessary and desirable. Capitalism promotes economic growth as our only hope of feeding and housing an expanding world population and improving our standard of living (a standard that has come to be defined strictly in economic terms). Corporate elites grow more powerful within this consensus on the desirability of economic growth (pp. 74-75).

The primary means of increasing profitability is expanding markets and adopting more efficient technologies to lower production costs (and thus control labor costs). However, even when industry moves to increase efficiency through technology designed to limit raw materials and energy input, Foster argues, these savings are more than offset by the expansion of industry itself. The growth of capitalism, Foster states repeatedly, has led to the growth of wastes of all kinds. Monopoly capitalism produces many products that have limited "use value." He reports that almost three-quarters of materials used in industrial economies end up as waste within a year (pp. 23-24). The whole point of capitalism is profitability, which can only be maintained through the continued expansion of markets and the commodification of all potentially profitable goods and services within the world system. Since the beginning of the 20th century, Foster reports that the world population has tripled, and the world economy has expanded approximately twenty-fold (p. 44).

However, serious environmental problems are not simply due to our numbers and consequent consumption increase and waste. The type of technologies used to manufacture goods, the type of agriculture used to grow and process food, and the type of transport used for goods and people are independent factors in determining our environmental impact. Burning fossil fuels and converting oil into thousands of synthetic substances have wreaked havoc with natural recycling systems, severely affecting human health, agricultural systems, and the planet's biodiversity (Foster, 1999, p. 120). The drive for profit has led capitalists to integrate science into the industrial production process, an integration that, true to form, pays little heed to the environmental consequences.

> New technologies have replaced older ones. Synthetic detergents have replaced soap powder; synthetic fabrics have replaced clothing made out of natural fibers (such as cotton and wool); aluminum, plastics, and concrete have replaced steel and lumber; truck freight has displaced railroad freight; high-powered automobile engines have displaced the low-powered engines of the 1920s and 1930s; synthetic fertilizer has in effect displaced land in agricultural production; herbicides have displaced the cultivator; insecticides have displaced earlier forms of insect control (p. 114).

Since World War II, capitalism has employed science to develop a production system that is hostile to the environment, a "counter-ecological" production system (p. 115).

To illustrate the hostility of monopoly capitalism to the environment, Foster cites America's automobile complex or the establishment of the automobile as the dominant mode of transportation. Corporate elites took up the quest to make cars and trucks the dominant mode of transportation for people and goods to maximize profitability. Acting at the behest of these elites, federal and state governments granted tremendous subsidies for road building and maintenance. General Motors and other interested corporations actively bought electric streetcar lines, dismantled them, and replaced them with buses. "The number of streetcar lines dropped from 40,000 in 1936 to 5,000 in 1955. Meanwhile, GM used its monopolistic control of bus production for the Greyhound Corporation, on the one hand, and its monopoly in the production of locomotives, on the other, to ensure the growing displacement of bus and rail traffic by private automobiles in intercity transport—essentially undercutting itself in intercity mass transit in order to make higher profits off increased automobile traffic" (p. 116). As a result of such corporate interests, the U.S. relies almost exclusively upon truck and automobile transportation for the ground transport of goods and people. Foster claims no other ground transport system is so inefficient, polluting, and wasteful of energy. However, no other system could have been so profitable to corporate elites.

Petrochemicals are another industry that has used science in the search for profit to the detriment of the environment. "Synthetic fibers, detergent, pesticides, and plastics are all products of the petrochemical industry, as are most toxic wastes" (p. 116). According to Foster, industry synthesized over 70,000 different chemicals, hundreds of which have made their way into the human organism. Most of these chemicals have not been tested for toxic effects, either singly or combined with other chemicals. In addition, Foster adds, the industry has become integral to modern manufacturing and a staple of modern agriculture—and all to severe environmental consequences (p. 116). (For a fascinating discussion of the impact of corporate capitalism on agriculture, see Berry, Wendell, 1977, *The Unsettling of America*.)

Within the system of capitalism, nature rarely enters the equation. Raw materials are commodities—only their exchange values matter. The environment has little value; pollution in the production process can be carted to landfills, dissipated in the air through smokestacks, or dumped into our streams, rivers, lakes, and oceans. Foster writes: "[T]he profit-making relation has become the sole connection between human beings and between human beings and nature. This means that while we can envision more sustainable forms of technology that would solve much of the environmental problems, the development and implementation of these technologies is blocked by the mode of production—by capitalism and capitalists. Large corporations make the major decisions about the technology we use, and the sole lens that they consider in arriving at their decisions is profitability" (pp. 123-124). Mainstream environmental movements miss this essential connection: Our environmental problems are inextricably linked to our social problems, and both are rooted in capitalism. Because they miss this connection, they call for purely technological solutions: smaller cars, moving away from our dependence upon fossil fuels, and recycling waste. They look at our environmental problems as purely technical problems to be addressed by more efficient management, technology, and technicians. Such organizations do not even seriously address economic growth. Foster asserts that no technological fix exists for unbridled economic growth in a finite environment (2002, p. 80). Instead, they seem to be putting faith in educating the public and, through them, corporate leaders in the vain hope that such enlightenment will naturally lead to a more environmentally friendly industrial system. Such idealism is refreshing in youth, but as a strategy for changing the world, it lacks touch with material conditions (Foster, 1999, p. 147; 2002, pp. 44-46 & pp. 74-75).

Foster asserts that the rapid deterioration of the global environment is due to the ever-expanding nature of capitalism. It is an economic system that knows no bounds that converts all to marketable commodities. Government attempts to regulate this system have generally failed because (1) modern governments are dependent upon the capitalist system for taxes, employment of the population, and increasing the wealth of the nation; (2) government officials and elected representatives are dependent upon capitalists for campaign contributions, and are susceptible to other forms of bribery; and (3) high government officials and elected representatives are often from the same elite social classes or dependent upon these classes for their position, consequently taking on similar ideologies, outlook, and interests.

Reform of the system can only be of limited value; while such reform can address some of the worst abuses, the underlying cause remains capitalism. It is not the abuses of capitalism that concern Foster. Capitalism itself is an abuse—for the few exploit the mass of people and the earth. The system cannot be reformed; it can only be destroyed and replaced; this can only occur with a real revolution. Unless we address the problem of capitalism, Foster argues, our environmental crisis will intensify to the point of social collapse (Foster, 1999, p. 129; Foster, 2002, p. 40, pp. 44-45, p. 67, & p. 90).

The Imperial Connection

John Bellamy Foster's Ecological-Marxism goes beyond the immediate concerns of capitalist firms within nation-states exploiting the environment and workers. Like Wallerstein, Foster in his book

Naked Imperialism: The U.S. in Pursuit of Global Dominance (2006) offers a Marxian analysis of the relations between core and peripheral nations that have grave consequences for environmental depletion and pollution, global inequality between and within nation-states, nuclear proliferation, and the likelihood of nuclear war. (This book, *Naked Imperialism* is a compilation of essays written for Monthly Review between November 2001 and January 2005.) In his analysis, Foster examines details of the historical and contemporary foreign policy of the United States of America. He finds that much of that foreign policy, particularly since World War II, has been aimed at strengthening American political, military, and economic power worldwide. Many of these actions have been taken in the name of spreading freedom and democracy around the globe, protecting American citizens or allies, or, more recently, preventing the spread of weapons of mass destruction. Foster asserts that these actions are primarily taken to serve the needs of American Capital; they aim to secure access to raw materials, markets, and labor—to expand American corporations' investment opportunities further. According to Foster, the United States of America is still the hegemonic power at the core of the world system. It uses its military, political, and economic power imperialistically, consistent with such historical empires as Britain and Rome.

The roots of American imperialism lie in capitalism and the capitalist world system. "From its beginning in the sixteenth and seventeenth centuries," Foster writes, "and even more so in the monopoly stage, capital within each nation-state at the center of the system is driven by a need to control access to raw materials and the labor in the periphery" (p. 109). While the specific mechanisms of imperialism vary historically, the goal of American imperialism today is the same as in the past. That goal is to invest in the economies of third-world nations to obtain raw materials and agricultural products at the lowest possible prices. To siphon off the economic surplus produced by these economies, exploit their people as a source of cheap labor (and use them as a threat to labor within the core). "Economies of the periphery are structured to meet the external needs of the United States and other core capitalist countries rather than their own internal needs" (pp. 13-14).

Foster reports that American imperialism had limited aims and goals within a well-defined sphere of influence until recently. This area excluded the Soviet sphere of influence and the Middle East's contested region. With the fall of the Soviet Union in 1989, the U.S. began an aggressive policy of extending its economic and political power through military means (pp. 15-17). Foster writes that another factor behind the intensification of American imperialism in the 1990s was the enormous military war machine that the United States built since World War II in its Cold War with the former Soviet Union. American capitalism had long depended on lucrative government contracts for weapon systems and war materials. How could this spending be supported without its former enemy? It was the removal of the Soviet check on American power that allowed the U.S. to expand its imperial ambitions. Its superior military gave it the tools to do so. U.S. capitalism incentivized the government to use this military to keep the government contracts coming and assure access to foreign markets and resources (p. 23).

In Foster's opinion, the George W. Bush administration does not represent a sea change in American foreign policy. It is not as if some neo-conservative cabal seized control of the American government and the military and has taken America in a new direction of military-imperialist expansion. Instead, the Bush II administration and its use of military force in expanding the American empire is consistent with the imperial drift of the last years of the 20th century. Bush II represents a continuation of American imperialism, a bipartisan foreign policy since World War II, becoming more aggressive with the fall of the Soviet Union. The terrorist attacks of September 11 only allowed the nation to become more militaristic and more open in its goals (p. 18).

It is challenging to strike the right note when dealing with the causes of the September 11 attacks upon America, particularly for an American audience. Foster opens his analysis with a clear statement that his discussion in no way is intended to excuse or condone terrorism itself. The attacks were "acts of utter, inhuman violence." They were "indefensible in every sense…Such terrorism has to be rid from the face of the earth" (p. 21). The issue is not the barbarity of the attacks but rather the root causes of terrorism and how best to stop it. The terrorism from the Islamic world, Foster asserts, is in direct response to Western imperialism. "In this view," Foster writes, "the terrorists attacking the World Trade Center and the Pentagon were not attacking global sovereignty or civilization (it wasn't the United Nations in New York that was attacked)—much less the values of freedom and democracy as claimed by the U.S. state—but were deliberately targeting the symbols of U.S. financial and military power, and thus of U.S. global power" (pp. 36-37).

As the dominant (hegemonic) nation at the core of the capitalist world system, America has had a long history of intervening in the Middle East through military, economic, and covert means. These interventions have been undertaken to assure continued access to the region's oil and markets. American interventions have consisted of the support of dictators to assure domestic

85

tranquility and the training and arming of these dictators to strengthen their rule. In addition, America had armed and trained terrorist groups when it suited American interests, such as in the 1980s when the Soviet Union invaded Afghanistan or Iraq invaded Iran. Consequently, the Taliban of Afghanistan, including Osama bin Laden and Saddam Hussein, were all one-time clients and friends of the U.S. state. Foster points out that support of Saddam Hussein even went as far as to allow U.S. companies to sell the dictator anthrax and other biological cultures for weapons production.

Moreover, this continued even after Saddam used chemical weapons against Iran and Iraq's Kurdish population (p. 88). "In Afghanistan," Foster writes, "the U.S. military is seeking to destroy terrorist forces that it once played a role in creating. Far from adhering to its constitutional principles in the international domain, the U.S. has long supported terrorist groups whenever it served its own imperialist designs, and has itself carried out state terrorism, killing civilian populations" (p. 37). The fact that the U.S. conducted a full-scale war in the region in 1990 and has since established permanent military bases in Saudi Arabia is seen by many "as an occupation of the holiest land of Islam," a fact that bin Laden and those that follow consider sacrilege (64). Consistent with Chalmers Johnson (2004), Foster believes that the projection of U.S. military power throughout the world causes "blowback," a metaphor for the unintended consequences of military and covert action upon the country that started that action.

Writing in December of 2002, before the second Iraq war, Foster casts doubt on any Iraqi weapons of mass destruction since such capabilities were destroyed in the first Iraqi war and the resulting UN inspections. Instead, Foster believed that the then-current push to invade Iraq came from two motives. First is controlling the region's oil since Iraq's reserves are second only to Saudi Arabia. Second, it demonstrated to the world that the U.S. had finally gotten over the Vietnam Syndrome and was now prepared to use its military power fully to pursue its interests (p. 85, 92). The invasion, of course, was extraordinarily successful. The occupation and pacification of the country were much less so; many, including Foster, termed it a disaster (pp. 133-142). Foster's opposition to the Iraq war on theoretical, moral, and practical grounds is also apparent throughout this collection of essays. Getting out of Iraq, Foster contends, will be difficult and dangerous (it was).

A significant problem sustaining American imperialism is keeping the population's support for the war. Keeping popular support for domestic and foreign policies that overwhelmingly serve the interests of elites is a chronic problem in democratic-capitalist societies. Force, of course, can be used only in times of crisis. It is far more common for governments to use ideology, propaganda, and other forms of manipulation to keep their populations supportive of the party line. Since America's first imperialist war (the Spanish-American War in 1899), Foster claims, the U.S. government has propagandized, lied to, and deliberately misled the population to gain its support. In its efforts to mislead, the government is aided by a mass media designed to dazzle and entertain, presenting news as isolated events, disconnected facts, or factoids without context or more significant meaning. "What little contextualization professional journalism does provide tends to conform to elite premises" (p. 28). Foster believes the lack of contextualization in the news is due to the concentration of media in a few enormously powerful corporations whose only goal is profitability.

A more significant problem sustaining an imperial foreign policy is the fleeting nature of hegemony within the capitalist world system. As Wallerstein has pointed out, the struggle to maintain military superiority eventually erodes the economic base for this superiority. To enforce its will, the U.S. has established military bases in more than sixty countries around the world; the original justification for these bases was to contain Communism. With the end of the Cold War, the bases have increasingly been used to project American power around the globe. Consequently, the U.S. spends more on its military than the next ten highest nation-states combined. Such military investment means less spending on education, basic research, social services, and industrial infrastructure. Foster asserts that these military bases are highly visible symbols of U.S. imperialism worldwide. People often perceive the U.S. bases as unwanted "intrusions on national sovereignty," which often interfere with the domestic politics of the host nations and serve as a staging area for the projection of U.S. power in their region (pp. 55-62).

In addition, opposition to hegemony comes from other core capitalist nations with material interests in opposing the reigning hegemonic power as they compete with that power and among themselves for markets and resources. The U.S. has been relatively unsuccessful in enlisting the support of its allies in recent military actions. Finally, opposition to American militarism is coming from public opinion around the globe. "The Vietnam Syndrome, which has so worried the strategic planners of the imperial order for decades," Foster writes, "now seems not only to have left a deep legacy within the United States but also to have been coupled this time around with an Empire Syndrome on a much more global scale—something that no one really expected. This more than anything else makes it clear that the strategy of the American ruling class to expand the American Empire cannot possibly succeed in the long run, and will prove to be its own—we hope not the world's—undoing" (p. 120).

For these reasons, military imperialism on the part of the U.S. will probably be short-lived. However, Foster points out that pulling out of Iraq will be extremely difficult because so much American military prestige is on the line. Right-wing mythology has grown around the American defeat in Vietnam that blames radicals and the media for their unwillingness to "stay the course" and bring the war to a successful conclusion. "So powerful has this right-wing, military understanding of the Vietnam War become," Foster writes, "that it is now a force to be reckoned with in the current war in Iraq." Regardless, continuing opposition from allies and enemies around the globe will probably cause the U.S. to tone down its militarism over time. Nevertheless, the sacrifice of life and treasure to military expansion and the impact such militarism has on American constitutionalism, allies, and enemies alike will be enormous (p. 25, pp. 55-62, & p. 167).

However, imperialism, Foster reminds us, does not just grow from the barrel of a gun. There are many forms of imperialism; those who associate it only with military domination or formal political control are mistaken. Marxists view imperialism—like capitalism itself—as a historical process (p. 101), an exploitative relationship between the core and the periphery. The form of these relationships changes through history and circumstance, but the essence of the relationship is still exploitative (p. 99 & p. 101). In this view, imperialism occurs through formal policies of core nation-states, including military conquest, colonization, and unequal trade agreements. However, it can also be informal in nature, manifesting itself in corporate investment and finance, often working through local elites and collaborators in peripheral societies.

> In the contrasting Marxist view, imperialism occurred not simply through states' policies but also through the actions of corporations and the mechanisms of trade, finance, and investment. It involved a whole constellation of class relations, including nurturing local collaborators or comprador elements in the dependent societies. Any explanation of how modern imperialism worked thus necessitated a description of the entire system of monopoly capitalism. In this view, informal control of countries on the periphery of the capitalist world system by countries at the center of the system was as important as formal control. Struggles over hegemony and rivalries among the leading capitalist states were continuous but took on changing forms depending on the economic, political, and military resources at their disposal (p. 103).

Under the rule of monopoly capitalism, both formal actions on the part of core states and everyday actions on the part of corporate entities of enormous resources and political influence are part of a system of exploitation. The goal is to extract the surplus from peripheral areas of the globe for the general benefit of core nation-states and the specific benefit of economic and political elites within those nation-states.

Recent globalization is more accurately perceived in the context of the capitalist world system. The global free market where corporations compete internationally, free from the restrictions or aid of government, is as mythical as a free domestic market. Globalization is the intensifying economic incorporation of peripheral areas into the capitalist world. Large corporations within core nation-states use their economic power and political access to strongly influence national and international policies consistent with the interests of corporate structures and the elite. Globalization is, therefore, on unequal terms (p. 46). "All the talk about globalization having integrated the world and disintegrated all centers, eliminating all sovereign powers, is largely illusion," Foster writes. "Nation state sovereignty and U.S. imperialism have not gone away but continue to exist in this new phase of capitalist globalization in an explosive mixture" (pp. 52-53). Globalization increases the rate of exploitation of the periphery; more surplus is taken to meet the core's needs. According to the Marxist view, inequality must rise within and between nations; conflict between the periphery and the core and class conflict within nation-states becomes "inevitable." This conflict has taken the form of revolution against puppet or collaborative regimes in the third world, military intervention on the part of the U.S. to suppress revolutions or to extend the control of dictators, and most recently, terrorism (p. 51).

Foster repeatedly asserts that imperialism is an integral part of the capitalist world system— as crucial to the system's survival as profit itself (pp. 73-81 & p. 145). In 1750, there were only minor differences in income between states within the center and those on the periphery. By 1930, the difference was 4:1, growing to 7:1 by 1980 (pp. 20-21). To characterize the modern capitalist system as having somehow broken with its imperialist foundation is an absurdity. While some point out that globalization has led to closing the gap between rich and some developing nations, Foster argues that it is an illusion. "China," for example, "once distinguished by its devotion to equality has become increasingly unequal so that by the end of the nineties, China's distribution of income closely resembled the maldistribution of income in the United States" (p. 79). Foster's data for this analysis comes from a World Bank distribution of income table for the U.S. (1997 data) and China (1998). This table shows that the highest 20 percent of income earners in both nations received over 46 percent of all income. The lowest 20 percent of earners received less than 6 percent. In addition, Foster cites worldwide income data showing that the bottom 85 percent of the world's population received less income (37.1%) in 1993 than in 1988 (41%). Those in the top 10 percent of income recipients received 50.8 percent of world income in 1993 compared to 46.9 percent in 1988, and this inequality appears to be rising. Rising inequality on both national and international scales is precisely what Marx predicted as capitalism intensifies and expands.

Our primary environmental and social problems are inextricably linked and rooted in capitalism. Environmental movements can only be truly effective if they connect their concerns of the exploitation and degradation of the earth with Capital's exploitation and degradation of workers and the poor, of the capitalist core's exploitation and degradation of peripheral nations and peoples. Make these connections, Foster asserts, and the solution becomes clear: the social control of the forces of production on a global scale or world socialism. If priority were genuinely given to protecting the environment and addressing the needs of the world's poorest—rather than amassing greater capital—economic "development would necessarily take on a radically different character" (p. 133). Only in such a society embedded in a socialist world system can the forces of industrial production be subordinated to genuine human needs. Only a socialist society would use science and technology to follow sustainability and environmental protection; only long-term planning can avert environmental catastrophe (Foster, 2002, p. 57). Because of the influence of elites on government, it cannot take us toward socialism. Only a concerted social movement focused on the connections between capitalism and environmental and human degradation can transform social systems (Foster, 1999, p. 137; Foster, 2002, pp. 81-82).

About Foster

This section is based on personal correspondence with Professor Foster in the fall of 2007. John Bellamy Foster was born on August 19, 1953, in Seattle, Washington, one of three children to William Edwin Foster and Jesse (Patricia) Ratcliffe (Jepson) Foster (later Patricia Bellamy Foster). His father was in the Civilian Conservation Corps during the New Deal and served in the U.S. Navy in the Pacific during the Second World War. He went to university on the GI Bill, worked for several years as a schoolteacher, and later as a state employee with a job processing worker compensation claims. John's mother was drafted into the British military during the Second World War. After the war, she immigrated to the United States and married his father. She found employment as an administrative secretary for the state government. Both were politically to the left, identifying with socialism. William voted for Henry Wallace and was a socialist New Dealer. Patricia was a member of the British Communist Party during the movement to open a second front in the Second World War and identified with the radical wing of the British Labour Party. During the McCarthyite witch hunt and for most of the two following decades, their left political views and history were kept private to protect the family, particularly the children, from possible political repercussions. John spent two years away from his parents in 1961-1963 at the Children's Asthma Research Institute and Hospital in Denver. Together, the family moved from Seattle to Raymond, Tacoma, and Olympia, Washington, finally settling in Olympia in 1964.

Foster was introduced to left political and economic analysis at an early age, primarily by his father. He was active in his high school years in academic debate and protests of the Vietnam War (including a hunger fast) and took part in the teach-ins of the first Earth Day in April 1970. The decline of the anti-war movement coincided with his enrollment at The Evergreen State College beginning in 1971. There, he studied political science, philosophy, history, economics, and journalism in a broad, interdisciplinary curriculum. A sense of demoralization—due to the winding down of the anti-war movement even as the United States continued to bomb Vietnam—led him briefly in the direction of solipsism and existentialism in the form of studies of Schopenhauer and Kierkegaard. Nevertheless, he mostly pursued a critical education encompassing Marxism and critical theory.

A turning point in his life occurred in 1973-74 in response to two historical developments: the growing economic crisis in the capitalist economy and the U.S.-directed coup in Chile against the socialist government of Salvador Allende. These events convinced him that the intellectual's responsibility required constant engagement with public issues and the confrontation of reality with reason. He devoted his major studies in this period to economics (both mainstream and radical). However, simultaneously, he wrote a series of articles exploring the U.S. role in the Chilean coup for the college newspaper, *The Cooper Point Journal*. He was involved with other students in organizing the Northwest Symposium on Chile. In this context, he met his fellow Evergreen student Robert W. McChesney, who introduced him to *Monthly Review* and to the work of Paul M. Sweezy and Harry Magdoff. Together with a small group of like-minded students, they engaged in intensive studies of the political economy of capitalism and socialism and were involved in critical journalistic studies (Foster became Business Manager and later Managing Editor of *The Cooper Point Journal*).

In 1976, Foster entered the political science graduate program at York University in Toronto, where he was to study political economy, political theory, history, and philosophy. He studied with Neal Wood, Ellen Meiksins Wood, Gabriel Kolko, Robert Cox, Robert Albritton, and other noted critical thinkers. Foster wrote his master's paper on "The Political Economy of Joseph Schumpeter: A Theory of Capitalist Development and Decline,"— later published in *Studies in Political Economy*. In 1979, while studying with Kolko, he authored a lengthy paper on *The United States and Monopoly Capital: The Issue of Excess Capacity,* based on the economic theories of Joseph Steindl, Paul Baran, and Paul Sweezy, and relating these to empirical data on excess capacity. He sent this to Paul Sweezy, who was enthusiastic about the work, and they struck up a lifelong correspondence and eventual collaboration. He published his first article, *"Is Monopoly Capitalism an Illusion?"* in *Monthly Review*, edited by Harry Magdoff and Paul Sweezy in 1981. Articles followed this in *The Quarterly Journal of Economics, Science & Society, Studies in Political Economy, the Review of Radical Political Economics,* and elsewhere. In 1984, Foster edited *The Faltering Economy: The Problem of Accumulation Under Monopoly Capitalism* with Henryk Szlajfer. In 1986, he published *The Theory of Monopoly Capitalism: An Elaboration of Marxian Political Economy*, based on his previous year's dissertation.

Having received his Ph.D., Foster was hired in 1985 as a Visiting Member of the Faculty at The Evergreen State College in the Political Economy Coordinated Studies Program. The following year, he became an assistant professor of sociology at the University of Oregon, where he was promoted to associate professor in 1991 and full professor in 2000. In 1989, he became a director of the Monthly Review Foundation Board and a member of the editorial committee of *Monthly Review*.

Beginning in the late 1980s, Foster began to refocus his research on the environment, first with work on the ancient forest crisis of the Pacific Northwest and after on the global ecological crisis and socialist approaches to environmental analysis. In 1994, he published his book *The Vulnerable Planet: A Short Economic History of the Environment.* This was followed by several articles on Marxism and ecology, notably "Marx's Theory of Metabolic Rift: Classical Foundations for Environmental Sociology" in the *American Journal of Sociology* in September 1999. This analysis was developed and expanded in his *Marx's Ecology: Materialism and Nature* in 2000 (which received the book award from the Section on Marxist Sociology of the American Sociological Association). Other work in this vein included *Hungry for Profit: The Agribusiness Threat to Food, Farmers, and the Environment,* edited with Fred Magdoff and Frederick H. Buttel in 2000, and *Ecology Against Capitalism* in 2002. From 1996 to 2001, he was co-editor of the journal *Organization & Environment.* In 2002, he received the Distinguished Contribution Award from the Environment and Technology Section of the American Sociological Association. In 2007, he served as chair of the Section on Marxist Sociology of the American Sociological Association.

In 2000, Foster and Robert McChesney (who in the intervening years had become one of the leading intellectual figures in the political economy of the media) joined Paul Sweezy and Harry Magdoff as co-editors of *Monthly Review.* In 2002, Foster became president of the Monthly Review Foundation. Following Paul Sweezy's death in 2004, Robert McChesney's resignation as co-editor soon after (he stayed on the board), and Harry Magdoff's death in 2006, Foster was left as sole editor of the magazine, supported by a talented editorial group.

Although Foster has continued his ecological research, the demands upon him as editor of *Monthly Review* induced him to resume his earlier work on the political economy of capitalism and imperialism. This led to several articles on the economy and the U.S. war machine. In 2006, he published his *Naked Imperialism: The U.S. Pursuit of Global Dominance,* which accounted for the expansion of the U.S. military's role in the world following September 2001. His latest contributions to *Monthly Review* have included an attempt to account for the new financially led phase of capitalism, which he has called "Monopoly-Finance Capital" (*Monthly Review,* December 2006 and April 2007). He lives with his wife, Carrie Ann Naumoff, and his two children in Eugene, Oregon.

Part 2: The Division of Labor & Anomie

The realm of Macro Social Theory encompasses a diverse array of thinkers, each contributing distinctive insights into the complex fabric of society. Emile Durkheim, a founding figure in sociology, laid the groundwork for many subsequent theorists with his seminal works on topics such as the division of labor and anomie. This introductory essay delves into a section of *Macro Social Theory* focusing on the work of four significant theorists—Emile Durkheim, Robert K. Merton, Robert Nisbet, and Neil Postman. By exploring their theories, we aim to uncover the commonalities shared between these recent thinkers and Durkheim, particularly in their understanding of the division of labor and the concept of anomie. Drawing out these connections, we shed light on the lasting influence of Durkheim's ideas and their relevance in contemporary macrosocial theory.

One of Durkheim's key contributions lies in his analysis of the division of labor, which he viewed as a central organizing principle in society. Durkheim argued that as societies progress, they experience a shift from mechanical solidarity, characterized by shared values and collective consciences, to organic solidarity, characterized by interdependence and specialized roles. The increasing division of labor facilitates this transformation as individuals become more specialized in their tasks and rely on one another for the functioning of society as a whole.

Robert K. Merton, a prominent sociologist of the mid-20th century, expanded on Durkheim's ideas, mainly through his functionalist perspective. Merton emphasized the importance of social institutions and their role in maintaining social order. Drawing from Durkheim's insights on the division of labor, Merton introduced the concept of functional prerequisites, which are the functions different social structures must fulfill to ensure societal stability. Merton's work further underscores Durkheim's notion of the division of labor as a vital mechanism for social cohesion and the smooth functioning of society.

Robert Nisbet, a sociologist known for analyzing community and social structure, also draws inspiration from Durkheim's ideas, specifically about social cohesion. Nisbet argues that social order and stability depend on strong communal bonds and shared values. In his work, Nisbet explores the impact of the division of labor on social integration and highlights the potential risks of excessive individualism and alienation. By emphasizing the significance of collective identity and community ties, Nisbet resonates with Durkheim's concern for maintaining social cohesion in the face of an increasingly specialized and fragmented society.

Neil Postman, a cultural critic and media theorist, offers a unique perspective on Durkheim's concept of anomie, which refers to normlessness and social disintegration. Postman focuses on the impact of modern media and technological advancements on cultural norms and values. He argues that the proliferation of mass media and the erosion of traditional cultural boundaries can lead to cultural anomie, where individuals feel adrift and lack a cohesive moral framework. Postman's analysis echoes Durkheim's concerns about the disruptive effects of rapid social change on social integration and collective conscience.

As we explore the works of Robert K. Merton, Robert Nisbet, and Neil Postman alongside Emile Durkheim's foundational theories, we witness the enduring influence of Durkheim's ideas on contemporary macrosocial theory. These theorists, each situated in different historical contexts, build upon Durkheim's analysis of the division of labor and anomie, extending and applying his concepts to shed light on the complexities of modern society. Their shared emphasis on social cohesion, the functional prerequisites of institutions, and the challenges posed by rapid social change demonstrate the continued relevance of Durkheim's insights. By examining these remarkable thinkers, we deepen our understanding of Durkheimian legacy within macro social theory and the ongoing dialogue sparked by his groundbreaking contributions.

Chapter 4: The Sociology of Emile Durkheim

Most sociologists consider Emile David Durkheim (1858-1917) one of the "big three" in the discipline, the other two being Karl Marx and Max Weber. However, I have often thought of his reputation as being over-inflated. I have had many arguments with colleagues on this score. They point out several contributions he has made to the field: (1) distinguishing and elaborating the field of sociology from the other social sciences; (2) his emphasis on empirical data to lend support to his theoretical speculations; (3) functionalism; (4) his focus on the division of labor and its consequences for social life; (5) his conception of anomie and its causes and consequences for human societies; (6) his sociology of religion which is still considered seminal; and (7) the collective conscience or the need for a common core of values and beliefs.

The collective conscience requires some explanation. First, disagreement over whether this should be "collective conscience" or "collective conscious." The confusion stems from "the word in French means both these things" (Collins & Makowski, 1989, p. 105n). This chapter will stick with "collective conscience" unless directly quoting others using "collective conscious." Second, a definition is necessary as modern sociologists rarely use the term (apart from discussing Durkheim). Collins and Makowsky say that the collective conscience is "a sense of belonging to a community with others and hence feeling a moral obligation to live up to its demands. We share feelings of right and wrong, inseparable from our feelings of belonging to a group, whether it be humanity, one's country, or one's family. The collective conscience does not mean that a group mind is hanging over our heads, but rather that people have feelings of belonging to a group" (p. 105n). This definition is fitting.

Some of Durkheim's accomplishments are found in earlier theorists. August Comte, for example, writes of the division of labor and how its development leads to a shift in social bonds from similarity to interdependence. Karl Marx has a far better grasp of how destructive of social solidarity the detailed division of labor can be. (Both Braverman ([1974] 1998) and Marvin Harris (1981) comment on this extensively.) T. Robert Malthus writes of the effect of population (and other components of society) on various parts of the social system and the whole in a distinctly functionalist manner. Malthus also uses available government data on birth and death rates almost 100 years before Durkheim. While Durkheim is the first to be accorded academic status as a sociologist, I did not believe that his contributions and insights rank him in the same league as such titans as Marx and Weber. Besides, while many sociologists treat Durkheim as a classical theorist, few contemporary [American] sociologists base their work extensively on his theory. Many contemporary sociologists are influenced by Marx or Weber—hardly anyone calls themselves a "Durkheimian" anymore. As Harry Alpert (1939, p. 213) wrote, "Durkheim is well known among American sociologists, but he is not known well."

Still, the influence of Durkheim on sociology in the last half of the twentieth century is formidable—particularly his functionalism, use of empirical data to support his arguments, and his conception of human nature and the problem of anomie. However, as I began writing this chapter, I have had to reevaluate Durkheim's place in the pantheon of classical theorists—he is far more insightful than I had previously thought. The turning point was reading Stjepan Mestrovic's interpretation and translation of his thought. (Reevaluation during the writing process is common; the writing process clarifies, refines, and expands the writer's thinking. It is an intensely intellectual interaction between the writer and the text.) For these reasons, I include a summary of his work heavily influenced by Mestrovic in this volume. Basic knowledge of Durkheim is essential for understanding sociocultural systems.

Human Nature

According to Durkheim, social facts (or social phenomena or forces) are the subject matter of sociology. Social facts are "*sui generis*" (of their own kind) and must be studied distinct from biological and psychological phenomena. Social facts can be defined as patterns of behavior that can exercise some coercive power upon individuals. "The determining cause of a social fact should be sought among the social facts preceding it and not among the states of individual consciousness" (Durkheim, [1895] 1950, p. 110). They are guides and controls of conduct external to the individual through group norms, mores, and folkways. Through socialization and education, these rules become internalized in the individual's consciousness. These social constraints and guides become moral obligations to obey social rules.

The key to Durkheim, Mestrovic argues, is his conception of human beings as "homo duplex," beings of two natures, the angel and the beast, the beast being the stronger of the two. In this concept of homo duplex, Durkheim was influenced by the philosopher Arthur Schopenhauer, who thought of this higher side of human nature as "reason" or the "mind." Durkheim gave this philosophy a strong sociological caste, asserting the social nature of the angel or higher side of homo duplex. Society or the social group gives the individual meaning, values, and moral guidelines. Without strong integration into social groups—not just normative consensus on the rules of behavior and shared values, but love and commitment on the part of the individual to these groups—the individual lacks solid moral guidance, and the ego or will is set loose upon the world. In such situations, men and women essentially exploit their fellow humans. "There are in each of us, as we have said, two consciences: one which is common to our group in its entirety which, consequently, is not ourself, but society living and acting within us; the other, on the contrary, represents that in us which is personal and distinct, that which makes us an individual" (Durkheim [1893] 1960, pp. 129-130). The first and "lower" part of that nature is that of "will," an id-like nature that is focused on the individual satisfaction of all wants and desires. (Mestrovic asserts many similarities between the social theories of Durkheim and Freud, two contemporaries who shared intellectual forebears, posited a similar dual nature of human beings, and so wrote extensively of a pervasive discontent with modern civilization.) Egoistic drives and desires are centered on the body; they recognize no interests but that of the individual actor, pushing the individual to satisfy all wants and desires even at the expense of the will of others (Mestrovic [1988]1993, p. 57 & p. 73). The will is a "tyranny of passions imposed by nature" (p. 54); it is the root of all human wickedness and evil, the source of immorality. The will seeks the satisfaction of all wants and desires. It knows no boundaries. This side of human beings quickly leads to a condition that Durkheim labels "anomie." "Left unchecked," Durkheim ([1897]1951) writes, "the will leads to suffering and despair: Unlimited desires are insatiable by definition, and insatiability is rightly considered a sign of morbidity. Being unlimited, they constantly and infinitely surpass the means at their command; they cannot be quenched. Inextinguishable thirst is constantly renewed torture" (cited in Mestrovic [1988] 1993, p. 63).

The other part of human nature is social in origin, the "collective conscience." This conscience is a collective moral system, a reality separate from the individual and comprised of ideas and values. For Durkheim, society consists of "representations" or ideas; these representations are not the simple collections of the beliefs and values of all humans who make up the society, but rather, these representations have a unique reality of their own, exerting an independent force on individuals. Society is "not the outcome of human agency nor material determinants. It is neither entirely objective nor subjective. And because the representation is a reality *sui generis*, not a mere reflector, it expresses its will—in part—independent of the will of human agents" (p. 13). The collective conscience disciplines the individual will, which limits individual desires and thus makes some satisfaction possible (pp. 87-88). For Durkheim, this collective conscience is essential in limiting the will, keeping the lower side of human nature in check and in line with the needs of social justice and order.

It is important to note that Mestrovic does not claim that Durkheim believes the needed morality cannot come from a rational source; in fact, rationality tends to erode the moral authority needed to restrain exploitive behavior. Instead, what is needed is a revival of traditional and emotional structures that can fully integrate people into society to keep them in check; love and commitment on the part of individuals toward social groups and institutions are needed most of all. The will is left to its own devices when it lacks integration and engages in barbarism and other exploitive behaviors to satisfy its whims. The continual conflict between our human senses and appetites and our socially instilled moral life—an ongoing and never-ending conflict between the will and the collective conscience—defines human existence, subjecting us to constant frustration, psychic pain, and regret.

Durkheim ([1914] 1973) writes that the dualism of human nature is painful, as evidenced by the conflict between our nature and society's demands on our behavior.

> Undoubtedly, if society were only the natural and spontaneous development of the individual, these two parts of ourselves would harmonize […] In fact, however, society has its own nature […] Therefore, society cannot be formed or maintained without our being required to make perpetual and costly sacrifices. Because society surpasses us, it obliges us to surpass ourselves, and to surpass itself a being must, to some degree, depart from its nature—a departure that does not take place without causing more or less painful tensions […] We must, in a word, do violence to certain of our strongest inclinations. Therefore, since the role of the social being in our single selves will grow ever more important as history moves ahead, it is wholly improbable that there will ever be an era in which man is required to resist himself to a lesser degree, an era in which he can live a life that is easier and less full of tension. To the contrary, all evidence compels us to expect our effort in the struggle between the two beings within us to increase with the growth of civilization (cited in Mestrovic [1988] 1993, p. 74).

This conflict, rooted in our dual nature, is ongoing and can never be finally resolved. Moreover, the struggle will get worse, Durkheim claims, as civilization progresses (p. 74).

Anomie

Durkheim characterized the modern individual as suffering from a weak collective conscience. This collective conscience does not provide adequate guidance and moral imperative to individuals' behavior. When social regulations break down, controlling individual desires and interests is ineffective; individuals are left to their own devices. Because of the dual nature of human beings—the id-like individual part that needs moral regulation to keep it in check—widespread deviance, despair, unhappiness, and stress result.

Anomie is our time's central social problem, yet it is largely neglected and misunderstood even by sociologists (p. xiii). Durkheim saw anomie as a "pervasive discontent" afflicting modern society, a "collective derangement" brought about by loosening social bonds upon people—the rise of individualism, the weakening of family, religion, and professional groups and associations. With modernity, economic institutions have increasingly taken center stage in social life; all other institutions have become mere appendages to modern economic systems. These economic systems—capitalist, communist, or socialist—do not provide moral guidance to the individual, instead promoting consumerism and economic self-interest, which only inflame desires and the will, making discontent far worse (p. xvi & p. 64).

Modernity, Durkheim argues, tends to weaken those traditional institutions that served to restrain egoism, eroding the commitment, fealty, and love that bind individuals to their institutions and, thus, their fellow humans. Thus, modernity weakens the collective conscience, promoting unrestrained egoism and allowing people to exploit one another freely; worse still, it unleashes unlimited desires that can never be satisfied. Mestrovic again quotes Durkheim ([1925] 1961, p. 42): "The totality of moral regulations really forms about each person an imaginary wall, at the foot of which a multitude of human passions simply die without being able to go further. For the same reason—that they are contained—it becomes possible to satisfy them. But if at any point this barrier weakens, human forces—until now restrained—pour tumultuously through the open breach; once loosed, they find no limits where they can or must stop. Unfortunately, they can only devote themselves to the pursuit of an end that always eludes them" (p. 71). According to Durkheim, modernity must necessarily lead to widespread unhappiness, suffering, and despair.

Durkheim identifies two major causes of the weakening of the collective conscience and the resulting anomie: the division of labor and rapid social change. Both are associated with modernity. In modern literature on anomie, the focus tends to be on rapid change experienced by individuals either up or down the social structure. Here, let us focus again on the division of labor. The individual in modern society is confronted with various groups with different values and goals, each of which competes for the individual's allegiance.

Compare the norms on premarital sexuality for females in more traditional societies (say, America in 1900) with contemporary American society. (The double standard on sexual behavior for males and females is part of our traditional morality; boys have always been given mixed messages.) In a traditional setting, the strength of the bond is more intense between a young woman and the relatively few groups to which she belongs. The message from all groups, families, churches, schools, and peers is virtually the same: "Don't do it." Compare this uniformity of messages with the conflicting messages girls receive in modern American society. In most families, the parent(s) message is: "Don't do it," although the message may be mixed if a teenager has older siblings. If she belongs to a traditional church, the message is the same. However, movies, television, and music video messages amount to "Everybody is doing it" (and are more beautiful and happier as a result). Media ads are encouraging: "Just do it!" connecting the product they are trying to sell with promises of sexual fulfillment. The school she attends and "Dear Abby" tell her: "Don't do it, but if you do, use a condom."

Moreover, her peer group, particularly if she has a boyfriend, encourages her to: "Do it." Consequently, the young woman is left to her own devices; consistent or strong group norms must discipline her desires and natural curiosity. Durkheim refers to this social condition as anomie, in which individuals are given weak, inconsistent, or incoherent normative rules.

A key point of Durkheim's concept of anomie is this: An increasing division of labor weakens the sense of identification and social bond within the wider community and weakens social constraints and moral guidance on human behavior. These conditions lead to social "disintegration"—high egocentric behavior, norm violation, and consequent de-legitimation and distrust of authority. In the final analysis, Durkheim's whole sociology revolves around this issue.

Mestrovic points out the heavy religious influence on Durkheim's concept of anomie: "Disobedience, willfulness, rebellion—these traits characterize man's original sin in Paradise. But these traits also characterize anomie. For Durkheim, the offense is against society, but for him, society is definitely on a symbolic plane with God" (65). The sacred nature of society is apparent when Durkheim wrote the following in *The Elementary Forms of Religious Life* ([1912] 1954, p. 162):

> It is not without reason. Therefore, that man feels himself to be double: he actually is double [...] In brief, this duality corresponds to the double existence that we lead concurrently; the one purely individual and rooted in our organisms, the other social and nothing but an extension of society [...] The conflicts of which we have given examples are between the sensations and the sensory appetites, on the one hand, and the intellectual and moral life, on the other, and it is evident that passions and egoistic tendencies derive from our individual constitutions, while our rational activity—whether theoretical or practical—is dependent on social causes (cited in Mestrovic [1988] 1993, p. 73).

Traditional religion promoted a bond between people; the erosion of traditional religion is one of the primary reasons for spreading discontent. "Durkheim," Mestrovic points out, "was a moralist—albeit a scientific moralist—who was sensitive to the pain and sorrow caused by immorality. He did not think of anomie as simple confusion but as evil. And he thought of it as evil because it unleashes the unrestrained will" (p. 75). Much of Durkheim's work constituted a search for new sources of morality, institutions, and belief systems that would bind humans to their fellow beings. "Durkheim was searching for moral rules that would exert a benign kind of constraint on the individual. He was aware that constraint connotes violence and pain, and he never took this price lightly" (p. 87). Durkheim's is not a straight-line evolutionary theory. In his conception, anomie and unrestrained egoism are as harmful to the individual as they are to the social system, and institutions (and individuals) react to the social disorder that results from the weakening of the collective conscience. Durkheim believed society's functional needs caused the emergence of new forms of social integration. Even modern sociocultural systems with a high degree of division of labor still need a common faith and collective conscience to integrate people into society.

Social Order

A central issue in Durkheim's work concerns the source of social order and disorder. Recall that according to Durkheim, the desires and self-interests of human beings can only be held in check by forces that originate outside the individual. "Thus, the more one has, the more one wants, since satisfactions received only stimulate instead of filling needs" (Durkheim [1897] 1951, p. 248). Durkheim characterizes this external force as a collective conscience, a shared social bond expressing the culture's ideas, values, norms, beliefs, and ideologies, institutionalized in the social structure and internalized by individual members.

> Society is not at all the illogical or a-logical, inherent, and fantastic being that has too often been considered. Quite on the contrary, the collective consciousness is the highest form of psychic life since it is the consciousness of consciousness. Being placed outside of and above individual and local contingencies, it sees things only in their permanent and essential aspects, which it crystallizes into communicable ideas. At the same time that it sees from above, it sees farther; at every moment of time it embraces all known reality; that is why it alone can furnish the minds with the molds which are applicable to the totality of things and which make it possible to think of them (Durkheim [1912] 1954, p. 444).

He elaborated on the cause and effects of weakening group bonds on the individual in his works, *The Division of Labor in Society* (1893) and *Suicide* (1897).

In *The Division of Labor*, Durkheim ([1893] 1960) identifies two forms or types of solidarity based on dissimilar sources. "Social life comes from a double source, the likeness of consciences and the division of labor. The individual is socialized in the first case, because, not having any real individuality, he becomes, with those whom he resembles, part of the same collective type; in the second case, because, while having a physiognomy and a personal activity which distinguishes him from others, he depends upon them in the same measure that he is distinguished from them, and consequently upon the society which results from their union" (p. 226).

Mechanical solidarity is "solidarity which comes from likeness," Durkheim writes, and "is at its maximum when the collective conscience completely envelops our whole conscience and coincides in all points with it." Durkheim claims this occurs in early societies with little division of labor. "[Mechanical solidarity] is strong only if the individual is not. Made up of rules which are practiced by all indistinctly, it receives from this universal, uniform practice an authority which bestows something superhuman upon it, and which puts it beyond the pale of discussion" (p. 228). Such societies are relatively homogenous. Men and women engage in similar tasks and daily activities, and people have similar experiences. In such societies, the few different institutions express similar values and norms that tend to reinforce one another. Mechanical solidarity, Durkheim adds, means that "ideas and tendencies common to all members of the society are greater in number and intensity than those that pertain personally to each member" (p. 228). Society's norms, values, and beliefs (or the collective conscience) are so homogenous that they confront the individual with such overwhelming and consistent force that there is little opportunity in such societies for individuality or deviance from this collective conscience. The collective conscience and individual conscience are virtually identical.

According to Durkheim, traditional cultures experienced high social and moral integration. Little individuation and social norms usually embodied in religion govern most behaviors. By engaging in the same activities and rituals, people in traditional societies shared common moral values, which Durkheim called a collective conscience (modern sociologists would refer to them as the norms and values of society, which individuals internalize). In traditional societies, people tend to regard themselves as group members; the collective conscience embraces individual awareness, and there is little sense of personal options.

The second form of solidarity Durkheim terms "organic." As society becomes more complex, individuals play more specialized roles and become more dissimilar in their social experiences, material interests, values, and beliefs. Individuals within such a sociocultural system have less in common; however, they must become more dependent on each other for survival. "Because the individual is not sufficient unto himself, it is for society that he works. Thus, is formed a very strong sentiment of the state of dependence in which he finds himself. He becomes accustomed to estimating it at its just value, that is to say, in regarding himself as part of a whole, the organ of an organism. Such sentiments naturally inspire not only mundane sacrifices which assure the regular development of daily social life, but even, on occasion, acts of complete self-renunciation and wholesale abnegation" (p. 228).

Organic solidarity develops as a by-product of the division of labor. "The co-operative society [organic solidarity], on the contrary, develops in the measure that individual personality becomes stronger. As regulated as a function may be, there is a large place always left for personal initiative" (pp. 228-229). The growth of individualism is inevitable due to the increasing division of labor. This individualism can develop only at the expense of society's shared values, beliefs, and normative rules—the sentiments and beliefs held by all. We also lose our sense of community or identity with the group by loosening these standard rules and values. The social bond is weakened, and social values and beliefs no longer provide coherent, consistent, or insistent moral guidance.

Although the diversity of norms and values can free the individual from tradition and the hierarchies of family, church, and community, the diversity also creates problems. According to Durkheim, if an individual lacks any social restraint, she will tend to satisfy her appetites with little thought of the possible effect her actions will have on others. Again, human wants and desires are insatiable, "the more one has, the more one wants, since satisfactions received only stimulate instead of filling needs (Durkheim, [1897] 1951, p. 248). Instead of asking, "Is this moral?" or "Does my family approve?" the individual is more likely to ask, "Does this action meet my needs?" The individual is left to find her way in the world—where personal options for behavior have multiplied as strong and insistent norms have weakened.

However, Durkheim asserts there are limits to this weakening of the collective bonds, "complete anomie or total normlessness, is empirically impossible" (Coser, [1971] 1977, p. 133). In the Division of Labor in Society, Durkheim states:

> Consequently, even where society relies most completely upon the division of labor, it does not become a jumble of juxtaposed atoms, between which it can establish only external, transient contacts. Rather the members are united by ties which extend deeper and far beyond the short moments during which the exchange is made. Each function they exercise is, in a fixed way, dependent upon others, and with them forms a solidary system. Accordingly, from the nature of chosen task, permanent duties arise. Because we fill some certain domestic or social function, we are involved in a complex of obligations from which we have no right to free ourselves. There is, above all, an organ upon which we are tending to depend more and more; this is the State. The points at which we are in contact with it multiply as do the occasions when it is entrusted with the duty of reminding us of the sentiment of common solidarity (Durkheim [1893] 1960, p. 227).

As levels of anomie rise within a society, some countertrends bind men and women to the social whole. Durkheim points to the State as a critical institution that performs this role.

Suicide

Durkheim insisted that the study of society must not rely on psychological factors alone (reductionism). Instead, the observer must consider social phenomena as a different class or level of fact. To show the power of these social facts in determining human behavior, Durkheim studied suicide. Before Durkheim, most perceived suicide as one of the most intensely individual acts, purely determined by psychological and biographical factors. However, psychological and biological facts cannot explain variations in suicide rates among racial, ethnic, religious, and occupational groups.

Durkheim reasoned that while suicide occurs in all societies, he saw that suicide rates for various groups within the same society are often different. These rates are remarkably stable over time. These differences and the stability of group rates indicated that something other than psychology was involved in the decision to commit suicide. Why is it that Protestants are more prone to suicide than Catholics? Why are there stable rates of suicide, year after year, within the same groups and societies? Why do rates differ between age groups within the same society? It is simply impossible, Durkheim insisted, to explain or interpret the characteristics and behaviors of human groups on a psychological or biological basis. Much of who we are, how we behave, and what we believe is due to social forces.

To explain differential rates of suicide in various religious and occupational groups, Durkheim studied how these groups brought about social cohesion and solidarity among their members. He hypothesized that a significantly higher rate of suicide in a particular group showed that the social cohesion of that group was weak and that its members were no longer protected during personal crises. By examining government data, Durkheim demonstrated that suicide varies with the degree of social integration.

Durkheim described two types of suicide based on the source of this perceived lack of cohesion. *Egoistic suicide* occurs among men and women not sufficiently integrated into social groups. Because they do not belong, they do not interact and take part; when confronted with a personal crisis, they must face it alone. They have not internalized the regulation and guidance nor have the social support needed to handle the stress.

The second type of suicide is based on the lack of group cohesion. Durkheim labels *anomic suicide*. Anomic suicide will likely occur when the group does not give the individual enough regulation and guidance. Protestantism, for example, "concedes a greater freedom of individual thought than Catholicism [...] it has fewer common beliefs and practices" (Durkheim [1897] 1951, p. 159). Because of this, Durkheim reasoned, we should see higher rates of suicide among Protestants as a response to these weaker rules of conduct and emphasis upon autonomy and individualism. Because the increasing division of labor weakens the traditional ties of community, religion, and family, this type of suicide is associated with modernity.

A third primary type Durkheim labeled *altruistic suicide*. This type of suicide occurs when the individual is tightly integrated into a group, and the group requires that individual to give up her life. It occurs among soldiers for their friends, nationalists for their countries, and true believers for their cause. While Durkheim was aware of the dangers of the breakdown of social order, he also realized that too much social control of individual behavior could be dangerous (Coser [1971] 1977, p. 135). Such cohesion is associated with traditional (or mechanical) societies, where the collective conscience is nearly synonymous with individual consciousness.

Contrary to the secondary literature, Mestrovic ([1988] 1993) maintains Durkheim did not claim that all varieties of social integration were beneficial in constraining the individual will (p. 117). Much like Ferdinand Tönnies' distinction between Gemeinschaft (community) and Gesellschaft (society), Mestrovic insists that Durkheim distinguishes between two types of integration. Tönnies' "Gemeinschaft" refers to groups based on close interpersonal relationships. In such groupings, people are bonded by kinship, friendship, or other bonds that evoke solidarity and togetherness. "Gesellschaft," on the other hand, refers to groups and organizations that are held together by instrumental goals. Tönnies saw modernity as being increasingly dominated by Gesellschaft organization. Mestrovic explains: "Essentially, Durkheim distinguishes sharply between two aspects of social integration, social contacts versus social bonds. The former increase as civilization develops, while the latter decline. Thus, modern man is ripped apart by two antagonistic forces. This dualistic understanding of social integration in Durkheim's thought has been completely missed by his contemporary commentators, yet it is what sets Durkheim's evolutionary scheme apart from other evolutionary theories of society" (p. 119). Simple social contacts do little to constrain the individual will; in fact, such contacts may serve to inflame the will; such integration is characteristic of modernity in which communal bonds have been weakened. Thus, the expectation that social integration alone will protect the individual from anomie is hopelessly naïve.

Another problem is relying on simple social integration to protect individuals from anomie. Individuals firmly integrated into a pathological society that encourages acts of violence, individual satisfaction, and exploiting others to satisfy individual wants and desires are not well served. Even societies with high social consensus and order can be evil or harmful to many individuals who make up that society. Such a case is modern consumer culture, which exposes children to such values at an early age, thus stimulating their desires beyond all hope of satisfaction (p. 119).

Durkheim posits that the growth of the modern economy is primarily responsible for eroding traditional institutions and actively promoting anomie in Western society. The commodification of social life has not only led to the weakening of traditional institutions such as religion and the family, which previously had placed some restraint on the egoistic desires of individuals, but it has replaced these traditional restraints with the promotion of egoistic desires. Modern capitalism enshrines self-interest—or unrestrained egoism—as an essential part of the economic system.

Mestrovic quotes Durkheim: "As there is nothing within an individual which constrains these appetites, they must surely be contained by some force exterior to him, or else they would become insatiable—that is morbid […] This is what seems to have escaped Saint-Simon. To him, it appears that the way to realize social peace is to free economic appetites of all restraint on the one hand, and on the other to satisfy them by fulfilling them. But such an undertaking is contradictory" (Durkheim, [1928] 1978, Le Socialisme, p. 213 cited by Mestrovic, p. 69). Both capitalism and socialism assume that man is a self-regulating economic animal (p. 129). By design, the capitalist economic system inflames desires, promotes egoistic behavior, and encourages unlimited acquisition. Amorality is the rule in economic life.

Durkheim's analysis of modern representative democracy is similar. The people's will, Durkheim argues, is as insatiable in political life as it is in economic life (p. 131). According to Durkheim, the State needs to be deliberative and reflective, a moderating force on the people's intense desires, passions, prejudices, and self-interests (p. 130). True democracy rests not on "rule by the people" but checks upon that will by a reflective and deliberative state. Mestrovic again cites Durkheim: "The more that deliberation and reflection and a critical spirit play a considerable part in the course of public affairs, the more democratic the nations. It is the less democratic when lack of consciousness, uncharted customs, the obscure sentiments and prejudices that evade investigation, predominate" (Durkheim, [1950] 1983, cited by Mestrovic, p. 131). Modern societies, Durkheim asserts, are held together by ideals of social justice held in the collective conscience. These ideals discipline individuals' desires and impulses; we must strengthen these ideals—and the attachment to them (p. 136).

For Durkheim, there is a difference between healthy individualism, based on the social side of homo duplex, and narcissism, based on the will or the lower side. Healthy individualism implies strong communal bonds that integrate the individual into a society where the collective conscience is a moving balance of values, beliefs, and ideas that constrain socially harmful impulses and desires and promote social justice. Because of the insatiability of the human will, these individual impulses and desires are also harmful to the individual. Modernity, on the other hand, stimulates the will and offers few constraints on satisfying individual impulses and desires; modernity stimulates narcissism. This narcissism is devastating to the individual and toxic to the social order (pp. 129-130).

With the passing of the traditional order, Durkheim saw the West in crisis. Christianity was increasingly being questioned, the traditional authority of family and community was being weakened, and the transition from feudalism to capitalism and monarchy to representative democracy was entering its final stages. Mestrovic (p. 71) again quotes Durkheim, this time from *Moral Education*:

> The notion of the infinite, then, appears only at those times when moral discipline has lost its ascendancy over man's will. It is the sign of attrition that emerges during periods when the moral system, prevailing for several centuries, is shaken, failing to respond to new conditions of human life, and without any new system yet contrived to replace that which has disappeared" (Durkheim [1925] 1961, p. 43).

> Whenever moral rules lack the necessary authority to exert, to a desirable degree, a regulatory influence on their behavior, we see society gripped by a dejection and pessimism reflected in the curve of suicides" (Durkheim [1925] 1961, p. 68).

> During periods when society is disorganized and, as a result of its decadence, has less power to exact the commitment of individual wills, and when, consequently, egoism has freer reign—these are calamitous times. The cult of the self and the notion of the infinite go together" (Durkheim [1925] 1961, p. 72).

Functionalism

For Durkheim, a society formed a unified system, with the various parts of the system fitting very closely together. Society is like an organism; all its parts are tightly meshed. The extreme system character envisioned by Durkheim can be seen in the following quote:

> But if there is one fact that history has irrefutably demonstrated, it is that the morality of each people is directly related to the social structure of the people practicing it. The connection is so intimate that, given the general character of the morality observed in a given society and barring abnormal and pathological cases, one can infer the nature of that society, the elements of its structure, and the way it is organized. Tell me the marriage patterns, the morals dominating family life, and I will tell you the principal characteristics of its organization" (Durkheim [1925] 1961, p. 87).

Therefore, there are two legitimate aims of social investigation. The first identifies a social phenomenon's historical causes or origins, and the second shows its functions for other parts of the social and whole systems. "The determination of function is [...] necessary for the complete explanation of the phenomena [...] To explain a social fact, it is not enough to show the cause on which it depends; we must also, at least in most cases, show its function in the establishment of social order" (Durkheim [1895] 1950, p. 97).

Determining the functions of social institutions and patterns of social facts was vital in Durkheim's sociology. "When […] the explanation of a social phenomenon is undertaken, we must seek separately the efficient cause which produces it and the function it fulfills. We use the word "function" in preference to "end" or "purpose" precisely because social phenomena do not generally exist for the useful results they produce. We must determine whether there is a correspondence between the fact under consideration and the general needs of the social organism, and in what this correspondence consists, without occupying ourselves with whether it has been intentional or not" (Durkheim, [1895] 1950, p. 95).

For example, Durkheim saw crime as a regular occurrence in any social system and serving some positive societal functions. First, crime and the reaction to crime, he asserts, provide society with a point of normative consensus. By condemning the crime, we reaffirm bonds among the non-criminal population, asserting that the group condemns and punishes the criminal action. The second function of crime is the drawing of boundaries for human behavior. By defining such boundaries and punishing those who cross them, we are strengthening the collective conscience. "Crime brings together upright consciences and concentrates them" (Durkheim [1893] 1960, p. 103). The third function of crime is to provide a certain amount of flexibility within society. "Where crime exists, collective sentiments are sufficiently flexible to take on a new form, and crime sometimes helps to determine the form they will take. How many times, indeed, it is only an anticipation of future morality—a step toward what will be" (Durkheim [1895] 1950, p. 71).

Religion

According to Durkheim, "a religion is a unified system of beliefs and practices relative to sacred things, that is to say, things set apart and forbidden--beliefs and practices which unite in one single community called a Church, all those who adhere to them" (Durkheim [1912] 1954, p. 47).

> At the roots of all our judgments, there are a certain number of essential ideas which dominate all our intellectual life; they are what the philosophers since Aristotle have called the categories of understanding: ideas of time, space, class, numbers, cause, substance, personality, etc. They correspond to the most universal properties of things. They are like the solid frame which encloses all thought; [...] They are like the framework of intelligence. Now, when primitive religious beliefs are systematically analyzed, the principal categories are naturally found. They are born in religion and of religion; they are a product of religious thought" (p. 9).

To discover the essence of religion and the functions it served, Durkheim studied animism, totemism (religious beliefs based on the worship of sacred objects which are often thought to possess supernatural powers), and other "primitive" beliefs." He concluded that all religions divide social life into two spheres: the sacred and the profane. He says nothing intrinsic about a particular object makes it sacred, and an object becomes sacred only when the community invests it with that meaning. Religion is "an eminently collective thing" and binds a community together (p. 47).

> Thus, something eternal in religion is destined to survive all the particular symbols in which religious thought has successively enveloped itself. There can be no society that does not feel the need to uphold and reaffirming at regular intervals the collective sentiments and the collective ideas which make its unity and its personality. Now this moral remaking cannot be achieved except by the means of reunions, assemblies, and meetings where the individuals, being closely united to one another, reaffirm in common their common sentiments; hence come ceremonies which do not differ from regular religious ceremonies, either in their object, the results which they produce, or the processes employed to attain these results.

> What essential difference is there between an assembly of Christians celebrating the principal dates in the life of Christ, or of Jews remembering the exodus from Egypt or the promulgation of the decalogue, and a reunion of citizens commemorating the promulgation of a new moral or legal system or some great event in the national life? (pp. 474-475).

Durkheim then goes a step further. Religion is not only a social creation; it is the power of the community being worshiped. So transcendent is the power of the community over the individual that people collectively give it sacred significance (pp. 488-496).

> Perhaps some will be surprised to see us connect the most elevated forms of thought with society: the cause appears quite humble in consideration of the value which we attribute to the effect. Between the world of the senses and appetites on the one hand, and that of reason and morals on the other, the distance is so considerable that the second would seem to have been able to add itself to the first only by a creative act. But attributing to society this preponderating role in the genesis of our nature is not denying this creation; for society has a creative power which no other observable being can equal. In fact, all creation, if not a mystical operation which escapes science and knowledge, is the product of a synthesis.

> Now, if the synthesis of particular conceptions which take place in each individual consciousness are already and of themselves productive of novelties, how much more efficacious these vast synthesis of complete consciousness which make society must be! A society is the most powerful combination of physical and moral forces, of which nature offers us an example. Nowhere else is an equal richness of different materials, carried to such a degree of concentration, to be found. That it is not surprising that a higher life disengages itself which, by reacting upon the elements of which it is the product, raises them to a higher plane of existence and transforms them" (p. 495).

By worshiping God, people are worshiping the power of the collective overall; we are worshiping society's transformative power over our very being.

According to Durkheim, religion is one of the leading forces that make up the collective conscience. Religious belief allows individuals to transcend the self and act for the social good. However, traditional religion was weakening under the onslaught of the division of labor; what could replace religion as the common bond?

> The great things of the past which filled our fathers with enthusiasm do not excite the same ardor in us […] In a word, the old gods are growing old or already dead, and others are not yet born [...] But this state of incertitude and confused agitation cannot last forever. A day will come when our societies will know again those hours of creative effervescence, in the course of which new formulae are found which serve for a while as a guide to humanity; and when these hours shall have been passed through once, men will spontaneously feel the need of reliving them from time to time in thought, that is to say, of keeping alive their memory by means of celebrations which regularly reproduce their fruits. We have already seen how the French Revolution established a whole cycle of holidays to keep the principles with which it was inspired in a state of perpetual youth […]
>
> There are no gospels which are immortal, but neither is there any reason for believing that humanity is incapable of inventing new ones. As to the question of what symbols this new faith will express itself with, whether they will resemble the past or not, and whether or not they will be more adequate for the reality which they seek to translate, that is something which surpasses the human faculty of foresight and which does not appertain to the principal question (pp. 475-476).

While men lose faith in the old religions, new religions will be born. "We must discover the rational substitutes for these religious notions that for a long time have served as the vehicle for the most essential moral ideas" (Durkheim, [1925] 1961, p. 9). All societies must express their collective sentiments, ideas, and ideologies in regular ceremonies. While the forms and symbols may change, religion is eternal.

Durkheim's Legacy

According to Stjepan Mestrovic, the world is in crisis, and sociology is having difficulty apprehending that crisis. "Nationalism, socialism, capitalism, and fundamentalism—the leading 'isms' that Durkheim tried to apprehend sociologically—are still causing turmoil in the world" (Mestrovic [1988] 1993, p. ix). The West is without a comprehensive system of morality. Everyone is left to his or her own devices, and there is little restraint on the individual's will. Crime has reached epidemic levels without a moral system that binds individuals to the social order; politics has become a game of power and dominance rather than governance and consensus. Economic competition has become unrestrained and often counter to the good of the social whole; violence in pursuit of individual "happiness" has become a way of life; suffering and discontent despite material abundance have become the norm.

According to Mestrovic, the Western world lives at the height of civilization and barbarism. Human knowledge today is more significant than ever; our understanding of nature and our universe has never been more accurate. Literacy has spread to the masses; higher education is increasingly made available to broader segments of the population. Our technology advances daily; we manipulate our environment to fashion goods and services at a scale unparalleled in human history. At the same time, we live in an era when wars kill thousands; divorce is rampant, inequality within and between nations is high; democratic governments engage in torture; and child abuse—sexual, emotional, and physical—has seemingly become epidemic. Mass murder on the part of governments has become commonplace; corporations exploit workers, customers, governments, and the environment. Murder and other forms of violent crime are at alarmingly high rates. Consumerism has become a way of life for many; drug use and abuse are epidemic, and politicians use lies and deception to get elected and govern. Moreover, the list could easily go on—go to any cable news channel on any given day, read a daily newspaper or a weekly news magazine—civilization is advancing, and barbarism is rising. Mestrovic asks, could the two be inextricably intertwined?

Civilization, or the creation of rational institutions through government to contain barbarism, is ineffective (p. xiv). Barbarism, or the "will" of the individual, cannot be constrained by such rationally constructed systems. The "heart" (egoism) is always more substantial than the "mind" (society); the constraining of the barbaric will can only be accomplished by other "habits of the heart" that are equally powerful (Mestrovic, 1993, p. 47). These habits of the heart, Mestrovic claims, are feelings of altruism and compassion, the other side of human nature that must be cultivated and given expression in our culture. Nevertheless, he warns, such altruism cannot be systematized. "But I cannot repeat often enough that they [Durkheim and Veblen] were against the neo-Kantian, rational, systematization of these benign traits. The moment that one tries to systematize compassion into socialism, for example, one has converted a benign trait into its opposite. This is because, according to Durkheim, any time we act from duty, fear, or any sort of compulsion, we are really acting based on egoistic self-interest, which is the basis for barbarism. Durkheim claims repeatedly in his writings that genuine human goodness must be sought spontaneously, for its own sake (p. 47).

For Mestrovic (and Durkheim), the problem becomes how we can foster the development of such empathy and compassion within the individual. This problem becomes particularly acute in that the development of civilization is eliminating the basis of such empathy by weakening traditional institutions such as family and community that instilled these values and strengthening economic institutions that inflame the egoistic will. Both Durkheim and Mestrovic argue that compassion cannot be learned; it can only be transmitted through example (Mestrovic, 1994, pp. 71-72). To do this, Durkheim advocated "the revival of guild-like associations and the family" to model compassion and foster its development within individuals; such development would bind the individual to others with bonds of love and commitment (Mestrovic, 1993, p. 181). Such guilds have yet to form, and the family, religion, community, and other institutions that functioned to bind the individual to the whole continue to be weakened in the West. Durkheim's aphorism that "The old gods are growing old or are already dead, and others are not yet born" is still true today (Durkheim, [1912] 1954, p. 475). Consequently, Western societies risk disintegration (Mestrovic, 1994, p. 72).

In addition to weakening the social bond that makes Western society more vulnerable to disintegration, social forces in the modern world promote Balkanization (fragmentation of nation-states into smaller and smaller states). Whereas the capitalist-industrial world promoted the consolidation of societies melding ethnic, religious, and racial groups into conglomerated nation-states and empires, new forces of sectarian religion and narrow nationalism focused on these more traditional identities are now actively promoting their disintegration. The Soviet Union and Eastern Europe fell to such forces; they will also increasingly threaten the West (p. 135).

Millions are seeking identity, values, direction, and meaning in the modern nation-state and not finding it. Millions have turned to sectarian religions and ideologies that glorify folk identity and advocate "suspicion, paranoia, and sometimes even hate of neighbors" (p. 8). In reaction to the decline of traditional universal religions that preached love and brotherhood, these fundamentalist faiths have attached themselves to political movements that look to separate from the dominant culture and set up a more homogenous social order. "The important point is that modernity produces its own nemesis. In seeking to establish order and eliminate sentiment, modernity paradoxically produces disorder, fragmentation, and heightened passions—in a word, the anti-modern (or the genuinely postmodern). This process is captured better by unorthodox historians such as Spengler and Toynbee who followed in the wake of Arthur Schopenhauer's [and

Durkheim's] formula that heightened rationality exacerbates the will (or passions) than by Kant's, Rousseau's, Comte's or the Cartesian formulas that rationality can eventually control or even eliminate passions" (p. 137). Again, it was Durkheim who encompassed all of this within his sociology. Durkheim made religion and the sacred a centerpiece of his thought; he pointed to the increasing division of labor as the key to modern society and economic development and the root cause of anomie and widespread discontent (p. 136). Modern sociologists have lost the critical insight that society is held together by irrational feelings of love, affection, attachment, empathy, and devotion to one another (Mestrovic, 1993, p. 248).

> The central insight of this lost trajectory is the horrifying idea that enlightenment cannot contain the forces of barbarism—that the will is stronger than rationality. If that is true, then all utopian schemes and efforts at social engineering are suspect. Modernity cannot take nature once and for all. Rather, human societies and culture are a part of nature. If anything like cosmopolitan humanity is to emerge, one that is mindful of the planet and of the human rights of all its citizens, it must learn to balance its barbaric tendencies with peaceable habits that have been ignored for too long (p. 278).

According to Mestrovic, this loss has had tragic consequences for sociology and Western society.

The spread of modernity has destroyed all bases for forming and maintaining a collective conscience necessary to bind the individual to society. The collective conscience guides individual behavior and desires in ways that benefit the group. With this weakening, the individual 'will' become increasingly unchecked and consistent with our folk wisdom of unchecked power, becoming increasingly egocentric, corrupt, decadent, and barbaric. "The collective consciousness no longer exists: it has succumbed to a process of fission, a Balkanization of social identity into fragmented group identities that are hostile to one another" (Mestrovic, 1997, p. xii). These groups often compete for our allegiance by debunking and attacking each other. Information supporting or attacking these groups' ideological positions or mythology is freely available to all; consequently, few can give unquestioned allegiance, and all causes and positions can be countered, ridiculed, discounted, or balanced with additional information (p. 62). The result is the spread of a personality that cannot take a long-term committed stand on anything, taking all views as relative (p. xv).

The weakening of the collective conscience also takes an emotional toll on the individual, according to Mestrovic, for the emotional bonds of individuals to the group are part of our very humanity. The weakening of the collective exposes us to the manipulation of our emotions by governments, corporations, and the culture industry (pp. 109-110). These cynical manipulations through the media evoke feelings of covetousness, community, pride, and other pseudo-emotions to harvest votes, poll numbers, commitment, or spending. The deliberate manufacture of pseudo-emotions among the populace is enabled by the development of television and other communications technologies; it has been made far more effective by the parallel collapse of the collective conscience (p. 126). "A social transformation has occurred from privately and passionately held rigid moral standards to a publicly and loosely held set of standardized feelings that are used in predictable ways depending upon social circumstances. This is evident from examining contemporary social interaction in the family, school, local and national political life, and also international affairs" (p. 52). This, Mestrovic claims, is a "neo-Orwellian" form of totalitarianism, one that is both efficient and effective (p. xv). Unlike totalitarianism based on terror, it does not rely on constant surveillance, secret police, or terror. It is difficult to oppose because it presents a happy, friendly face to the manipulated (p. 67).

Much of Mestrovic's writings are philosophical explorations of Durkheim's sociology and its relevance to understanding the present crisis of Western societies. Along with Durkheim, Mestrovic asserts that men and women are born with two natures: a strong ego or will and a mind or spirit that seeks to make sense of the world. The will is our animal nature, our drive to satisfy our biological needs. The mind or "collective conscience" primarily comes from the groups and organizations that give us life. Without strong integration into such social groups, that is, without the bonds of love and commitment that promote the internalization of moral guidance, the ego/will is loosed upon the world without mercy. Humans exploit the natural and social world without check; since unchecked desires can never be satisfied, rampant anti-social behavior contradicts human welfare, and unhappiness and misery (anomie) become general social conditions. The morality needed to check this condition cannot come from rational sources—one cannot legislate, teach, or contrive institutions to instill morality; in fact, rationality tends to weaken other traditional institutions that are the source of the needed moral authority.

Consequently, many fall prey to factions that give meaning and identity to the individual but at the expense of the social whole. Governments and corporations cynically manipulate others in search of meaning and identity for power and wealth. What is needed, both Durkheim and Mestrovic argue, is the birth of new social structures that can inspire the love and commitment of people and fully integrate people into the social whole. Lacking this integration, the will is left to its own devices and engages in barbarism and other exploitive behaviors in a futile attempt to satisfy its whims.

Most contemporary sociologists give only lip service to Durkheim; he is viewed as one of the discipline's founders; while isolated insights are used in social psychology, few contemporary sociologists have been heavily influenced by his macro theory—though Mestrovic is an obvious exception. In the 1930s, Talcott Parsons made Durkheim the centerpiece of his functionalist theory. This school of thought flourished for 30 years with advocates like Robert K. Merton, Kingsley Davis, Robert Nisbet, David Riesman, and Wilbert Moore. However, the appeal of this perspective has now faded. One of the issues with functionalism is that it has come to be identified with the status quo and conservatism among American sociologists. As Merton will show, this is not necessarily so, but the belief is there. It is also true that social theory is somewhat subject to fashion. This book will examine one of the best functionalists, Robert K. Merton, who styled himself a "Durkheimian" and thus borrowed heavily from him. Then, we will look at the social theory of Robert Nisbet, whose foundation in classical social theory was dramatically influenced by Durkheim. As a third contemporary advocate of Durkheim's thought, I have decided to go outside sociology. Neil Postman was a maverick communications theorist and general social critic who borrowed heavily from Durkheim's sociology. Durkheim, like functionalism, seems very much out of fashion among modern macro sociologists, and I consider the field poorer for this fact. The decision to include Postman was a challenging one. He is more of a generalist and social critic than a theorist, and social theorists (who are likely to be reviewers of books like this) tend to be a stuffy lot. Nevertheless, Postman is innovative and fun, and many of Durkheim's insights sparkle in his prose. A thorough review of the work of these three will reveal the continuing relevance of Durkheim's macro-social theory.

Chapter 5: Robert K. Merton's Functional Analysis

Robert King Merton (1910-2003) is a self-styled "Durkheimian," writing very much in the functional tradition. In conceiving society as a system, it becomes natural to see it as composed of interrelated parts whose operations have consequences on each other and the entire system itself. For example, examining a system like the human body makes it readily apparent that the various organs are interrelated and impact the body's overall health. So is it with sociocultural systems. Functional analysis results from thinking of society as a total sociocultural system, and functionalism analyzes social phenomena regarding their effect on other phenomena and the sociocultural system.

The functional orientation has long been implicit in biology, physiology, and the social sciences of anthropology, economics, and sociology (Merton, [1948] 1968, p. viii). Social scientists as diverse as Malthus, Spencer, Marx, Durkheim, and Weber have each described the interrelationships between social phenomena. To take a famous example, Weber wrote of the effect that a religious belief, the "Protestant Ethic," had on the rise of capitalism. In a more explicit functional reference, Durkheim wrote of the "functions" of criminal punishment in terms of its impact upon criminal behavior and its effect on society (it serves to bind society together, making explicit the rules and building consensus around these rules). Many contemporary social scientists, including those featured in this book, continue to engage in functional analysis.

Robert K. Merton's signal contribution to functionalism lies in his clarification and codification of functional analysis. Specifically, Merton (1) strips functionalism bare of the unexamined (and insupportable) assumptions of many of its practitioners, (2) broadens the analysis to incorporate change as well as stability, (3) makes critical distinctions between functions and personal motives, (4) develop a descriptive protocol for functional analysis to guide the analyst in social observations, and (5) engages in the functional analysis of a variety of sociocultural phenomena to demonstrate the utility of the perspective as well as to further understanding of the phenomena under investigation. This chapter examines Merton's contributions to the clarification of functional analysis.

Faulty Assumptions

One of the charges hurled against functional analysis in the 1940s and 1950s, and still echoed today, is that functionalism is an inherently conservative perspective devoted to preserving the status quo. Merton suggested this charge because analysts, chiefly in anthropology, have adopted three untenable and unnecessary postulates to the functional orientation. These postulates are first that all widespread activities or items are functional for the entire sociocultural system; second, that all such prevalent activities and cultural elements have sociological functions; and third, that the items are necessary for maintaining that system (p. 79). Merton examined these postulates and found them inconsistent with logic and observation.

The postulate of functional unity—that all prevalent activities relate positively to the social whole—may well be tenable in social anthropology, Merton asserted, in which the analyst is chiefly concerned with highly integrated, homogeneous, nonliterate societies (p. 82). It does not hold, however, for more complex heterogeneous societies. Functional unity, Merton stated, cannot be assumed; at most, it is an empirical question to be determined by social research. Further, some social or cultural items can have functions for some groups within a sociocultural system and not for others. Therefore, the analyst must delineate the group or groups for which a given sociocultural item is functional. Such items often have diverse positive and negative consequences on various groups and the sociocultural system (pp. 81-84).

Merton found the second postulate that all widespread items of the sociocultural system perform vital functions for that system equally invalid. Although widespread sociocultural forms may be functional for society, they are a problem for investigation; they cannot be assumed. Instead, Merton offered a "provisional assumption" that widespread and persisting sociocultural forms have a "net balance" of positive over negative consequences. This net balance will hold either for society as a whole or for elite groups within society that are powerful enough to "retain these forms intact" through "direct coercion or indirect persuasion" (pp. 85-86). Here, Merton pointed out that power differentials exist within sociocultural systems and that sociocultural forms and practices that benefit powerful groups may negatively affect other groups within society or even the total sociocultural system.

The final postulate of the indispensability of cultural items for maintaining the sociocultural system is also problematic. Merton asserted that sociocultural systems might have functional needs or prerequisites, but various forms may meet these needs. Calling it a "major theorem of functional analysis," Merton asserted that "*just as the same item may have multiple functions, so may the same function be diversely fulfilled by alternative items*" (pp. 87-88, emphasis in the original). There are a variety of ways to fulfill any function. Although these ways are not limitless (they are subject to structural constraints), no single social institution, cultural form, or widespread practice is indispensable; there is a range of "functional alternatives" or "substitutes" (pp. 106-107).

Merton claimed that the unexamined use of these postulates, singly or combined, has given rise to the charge that functional analysis is a conservative perspective adopted by social scientists committed to defending the current social order. However, Merton admitted to another reason the conservative label seems apt for the traditional functional perspective: Traditional functionalism seems wholly focused on social stability rather than change (pp. 91-94).

Incorporating Change

Merton maintained that such a focus on stability would give the analyst a conservative orientation, and focusing on change alone would lead the analyst toward a radical orientation. Functionalism, in and of itself, Merton claimed, is neither (p. 94). However, traditional practitioners, working with the limited concept of function alone, tend to focus on stability. To offset this focus, Merton introduced the concept of "dysfunction"(p. 94). Whereas functions contribute to the adjustment of the system, dysfunctions are those consequences that lead to instability and change (p. 105).

The analyst must recognize, Merton asserted, that institutional structures and cultural elements are interrelated and mutually supporting and that the dominant orientation of sociocultural systems is toward stability. However, to recognize this is not to give affirmation to all elements of the status quo (pp. 94-95). Change is also a part of sociocultural systems. "As we survey the course of history, it seems reasonably clear that all major social structures have, in due course, been cumulatively modified or abruptly terminated. In either event, they have not been eternally fixed and unyielding to change" (p. 95). Merton insisted that social structures can only be analyzed regarding statics (stability) and dynamics (change). The concept of dysfunction allows functional theory to focus on change.

The concept of dysfunction is based on tension, strain, or contradictions within component elements of sociocultural systems. Dysfunctional elements create pressures for change within the system (p. 176). Sociocultural items or practices may be functional for some groups and dysfunctional for others, often producing conflict within the system. Examining functions and dysfunction causes the analyst to focus on the range of units (people, groups, subgroups, statuses, and the entire society) that the item impacts (p. 106).

Social mechanisms within the system, including the interrelation and mutually supporting elements, operate to keep these strains in check, attempting to limit or minimize the change in the social structure. However, such mechanisms are not always effective, and the accumulation of stress and resulting conflict often causes systemic change. One of the primary goals of functional analysis is to identify these dysfunctions and examine how they are contained or reduced in the social system and how they sometimes cause systemic or fundamental change (p. 107).

Functions and Motives

The failure to distinguish between functions and motives is one of the chief sources of confusion for students of functionalism. "Functions are those observed consequences which make for the adaptation or adjustment of a given system; and dysfunctions those observed consequences which lessen adaptation or adjustment of the system" (p. 105). (The observer Merton implicitly refers to is the social scientist.) Motive, on the other hand, is the subjective orientation of the actor engaged in the behavior. The two are quite different, though traditional functional analysts have often used the terms interchangeably (p. 114).

The difference in function and motive can readily be seen in T. Robert Malthus's analysis of the double standard of sexual behavior. The origin of the "superior disgrace" attached to a woman's breach of chastity is due to the biological fact of childbirth. A woman who had sex ("connected") with a man who would not agree to support any resulting children would eventually bear children who would burden society. To prevent the recurrence of such a burden, Malthus maintained, men have punished such sex with disgrace. Malthus pointed out that the double standard is a breach of "natural justice" (it is dysfunctional for women). However, it is consistent with limiting population growth to what the environment can sustain. The double standard, Malthus added, gives rise to other beliefs regarding "female delicacy" and cultural values that justify the practice. These beliefs and values take on a life of their own. They serve to motivate people to condemn the unmarried sexual behavior of women "and operate with the greatest force on that part of society [among the upper classes] where, if the original intention of the custom were preserved, there is the least real occasion for it" (Malthus, [1798] 2001, p. 216). In the case of the upper classes, the personal motivation for judging female sexual behavior differently than male, Malthus pointed out, bears no relationship to its function for society.

Several other points of interest about Malthus's example touch upon Merton's brand of functionalism. By detailing this functional analysis of the double standard, Malthus was not advocating that it is right or just, only that the belief system is functional for a society that must limit its population. Nor was Malthus saying this belief is irreplaceable to the rest of the system and thus cannot be changed. Malthus wrote about other ways—technological and social—that serve to limit population growth. Also, note that whereas the double standard is functional for the entire society and men, it is dysfunctional for women. As most students today would readily agree, the double standard is passing in most Western societies. What is causing this change? New social practices, such as using more effective birth control techniques, make the double standard unnecessary (other cultural items are fulfilling the function of limiting births). Also, because of its dysfunction to a sizable portion of the population, the double standard created some strain (tension, contradictions) in the sociocultural systems of the West and ultimately became a source of active conflict.

There are times, however, when the objective consequences identified by the social scientist coincide with the subjective motivations of the individuals involved in the activity. In other words, at times, functions and motives are the same. Merton coined two terms that capture the necessary distinction: "Manifest functions are those objective consequences contributing to the adjustment or adaptation of the system and are intended and recognized by participants of the system; Latent functions, correlatively, being those which are neither intended nor recognized" (Merton [1948] 1968, p. 105). Dysfunctions, of course, can be latent as well. With the addition of these two concepts, Merton asserted, the functional analyst is now equipped to explore the critically (and theoretically) critical area of the "unintended consequences" of social action (p. 105).

One of the significant advantages of the distinction between manifest and latent functions is that it aids in identifying and explaining seemingly irrational social behavior (p. 116). On the surface, behaviors such as the Hopi ceremonials to bring rain (p. 118) or the Hindu worship of cows (Harris, 1974, pp. 11-32) are irrational behaviors that bear no relationship to their avowed purpose. Consequently, outsiders (including many social scientists) tend to label such behavior as mere "superstition" or "primitive behavior." However, it serves many latent functions for specific groups or societies. The persistence of these irrational behaviors lies with these latent functions rather than the manifest functions that people cite as their primary motivation.

Merton illustrated this point by discussing the latent functions fulfilled by the Hopi rain dance (Merton, [1948] 1968, pp. 118-119). Citing the work of Durkheim, Merton pointed out that such ceremonials are essential for expressing group sentiment and are a fundamental source of group unity. This latent function is far from the minds of the Hopi participating in the ceremony. Nevertheless, this function is vital in understanding the persistence of the ceremony as a social form. Merton suggested that sociologists can make distinctive contributions to understanding human societies by focusing on latent functions. The exploration of latent functions points the analysis toward theoretically essential issues. Inquiry into latent functions can advance knowledge of sociocultural systems (pp. 119-122).

Marvin Harris has had remarkable success relating sociocultural practices and beliefs to the functional consequences of these practices and beliefs. Using terminology similar to Merton's latent and manifest functions, Harris has made a critical distinction between *etic* consequences (imputed by outside observers) and *emic* motivations by the participants. Harris's functionalism, very much a part of his theory of cultural materialism, is used to identify the functions and dysfunctions of a variety of sociocultural items either for the benefit of powerful groups or for the adjustment of entire sociocultural systems (see especially *Cows, Pigs, Wars and Witches*, and *Cannibals and Kings*). The resulting insights are often stunning.

Description in Functional Analysis

Merton, always concerned with the relationships between theory and methods, attempted to summarize the data types needed to be collected to perform functional analysis. What data types must be included in observations, and what data can be safely excluded? To answer these questions, Merton reviewed several cases of functional analysis, specifically a Hopi Indian rain ceremony, the American romantic love complex, and Thorstein Veblen's analysis of conspicuous consumption, to codify the data types needed to engage in functional analysis (pp. 109-110). Merton identified five items in the "descriptive protocol" for functional analysis.

First, the analyst should systematically account for the pattern of behavior of interest and the people participating in the behavior. This account should include a detailed description of the social status of participants and onlookers and the types and rates of their interactions. These descriptions, Merton claimed, go a long way toward suggesting functional interpretations (p. 110).

The second item of the descriptive protocol calls for the analyst to explore other patterns, those of other sociocultural systems that represent alternative ways of dealing with the problem under study (p. 110). For example, Merton pointed out that the "romantic love complex" as the basis for American marriage excludes other patterns for choice of mates, such as parental selection or marriage as an economic alliance. By comparing the American pattern to these other cultural forms, the analyst often can tease out the different structural positions that benefit (functions) or are hurt by (dysfunctions) the cultural form under analysis.

The third item in the protocol describes the various meanings that the pattern of behavior has for the various participants and group members. Such meanings often give the analyst clues as to the social functions of these sociocultural items (pp. 111-112). The fourth protocol is for the analyst to give an account of the motivations of the people who both conform or deviate from the pattern under study. Again, these personal motives should not be confused with social functions but serve a functional analysis purpose. "Inclusion of motives in the descriptive account helps explain the psychological functions subserved by the pattern and often proves suggestive with respect to the social functions" (p. 113).

Finally, the fifth item describes any regularities of behavior associated with the pattern under study. The participants may not recognize such behavior as related to the pattern. These "unwitting regularities" often lead to discovering latent functions (p. 114). Merton most fully illustrated the utility of the descriptive protocol by extracting from Veblen's functional analysis of the pattern of "conspicuous consumption":

> The cultural pattern of conspicuous consumption: the conspicuous consumption of relatively expensive commodities "means" (symbolizes) the possession of sufficient wealth to "afford" such expenditures. Wealth, in turn, is honorific. Persons engaging in conspicuous consumption not only derive gratification from direct consumption but also from the heightened status reflected in the attitudes and opinions of others who observe their consumption. This pattern is most notable among the leisure class, i.e., those who can and largely do refrain from productive labor (this is the status or role component of the description). However, it diffuses to other strata who seek to emulate the pattern and who likewise experience pride in "wasteful" expenditures. Finally, consumption in conspicuous terms tends to crowd out other criteria for consumption (e.g., "efficient" expenditure of funds). (This is an explicit reference to alternative modes of consumption obscured from view by the cultural emphasis on the pattern under scrutiny.) (p. 112).

The functions of conspicuous consumption identified by Veblen are derived from his descriptive account of the phenomenon consistent with Merton's protocol. Veblen's description includes the statuses of the participants, alternative forms of behavior that have been crowded out, the meanings the participants and observers themselves ascribe to the behavior, and the participants' motivations

(p. 112). The manifest function of buying these goods—as superior ways of satisfying the needs for which the goods are designed—is consistent with these personal motivations. However, Veblen went beyond that by identifying the latent functions of conspicuous consumption: The consumption of these goods enhances or advances their social status; their consumption is an open display of wealth and financial strength to their fellows (pp. 123-124). Such an analysis describes complex human behavior, making it plain that "social life is not as simple as it first seems" (p. 122).

Anomie Theory

"Social Structure and Anomie" was published in 1938 and is Merton's most widely disseminated work within sociology. Merton's primary goal in this article was to extend functional theory to cover change by introducing the concept of dysfunction into the analysis. A dysfunction is based on tension, contradictions, or strain between elements of the sociocultural system, and anomie, a concept Merton borrowed from Durkheim, can result from such system contradictions.

Merton argued that deviant behavior—behaviors that do not conform to significant norms held by most of the members of a group or society—is a product of sociocultural forces rather than inherent within individuals. Freudian and other psychological theories, Merton claimed, posit that the different rates of deviant behavior in various groups in society are the result of the random distribution of pathological personalities in these groups (pp. 175-176). In contrast, Merton claimed that deviant behavior is created by tensions among (a) cultural values that strongly emphasize specific goals, (b) social norms and mores that proscribe approved avenues for attaining these goals but are not adequately emphasized, and (c) a social structure that systematically denies access to these goals for large numbers of people (p. 188).

Like Durkheim with suicide, Merton pointed out that the rates of deviant behavior vary across different societies. Even within societies, diverse groups have different rates and patterns of deviance. These different rates of deviant behavior between societies and among groups within societies rule out a simple psychological or biological interpretation. Different rates among groups demand a sociological explanation (pp. 185-186). "Our primary aim is to discover how some social structures exert a definite pressure upon certain persons in the society to engage in non-conforming rather than conforming conduct" (p. 186).

Merton identified two central elements of cultural systems. The first is cultural values and goals that a given sociocultural system defines and propagates as desirable. These goals are reinforced by dominant and prestigious institutions—family, school, church, mass media, and workplace (pp. 190-191). Consequently, the various members of society are socialized into these goals and values, integrating them (in varying degrees) into their very personalities (pp. 186-187). Often, the cultural values and goals thereby become their values and goals.

The second element of the cultural system consists of the approved avenues for attaining these goals. These approved avenues are consistent with other dominant values and sentiments within the sociocultural system (of the population at large or powerful groups within that population). They are often institutionalized into the normative structure of society, prohibiting individuals from striving for goals that might hurt the group (fraud or the use of force), go against the interests of elites, or violate other critical cultural values (p. 187).

These two elements of cultural systems, the culturally approved goals and approved means to attain them, vary independently. Cultures can place tremendous stress on the goals without much stress on the institutional means to channel the individual striving for these goals in a manner consistent with other societal values (p. 187). For example, in sports, when great emphasis is placed on winning and little on fairness and following the rules of the game, cheating and poor sportsmanship can become epidemic. Just how readily athletes and coaches will give into this temptation when there is little chance of being caught is evidenced by the scourge of performance-enhancing drugs, particularly the rash of designer drugs for which tests have yet to be devised. Cultures could also place excessive stress on the institutionalized means with little stress on the goals. In such a society, conformity to the rules themselves becomes the goal. Tradition and custom tightly bind such a society. Social stability and resistance to change, at least for a time, become the norm (pp. 187-188).

Most societies exist between these extremes, with cultural goals and institutionally prescribed means in some rough balance (p. 188). Societies that maintain this rough balance are well-integrated and consequently have low rates of deviance and social change. Merton's concern in the anomie essay is with the type of society that places heavy emphasis on cultural goals without putting much emphasis on the approved institutional means to attain these goals. Such societies are mal-integrated cultures (p. 188). Merton also wrote about the other polar extreme—excessive emphasis upon the means with little emphasis on the goals—in his essay on the bureaucratic personality, summarized in this chapter.

Consequently, in such societies, individuals receive little guidance on how to obtain these highly desirable goals. Merton maintains that rates of deviance (and change) in such societies should be high.

> No society lacks norms governing conduct. However, societies differ in the degree to which the folkways, mores, and institutional controls are effectively integrated with the goals that stand high in the hierarchy of values. The culture may lead individuals to center their emotional convictions upon the complex of culturally acclaimed ends, with far less emotional support for prescribed methods of reaching out for these ends. With such differential emphases upon goals and institutional procedures, the latter may be so vitiated [weakened] by the stress on goals as to have the behavior of many individuals limited only by considerations of technical expediency. In this context, the significant question becomes: Which of the available procedures most efficiently nets the culturally approved value? The technically most effective procedure, whether culturally legitimate or not, becomes typically preferred to institutionally prescribed conduct. As this process of attenuation continues, society becomes unstable, and there develops what Durkheim called "anomie" (or normlessness) (pp. 188-189).

Merton added that American Society is approaching this extreme, emphasizing material success and comfort and little on institutional means of attaining it. Consequently, one would expect higher levels of deviance in American Society (concerning achieving the goal of wealth and success) compared to sociocultural systems that have these two cultural components more balanced. In addition, Merton posited that this "demoralization" affects groups within the same society differently, depending upon the extent of the members' exposure and internalization of the two components of the cultural structure (p. 190 & p. 224). Thus, the imbalance between cultural goals and means stems from two sources. This imbalance originates in the differential emphasis placed on the goals and means within the entire sociocultural system. However, within a mal-integrated culture, it is exacerbated by an imbalance in emphasis within groups and subcultures.

The success ethic has been incorporated into the very fiber of American Society (p. 222). Merton asserted that Americans are "bombarded" by school, workplace, and family messages, urging them to strive for the American dream despite repeated failure. These messages constitute a social force encouraging individuals to "never give up," "try, try again," and to maintain their lofty ambitions at all costs (pp. 190-193). Merton asked how individuals respond to a culture in which they are continually urged to succeed monetarily without a corresponding emphasis upon the legitimate or institutional means for doing so. What are the consequences of this mal-integrated culture for individual behavior? Table 5.1 shows the typology of Merton's modes of individual adaptation.

Table 5.1: A Typology of Modes of Individual Adaptation

Modes of Adaptation	Cultural Goals	Institutional Means
Conformity	+	+
Innovation	+	−
Ritualism	−	+
Retreatism	−	−
Rebellion	±	±

Merton contended that most people would conform to the dictates of the cultural goals and institutional means, even in a society such as the United States, where success goals and means are mal-integrated. Countervailing forces, sanctions, and alternative goals can and do keep people integrated into the culture (p. 237). Still, many individuals must adapt, particularly within groups in society that are blocked from access to legitimate means to attain their goals (p. 194).

Concerning the goals of monetary or material success, innovators are those individuals who have accepted the great American dream of wealth but have not fully internalized the culturally approved means to attain this goal. Merton suggested that a fine line often exists between sharp business dealings and practices that violate the law (p. 195). White-collar and organized crime, such as gambling and vice, represent innovative ways of attaining success. An individual is particularly likely to adapt through innovation when culturally approved avenues have been blocked (pp. 199-200).

Merton contended that the lack of opportunity does not cause deviant behavior but the lack of opportunity in the context of an exaggerated cultural emphasis on achieving material success. Rigid caste societies may restrict mobility more than the American class system, but without the emphasis on material success attainable by all, such cultures produce far less deviance (pp. 200-201). Deviance is, therefore, a dysfunction of American culture's heavy emphasis on the goal of success. This adaptation mode is based on the failure to internalize the culturally legitimate means to material success while internalizing the success goals themselves (p. 203). Many have not fully internalized these cultural mores and norms due to failures in the socialization process. Merton argued that American culture does not properly emphasize legitimate means, and often, subcultures even less so. Consequently, the individual responds to the cultural pressure to succeed by bending, stretching, or breaking the rules.

However, most people have internalized both the goal of success and the legitimate means. In these cases, frustration is far more likely to lead to the third adaptation mode, ritualism. When blocked from achieving success goals, such men and women will stick to legitimate means and go through the motions. Merton contended that the heavy emphasis the lower middle classes place on socializing the young in obedience predisposes them to this adaptation mode (p. 205).

Merton described retreatism as probably the least common of the adaptation responses. The category consists of society's dropouts: psychotics, tramps, and substance abusers, and they have given up on both the culturally prescribed means and the goals (pp. 207-208). Merton viewed retreatism as a way of escaping society's demands.

The final category, rebellion, consists of rejecting goals and means and advocating new standards and goals to take their place. Rebellion is based on alienation from established cultural goals and institutional means. "In our society, organized movements for rebellion apparently aim to introduce a social structure in which the cultural standards of success would be sharply modified, and provision would be made for a closer correspondence between merit, effort and reward" (p. 209).

Before leaving the topic of Merton's anomie or stress theory, several points should be emphasized. Merton used monetary success as an example. Do not mistake the example for the theory. According to the theory, any cultural goal with an extreme emphasis on achievement without a corresponding emphasis upon institutionalized (or legitimate) means will result in anomie (p. 220 & p. 235). For example, Americans emphasize the desirability of romantic love as the foundation of marriage. The legitimate means of achieving this goal are dating, courtship, and marital bliss. Not everyone has fully internalized the culturally approved goals and means; many are biologically or psychologically unsuited for attaining the goal. Do the modes of individual adaptation have any relevance to this goal–means imbalance?

Merton's anomie theory is not intended to be a theory of all deviant behaviors. One of Merton's middle-range theories focuses on limited forms of crime, delinquent, and deviant behavior (some of which do not violate any law) (pp. 231-232). Other types of deviant behavior may result from social, psychological, or biological forces. Not all deviant behavior, Merton points out, is dysfunctional to the sociocultural system or the individual (p. 237).

The different modes of adaptation discussed by Merton do not refer to personality types. Instead, the modes of adaptation refer to role behaviors in specific situations in which the individual is engaged, adaptations to situations in which the goals are strongly encouraged by the culture, but the legitimate means are not given emphasis or have not been adequately internalized (p. 194).

Merton's conception of anomie is a particular case of Durkheim's more general concept. Merton's concept is limited to the stress produced when there is a disjunction between cultural goals and prescribed means to achieve them. Like Durkheim's original conception, culture does not give individuals sufficient guidance for proper role behavior. Merton was aware of other situations in which the culture fails to give proper guidance that is not due to a goal–means disjunction (p. 217 & p. 242).

Merton's anomie theory is centered on some sociocultural sources of deviant behavior. Everyone subjected to this pressure does not necessarily respond with deviant behavior. Consistent with Durkheim's original formulation, countervailing forces—alternative goals, sanctions, and other social mechanisms—bring people back into conformity. The most common response in any sociocultural system is conformity (p. 237).

Increasing levels of deviant behavior weaken institutional norms, thus increasing anomie, leading others to deviate from sociocultural norms. This feedback process results in cumulatively rising rates of deviance if counteracting control mechanisms are not instituted (pp. 234-235).

Finally, the theory is rooted in functional analysis. Cultural goals, values, mores, and norms constitute social forces that push people into specific, predictable paths of behavior. These elements are institutionalized in the structure and internalized through the individual's socialization. The extent of institutionalization and internalization varies across cultures and subcultures. Regardless, these forces produce the overwhelming conformity of human behavior, making social life predictable and possible. At the same time, Merton demonstrated that the malintegration of these same forces creates the conditions for social deviance and general social change. The malintegration of these cultural elements creates functions and dysfunctions for the individual and society.

Bureaucratic Personality

In *Bureaucratic Structure and Personality*, Merton examined the functions and dysfunctions that bureaucratic structures perform for individuals and entire sociocultural systems (p. 177). How do such structures constrain the behaviors of individual officeholders and the people subject to these officers? What impact do such structures have on the broader sociocultural system? To address these questions, Merton first described the structure and growth of bureaucratic organizations in classic Weberian terms.

The importance of addressing these issues is evident in the increasing bureaucratization of Western Society (p. 259). Citing Weber, Merton argued that social relations are increasingly subject to bureaucratic coordination. Through bureaucracy, Merton asserted, people are yoked to the production of goods and services (pp. 250-251). More people are separated from the means of production—soldiers from their weapons, blue-collar workers from their tools, salespeople from their customers, and scientists from their technical equipment. To work, one must be employed by an organization capable of amassing capital and providing the coordination necessary for these large and complex undertakings. Merton concluded that, increasingly, to live, people must be employed by massive public and private bureaucracies.

Merton draws heavily on Weber's work on rationalization and bureaucracy. As we will see, Weber believed that the separation of the worker from the forces of production, documented by Marx, had little to do with the ownership of the forces of production but was a consequence of bureaucracy and the rationalization of social life. Marx asserted that capitalism has led to the "expropriation" of the worker from the mode of production. He believed the modern worker was not in control of his fate and was forced to sell his labor (and thus his "self") to private capitalists. Weber countered that loss of control at work was an inevitable result of any system of rationally coordinated production. Weber argued that men could no longer engage in socially significant action unless they joined a large-scale organization. In joining organizations, they would have to sacrifice their desires and goals for the organization's impersonal goals and procedures. By doing so, they would be cut off from a part of themselves and become alienated. Also, in line with Weber, Merton described an ideal bureaucracy, highlighting the following characteristics (pp. 249-252): 1) hierarchical offices, functionally interrelated; 2) rules of procedure and responsibility; 3) impersonality and formality of relationships; 4) division of labor; 5) appointment and advancement based on achievement; and 5) efficiency.

Written rules are essential in understanding bureaucratic efficiency. The rules are constantly being refined and generalized to encompass a wider variety of cases to avoid the necessity of constant instruction and decision-making at the top. This generalization of rules is intended to provide clear and consistent guidance to decision-makers at various levels of the hierarchy. Thus, there is a strong emphasis within bureaucratic structures to follow prescribed rules and regulations to assure uniformity and efficiency in decision-making.

What is the effect on the individual officeholder of being subjected to a social structure that stresses procedural means with little emphasis on the goals? Note that this is a component of the goals-means typology of anomie theory; in this case, the imbalance involves excessive stress on the means and little stress on the goals. Such an emphasis is likely to produce ritualistic behavior. As described by Merton, the impact of bureaucratic structure on the personality of officeholders is guided by his Anomie Theory. Following the rules becomes an end–in–itself. What was instituted to attain the bureaucracy's goal efficiently impedes that achievement. The bureaucrat becomes rigid, unable to make exceptions or decisions that do not fit standard categories. Decision-making becomes a ritualized process of forms and standardized procedures. This tendency toward ritualized adherence to the rules is buttressed by a bureaucratic system that stresses incremental salaries and promotions based on seniority and adherence to these rules (pp. 253-255).

According to Merton, the bureaucratic structure also induces an "esprit de corps" by minimizing competition within the organization (through seniority) and engendering a feeling of common cause. Thus, informal loyalties develop, and the occupants of the offices begin to identify with one another, defending each other and their interests from outsiders. This defensiveness is active whether these outsiders are elected officials charged with setting the direction and goals for the bureaucracy itself, stockholders, or the customers or clientele they are supposed to serve (p. 255).

Still, another dysfunction of bureaucracy is caused by the emphasis bureaucratic organizations place on depersonalized treatment of individuals (p. 256). Although this quickly can be taken to extremes, the need to treat clients and colleagues as representatives of categories rather than as individuals is at the heart of efficiency and fairness. Professors are to grade their students based on academic performance, not their personalities, physical attractiveness, or power connections. Promotion based on these personal characteristics does not further the cause of either education or fairness. To violate these precepts is to violate not only bureaucratic rules but also rules that most bureaucratic functionaries have internalized. On the other hand, clients (and students) are interested in being treated in terms of their individual characteristics and problems.

Thus, the bureaucratic characteristic of impersonality functions to promote fairness and efficiently attain bureaucratic goals. The efficient attainment of goals is the primary characteristic of bureaucracy. Contrary to widespread belief, they are highly efficient in making money, graduating students, or licensing drivers. Their reputation for inefficiency lies in their inability to deal with cases outside the norm, individuals with unique problems. Nevertheless, an ideal bureaucracy is constantly refining its rules and processes to encompass more of these exceptional cases.

Its dysfunction to individuals is that the bureaucrat (and the organization) is often perceived as cold, uncaring, unresponsive, haughty, and overbearing. Merton concluded that bureaucracies are increasing in size and scope and should not be the sole reason sociologists study such organizations. Studying the interaction of such organizations with personality will increase understanding of modern social life (pp. 258-259).

Protestant Ethic and the Spirit of Science

Initially beginning in his graduate studies, Merton's work in the sociology of science ultimately defined the specialty. His study on Puritanism, pietism, and science exemplifies Merton's sociology. This study was based on functional analysis, looking at religious ideas and ideologies' impact on science and the whole sociocultural system.

The study addresses the unintended consequences of social actions—in this case, the latent functions of Protestant ethics in fostering science development. It is empirical; Merton used historical documents to demonstrate his case. Though it is a study in macrosociology, it is a theory of the middle range, limiting its vision to a single time and place. Moreover, the study builds solidly on a classical foundation, reworking Weber's theory of one of the causes of capitalism.

Merton's thesis on the Protestant ethic is that Puritan values "demanded in their forceful implications the systematic, rational, and empirical study of nature for the glorification of God in His works and for the control of the corrupt world" (pp. 628-629). Merton used two strategies to demonstrate the viability of his hypothesis. First, by examining historical documents, he demonstrated that the values of Puritanism were highly consistent with the ideals and methods of science. Secondly, Merton presented empirical evidence that the founders of science, both in England and on the continent, were men of Protestant backgrounds (p. 628).

According to Merton, five Protestant values directly promoted the scientific revolution: 1) glorification of God; 2) concern for the welfare of man; 3) exaltation of the faculty of reason; 4) respect for empiricism; and 5) faith in order. Merton provided evidence that these values were integral to the Puritan ethic, and each played a prominent role in early scientific studies.

There is little doubt that 15th and 16th-century scientists were primarily motivated in their studies for the greater glorification of God and a concern for the welfare of humanity. Merton cited writings of Bacon, Boyle, Willoughby, Sprat, Wilkins, and Ray to this effect (pp. 629-631). Each of these men dedicated their works to the glory of God and attempted to justify their science to their creator through their religious values. The study of nature, their writings suggested, was an attempt to understand God's handiwork and use nature for humankind's benefit (pp. 631-633).

Puritanism also fostered the faculty of reason. More critically, Merton added, the Puritan ethic made this rationalism "subservient" to empiricism. Rationalism and empiricism are the very foundations of modern science. Finally, Puritanism shared the basic assumption of order to nature with the new science. For both Protestants and scientists, this natural order revealed the hand of God (pp. 633-636).

Whereas Merton demonstrated excellent compatibility between the values of Puritanism and early science, the real empirical test of the hypothesis is the extent to which Protestants are found in the ranks of early scientists. Here, the evidence is overwhelming. The leading figures of the founders of the Royal Society were strongly influenced by Puritanism (pp. 637-638). Merton cited Dean Dorothy Stimson, who arrived at similar conclusions:

> She points out that of the ten men who constituted the "invisible college" in 1645, only one, Scarbrough, was non-Puritan. There is some uncertainty about two others, though Merret had Puritan training. The others were all definitely Puritan. Moreover, among the original list of members of the Society of 1663, forty-two of the sixty-eight concerning whom information about their religious orientation is available were Puritans. Considering that the Puritans constituted a relatively small minority in the English population, the fact that they constituted sixty-two percent of the initial membership of the society becomes even more striking. Dean Stimson concludes: "that experimental science spread as rapidly as it did in seventeenth-century England seems to me to be in part at least because the moderate Puritans encouraged it"(pp. 638-639).

The Protestant ethic, Merton concluded, is strongly correlated with the scientific revolution and technological development. "Hence the two fields were well integrated and, in essentials, mutually supporting, not only in seventeenth-century England but in other times and places" (p. 649).

Middle Range Theory

Merton's advocacy of theories of the "middle range" is the most controversial aspect of his sociology (pp. 53-54). Theories of the middle range, Merton asserted, are limited in scope. They do not attempt to account for all social stability, change, and organization across all sociocultural systems. Instead, they focus on limited problems and processes (p. 51).

To say that theories of the middle range are limited in scope does not mean that they are mere empirical generalizations. Merton conceived these theories as an intermediate between research hypotheses and more inclusive theoretical systems (p. 39). According to Merton, social scientists are not yet ready to develop all-inclusive theoretical systems; they have yet to accumulate the necessary knowledge. Merton stated that the best social scientists can do today is "develop special theories applicable to limited ranges—theories, for example, of deviant behavior, the unanticipated consequences of purposive action, social perception, reference groups, social control, the interdependence of social institutions—rather than to seek immediately the total conceptual structure that is adequate to derive these and other theories of the middle range" (p. 51). From these middle-range theories, more general conceptual schemes will evolve.

In addition to his work, Merton placed the works of some well-known classical authors in this category. Theories of the middle range include Durkheim's *Suicide* (according to Merton, an exemplar of the genre) and Weber's *The Protestant Ethic and the Spirit of Capitalism*. Weber's *Protestant Ethic*, for example, "...deals with a severely delimited problem—one that happens to be exemplified in a particular historical epoch with implications for other societies and other times; it employs a limited theory about the ways in which religious commitment and economic behavior are connected; and it contributes to a somewhat more general theory of the modes of interdependence between social institutions" (pp. 63-64).

Merton maintained that what usually passes for theory in the social sciences are "general theoretical orientations" rather than tightly knit theories amenable to critical empirical testing. They indicate the types of variables and relationships the analyst should be concerned with and the tentative framework that provides the context for empirical inquiry. Merton characterized these general theoretical orientations as "indispensable" (p. 142). However, they provide only a broad context; it is up to the researcher to specify particular variables and relationships. "Such general orientations may be paraphrased as saying in effect that the investigator ignores this order of fact at his peril. They do not set forth specific hypotheses" (p. 142). Merton noted that many middle-range theories are consistent with several broad theoretical schemes. Consequently, such general theoretical orientations have only an indirect effect on empirical research; such research has a minor impact on the formulation and refinement of these theoretical orientations (pp. 68-69).

Merton was widely criticized for his views on middle-range theory, some interpreting it as a call for lowering intellectual ambitions, others as a condemnation of macro social theory, and still others as the development of specialized mini-theories fragmenting the field. However, the relations between theory and research are at the heart of Merton's concern. Sociologists, Merton maintained, tend to be in one of two camps.

> On the one hand, we observe those sociologists who seek, above all, to generalize and find their way as rapidly as possible to formulate sociological laws. Tending to assess the significance of sociological work in terms of scope rather than the demonstrability of generalizations, they eschew the "triviality" of detailed, small-scale observations and seek the grandeur of global summaries. At the other extreme stands a hardy band who do not hunt for the implications of their research too closely but remain confident and assured that what they report is so. To be sure, their reports of facts are verifiable and often verified, but they are somewhat at a loss to relate these facts to one another or even to explain why these, rather than other, observations have been made. For the first group the identifying motto would at times seem to be: "We do not know whether what we say is true, but it is at least significant." Moreover, the radical empiricist's motto may read: "This is demonstrably so, but we cannot indicate its significance" (p. 139).

Merton's focus on middle-range theory urged sociologists to be both significant and true.

About Merton

Robert K. Merton was born in South Philadelphia on July 4, 1910. His parents were working-class Jewish immigrants from Eastern Europe. His boyhood was poverty, though he recalled a childhood full of cultural opportunities at the nearby Carnegie Library, the Academy of Music, and the Philadelphia Museum of Art. He wrote, "that seemingly deprived South Philadelphia slum was providing a youngster with every sort of capital—social capital, cultural capital, human capital, and, above all, what we may call public capital—that is, with every sort of capital except the personally financial" (Merton, [1994] 1996, p. 346).

His birth name was Meyer R. Schkolnick, but after taking up magic at 14, he first became Robert K. Merlin and then Merton in the early 1920s. Receiving a scholarship to Temple University, he "chanced" into a sociology class by George E. Simpson, where he found his subject. Simpson took him on as a research assistant and encouraged him to attend professional meetings where he met the Russian sociological theorist and émigré Pitirim Sorokin. Sorokin encouraged him to apply for graduate school at the new sociology department he was forming at Harvard. Upon graduating from Temple in 1931, Merton received a scholarship to attend Harvard and was Sorokin's research and teaching assistant. One of his first assignments for Sorokin was to author papers on French sociology. Here, Merton first discovered Durkheim, which "resulted in my becoming a transatlantic Durkheimian and laid the groundwork for what would become my own mode of structural and functional analysis" (p. 350). At Harvard, Merton also worked with George Sarton, a prominent science historian. For his dissertation, Merton chose the topic of *Technology and Science in Seventeenth Century England*, which began the specialty of the sociology of science and his lifelong interest in it.

At Harvard, Merton also met Talcott Parsons. At the time, Parsons was a young instructor, Merton reported, who was beginning to lecture on the ideas that would later form the core of *The Structure of Social Action*. Although Merton was much impressed with Parsons, he became critical of his theorizing mode and writing style. He found Parsons's theory far too remote and obscure to guide empirical inquiry. Parsons's grand theory was uppermost in his mind when Merton wrote of the need for theory of the middle range.

It is interesting to note that C. Wright Mills expressed similar concerns regarding the relationships between theory and research in *The Sociological Imagination* as does Merton in his essays on theories of the middle range, empirical research, and their inter-relationships. However, they would disagree over various definitions. C. Wright Mills used the term *grand theory* to refer to similar systems of theoretical thought that Merton labeled "total sociological systems." Merton was referring obliquely to the work of his good friend and mentor, Talcott Parsons. Mills was, of course, more direct in his criticism of Parsons.

Mills' concept of "abstracted empiricism," or the reification of empirical method, echoes Merton's concern over simple empirical generalizations. However, Mills' critique was directly aimed at Paul Lazarsfeld, Merton's long-time research collaborator. Mills never extended his criticisms to Merton's work. He does not address Merton's theories of the middle range in *The Sociological Imagination*, though it was a controversial paper in sociology at the time. Mills seems to have been the most respectful and reserved of all his colleagues with Merton. For example, in 1949, Mills praised Merton's first edition of *Social Theory and Social Structure*. "Although in my distracted and benumbed condition it's hard to read anything with strict attention, over the last few days I have read all the new matter in your book and some of the older materials. It was very depressing. I hadn't realized (in fact I had for some reason been refusing to examine the point) how very far I had wandered from really serious work in our discipline" (Horowitz, 1983, p. 82). Merton thought Gerth and Mills' book on social psychology, *The Psychology of Social Institutions* (1953), a work of systematic analysis and wrote the introduction to the volume. Although he supported and complemented Mills' work *White Collar* and *The Power Elite*, Merton thought they were too journalistic. Merton considered Mills' *Causes of World War III* and *Listen Yankee* as straight journalism (Merton [1948] 1968, pp. 65-66n).

Merton and Mills spent most of their professional lives at Columbia University as long-term colleagues, both struggling for the soul of the discipline. Merton and Paul Lazarsfeld brought Mills to Columbia to work at the Institute for Social Research. Horowitz (1983, p. 74) commented that Merton often acted as a calming influence in a department much troubled by Mills. Mills favored "taking it big," but Merton was more interested in connecting theory to empirical checks. Just as Mills' *The Sociological Imagination* promotes Mills' type of sociological inquiry, Merton's essays on theories of the middle range are justifications for his. However, both were strong advocates for their style of scholarship, and neither defined his style as the only legitimate way of doing sociology.

Parsons, too, Merton admitted, led him to adopt a style he has called "oral publication." Merton considered teaching a form of scholarship in which he would work out ideas in lectures and seminars with students, each semester revising and editing and producing a new edition. Only after years of refining his ideas this way would he commit himself to print. "I notice that a dozen years raced by between the time I first lectured on 'manifest and latent functions' at Harvard, and the time those ideas took printed form in a 'paradigm for functional analysis" (Merton [1994] 1996, p. 351)

Upon graduation from Harvard (1936), Merton spent a brief period as an instructor there, spent two years at Tulane (as a young department chair), and then, in 1941, joined the faculty at Columbia. While at Columbia, Merton helped build one of the most prominent sociology departments in the country and began his long collaboration with Paul Lazarsfeld, a mathematically minded methodologist. For more than 30 years, the two entered "a continuing program of theory-guided and methodologically disciplined empirical social research on a wide variety of substantive problems" (p. 355). Their studies included radio and TV propaganda, voting decisions, mass communications, and racial integration. Their students at Columbia in the 1940s and 1950s included Lewis Coser, James Coleman, Peter Blau, Rose Coser, and Seymour Martin Lipset. In addition to his authored work, Merton was quite active in editing books and articles, estimating in his autobiographical essay that he had edited some 250 books and approximately 2,000 articles for his colleagues and former students.

The breadth of Merton's scholarship is awe-inspiring. Although the sociology of science remained his specialty, he wrote in disparate fields such as bureaucracy, deviance, knowledge of knowledge, applied sociology, communications, medical sociology, reference group theory, stratification, and methodology. He is responsible for developing critical sociological concepts such as manifest and latent function, self-fulfilling prophecy, role model, and serendipity in science. He even managed a crucial innovation in research methodology, developing with Marjorie Fisk and Patricia Kendall the "focused group interview" that has become the favored technique of corporate and political marketing research.

Active in scholarship all his life, Robert K. Merton died at 92 on February 24, 2003. He was a much beloved and respected man within the academe. In its obituary, the *American Sociological Association's Footnotes* called him "one of the most influential sociologists of the 20th century." He was a National Academy of Sciences member and a past president of the American Sociological Association. One of his most notable awards was the nation's highest scientific honor, the National Medal of Science, in 1994. Merton was the first sociologist to receive this honor.

Chapter 6: Robert A. Nisbet's Leviathan

Though one can find elements of other classical theorists in his writings, Robert A. Nisbet (1913-1996) is primarily a follower of Emile Durkheim. This influence can be seen in his basic understanding of modern sociocultural systems and their drift. He contends that society is increasingly dominated by large-scale administrative systems, severely weakening traditional groups and organizations. This concentration and centralization of social and political power and the consequent weakening of institutions that formerly mediated between the individual and centralized power have devastated democracy, freedom, and human welfare.

In his first book, *The Quest for Community* ([1953] 1990), he makes known his primary concern about the direction of social development: the expansion of administrative power, particularly government, and the consequent weakening of traditional groups and organizations. It was a concern he expressed over the next four decades. Initially, his primary concern was parallel to Durkheim's: the impact that this weakening of primary group ties had on the normative structure of society and the consequent lack of integration of individuals into the social order. However, over the years, he focused more on this shift's impact on representative government and individual liberty.

The Decline of Intermediate Organization

The present structure of the State began to gain overwhelming dominance in the West with the French Revolution, he argues. In his first book, Nisbet capitalizes "State" to denote the modern political State; modern States differ from traditional states in that government is greatly enlarged in its functions and powers and has become highly bureaucratic and centralized. Since the French Revolution, the State has taken over more functions from traditional organizations and groups such as the extended family, neighborhood, class, and regional authority. Nisbet conceives of the centralization of power in the hands of the State as both diminishing individual freedom and as "a retreat of authority" in the traditional primary groups, which are the essential components that make up the whole society. In these groups, the individual has roots, is formed, and internalizes society's norms, values, ideologies, and outlook. Social disorganization—the decline of the family, community, and other traditional primary groups is more appropriately thought of as the wearing away of these authorities caused by the "absorption" of their functions by the State (Nisbet 1970, p. xxvii). While Nisbet's focus is on State power, he understands that "changes and dislocations" in other sectors of society—technological, economic, and religious—also contribute to this centralization of bureaucratic authority and weakening of primary groups (Nisbet, [1953] 1990, 43-44). The enlargement and centralization of State bureaucratic power has dramatically affected other forms of social organization. The social fabric becomes frayed. "Threads are loosened by the tightening of power at the center" (Nisbet, 1988, p. 84). Without a common bond, individuals increasingly take advantage of one another; relationships become commodified, increasingly relying upon contracts and cash rather than loyalty and commitment. "As the blood rushes to the head of society," Nisbet says, "it leaves anemic the local and regional extremities" (p. 85).

He argues that this enlargement and centralization of State power are the root causes of these intermediate institutions' loss of authority and function and have two principal effects. The first is the weakening of local and regional checks on further centralization. The second is the isolation and alienation of the individual and their consequent powerlessness (Nisbet, 1975, p. 195). Further, this centralization of power, a power that is external to both local groups and the individual, makes it difficult to establish a true community. Nisbet explains that people gather in lasting groups and associations to do things they cannot do alone. When centralized power relieves these local groups of these functions, it undermines the foundation for community, leaving local groups without function or authority, "what else but the social horde and alienation can be the result?" (Nisbet, 1970, pp. xxviii-xxix). An ideology of bureaucracy has pushed this centralization and enlargement of power. This ideology promotes centralization, formal hierarchy, written rules of conduct and authority, and impersonal administration based on military models of human organization. Government bureaucracy has come from two primary sources: Nisbet argues mass war and the creation of the welfare state (Nisbet. 1975, p. 59). As Tocqueville, Marx, and Weber predicted, bureaucracy is now firmly in control. One need only look at the thousands of miles of bureaucratic corridors and millions of offices in Washington to recognize that bureaucratic organization reigns supreme (Nisbet, 1970, p. xxvii; Nisbet, 1975, pp. 53-54).

This fundamental view of modern sociocultural systems is remarkably similar to the sociology of C. Wright Mills. This similarity is remarkable because Mills is a staunch Weberian and is widely seen as a left-wing radical in American sociology. Nisbet is the opposite: a self-described libertarian with vastly different political loyalties and policy prescriptions. They differ in their view of who has the upper hand in the State and Capital relationship. Mills focuses on the "Power Elite," the people at the top of enlarged and centralized bureaucracies of three dominant institutional sectors of American society—government, military, and economic--and finds that of the three, the economic is often dominant. Nisbet's initial focus is upon the State as a unified "Leviathan." He believes that the political State has rapidly absorbed military, economic, political, and social power in transforming all social organizations in the West (Nisbet, [1953] 1990, p. xxxiii; 1955, p. 154). In later writings, he details the interrelationships between State, economic, and military power in language highly reminiscent of Mills, although constantly asserting that State power is dominant in economic activities and has been since the rise of capitalism itself. However, there are many similarities in their analyses as well. Like Mills, Nisbet also recognizes that war and the military caste of mind are responsible for the tremendous centralization of government and the economy and makes military adventure far more likely (Nisbet, [1953] 1990, pp. 94-95; 1975, p. 56, p. 154; 1988, p. 105). Also, like Mills, in his later writings, Nisbet shares with Weber the concern that this concentration of power is counter to democracy and freedom. Beginning only with military power, it is the State's later absorption of political, economic, kinship, and religious functions, as well as the State's dislocation or outright destruction of traditional authority structures, that has led to the decline of community, freedom, and democracy ([1953] 1990, pp. xxxiii-xxxiv).

Nisbet's initial concerns, however, are far more Durkheimian: the concentration and enlargement of bureaucratic authority have led to the loss of community that is so keenly felt in the West. Nisbet argues that social ties such as family, religion, and community remained vibrant and intact for thousands of years. It was only at the end of the eighteenth century, with the democratic and industrial revolutions, that these primary institutions began to weaken. These revolutions went to the core of the social bond and "went right to man's most ancient and cherished sources of identity" (Nisbet, 1975, p. 79). While the State and the economy have sought to replace these ties with more formal mechanisms of identity and sources of inspiration and loyalty, these organizations still need to inspire or bind the individual to the larger group. Nisbet complains that more Americans are only loosely attached to traditional primary groups; consequently, they no longer share in such traditional values as commitment, loyalty, and community, and so are increasingly ruled by the "cash nexus" (Nisbet, 1988, pp. 85-95). All of which could have easily been penned by Mills.

In *The Quest for Community* (1953), Nisbet is primarily concerned with the psychological consequences of increasing individualism and social disintegration at the local and regional levels. "How extraordinary, when compared to the optimism of half a century ago, is the present ideology of lament," Nisbet remarks. "There is now a sense of disorganization that ranges all the way from the sociologist's concern with disintegration of the family and small community to the religious prophet's intuition that moral decay is enveloping the whole of Western society" (Nisbet, [1953] 1990, p. 7). The modern individual has been freed from traditional hierarchies of class, religion, locality, and kinship, but this freedom has brought insecurity, disenchantment, and alienation. Citing Durkheim, Nisbet points out that such individualism has led to "masses of normless, unattached, insecure individuals who lose even the capacity for independent, creative living" (p. 12). This anomie is because these traditional hierarchies precede and form individual consciousness. Nisbet argues that they are the institutions that shape the individual's values, beliefs, and behavior. In primary groups, men and women are shaped—their personalities, wants, "needs," and drives are fashioned (Nisbet, 1975, p. 270). When governments rob men and women of this community context, it is not freeing them but banishing them to lives of alienation, loneliness, passion, fear, and manipulation (Nisbet, [1953] 1990, p. 22). Moreover, this has led to a search for community, belonging, and an escape from impersonality and anonymity (pp. 25-28).

This search for community, Nisbet argues, goes a long way toward explaining the appeal of communism for some. Such an individual is searching for certainty and solid membership in a human association. "The greatest appeal of totalitarian party, Marxist or other, lies in its capacity to provide a sense of moral coherence and communal membership to those who have become, to one degree or another, victims of the sense of exclusion from the ordinary channels of belonging in society" (32). A similar argument can be made for the appeal of fundamentalist religious groups of Christian, Muslim, or other varieties. Furthermore, there is the communal appeal of war, Nisbet claims, a longing for a national purpose, for bonding as a nation against a common enemy. While the horror of modern warfare is genuine, so is the communal appeal for war. For soldiers, the appeal is more direct: the experience of military organization, bonding with comrades, and, in contrast to civilian pursuits, a life charged with moral meaning and purpose (pp. 36-37).

The small, personal relationships in primary groups are in sharp decline, "relationships that mediate directly between man and his larger world of economic, moral, and political and religious values" (p. 44). Such values are made meaningful in these small groups and associations. Here, they are internalized and become a part of the self. Traditional primary groups—family, local community, church—have given over many of their functions (education, elder care, welfare) to the State and the economy and have consequently become irrelevant and meaningless in the lives of many. Traditionally, these groups have served to mediate between the individual and the larger society; these groups have formed individual moral and personal character. "Within such groups have been engendered the primary types of identification: affection, friendship, prestige, recognition. And within them also have been engendered or intensified the principal incentives of work, love, prayer, and devotion to freedom and order" (p. 45). With their decline in functional and psychological significance in the lives of many, men and women are forced to search for status, belonging, and security within large impersonal bureaucratic organizations; status and security that was once freely given, Nisbet says, in their primary group associations (pp. 44-45). It should be emphasized here that Nisbet is not asserting that such interpersonal relationships are declining in number. Instead, he claims they are declining in functionality and psychological significance. "…it is becoming apparent that for more and more people such relationships are morally empty and psychologically baffling" (47).

The most fundamental problem of our age, Nisbet argues, is that primary social groups no longer have a role in our economic-political system. In a traditional society, they held the allegiance of their members because they were essential in distributing goods, labor, power, and authority within the society. They served as the mediators between the larger economic and political institutions of society and the individual. "Our present crisis lies in the fact that whereas the small traditional associations, founded upon kinship, faith, or locality, are still expected to communicate to individuals the principal moral ends and psychological gratifications of society, they have manifestly become detached from positions of functional relevance to the larger economic and political decisions of our society" (p. 48). They no longer play a significant role in supplying mutual aid, production, childcare, education, distribution of goods, and welfare. Such groups still need to develop new functions that people find essential.

Nevertheless, we still expect individuals to identify with these groups, internalize their values, and gain a sense of belonging and community through participation. New organizations arise, but their functional utility is limited. Relations tend to be based on a cash or legalistic basis; thus, their bonding power is weak. The individual has been emancipated from outmoded customs and the stifling effects of local and regional communities. However, the individual has also been freed from group identity, moral and cultural certainties, solidarity, and meaning. The nation-state and nationalism thus come to fill the psychological need of the individual to identify with something more significant than the self (p. 51).

The family in the West is an excellent example of the decline of primary groups. A family is a group of individuals related to one another by blood ties, marriage, or adoption. Families form an economic unit, and the adult members handle raising children. All societies involve some form of family, although the form the family takes is widely variable. Nisbet claims that the symbolic importance of the family is still significant. However, it has been pared down from an extended family to a single nuclear unit, and this nuclear unit has little functional relevance to larger economic or political institutions in Western society (p. 53). This nuclear unit is bound together based on romantic love, a rather insubstantial foundation. In a traditional society, the family is bound together by such ties as duty, obligation, and protection. These bonds are reinforced and reenacted daily through the exchange of mutual aid and protection (Nisbet, 1975, pp. 256-277). "The family is a major problem in our culture simply because we are attempting to make it perform psychological and symbolic functions with a structure that has become fragile and an institutional importance that is almost totally unrelated to economic and political realities of our society" (Nisbet [1953] 1990, 55). The family has lost all functions save two: 1) it is an institution where we can express personal romance and sexuality, and (2) it has become a haven in a cold and impersonal world. Other personal relationships are unlikely to shoulder household burdens, deflect emotions, care for children, care for aged parents, counsel adolescents, and help family members cope. The functions of the extended kinship system have been taken over, to a considerable extent, by formal service organizations staffed by professionals steeped in the ideology of individualism, which has no personal stake in marriage itself. The primary function remaining is that it has become the center of our emotional life. As such, it has become extremely unstable.

Why have extended families lost these functions? Nisbet's answer focuses on the State co-opting the functions of the family. He gives only passing attention to economic conditions—the transition from an agricultural to an industrial society—in which individuals must move from one end of the country to another to pursue their careers. By casting the family adrift from an extended kinship system, industrial society has created an extremely mobile population--both physically and socially. Since the couple must live alone, it is appropriate for them to select one another based on romantic love rather than utilitarian-extended family requirements based on alliances, economics, or custom. So, an alternative view would be that the extended family was weakened by social forces (geographic and social mobility, the increasing division of labor) and could no longer fulfill its traditional functions, so the State and the economy stepped in to fill the vacuum. Or is it possible that both processes are responsible? Regardless, Nisbet argues that the family, not the individual, is the fundamental foundation of society. Without a solid and viable extended family system, Nisbet doubts that advanced civilization is long possible. Moreover, again, the enlargement and growth of the State are responsible for the family's loss of functions and its precipitous decline (Nisbet, 1975, p. 260).

Nisbet rarely focuses on economic growth and how it has contributed to this weakening of primary group bonds. Industrial society and its detailed division of labor, now even affecting professional jobs, often requires the individual to move from one region of the country to another. Such geographic movement is undoubtedly a significant factor in weakening ties between extended family members and increasingly nuclear family members. As Durkheim pointed out, the intensification of the division of labor also leads to cultural and moral divisions between people. However, while Nisbet does focus on the State, it should be remembered that he considers the State a Leviathan, incorporating and subsuming economic, military, and educational functions (among others) as it continues to enlarge and centralize.

Nisbet maintains that a similar loss of function has also happened to the local community and neighborhood. Furthermore, their decline in functional importance has come with a loss of social cohesion, a foundation on which our economic and political institutions were based. The family and community supplied the mutual aid and support needed for capital accumulation in the nineteenth century. To have psychological meaning to individuals, the community must have some functional significance. "And, quite obviously, local community has been no more functionally important than kinship in the kind of society that the industrial and political revolutions brought into being. State and economy alike have, in effect, bypassed family and community to go straight to the individual, thus leaving him so often precariously exposed to the chilling currents of anonymity and isolation" (Nisbet, 1975, p. 85). The family and community instilled the incentives and values needed to discipline people to hard and monotonous work, savings, voting, and other forms of political participation (Nisbet, [1953] 1990, pp. 60-61). While rationalists have long believed that these incentives and motivations are present in the individual from birth, we are beginning to learn that this is not so. Nisbet says that such motivations result from socialization in primary social groups, that is, groups in which the members have close personal relations with one another. Such primary groups have a functional importance in the lives of the individuals involved, and because of this, they also carry significant moral weight (p. 62). The evidence does not support the assertion that new groups and associations have arisen to replace community and family; the unaffiliated may become the norm. The associations that seem to be on the rise—industrial corporations, government agencies, and educational institutions, are all bureaucratic and, in the main, do not engender the personal loyalty, commitment, and identity of the older primary groups (p. 63). The problem, then, is not simply the decline of traditional primary groups but the failure of modern social structure to foster new groups at the primary level to perform their functions (pp. 63-65). However, Nisbet is overlooking the impact of science, technology, and urbanism on the detailed division of labor and this impact on geographical and social mobility. Consequently, primary groups weaken along with the values that such groups promote. Instead, Nisbet asserts that the fault lies entirely with the modern State's development.

Nisbet claims that one can only understand the present by referencing the past. "The Historical past has a persistent and penetrating influence upon the behavior of any generation [...] If we would diagnose our own age we had better do so historically, for history is the essence of human culture and thought" (pp. 70-71). Modern kinship, community, and religious institutions have evolved from the far more vibrant institutions of the Middle Ages. They have been changed and adjusted by historical events and in response to other institutions' modifications, adjustments, and adaptations (p. 73). In medieval society, small groups, not the individual, were the basic building blocks of society. The small group—family, guild, church, class, urban neighborhood, or village community—had functional relevance in allocating labor and distributing resources to support life's necessities. These groups, therefore, had absolute authority in daily life, and individuals were deeply committed to the group's norms, values, and way of life. Centralized authority in the medieval era was distant and weak. Therefore, the individual and the centralized State were subordinated to these groups. Nisbet reports that taxes and fines were levied upon the family; it was the family that received the honors and accolades of its members' achievements.

Further, it was within the family that individual occupation and marriage decisions were made; the extended family and broader community raised the children. Even property, Nisbet reports, was owned by the family rather than its members and, therefore, could only be quickly sold with the family's approval (p. 74). The history of the West, Nisbet says, is primarily composed of the successive emancipation of individuals from these "fetters" of community life (pp. 73-74). At the same time, the State took over many of its former functions, dealing directly with individuals rather than through these intermediate institutions.

Sacred & Profane

Like Durkheim, Nisbet believes that the distinction between the sacred and the profane is of profound significance. To give an institution sacred significance is to remove it from considerations of practical utility or the everyday. Examples of the sacred include human life, community, family, or the nation-state. Almost anything, Nisbet says, can be given sacred significance, but anything sacred can also be lowered into the purely utilitarian or the profane. "Rightly did Durkheim declare that the sacred but the other side of the coin on which community is written," Nisbet writes. "Human aggregates are possible, or at least conceivable, without a sense of the sacred, but not, Durkheim declared, community" (Nisbet, 1975, p. 87).

Nevertheless, there is a conspicuous erosion of the sacred in the modern world due to the decline of primary groups. The social bond is essential to experiencing the sacred. This erosion of the sacred is evidenced by changes in our ritual celebrations, which have lost their sacred significance over the years. "Christmas, Easter, and Halloween are today but impoverished reminders of a time when the year was rich in celebration of seasons—and, far more important, of human community and its relation to the forces of nature" (p. 86). This commodification and commercialization of the sacred is the epitome of the profaning of the culture; it represents a "desecration and dishonor" of the social bond (Nisbet, 1988, pp. 107-108).

The Rise of the State

Many see the rise of capitalism as the prime mover in modern history, a rise responsible for creating a consumer culture of atomized individuals, transforming the social bond into a cash nexus. Marxists and other economic determinists argue that technological change caused the rise in power of the bourgeoisie, who transformed the social order through their economic activities and wealth accumulation. They claim it is from these economic interests that rationalization, commercialization, and bureaucratization have all sprung and completely transformed the social world (Nisbet, [1953] 1990, pp. 87-88). But Nisbet disagrees. He recognizes that factories, markets, and the rapid development of innovative technologies have radically transformed traditional society. However, Nisbet maintains that the State has fostered capitalism's establishment and continued growth in the West. The State has defined legal contracts, established a system of laws, common currency, weights, and measures, regularized and promoted trade within and between societies—often through its police and military power, and established tax and tariff rates favorable to business. Moreover, the State assures domestic tranquility throughout its territories and assures that social life becomes based upon bureaucratic values of impersonality, calculability, and efficiency, thus suitable for business (pp. 94-95). This view of the role of the State in the beginnings of capitalism is very much in line with Max Weber's view on the rise of capitalism—once he expands the Protestant Ethic hypothesis. (See, for example, Weber's (1927) *General Economic History.*)

It is the rising power of the State, Nisbet claims, which is the prime mover in modern society, a revolutionary movement that cannot be explained through simple economic determinism (77). The rising power of the State has promoted the development of capital and increasingly placed limits on the rights and responsibilities of primary groups and institutions that were formerly intermediate between the individual and the State (p. 89). Nisbet insists that the State is now the prime mover in history, a Leviathan that has assumed all political, economic, and social power (pp. 89-94). Nisbet goes on: "It is in these terms, indeed, that one historian has been led to wonder how far capitalism was the work of businessmen at all, and how far it was the consequence of the overthrow of the medieval system by the military might of the absolute State" (p. 95). This view of the omnipotent State is similar to Wallerstein's world-systems theory.

The earliest function of the State was in war; in an analogy worthy of the SAT, Nisbet says that war is to the State as religion is to the church (p. 91). In true Durkheimian fashion, Nisbet later writes extensively about the functions of war (Nisbet, 1988, pp. 5-15). Nevertheless, over time, other functions were added to the State's war-making powers: first legal and judicial, then economic and religious. Nisbet describes a long-term evolutionary process of the State moving from an exclusively military organization to pick up added functions gradually—usually taking these away from traditional institutions—until it provides, decides, or regulates almost all aspects of social life (p. 91). Nisbet points out that the process is not smooth or continuous. Often moving in fits and starts—external wars and internal conflict between institutions, charismatic figures, and historical events either slow the aggrandizement of State power or speed it up—but the long-term process is straightforward (p. 91).

Before the modern era, the central government's power was hampered by the existence of the town, guild, clan, and church. As the medieval period ended, the State came into conflict with one and then another of these institutions. This conflict was built into the very structure of the society, Nisbet argues, as local institutions "claiming limited jurisdiction over its members" necessarily came into conflict with centralized authority that "seeks to consolidate all important authorities within that territory" (p. 107). The State became the successor to the church as the principal institution by which human beings fulfill their aspirations and regulate their lives. "One would have to go to religion to find anything comparable to Western man's willingness to make sacrifices, of property and life when necessary, in the name of political patriotism" (Nisbet, 1975, pp. 3-4). There is no question, Nisbet explains, that this rise of State power—at least to date —is associated with some resplendent gains in individual liberty and equality, releasing many from the oppressive constraints of community, family, and class (Nisbet, 1988, p. 67). This power is what makes the State revolutionary in character. It frees people from local constraints and tries to assimilate them as individuals into an all-encompassing national State. However, in the "still ongoing process," the power of the State becomes unchecked and absolute, and the exchange of real community for citizenship leads to massive problems of alienation and anomie
and ultimately to the loss of all meaningful freedoms (Nisbet, [1953] 1990, p. 108).

The Twilight of Authority

True to his roots in Durkheim, Nisbet believes that the West is moving into a twilight period when our social institutions decline. People are losing their sense of being rooted in the culture; anomie, individualism, corruption, hedonism, and a sense of disintegration are becoming widespread (Nisbet, 1975, p. v). Our political community—government, of course, but also our entire system of rights, protections, responsibilities, and liberties—once enjoyed the loyalty and trust of the citizenry to the degree that can only be likened to the commitment that medieval believers made to their religious institutions. Nevertheless, like religious commitment in the past, the political community is rapidly losing legitimacy and effectiveness. Moreover, our way of life is increasingly at risk (pp. 3-4). Our government is now viewed with suspicion and outright hostility by a growing segment of the citizenry. The United States government is now widely seen as mainly unresponsive to the people's will, structured to benefit the already rich and powerful, and serving the interests of the privileged (pp. 4-5). Nesbit certainly does not bemoan the decline of the State itself. He does, however, find it tragic that the liberties and rights that the State guaranteed might well be lost.

The crisis of authority, as detailed by Nisbet, refers to several interrelated phenomena. First, the State has hollowed out all functional authorities intermediate to it and the individual. Second, these primary group ties have been replaced by ties promoted and regulated by the State: money, market, and contract. In such a milieu, individual desires become stimulated. Third, the weakening of primary groups cuts the individual off from traditional sources of identity and severely weakens the formation of morality and character, thus causing the atomization of human behavior, widespread alienation, and deviance. The individual is thus left with little guidance. All forms of social authority and hierarchy have been weakened and are ineffectual, and anomie has become widespread. Fourth, the State increasingly fails to evoke feelings of identity, solidarity, discipline, and patriotism through manipulation and further centralization, bureaucracy, and leveling. Fifth and finally, in response to rising rates of crime, disorder, and terrorism from disaffected groups both domestically and internationally, the State takes on an increasingly military caste, becoming involved in military adventures abroad and ever more bureaucratic and totalitarian.

Evidence of a revolt against political authority in the West is widespread. Nisbet cites the rise of fundamentalist, Pentecostal forms of religion, which are often hostile to the political caste of mind—forsaking the authority of the political State whenever it clashes with religion. The reinvigoration of ethnicity, local and regional authority, community and neighborhood, and family are all evidence that the State is under attack. "I do not doubt that the ethnic, religious, and social phenomena I describe have many sources," Nisbet writes. "But surely a major one is repudiation of the political state and of the whole pattern of thinking that has been associated with the state for more than two centuries" (p. 11). Echoing Durkheim, Nisbet asserts that this is a recurring pattern in history; as people become alienated from dominant institutions—State, church, or clan—they begin to give their allegiance to other forms of community. Throughout history, there has been a succession of dominant authorities in sociocultural systems: first kinship or clan, then the State (in the ancient world), then religion (medieval), then the State (modern) (p. 13). He believes that the political State is now in decline and being replaced by totalitarianism—an authoritarian government that tries to regulate every aspect of social life.

The decline of political order is also apparent in the rise of multinational corporations. Such corporations are almost entirely independent of the laws of any one nation-state. Nisbet claims that their power, reach, and size are only partly responsible for their freedom from state control and regulation. A large part of their independence is because governments no longer have the allegiance, confidence, or respect of their people and are thus rapidly losing their authority (p. 13). Nisbet asserts that there is a greater gulf now between citizens and the State than ever since the French Revolution (p. 14). Throughout the 20th century, the government of the people relied upon manipulation and deception; as more people shared this belief, confidence and trust in government and society were weakened. Nesbit traces the manipulation and lying back to Woodrow Wilson (as he does the massive intrusion of the federal government into the economy and other aspects of social life). Wilson's 1916 reelection was based on the lie that he would not become entangled in World War I. This record of lying and manipulation becomes thicker the closer we approach the present (it would be easy to demonstrate that it has continued unabated—if not strengthened—since 1975 as well). (See Nisbet 1988 for an extensive discussion of American political history in the 20th century.)

Another sign of the crisis of authority in the West is the rise of "democratic royalism." Here, Nisbet refers to the pomp and circumstance surrounding the American presidency. Specifically, the attention and focus society gives to every word and act of the person holding the office, even on the most trivial matters. He calls it a presidency with a "carefully cultivated image of democratic, popular roots of power" (p. 30). He is referring to an "Imperial Presidency" that has slipped the checks of other institutions on its powers (pp. 27-29). Indeed, its powers have significantly increased since Nisbet's writings. Throughout history, the rise of royalism—as in Greece, Rome, and the European monarchies in the Middle Ages—is associated with the corresponding weakness of representative institutions (p. 27).

Also associated with democratic royalism is using federal agencies such as the FBI (Federal Bureau of Investigation) and the National Security Agency (NSA) by the executive branch to put citizens under constant surveillance. This practice goes back to Franklin Roosevelt and indeed runs to the present—always justified, Nisbet adds, under the claim of national security (p. 31). Also associated with democratic royalism is the employment of extra-constitutional aides and assistants who often wield more power than Cabinet officers. Such aides are not subject to Congressional approval or oversight. These aides give loyalty and allegiance to the person holding office rather than to the office or the country (p. 33). An added sign of democratic royalism is the growing practice of protecting the president "from unwelcome news, advice, counsel, and even contact with officers of government" (p. 34). Democratic royalism is increasingly shown in the architecture of Washington; the buildings' sheer size and grandiose styles indicate our rulers' mindset. Nisbet believes that democratic royalism, despite setbacks such as Watergate, will continue to spread and intensify as representative democratic government loses allegiance and commitment (pp. 34-35).

Another sign of the crisis of authority, with relevance for today, is the decline of "forms." Forms are the traditional, legal, or accustomed ways of government, the respect for the office, procedure, law, opposing parties, consultation, and open communication within executive agencies and between branches of government. "Forms are, above all else, powerful restraints upon the kinds of passion which are generated so easily in religion and politics. Few things are more obvious in the recent history of the United States than the quickened decline of forms in all spheres of social life, but particularly, and most decisively, in the political" (p. 37). The decline of forms has continued well into the 21st century with extreme partisanship and the rise of the national security state after 9/11. According to Nisbet, this decline is associated with impatience with the pace of democratic government and viewing various agencies and coequal branches as impediments to the will of the executive. Democratic forms come to be viewed as standing in the way of achieving important goals. Once these forms are flouted, they lose all restraining forces on centralized power (pp. 37-39).

Nisbet thinks there is little ideological difference between America's two major political parties. They represent two separate power blocs, each with a lust for office. Politics in America has become tactical warfare over elections—and elections have taken on an endless character. He argues that there is no longer a consensus on this warfare's boundaries (or forms) and little willingness or strategic advantage to compromise with one another. Thus, we have extreme partisan warfare over Supreme Court nominees, national security, war, social security, and every other political, social, cultural, or economic issue that arises (pp. 39-52). "Since there is no true political ideology held by either party, there has been an ever-intensifying focus on the personality and charismatic qualities of the political leader and "an increasingly savage struggle between factions variously termed "Left" and "Right" but which, like those of the late Republican Rome, reflect little more than the lust for power and its capture through whatever means" (p. 52).

However, another sign of the crisis of authority in the West is the decline of patriotism in many circles. Patriotism, Nisbet explains, is the emotional and spiritual bond that holds the political community together. In America, it was a powerful bond indeed. Since the French Revolution, patriotism has been based on the work of intellectuals who wrote histories, songs, slogans, and speeches that roused an emotional attachment and passion for the State. Many in this class were won over to the national State because it rose in opposition to hated feudal institutions of nobility, church, and clan. "But what the intellectual class gives, it can take away!" (p. 68). Starting in the early part of the 20th century, ever more significant numbers of intellectuals have withdrawn their support, as have many citizens. Citing Edmund Burke, Nisbet points out that it is difficult for a highly centralized State to inspire loyalty and solidarity. Local institutions such as the family and community naturally inspire such identification and, when running effectively, transfer this identification to the broader community. Democracy was founded upon cultural traits rooted in primary group association. Traits necessary for self-government—respect for the role of reason in human affairs, self-discipline, and self-restraint—all are rooted in the individual's participation in such vibrant groups as the extended family, community, church, and voluntary associations. By weakening these primary group ties, the State undermines its democratic foundations (pp. 76-77).

In addition, the State still needs to live up to its promise. "The political order, swollen by economic and social responsibilities, so many of which it performs ineffectually and at awesome cost, has manifestly lost the capacity to do at least one of the things for which it is uniquely fitted: maintain internal order" (p. 71). Like Durkheim, Nisbet associates anomie with a rise in affluence. Poverty exerts limits on individual hopes and desires; affluence not only destroys these limits but also promotes a set of rising expectations. A consumer culture further inflames desires that quickly become insatiable (p. 95). Affluence and the rise of consumer culture have weakened institutions such as religion, family, community, and neighborhood that used to tamp down individual desires. Each of these institutions gave the individual a sense of roots, which "discouraged" the ambitions of many to achieve higher social or economic status and redirected their desires along other avenues (p. 100). With the decline of these institutions, the individual is left without limits, direction, or guidance; consequently, many do not internalize social norms and values. "Unless and until a degree of internalization is achieved that makes one's conduct seem almost totally self-willed," Nisbet says in a passage worthy of Durkheim himself, "cultural processes cannot be said to be working very effectively. And yet, this said, there is no avoiding the fact that the elements of culture, including the very deepest ones, are outside the individual, waiting, as it were, to become through complex means of interaction, constitutive parts of mind and personality. And in all this coercion, authority, and discipline are crucial, in whatever degree they may operate" (p. 95). With the decline of primary groups and their authority structures, pathologies such as egoism, eccentricity, and subjectivism have become more widespread, and deviance and crime have increased.

The New Totalitarianism

Nisbet cites Weber's assertion of the ongoing conflict between democracy and bureaucracy: democracy promotes bureaucracy. Such organizations are necessary to provide the coordination and control desperately needed by complex societies (and huge populations). Such functions as the administration of justice, education, voting, and other complex administrative tasks could only be carried out with bureaucratic coordination. However, while modern societies depend on these organizations, bureaucracy undermines human freedom and democracy (pp. 54-56). Over time, State bureaucracy becomes resistant to the rule of elected officials—the bureaucracy is permanent and will always be there, and elected officials are transient. The result, Nisbet asserts, is that elected officials often engage in demagoguery and violation of form to get their way. At the same time, most office seekers promise to cut bureaucratic waste and downsize staff, bureaus, and departments, but once in office, they rarely do.

Western governments' bureaucratization primarily comes from war and social reform (p. 59). Nisbet predicts that this trend will continue. The rise in crime and the increasing threat of terror will cause the United States and other Western countries to increasingly turn to military forms of government to restore confidence in the ability of the government to protect its citizenry. The rise in crime is predicated upon the rise in anomie as norms and values fail to be internalized and lose effectiveness in disciplining egoistic individuals. The predicted increase in terrorism is based on the centralization and enlargement of power in Western (and other) governments; revolution from disaffected groups is now virtually impossible (pp. 61-64). Such blockage makes it "probable that mindless, purposeless terror is filling the vacuum left by receding revolutionary hope as an end in itself" (p. 63).

Like C. Wright Mills, Nisbet believes the military caste of mind increasingly dominates our government. The threat of terrorism, the decline of civil authority, and the breakdown of family and community structures of authority all lead to the rise of militarism. Nisbet asserts that if terrorism continues to increase in the coming decades as rapidly as it had in the decade before his writing, he could not conceive of representative democracy surviving. He did not predict that the terrorists would win but that the U.S. would feel compelled to abandon its Bill of Rights. Today, many argue that this has happened, pointing to the Patriot Act and corporate instances of surveillance and tracking.

As evidence for the rise of militarism, Nisbet points to the increased incidence and intensity of war in the 20th century. Also evident is the increase in the "size, reach, and sheer functional importance of the military" in modern times. To believe that such an institution increasing in our midst has not severely impacted other parts of the sociocultural system—domestic and foreign policy, the economy, and civil and cultural life—is ludicrous (Nisbet, 1988, p. 1). By 1988, Nisbet called the U.S. an "imperial power," likened to Great Britain in the eighteenth century. Like Mills before him, Nisbet saw the militarism of the federal government as one of the greatest threats to freedom in this country and abroad. "To imagine that the military's annual budget of just under a hundred billion dollars does not have significant effect upon the economy is of course absurd, and it may be assumed that with respect to the military as with any other institution, beginning with the family, what affects the economic sphere also affects in due time other spheres of life" (Nisbet, 1975, pp. 147-148). (In 2023, many estimate that the total U.S. military budget, including national security expenditures, is over one trillion dollars.)

Nisbet concludes that such a military establishment will significantly and continuously affect the entire sociocultural system. The militarization problem would not be so critical if we only had to face the increasing centralization of government and the related decline of intermediate authority. Alternatively, it would not be critical if we only faced increased military and terror threats abroad. "But the fact is, both of those conditions are present, and in mounting intensity, and against them any thought of arresting or reversing the processes of militarization of society seems rather absurd. The industrial-academic-labor-military complex President Eisenhower referred to in his farewell remarks has become vastly greater since his presidency, and the military's ascendancy in this complex becomes greater all the time, though not, as I have noted, without much assistance from each of the other elements" (p. 193). The "military-industrial complex" and the "scientific-technological elite" that Eisenhower spoke of means that research universities and institutes, corporations, the military, and government leaders all have a personal stake in a large military, sophisticated weapons systems, and war (Nisbet, 1988, pp. 24-28). No nation, Nisbet warns, has ever managed to retain its "representative character" along with a massive military establishment; the U.S. will not be an exception (p. 39).

Also, like Mills, Nisbet sees the intellectual class as complicit in supporting the military State. Under Wilson and later Roosevelt, intellectuals were brought into government service and supported centralizing power in the federal government (and increasingly the executive branch). They increased this support for the militarization of that power in World War II, the Cold War, and increasingly in the war on terror. Aside from designing the programs, staffing the upper levels of the bureaucracies, creating the strategies, and setting foreign and domestic policies, the intellectual creates the slogans and ideologies that motivate the masses, spin the moralizing and rationalizations necessary for war, and define the crises and the strategies of conflict (Nisbet, 1975, p. 190). Few intellectuals have the independence of mind or the will to oppose either centralization or militarization. With the notable exception of Marx, the founders of sociology—Durkheim, Spencer, Weber, and Sumner—were all extremely skeptical of centralization and the State. Nevertheless, modern practitioners of the social sciences, almost without exception, look to the centralization and enlargement of the State as if it were part of the natural order of sociocultural systems (p. 249).

Nisbet is not predicting the evolution of American society into something akin to Nazi Germany; instead, he sees America rapidly moving toward "legal and administrative tyranny" (Nisbet, 1988, p. 57). Nisbet sees power in contemporary America as becoming "invisible," removed first from family and community to elective office. However, it is now increasingly placed in the hands of the many State bureaucrats who regulate the economy, educational institutions, and medical facilities—our very social existence. The reason that this power has become invisible is two-fold. First, it is done in the name of humanitarian goals, with the government as protector and friend; and second, the State manipulates the media, the educational system, and the minor details of life so that the will of the State becomes internalized by the individual (Nisbet, 1975, pp. 195-197). "The greatest power," Nisbet writes, "is that which shapes not merely individual conduct but also the mind behind the conduct. Power that can, through technological or other means, penetrate the recesses of culture, of the smaller unions of social life,

158

and then of the mind itself, is manifestly more dangerous to human freedom than the kind of power that for all its physical brutality, reaches only the body" (pp. 226-227).

The most revolutionary change of the twentieth century, Nisbet asserts, is that power and authority have been transferred from the offices of constitutional government to bureaucracies "brought into being in the name of protection of the people from their exploiters" (195-196). This "softening" of power, placing the velvet glove over the iron fist of the State, makes such power much more difficult to detect or oppose (p. 223). "In the name of education, welfare, taxation, safety, health, and the environment, to mention but a few of the laudable ends involved, the new despotism confronts us at every turn" (p. 197). The new totalitarianism is not based on terror or external force, although the police powers of the State ultimately undergird its authority. An organization that depends on the constant use of force and intimidation to discipline its members is highly inefficient and ultimately ineffective. A system based solely on force must expend too much energy policing its members; it stifles initiative and provides an obvious target for rallying opposition. Instead, the new totalitarianism is founded upon the ever more sophisticated methods of control given us by science (including social science) and technology based on manipulation. Nisbet asserts that government power is far greater today than ever, but it is more indirect, impersonal, and based on manipulation rather than brute force (p. 223). While the old totalitarianism is based on force and terror, the new totalitarianism is based on the art of manipulation. The bureaucratic growth of the State to absolute power and authority over the masses is even more absolute than old forms of totalitarianism because it encompasses humanitarian concerns (Nisbet, 1988, p. 61). The new totalitarian State uses technologies of mass media, advertising, and propaganda to control its population and to get them to mobilize, believe, and act following the wishes of the State.

The quaint old forms and trappings of democracy--elections, supreme courts, Congress, and the Constitution--will remain in place. The traditional names and slogans will continue to be called upon and broadcast; freedom and democracy will continue to be the theme of presidential speeches and editorials. Moreover, certain freedoms will reign. "There are, after all, certain freedoms which are like circuses. Their very existence, so long as they are individual and enjoyed chiefly individually as by spectators, diverts men's minds from the loss of other, more fundamental, social and economic and political rights" (Nisbet, 1975, p. 229). However, Nisbet asserts this is simply an illusion of freedom, yet another way of softening power. As in the present, political scientists

159

and sociologists will continue to debate the totalitarian hypothesis. Nevertheless, it will be democracy and freedom in a trivial sense, unimportant and subject to "guidance and control" or manipulation by the State (Nisbet, [1953] 1990, p. 185).

The first condition for the totalitarian State's rise is that intermediate groups be severely weakened or destroyed. "We may regard totalitarianism," Nisbet writes, "as a process of the annihilation of individuality, but, in more fundamental terms, it is the annihilation, first, of those social relationships within which individuality develops. It is not the extermination of individuals that is ultimately desired by totalitarian rulers, for the new order needs individuals in the largest number. What is desired is the extermination of those old social relationships which, but for their autonomous existence, must always constitute a barrier to achieving the absolute political community (p. 179).

The second condition is that the State extends its administrative structure, control, and regulation to all aspects of social life—aspects that used to be the purview of these intermediate groups (p. 182). Any new groups or associations formed must be subject to the regulation and control of the State. Intermediate groups become "plural only in number, not in ultimate allegiance of purpose" (p. 186). Furthermore, this destruction and cooptation of intermediate organizations is the true horror of totalitarian rule, for it destroys the foundation of identity, individual morality, protection from arbitrary rule, and freedom. Intermediate institutions, Nisbet argues, are essential in inspiring individuals to restrain their appetites, internalize social morality, and thus make civil society possible. Intermediate institutions also formed the walls that contained the State's appetite for power (Nisbet, 1975, p. 74). Therefore, "total political centralization can only lead to social and cultural death" (Nisbet, [1953] 1990, p. 187).

Nisbet sees the trend toward militarism, centralization, and the weakening of primary groups as inexorable. He is skeptical that there will be any significant and long-lasting reversal of these trends soon. However, he does offer some hope. Echoing Weber, he says that a charismatic—a prophet, a genius, or a maniac—might well stop or even reverse the trends (Nisbet, 1975, p. 233). He also echoes Durkheim's claim that people cannot long endure elevated levels of anomie. "Human beings cannot long stand a vacuum of allegiance, and if, as seems evident enough, the political state in its present national, collective, and centralized form is no longer capable of fulfilling the expectations and supplying incentives, human beings will surely turn, as they have before in history, to alternative values and relationships" (p. 283).

Nisbet advocates for the cultural disease he has so thoroughly described as institutional reform based on the principles of libertarianism and pluralism. He states that distinctive institutions—economic, educational, family, and religious—must be left as free as possible from the regulation and dictates of the State. He advocates a decentralization program, devolving powers from the federal government to the states and from the states to local community organizations. He calls for the strengthening, re-creation, or creation of practical intermediate associations, groups, and communities that can buffer the effects of the State upon the individual. Such groups must have functional importance in distributing goods and services, for only then can such groups stimulate solidarity and commitment from individual members (p. 278). This call for the revitalization of primary groups parallels Durkheim's call.

Nisbet asks us to give up our passion for equality and recognize that hierarchy is part of the social bond and essential for social order and the transmission of our culture across generations. He calls for a recommitment to tradition, abandoning attempts to regulate every aspect of life through formal law and administrative regulation and relying upon custom and folkway in their stead. "Pluralist society is free society exactly in proportion to its ability to protect as large a domain as possible that is governed by the informal, spontaneous, custom-derived, and tradition-sanctioned habits of mind rather than by the dictates, however rationalized, of government and judiciary" (p. 240). We are becoming a nation of lawyers; our relationships are increasingly adversarial and defined by legal codes or administrative decrees. However, freedom, liberty, and authority are all rooted in tradition and primary group association, and we must return to this foundation.

Furthermore, Nisbet believes it is in our power to return, for there is no social problem that is not in our power to correct. "It is not as though we are dealing with the relentless advance of senescence in the human being or the course of cancer. Ideas and their consequences could make an enormous difference in our present spirit. For whatever it is that gives us torment […] it rests upon ideas which are as much captive to history today as they ever have been. The genius, the maniac, and the prophet have been responsible for more history than the multitudes have or ever will. And the power of those beings rests upon revolutions in ideas and idea systems" (Nisbet, 1988, pp. 134-135).

About Nisbet

Robert Alexander Nisbet was born in Los Angeles on September 30, 1913, the oldest of three boys born to Henry and Cynthia Nisbet. His father managed a retail lumber yard, and Robert was raised in modest circumstances in Maricopa, a small California desert town. The family stressed education, and Robert and his brothers were encouraged in their studies and expected to attend college. 1927 the family moved to San Luis Obispo, where he did well in a demanding high school program. Upon graduation and a year at junior college, he began at the University of California at Berkeley in 1932. His association with Berkeley proved both long and fruitful. He completed his bachelor's degree in 1936, his M.A. in 1937, and his Ph.D. in 1939. Upon obtaining his Ph.D., he accepted an instructor's position, rising through the ranks to full professor there in 1953. By Perrin's account, Nisbet was an excellent teacher. The Department of Social Institutions (later renamed the Department of Sociology) was headed by Frederick J. Teggart, Nisbet's mentor and dissertation advisor. "Young Nisbet consciously modeled himself after Teggart. Among other things, Nisbet inherited his view of history and his approach to studying social change directly from Teggart. The Ph.D. dissertation ("The Social Group in French Thought") he wrote under Teggart's direction marked the beginnings of his enduring interest in intermediate social structures" (Perrin, 1999, pp. 702-703).

Nisbet served in World War II, enlisting in the Army in 1943 and served in the Pacific, eventually becoming staff sergeant. Nisbet maintained close communication with his department throughout his service and was instrumental in its transformation into a sociology department. In 1946, he became acting chair of the department and assistant dean for the College of Letters and Science. In 1953, he left Berkeley to become the founding dean of the College of Letters and Science at the new Riverside campus of the University of California, later becoming vice chancellor there in 1960. In 1963, he left academic administration, believing that "administrative work, sufficiently prolonged, has a sterilizing effect upon the creative or the scholarly mind" (703). After a Guggenheim Fellowship, which allowed him to spend a year at Princeton University, he returned to Riverside. Over the next eight years, he completed "dozens of articles and reviews, as well as some seven books" (704). After 30 years, Nisbet retired from the University of California in 1972, first accepting a position at the University of Arizona and then moving on to the Albert Schweitzer Chair at Columbia University in 1974, working with Robert K. Merton. While at Columbia, Nisbet taught both history and sociology. At the age of 65, he retired from university teaching. He moved to Washington in 1978 and became affiliated with the American Enterprise Institute, a conservative think tank, until 1986. Even after full retirement from university and think tank, Nisbet continued to write until his death from prostate cancer on September 9, 1996, just 21 days shy of his eighty-third birthday. His scholarship included over twenty books, over 150 articles, book chapters, and review essays. More than a serious academic, Nisbet was a public intellectual, writing for a broad general audience.

Chapter 7: Neil Postman's Technological Determinism

In this chapter, we will examine the work of Neil Postman (1931-2003), whose social theory returns repeatedly to the theme of technological change driving changes in structure and culture. Postman repeatedly asserts that regardless of the intentions of the users (or the owners), technology always has unintended consequences, both positive and negative, and that these consequences are rarely evenly distributed throughout society. Postman calls this the "Frankenstein Syndrome," in which technology is developed for a limited and specific purpose. "But once the machine is built, we discover—sometimes to our horror, usually to our discomfort, always to our surprise—that it has ideas of its own" (Postman [1982] 1994, 21). Inevitably, modern technologies cause changes in institutional structures, ideas, ideologies, beliefs, and even habits of thought. Postman asserts that these changes are generally true of technology, especially communications technologies.

Postman was a communications theorist who wrote in the latter third of the 20th century and was influenced by Lewis Mumford, Jacques Ellul, Norbert Elias, Elizabeth Eisenstein, Marshall McLuhan, and Harold Innis. The most significant classical theoretical influence is Durkheim, whose influence is evident though perhaps indirect. For Postman, the prime movers in sociocultural change are technology and consequent changes in the division of labor; these combined forces change social structures and, ultimately, the very character of the men and women who inhabit the society. Classic anomie, as defined by Durkheim—that is, anomie rooted in the increasing division of labor and the consequent weakening of traditional social structures—also plays a prominent role in Postman's social theory.

The Socialization Process

In his most provocative book, *The Disappearance of Childhood*, Postman explains why the dividing line between childhood and adulthood is rapidly eroding in contemporary society and why the social role of the child may well disappear in modern industrial society. He points out that his contribution to this topic is not documenting this erosion, as many observers have marked the disappearance. Instead, his contribution explains childhood's origin and the reasons for its decline

(p. xii). Specifically, Postman posits that both the rise of the social role of the child and its consequent decline are rooted in changes in communications technology. The invention of the printing press and the spread of print culture were the primary causal agents in the rise of childhood. Replacing print culture with an electronic medium in which imagery is the main conveyor of information is the primary agent in its decline (pp. xii-xiii).

Postman states that there is no sharp distinction between children and adults in a world dominated by oral tradition. In such a world, childhood ends at about seven when the child has mastered speech (p. 15). At seven, "the medieval child would have had access to almost all of the forms of behavior common to the culture" (p. 15). Save for sex and war, medieval youth would fully partake in adult life, sharing in games, work, play, and stories. The culture did not have a need or means of keeping information away from youth. There were few secrets between the generations: the youth fully entered adulthood at age seven. Because it is an oral culture, Postman asserts, there is no need to prolong the socialization process so that youth can master reading and esoteric knowledge beyond the immediate local culture. Thus, there was no need for educational institutions in which youth were segregated from adults and age-graded so that they could master both readings and be gradually exposed to the harsher ways of the world. There was no well-developed concept of shame because all had ready access to oral information.

With the invention of the printing press in about 1450 and the spread of literacy, the "communication environment" rapidly changed (p. 28). Literacy gradually became a great divide among people; becoming literate meant becoming a fully functioning adult and engaging in a new world of facts, impressions, and opinions beyond the local milieu. More than this, Postman says, "typography was by no means a neutral conveyor of information" (p. 32). Instead, printing changed the very organization and structure of thought. "The unyielding linearity of the printed book—the sequential nature of its sentence-by-sentence presentation, it is paragraphing, its alphabetized indices, its standardized spelling, and grammar" promoted "a structure of consciousness that closely parallels the structure of typography" (p. 30). With the spread of literacy, young and old began to live in different worlds; one now had to achieve adulthood by mastering literacy and the habits of mind it promoted. To do this, Postman adds, required the development of institutions to provide this education, making the creation of childhood necessary (p. 36).

The relationship between the spread of literacy, the development of schools, and the growing conception of childhood as a part of the life cycle is incontrovertible (p. 39). Over the next few centuries, adults took increasingly formal control over the socialization of youth, setting forth more stringent criteria for attaining adulthood. Postman asserts that childhood begins as a middle-class phenomenon, and parents have the resources to encourage its development (p. 45). He also remarks upon the abuse of lower-class children in the West through the 19th century (p. 54). Nevertheless, the concept of childhood spreads with mass literacy and schooling and eventually reaches the lower classes. Schools required youth to undergo strict discipline to sit quietly in neat rows, hands folded on the desk to facilitate this formal learning. "The capacity to control and overcome one's nature became one of the defining characteristics of adulthood and therefore one of the essential purposes of education, for some, the essential purpose of education" (pp. 46-47).

At the same time, the family gradually became organized around childhood and schooling, and both the family and school promoted the idea of discipline and restraint of bodily functions. Citing Norbert Elias, Postman adds that a clear distinction was drawn between private and public behavior. Shame and embarrassment became associated with sexual behavior and other biological functions. They developed a whole vocabulary of words deemed too sensitive for children's ears. Adults "began to collect a rich content of secrets to be kept from the young: secrets about sexual relations, but also about money, violence, about illness, about death, about social relations" (pp. 48-49).

The family and the school maintained this monopoly on the control of information and experience of the child. Print culture easily maintained this monopoly in which basic reading was challenging to master, and age-graded exposure to more in-depth and complex information was carefully monitored. Literature dealing with adult themes and secret knowledge was of sufficient complexity to deter children's entry until they had undergone years of training in reading, vocabulary, and syntax (p. 79). "The maintenance of childhood depended on the principles of managed information and sequential learning" (p. 72). However, this monopoly crumbled with the advent of electronic information, mainly when television was introduced directly into the home (pp. 78-79).

Television, Postman points out, is a visual medium that requires no training and is available to be viewed and understood by all. "In learning to interpret the meaning of images, we do not require lessons in grammar or spelling or logic or vocabulary. We require no analogue of the McGuffey Reader, no preparation, no prerequisite training. Watching television not only requires no skills but develops no skills" (p. 79). The barriers between adulthood and childhood are eroded;

there is no longer the possibility of segregating information from the young. All are exposed to the adult world—murder and mayhem, lust and titillation, greed and consumerism—through television melodrama and comedy, talk shows, game shows, news shows, "reality" shows, and commercials (p. 80). These shows run on hundreds of stations twenty-four hours a day, seven days a week. Most compete for a wider audience, and much of this competition consists of creating new and novel situations, information, and images to attract and hold that audience (p. 82). Thus, television constantly seeks to push the envelope by depicting all manner of human behavior, ideas, and lifestyles. Nothing is held back, and all have access. Moreover, Postman adds that without secrets or any sense of shame, childhood must necessarily disappear (p. 80). Postman says that the exclusivity of information and knowledge primarily defines groups their members share, and adults no longer enjoy such exclusive knowledge (pp. 84-85).

To say that television has significantly changed youth's socialization process is also to claim that it has also changed the meaning and form of adulthood (pp. 50, 63, & 98). In *The Disappearance of Childhood,* Postman first broaches the theme of electronic media changing the character of the people inhabiting society. Adult intellectual and emotional capacities emphasize emotional responses to political candidates, consumer products, and social issues instead of rational interest, logic, reflection, and reason (pp. 98-102). Electronic media reduces the complexity of any subject to simple slogans; politics becomes trivialized to personality and images (p. 107). Postman asks, "What is the effect on grown-ups of a culture dominated by pictures and stories? What is the effect of a medium that is entirely centered on the present, that has no capability of revealing the continuity of time? What is the effect of a medium that must abjure conceptual complexity and highlight personality? What is the effect of a medium that always asks for an immediate, emotional response?" (117). More generally still, Postman asks, "What is the effect on an entire culture of a society that has given full reign to technological progress?" (pp. 145-146). It is to answer these questions that drive all of Postman's writings.

The Medium and the Message

In *Amusing Ourselves to Death,* Postman (1985) continues to examine the effects of the new communications technology, though he broadens his inquiry to include the entire culture. While he does not go as far as adopting Marshall McLuhan's line that "the medium is the message," Postman strongly believes that the medium necessarily strongly influences the messages it transmits. A medium, Postman explains, is to technology as the mind is to the brain. "A technology, in other words, is merely a machine. A medium is the social and intellectual environment a machine creates" (p. 84). Postman argues that the form of public discourse, whether primarily through the technology of the printed word (newspapers, pamphlets, and books) or electronic through radio or television, will impact the ideas expressed and received. Further, those ideas readily expressed through the dominant media soon become the dominant ideas within the culture (Postman, 1985, p. 6).

> To say it, then, as plainly as I can, this book is an inquiry into and a lamentation about the most significant American cultural fact of the second half of the twentieth century: the decline of the Age of Typography and the ascendancy of the Age of Television. This change-over has dramatically and irreversibly shifted the content and meaning of public discourse, since two media so vastly different cannot accommodate the same ideas. As the influence of print wanes, the content of politics, religion, education, and anything else that comprises public business must change and be recast in terms that are most suitable to television (p. 8).

Any communication medium emphasizes specific ideas, ways of thinking, and outlooks. Dominant media, therefore, goes a long way toward determining the content of the culture (p. 9).

Postman argues that any medium determines the structure of discourse by demanding certain kinds of content of the messenger and favoring certain traits of personality, exposition, and intelligence (p. 27). In societies dominated by print, the demands on the communicator are of logical, linear thought, with ideas building upon one another in logical sequence and order. In such cultures, ideas are debated and discussed, even in oral debate, consistent with the rules of logic in a thorough, comprehensive manner. The demands of those receiving the communication are equally exacting. First, the audience in a print culture must master basic literacy. They also had to acquire some familiarity with history, rhetoric, and philosophy to provide the context for understanding complex communication. A second demand was for attention—19th-century audiences for political and religious speeches were often subjected (treated) to hours of speeches and debate (p. 45). Postman uses the Lincoln-Douglas debates for a Senate seat in Illinois as the 19th-century ideal of this sophisticated discourse. He marvels at the rhetorical skills of debaters and the audiences' listening and comprehension skills for these debates that last hours. The debates were full of historical, political, and literary references, demanding great attention and concentration from the audience. More remarkably, the audience did not get to vote directly for these candidates, as the state legislature selected a state's senators. Postman adds that Speeches, like their print counterpart, were often intricate and subtle, requiring high levels of aural comprehension (p. 45).

Postman points to 18th and 19th-century America as a prime example of such a print-based culture. "We might even say that America was founded by intellectuals, from which it has taken us two centuries and a communications revolution to recover" (p. 41). In early America, the influence of the printed word was dominant not only because of the sheer quantity of printed matter—pamphlets, newspapers, books—but most especially because of their monopoly (41). Postman asserts that this print culture produced habits of mind on the part of both leaders and the broader public, encouraging serious public discussion and debate of substantive issues. Leaders and the broader public could also better manage such complex discussions and debates (p. 51). Postman declines to assert that the changing media causes changes in the brain's structure and, thus, the mind's cognitive processes. However, he recognizes that Marshall McLuhan, Walter Ong, and Julian Jaynes have made such claims. He is sympathetic to such arguments, but his theory is based on the hypothesis that the changing media only causes changes in the structure of public discourse (p. 27).

"Public business was channeled into and expressed through print, which became the model, the metaphor and the measure of all discourse. The resonance of the lineal, analytical structure of print, and in particular, of expository prose, could be felt everywhere" (p. 41). The written word was the measure of all public discourse; 19th-century politicians and other public figures— scientists, churchmen, lawyers, and captains of industry—were primarily known by what they had written or what was written about them, not by their pictures or other images (pp. 60-61). In sum, a medium strongly influences the message it carries, and a print-based medium emphasizes exposition, logical coherence, sequential development, objectivity, and reflection (p. 63). Toward the end of the 19th century, Postman claims, print-based culture began to pass, to be progressively replaced by electronic media (p. 63). As a culture moves from an emphasis on print to one based on graphical images presented directly into the home, Postman claims, its emphasis, ideas, and even truths pass from exposition to "show business."

Postman characterizes the dominant ideas and ways of thinking fostered by electronic communication as "dangerous nonsense" (p. 16). As is readily apparent, Postman is no relativist in this matter (p. 27). He views print as a superior medium for the exposition of complex ideas; he believes that it has a far "healthier influence" on societies than when electronic media dominate the discourse. Indeed, Postman believes "that we are getting sillier by the minute" (p. 24). He claims that with the coming of the telegraph, news began to emphasize speed, quantity, novelty, and distance in reportage, often at the expense of relevance and coherence (p. 67). Combined with the graphics revolution, photography, motion pictures, and then radio and television, the new electronic media present a world bordering on seeming chaos (p. 70). Stories and headlines come from all parts of the globe, often isolated from any coherent context or connection to the local (p. 70). Postman characterizes this as a "peek-a-boo world" in which stories and images constantly vie for our attention and are quickly forgotten (p. 77). This new electronic media does not merely supplement the old print culture; it supplants it. In time electronic media becomes the "dominant means for construing, understanding, and testing reality" (p. 74).

Television carries this to the extreme, combining images, sound, and immediacy and bringing it directly into the home (p. 78). "And most important of all, there is no subject of public interest— politics, news, education, religion, science, sports—that does not find its way to television. Which means that all public understanding of these subjects is shaped by the biases of television" (p. 74). The images of the world as given by television have become so ingrained that they now seem normal, right, and natural. The art of show business has become a part of politics, news, religion, marketing, corporate relations, and governance. Incoherence, triviality, irrelevance, image, and manipulating behavior through stimulating emotions of lust, greed, and fear have become the order of the day. Television delivers a steady stream of fast-moving images of constant novelty, most of which are aimed at stimulating emotional rather than intellectual responses (p. 86). "It is in the nature of the medium that it must suppress the content of ideas in order to accommodate the requirements of visual interest; that is to say, to accommodate the values of show business" (p. 92). However, the problem is not confined to television, for we have come to expect similar stimulation from our daily experiences—it is the standard by which we judge all interactions (p. 87).

Through television, Postman claims that our culture comes to know itself, and how it depicts the world becomes the measure of all—onscreen and off. Just as print once determined the form of political, economic, and religious discourse, television now becomes the model (p. 92). The demands on the messenger, whether on the tube or in person, are similar—play to the broadest possible audience, appeal to emotions, and, more than anything else, entertain! (p. 98). Image replaces reality, and manipulation and showmanship replace leadership (p. 97). People exposed to a constant diet of television—its "news," entertainment shows, and commercials —are being socialized into expectations about reality. "For example, a person who has seen one million television commercials might well believe that all political problems have fast solutions through simple measures—or ought to. Or that complex language is not to be trusted, and that all problems lend themselves to theatrical expression. Or that argument is in bad taste, and leads only to an intolerable uncertainty" (p. 131). People exposed to a steady diet of news might believe that the world is far more crime-ridden and violent than it is or that our social and political problems have no real connections between them. People exposed to a steady diet of sports and other entertainment may raise their expectations about social life and its conduct, which bears little resemblance to real life. They are constantly exposed to black-and-white issues with few shades of gray, heroes and villains, and straightforward solutions to all problems.

The evidence presented by Postman for the trivializing of various American institutions by the entertainment requirements of television is overwhelming. Television news is introduced and often interspersed with music, each story typically introduced by a news anchor presenting one story after another with little context and few connections between them (p. 102). American newspapers and news magazines adopt similar formats and features—shorter stories and a greater focus on novelty, imagery, and variety. The result is that Americans are among the most entertained and least informed people on the planet (p. 106).

Other institutions have restructured themselves to accommodate the necessity of entertaining the audience, such as religion, education, marketing, politics, and government. For example, Postman says about religion on television: "The first is that on television, religion, like everything else, is presented, quite simply and without apology, as entertainment. Everything that makes religion a historic, profound, and sacred human activity is stripped away; there is no ritual, no dogma, no tradition, no theology, and above all, no sense of spiritual transcendence. On these shows, the preacher is tops. God comes out as second banana" (p. 117). The new electronic communications have profoundly affected education as well. By monopolizing their time and attention, television affects the reading habits of the young (p. 141). More than this, however, by instilling in teachers and students the expectation that all teaching (and learning) must be entertaining, the age of electronics has seriously affected the classroom and eroded the self-discipline needed throughout the learning process (pp. 125-146). Students find it increasingly difficult to master complex material because they have not developed sufficient critical reading and thinking skills or the self-discipline needed to acquire them.

Capitalist enterprises seek to sell products not by informing potential customers of the benefits of their product but rather by projecting ideal images to appeal to their potential customers' hopes, dreams, fantasies, or fears (p. 128). This appeal is quite different from early capitalism, Postman argues, in which both parties in economic exchange were well-informed and rational (pp. 126-27). Politics plays a similar game. Candidates do not simply offer up an image of themself; instead, they (and their handlers) try to craft and project an image that has been market-tested to appeal to an audience (p. 134). The goal is to project this image in speeches and debates and to sell the candidate through commercials, using imagery and emotional appeal similar to the techniques used to sell deodorant. Candidates attempt to wrap themselves in the flag and project an image of optimism and confidence, honesty, good-natured humor, and charm; one of the hot questions of the 2000 presidential race among journalists (and thus voters): "Which one of these men would you like to have a beer with?" In this one, Bush won easily.

Culture and Technology

In his writings, Postman gradually broadens his inquiry on technology. First, he focuses on the impact of changes in communications technology on childhood. Postman then examines the impact of new electronic communications on social discourse. Finally, he moves from a focus almost exclusively on communications technology to a broader view of the impact of technological change on the entire culture. Throughout, however, Postman remains consistent in his view that ideas and ideologies are strongly associated with the use of technology and that changes in technology necessarily produce changes in social structures, institutions, and cultural ideologies and beliefs. Postman believes that it is self-evident that 20th-century technology has transformed sociocultural life in America. The industrialization of agriculture, mass production of consumer goods, new modes of transportation and distribution, office machinery and the computer, and electronic communications have dramatically impacted economic, political, and social life. All technologies have functions and dysfunctions, manifest and latent. The public has yet to examine potential technologies beyond their manifest functions, that is, what the inventor intended the machine to perform. In addition, Postman adds, the functions and dysfunctions (or the "benefits and deficits") are not evenly distributed throughout the population. Some benefit far more than others from technological change; some are profoundly hurt (Postman, 1992, p. 9).

The automobile, for example, had a manifest function of providing transportation for the individual. No one anticipated then that the widespread adoption of the automobile would dramatically change our landscape, air quality, living patterns, and sexual behavior and provide new outlets for expressing ourselves and our status. The fact that most social change caused by technology was unanticipated by both inventors and the adapting public was excusable in the early part of that century. "But it is much later in the game now, and ignorance of the score is inexcusable. To be unaware that a technology comes equipped with a program for social change, to maintain that technology is neutral, to make the assumption that technology is always a friend to culture is, at this late hour, stupidity plain and simple" (Postman, 1985, p. 157).

Postman (1992) also argues that technological change is "ecological." By this, he means that because we are dealing with a sociocultural *system*, a change in one significant part of that system will cause changes in other parts. Thus, innovative technologies can create changes throughout the sociocultural system to change "everything" (p. 18). Finally, Postman believes that ideas and ideologies are strongly associated with the technologies we use. Citing Marx several times in his writings to sharpen the point, Postman asserts that technologies are a part of the material conditions that determine mental life and create how reality is experienced. He writes:

> But obviously I do not mean to say that print merely influenced the form of public discourse. That does not say much unless one connects it to the more important idea that form will determine the nature of content. For those readers who may believe that this idea is too 'McLuhanesque' for their taste, I offer Karl Marx from *The German Ideology*. 'Is the *Iliad* possible,' he asks rhetorically, 'when the printing press and even printing machines exist? Is it not inevitable that with the emergence of the press, the singing and telling and the muse cease; that is, the conditions necessary for epic poetry disappear?' Marx understood well that the press was not merely a machine but a structure for discourse, which both rules out and insists upon certain kinds of content and, inevitably, a certain kind of audience (Postman, 1985, pp. 42-43).

Postman classifies societies into three types: "tool-using cultures, technocracies, and technopolies" (Postman, 1992, p. 22). Tool-using cultures have strict controls on the development and utilization of technology, subordinating their use to cultural institutions, traditions, and beliefs (p. 23). He adds that tools are fully integrated into the culture on the culture's terms, not the terms of the technology (p. 25). In addition, tool-using cultures tend to have a solid unifying theology that provides an overarching meaning to life, a metaphysical belief that protects the people from the lure of technological progress or plenty (p. 26).

Technocracies are far more tool-centered, according to Postman. "Everything must give way, to their development. The social and symbolic worlds become increasingly subject to the requirement of that development. Tools are not integrated into the culture; they attack the culture" (p. 28). In technocracies, all social structures, institutions, and cultural beliefs are under assault by technological forces, and all must make serious adjustments to accommodate technological change (p. 28). Postman dates the beginning of technocracy with Bacon, who advocated advancing science and technology to improve the material condition of humanity (p. 35). Postman notes that Bacon, too, saw the power of technology to transform social life, quoting one of the more famous passages from Bacon's work:

> It is well to observe the force and effect and consequences of discoveries. These are to be seen nowhere more conspicuously than in those three which were unknown to the ancients, and of which the origin, though recent, is obscure; namely, printing, gunpowder, and the magnet. For these three have changed the whole face and state of things throughout the world; the first in literature, the second in warfare, the third in navigation; whence have followed innumerable changes; insomuch that no empire, no sect, no star seems to have exerted greater power and influence in human affairs than these changes (p. 37).

In addition to the connection between technology and material advances, technocracy also fostered the idea of the inevitability of progress and weakened the hold of tradition on social life (p. 45). More emphasis was placed on speed and time, and technology became the means to conquer both (p. 45).

Technopoly arose at the beginning of the 20th century, with Postman marking its start with the publication of Frederick Taylor's book, *The Principles of Scientific Management*, in 1911 (p. 51). As we have seen in the chapter on Harry Braverman, Taylor's primary goal in his "scientific" management was to maximize the worker's efficiency through technical measurement and calculation, simplifying work tasks, and close supervision. Taylor and his followers made "the first clear statement of the idea that society is best served when human beings are placed at the disposal of their techniques and technology, that human beings are, in a sense, worth less than their machinery" (p. 52). With Technopoly, all social life—structures, cultural beliefs, and values—become subordinate to technology and technique (p. 52). Nevertheless, while Taylor gave voice to the philosophy of this "brave new world" of Technopoly, America was fertile ground for its development (pp. 52-53).

Postman identifies three interrelated reasons why America became the first society to transition to Technopoly and had so thoroughly embraced it as a way of life. First, Postman says, is the distrust Americans have always had for limits and constraints, a part of the national character that rebels against natural and social limits on human behavior. A second reason for the love affair with technology is that American capitalists quickly seized on the new technologies and developed them to their fullest, far quicker than capitalists from other nations. Postman believes their ardor was related to the American character and distrust of constraints. It may also be because, unlike European capitalism, American capitalism had no remnant feudal institutions or significant socialist parties to moderate capitalist development. In addition to developing these technologies, these captains of industry also pushed the philosophy of efficiency, productivity, and unrestrained capital development. A third reason for Technopoly's success in America was technology's apparent accomplishment in delivering the good life. Early twentieth-century technology delivered goods and services that were convenient, comfortable, quick, hygienic, and in abundant quantities (p. 54).

As technology develops, more information is discovered and made available through a proliferation of media. Moreover, with the development of the telegraph and the graphics revolution, the character of information began to change. "Here was information that rejected the necessity of interconnectedness, proceeded without context, argued for instancy against historical continuity, and offered fascination in place of complexity and coherence. And then, with Western culture gasping for breath, the fourth stage of the information revolution occurred, broadcasting. And then the fifth, computer technology" (p. 69). With so much information vying for attention, all coherence is lost, and the world becomes a collection of improbable events (p. 70).

The flood of information corrosively affects traditional social institutions' ideologies, theories, and legitimations (p. 83). This weakening of traditional institutions and beliefs makes the information explosion especially harmful (p. 54). Unfortunately, Postman does not connect the growth in technology with the decline in traditional institutions like the family, religion, and community, though this can easily be done. He specifically mentions the rise of evolutionary theory, which challenges (at least for some) the faith in a creator God. Postman also mentions Nietzsche's philosophy that God is dead. However, he has in mind far more.

Postman argues that one of the primary functions of social institutions is to control the flow of information, to direct people in how much weight and value to give to it, and to fit new information into an overall worldview or meaning of life (p. 73). As technological change has weakened traditional social institutions—such as the family, religion, and community—this control of information is lost. "Information loses its use and therefore becomes a source of confusion rather than coherence" (p. 73). With the proliferation of information and the weakening of traditional institutions, a coherent worldview becomes more problematic to attain and maintain; people are exposed to constant contradiction and chaos. What results are a general breakdown in social tranquility and purpose and a lack of guidance in "moral" behavior (p. 72, 79). In other words, what results is a structural condition that Durkheim characterized as anomie. As an aside, Postman notes that sociologists have difficulty grasping the idea that weakening social institutions makes people vulnerable to chaos and disorder. This charge is curious because Durkheim bases anomie theory on weakened institutions that fail to provide adequate guidance to their members, thus making them vulnerable to conflicting ideas and social stress. Durkheim also identifies technological change and its impact on the division of labor as one of the primary causes of anomie within a society.

To counter this decline in traditional control, American Technopoly has come to rely ever more heavily upon the more formal coordination, regulation, and control of the bureaucratic organization (p. 83). Citing Weber, Postman points out that the goal of all bureaucracy is to focus on efficiently attaining the organization's goals—all other goals, moral considerations, values, and beliefs are subordinate or even "irrelevant" to the goal of efficiency (pp. 84-85). These bureaucracies employ legions of administrators to staff offices and execute their rules to coordinate American society. Thousands of experts, specialists, and paraprofessionals are needed to provide health care, education, welfare, environmental regulation, defense, law enforcement, tax collection, and counseling.

In creating order out of the chaos caused by the rapid proliferation of information, bureaucracy and its administrators and experts are aided by developing "technical machinery." "Technical machinery is essential to both the bureaucrat and the expert, and may be regarded as a third mechanism of information control. I do not have in mind such "hard" technologies as the computer—which must, in any case, be treated separately, since it embodies all that Technopoly stands for. I have in mind "softer" technologies such as IQ tests, SATs, standardized forms, taxonomies, and opinion polls" (p. 89). The growth of these social technologies (and bureaucracy and specialization are just further examples of such technologies) has been concurrent with the decline in the power of traditional social institutions to provide guidance in the organization and maintenance of a coherent worldview.

Rather than provide a substitute worldview of power and scope to bind men and women to the social order, the growth of bureaucratic organization and its tools has only added to the disorder (pp. 90-91). Technopoly has given us only the glories of technological progress in place of the grand religious, philosophical, or patriotic narratives of the past. According to Durkheim, these grand narratives (religion or a belief in the sacred in Durkheim's terminology) are essential in inspiring men and women to transcend their egoistic interests, bind them to the group, and limit their desires. However, the goal of education has become merely economic development for society and a decent job for the individual (p. 174). A respectable job is increasingly defined as providing plenty of money for high consumption. We have sold our human heritage—our traditions, values, and meanings—for convenience and comfort.

The Need for Grand Narrative

Recall that Durkheim argued that religious belief (broadly defined) is essential in inspiring men and women to transcend their egoistic interests, bind them to the group, and limit their desires. Postman (1995) titled the last major work before his death *The End of Education*. By "the end," Postman refers to the purpose or function of education, not its demise. His thesis is that educational reformers focus far too much on means and methods of education without giving much thought to the ends—what we are trying to do in the schools. Postman expands on this Durkheimian theme of the need for an inspiring narrative that transcends the individual to commit to ideals apart from self-interest. Individuals must have a "great narrative, one that has sufficient credibility, complexity, and symbolic power to enable one to organize one's life around it" (6). While religion has been the chief source of these grand narratives of the past, Postman asserts that other sources, including myth, science, government, and the humanities, may also serve (Postman, 1992, p. 172). Consistent with Durkheim, Postman discusses how the grand narratives of the past are failing due to processes of modernity. Again, in Durkheimian terms, Postman establishes why such narratives are essential for sociocultural systems and individuals' mental, spiritual, and physical health. Finally, he proposes education as the one institution capable of conveying such grand narratives to the broader population. He asserts that the liberal arts—humanities, sciences, social sciences, philosophy, and the arts—can be their only source.

The grand narratives of the past are dying due to modernization; technological change has multiplied information while severely weakening traditional institutions that provided coherence and meaning by filtering and organizing this information. Paraphrasing Durkheim, Postman writes: "Old gods have fallen, either wounded or dead. New ones have been aborted" (Postman, 1995, p. 23). However, it is not that the individual is left to her own devices in the modern era, for some narratives seek to guide the individual's behavior. Moreover, this is where the schools come in. Public education serves not merely the public; it forms or molds that public. "The question is, what kind of public does it create? A conglomerate of self-indulgent consumers? Angry, soulless, directionless masses? Indifferent, confused citizens? Or a public imbued with confidence, a sense of purpose, a respect for learning and tolerance?" (p. 18). What is the end (function) of education?

Unfortunately, the schools' most potent and pervasive narrative is promoted by our economic system, which advocates hyper-consumerism. Even the old symbols of previously dominant narratives are used to sell products. For example, God is used to selling hotdogs, wine, the nation's flag, and images of great presidents to sell everything from cars to sheets. Postman likens commercials to "parables" and claims many have a common theme: "...the root cause of evil is technological innocence, a failure to know the particulars of the beneficent accomplishments of industrial progress. This is the primary source of unhappiness, humiliation, and discord in life" (p. 35). Such commercial exploitation of symbols from the past's grand narratives weakens their hold and dissipates their power. "There can, of course, be no functioning sense of a great narrative without a measure of respect for its symbols" (p. 25). For example, here is the product description for a "Deluxe Jesus Action Figure" found online in 2008: "He turns water into wine folks! [...] this Jesus deluxe action figure stands 5 1/4-inches tall and features glow in the dark hands! He comes in an illustrated window box and includes eight accessories: a jug, 2 fish, and five loaves of bread!" Again, echoing Durkheim, Postman calls this "erosion of symbols, this obliteration of the difference between the sacred and profane." He believes it to be another effect of the narrative crisis (p. 25). Consequently, consumerism has become the ultimate purpose of life for many.

This consumer focus of society has pushed schools to become the training ground preparing the next generation of consumers. Taxpayers are increasingly persuaded to pay for education as an investment in future economic development for the state; students are persuaded to endure it as training for a career, an investment in their economic future; increasingly, the content and purpose of education have become career training. As meaning and purpose for life, it is a thin gruel.

Another "god that has failed" society and its schools is the "god of Technology." Filling children's heads with information and factual knowledge should not be the primary purpose of schools. Memorization is a low level of knowledge, and while a certain amount must be done, it should be more of a byproduct of learning rather than its focus. However, for many, Postman reports, particularly those who are taken with computer technology, information has been construed as power, and the chief purpose of the schools is to teach children how to access it (p. 42).

Many supporters of educational technology are paid shills of the computer industry or have been seduced by their arguments. In the 1990s, the educational establishment was giddy about teaching "computer literacy" and integrating information technology into all subject areas. There was fear that children who did not acquire these "skills" would forever be left behind in the competitive race for grades and jobs (and thus unable to consume on a whim). These "skills" are not comparable to the skills and discipline needed to acquire literacy. What our children need to learn about technologies, Postman asserts, "…is not how to use them but how they use us" (p. 44).

Nevertheless, another purpose of education that recently gained currency is to use the schools to promote multiculturalism. While Postman supports making students aware of cultural differences, he does not believe it is a narrative worthy of an "exclusive" focus (p. 51). Too often, Postman asserts, the narrative devolves into a message of separatism and tribalism. This narrative does little to mold a public of social responsibility, justice, commitment, empathy, and personal restraint.

According to Postman, the individual consequence of the lack of coherent and consistent inspiration and moral guidance from narrative includes suicide, alcohol, other drug abuse, violence among our youth, "impenetrable egoism," and other forms of escape (pp. 12-13). (This list could have easily come from Durkheim.) Postman points out that education for a job, greater consumer power in the future, navigating the information society, and glorifying and celebrating ethnic and religious diversity are all "gods that have failed." They fail to inspire individuals to transcend narrow self-interest and strengthen "the spiritual basis of the American Creed" (p. 18).

The narratives that Postman puts forward are intended to combat modern anomie. "My intention is to offer an answer in the form of five narratives that, singly and in concert, contain sufficient resonance and power to be taken seriously as reasons for schooling. They offer, I believe, moral guidance, a sense of continuity, explanations of the past, clarity to the present, hope for the future. They come as close to a sense of transcendence as I can imagine within the context of public schooling" (p. 62). These narratives form the organizing principle behind education, supporting the shared culture that unites us. Those interested in the straightforward narratives that Postman advocates can check out *The End of Education* from the library. They are all part of the Western tradition and have all proven to be of sufficient power to inspire many. They are all narratives woven from the traditional liberal arts—the sciences, humanities, social sciences, literature, philosophy, and history. Postman calls for the liberal arts to be taught as they are genuinely practiced, as explorations in the human condition, knowledge for the sake of knowledge.

Postman has a unique view of the social sciences, particularly for one who holds them in high regard. Unlike the movement of planets or the process of photosynthesis, human affairs are not governed by immutable laws. Instead, human behavior is always a product of intelligence interacting with the natural and social environment. For this reason, there are some predictability and patterns in human behavior, but human behavior is never "determined." Therefore, according to Postman, social science is not a science but a social narrative, a form of storytelling that helps people interpret their world. "Unlike science, social research never discovers anything. It only rediscovers what people once were told and need to be told again. If, indeed, the price of civilization is repressed sexuality, it was not Sigmund Freud who discovered it. If the consciousness of people is formed by their material circumstances, it was not Marx who discovered it. If the medium is the message, it was not McLuhan who discovered it. They have merely retold ancient stories in a modern style" (Postman, 1992, p. 157). Moreover, Postman believes himself very much a part of this tradition.

About Postman

Neil Postman was born in Brooklyn in 1931, the youngest of the four children of Bea and Murray Postman. (Information for this brief biography was taken from Strate (2003), Rosen (2003), and the Eulogy for Neil Postman delivered by his son, Andrew, on October 8, 2003.) He received his BS from the State University of New York at Fredonia and his MA and Ed.D (1958) in English Education from Teacher's College at Columbia University. From 1959 until his death, he was a professor in the School of Education at New York University. He founded the Media Ecology program in 1971 and was chair of the Department of Culture and Communication until 2002.

In his over forty-year tenure at NYU, Postman authored twenty books and over two hundred articles and gave thousands of lectures and presentations worldwide. His first book, *Television and the Teaching of English* (1961) was written in the early days of television. However, even then, he recognized that it was a medium of unprecedented power that could easily overshadow the influence of the traditional classroom. Postman's first critical success came with 1969's *teaching as a Subversive Activity* (with Charles Weingartner), in which they advocated inquiry-based teaching rather than the rote memorization of facts. All his writings and lectures show his lifelong fascination with technology, media, and education.

By all accounts (numerous tributes on the Internet by former students), Postman was an excellent teacher, using humor and questioning to encourage students to think. "There's no accounting for what you absorb from such a man," Jay Rosen, a former student and then colleague, writes, "for he knew the two secrets of all great teachers: things no Teacher's College can teach: First, you don't put knowledge into people, you draw it out. (Which is why personality was his one and only classroom 'method.') Second, if you can manage to conceal, artfully, some crucial part of what you are saying, then young people who are listening really, really hard will make it their business to find you out. And that's when you can really teach them. I must have heard it a thousand times. 'It's not that simple,' the student says to Postman. 'Oh?' And right there, the drawing out begins" (Rosen, 2003).

Compared to most academics, Rosen writes, Postman had no real specialty. His philosophy of education was that of the liberal arts. "As he explained it to me," Rosen (2003) writes, "'We're just trying to give people a good liberal arts education.' Which, he further argued and easily demonstrated himself, was precisely the tool needed to understand the gathering beast [...] the Media. In an age of specialization, this is different from how academic life works. But his did." A broad based liberal arts education is also the exact tool is needed for understanding sociocultural systems. Postman was a public intellectual of the first order; widely read in numerous fields, he managed to take complex ideas and theories of others, combine these with his unique insights, and write in an accessible style for a far broader audience than academics.

Postman refused to adopt any technology that claimed to be an improvement on something he did not think needed to be improved. He authored his books and essays in longhand on a legal pad with a felt-tipped pen. He never owned a computer and had no use for such innovations as email, the internet, electric car windows, or cell phones. He was an elegant writer—I believe him to be one of the best I have encountered among social theorists. He was also an excellent teacher, speaker, gifted athlete, and human being.

Part 3 Rationalization & Bureaucracy

Within the realm of Macro Social Theory, a constellation of thinkers has emerged, each offering unique perspectives on the intricate workings of society. Max Weber, a towering figure in sociology, delved deeply into the concepts of rationalization and the irrationality embedded within this process. This introductory essay focuses on a section of Macro Social Theory, examining the work of four significant theorists who worked from the Weberian playbook— C. Wright Mills, Norbert Elias, George Ritzer, and Roderick Seidenberg. By exploring their theories, we aim to unveil the commonalities shared between these recent thinkers and Weber, specifically regarding the rationalization process and its paradoxical consequences. In doing so, we illuminate Weber's ideas' lasting influence and significance in contemporary macrosocial theory.

Max Weber's analysis of the rationalization process remains a cornerstone of sociological thought. Weber argued that modern societies increasingly embrace rationality as the dominant mode of organizing social, economic, and political systems. He recognized the benefits of rationalization, such as efficiency and predictability, but also highlighted its potential for unintended and irrational outcomes. Weber's exploration of the multifaceted dimensions of rationalization laid the groundwork for subsequent theorists to delve further into this complex phenomenon.

C. Wright Mills, a prominent sociologist of the mid-20th century, drew inspiration from Weber's ideas on rationalization while examining power dynamics within society. Mills explored how the rationalization process, particularly in political and economic spheres, can concentrate power in the hands of a few, giving rise to what he termed the "power elite." Mills, like Weber, acknowledged the irrationality inherent within the rationalization process, as the concentration of power leads to the distortion of democratic principles and the erosion of individual agency.

Influenced by Weber's ideas, Norbert Elias contributed to the study of social processes through his concept of figurational sociology. Elias examined the interplay between rationalization and social change, emphasizing the shifting balance of power and interdependence within social networks. Elias, like Weber, recognized that rationalization has positive and negative consequences, leading to new forms of irrationality and power imbalances. His work deepens our understanding of the complexities inherent in the rationalization process.

George Ritzer, a contemporary sociologist, builds upon Weber's analysis by exploring the concept of "McDonaldization." Ritzer argues that contemporary society exhibits a process of rationalization exemplified by fast-food restaurants like McDonald's. He highlights the spread of efficiency, calculability, predictability, and control throughout various spheres of life, from education to healthcare and beyond. Ritzer, influenced by Weber's ideas on rationalization, examines the paradoxical outcomes of this process, such as the homogenization of experiences, loss of authenticity, and the dehumanization of social interactions.

New to this edition of *Macro Social Theory* is a chapter on Roderick Seidenberg, an architect who developed a theory of social evolution based on Weber's rationalization process. Seidenberg's theory is one of increasingly effective, efficient, and coordinated organizational control of human thought and behavior beginning in human prehistory, continuing through historical times, and leading to a post-history of total organization. Looking at social evolution over millennia, Seidenberg makes the case that the locus of control of individuals is increasingly shifting from internal to external social controls on thought and behavior.

As we explore the theories of Mills, Elias, Ritzer, and Seidenberg alongside Max Weber's foundational ideas, we witness the enduring influence of Weber's concepts of rationalization and the irrationality inherent within it. These thinkers, situated in diverse historical contexts, engage with Weber's insights to deepen our understanding of the multifaceted nature of rationalization and its consequences in contemporary macro-social theory. Their shared emphasis on power dynamics, the unintended consequences of rationalization, and the potential for dehumanization attests to the lasting relevance of Weber's ideas. Through their contributions, we gain new perspectives on the complexities of the rationalization process and its impact on individuals, societies, and the modern world.

Chapter 8: Verstehen: The Sociology of Max Weber

According to the standard interpretation, Max Weber (1864-1920) conceived of sociology as a comprehensive science of social action (Weber [1921] 1968, p. 4). I created the first draft of this essay as part of a website on Weber in 1996 for my students in social theory. My interpretation is relatively standard; it was initially informed by information and insights from secondary and primary sources, mainly including Coser ([1971] 1977) and Aron (1970). In summarizing this information, I present Weber reasonably coherently and comprehensively, using language and structure for the generalists amongst us. It has grown in the telling. "Verstehen" is a German word meaning to understand, perceive, know, and comprehend the nature and significance of a phenomenon. Weber used the term to refer to the social scientist's attempt to understand the intention and the context of human action.

Weber's initial theoretical focus is on the subjective meaning that humans attach to their actions and interactions within specific social contexts. In this connection, Weber distinguishes between four significant types of social action: (1) wertrational, (2) affective or emotional action, (3) traditional action, and (4) zweckrational. The first, wertrational, is characterized by striving for a value that may not be rational but is pursued through rational means. The values come from within an ethical, religious, philosophical, or even holistic context—they are not rationally "chosen," though the means to attain the goal are rational. The classic example in the literature is an individual seeking salvation by following a prophet's teachings. A more secular example is a person who attends a university because they value the life of the mind. This value may have been instilled in them by parents, previous teachers, or a chance encounter.

Affective action is based on the emotional state of the person rather than the rational weighing of means and ends. Sentiments are potent forces in motivating human behavior. Keeping consistent with our previous examples, attending university for the community life of the fraternity or following one's boyfriend to school would be examples of action motivated by emotions. The third type of action Weber calls "traditional action." This action is guided by custom or habit. People engage in this action often unthinkingly because it is simply "always done." Many students attend university because it is traditional for their social class and family to attend—the expectation was always there, and it was never questioned.

The final type of action, zweckrational, is an action in which both the goal and the means to attain the goal are rationally chosen. It is often exemplified in the literature by an engineer who builds a bridge as the most efficient way to cross a river. A more relevant example is the modern goal of material success many young people seek today. Many recognize that the most efficient way to attain that success is through higher education, so they flock to universities to get a good job. Zweckrational can best be understood as "technocratic thinking," in which the individual strives to find the most efficient means to whatever ends are necessary (by the individual, the social milieu, or an organization). When formal rationality is the motivating force, other considerations—such as long-standing traditions, human values derived from philosophy or religion, or human emotions—do not enter the calculation (Weber, [1921] 1968, pp. 24-25).

Weber's typology is intended to be a comprehensive list of the types of meaning men and women give to their conduct across sociocultural systems. As an advocate of multiple causes of human behavior, Weber knew that a mix of these motivations causes most behavior. Even today, when many believe it is careerism alone that motivates their attendance, university students have a variety of reasons for attending. University marketing attempts to appeal to all these motivations in their advertising: rolling hills, beautiful people for students and professors, career training, numerous social activities and entertainments, and the ubiquitous "tradition of excellence." (I am always struck by the number of classes held outdoors or in technical laboratories in the brochures. It would seem that the plain classroom has become rare.)

Nevertheless, Weber went further than a mere classification scheme. He developed the typology because he was primarily concerned with modern society and how it differs from past societies (p. 436). Weber proposed that the essential distinguishing feature of modern society was a characteristic shift in the motivation of individual behaviors. In modern society, he claimed, the efficient application of means to ends, or zweckrational, has come to dominate and replace other motivators of social behavior. His classification of types of action provides a basis for his investigation of the social evolutionary process in which behavior had come to be increasingly dominated by goal-oriented rationality (zweckrational)—and less and less by tradition, values, or emotions. When behavior is motivated by a mix of traditions, values, emotions, and goal orientation, Weber calls this "substantive rationality." When motivated solely by zweckrational, he labels this formal rationality. The "rationalization process," or simply "rationalization," is the increasing dominance of zweckrational as a motivating force in human thought and behavior. His sociology can be likened to an epidemiological study focused on rationalization—its causes, symptoms, spread, and prognosis. Weber would probably reject the disease metaphor, but it seems consistent with his views of rationalization—it is destructive of traditional social structure and character. Weber occasionally expressed sorrow regarding their passing.

"Within the realm of social action, certain uniformities can be observed," Weber writes, "that is, courses of action that are repeated by the actor or (simultaneously) occur among numerous actors since the subjective meaning is meant to be the same. Sociological investigation is concerned with these typical modes of action. Thereby it differs from history, the subject of which is the causal explanation of important individual events; important, that is, in having an influence on human destiny" (p. 29).

Because of this initial focus on the motivation of social action, Weber is often considered an "idealist" who believes that ideas and beliefs mold social structure and other material conditions (see Harris 1998 and Carneiro 2003). However, he committed himself to no such narrow interpretation of sociocultural causation. He is far subtler than that. Instead, Weber's system is one in which material interests and ideas are in constant interaction with one another. "Not ideas, but material and ideal interests, directly govern men's conduct. Yet very frequently the 'world images' that have been created by 'ideas' have, like switchmen, determined the tracks along which action has been pushed by the dynamic of interest" (Weber, [1948] 1958, p. 280). Weber believed that the shift in human motivation is one of both cause and effect occurring in interaction with changes in the structural organization of society. The major thrust of his work is to identify the factors that have brought about this rationalization of the West. While his sociology begins with the individual motivators of social action, Weber does not focus exclusively on idealism or the micro-sociological level of analysis. While he proposed that the essential distinguishing feature of modern society is best viewed in terms of this characteristic shift in motivation, he rooted the shift in the enlargement and intensification of bureaucratic organization.

> We cannot here analyze the far-reaching and general cultural effects that the advance of the rational bureaucratic structure of domination, as such, develops quite independently of the areas in which it takes hold. Naturally, bureaucracy promotes

a 'rationalist' way of life, but the concept of rationalism allows for widely differing contents. Quite generally, one can only say that the bureaucratization of all domination very strongly furthers the development of 'rational matter-of-factness' and the personality type of the professional expert. This has far reaching ramifications (p. 240).

The greater size and complexity of sociocultural systems and the consequent need for greater coordination and control of society's economic and political functions bring about this bureaucratic growth.

> Bureaucratization is occasioned more by intensive and qualitative enlargement and internal deployment of the scope of administrative tasks than by their extensive and qualitative increase [...] The growing demands on culture, in turn, are determined, though to a varying extent, by the growing wealth of the most influential strata in the state. To this extent increasing bureaucratization is a function of the increasing possession of goods used for consumption, and an increasingly sophisticated technique of fashioning external life—a technique which corresponds to the opportunities provided by such wealth. This reacts upon the standard of living and makes for an increasing subjective indispensability of organized, collective, inter-local, and thus bureaucratic, provision for the most varied wants, which previously were either unknown or were satisfied locally by a private economy (pp. 212-213).

Bureaucracy—on behalf of the state in carrying out its military, taxation, welfare, or educational functions or on behalf of the capitalist in producing and distributing goods and services—is the primary vector or carrier of rationalization.

Ideal Type

Weber's discussion of social action is an example of using an ideal type. An ideal type provides the primary method for historical-comparative study. It does not refer to the "best" or some moral ideal but to typical or "logically consistent" features of social institutions or behaviors. There can be an "ideal type" casino or an ideal religious sect, an ideal type dictatorship, or an ideal democracy (none of which may be "ideal" in the colloquial sense of the term). An ideal type is an analytical construct that serves as a measuring rod for social observers to determine the extent to which concrete social institutions are similar and how they differ from some defined measure (Gerth and Mills [1948] 1958, p. 59).

The ideal type involves determining the features of a social institution that would be present if the institution were a logically consistent whole, not affected by other institutions, concerns, and interests. "As general concepts, ideal types are tools with which Weber prepares the descriptive materials of world history for comparative analysis" (p. 60). Weber explains: "An ideal type is formed by the one-sided accentuation of one or more points of view and by the synthesis of a great many diffuse, discrete, more or less present and occasionally absent concrete individual phenomena, which are arranged according to those one-sidedly emphasized viewpoints into a unified analytical construct [...] In its conceptual purity, this mental construct [...] cannot be found empirically anywhere in reality (Weber, [1903-1917] 1949, p. 90). The ideal type never corresponds to a concrete reality but is a description to which we can compare reality.

For example, social science literature uses the concept of "ideal capitalism" extensively. According to the ideal type, capitalism consists of five basic features: (a) private ownership of all potentially profitable activity; (b) pursuit of profit; (c) competition between private companies; (d) government enforcement of contracts; and (e) non-interference of government in economic affairs (the latter being more of a convenient myth for the capitalist, than actual reality). All capitalist systems deviate from the theoretical construct we call "ideal capitalism." Even the U.S., often considered the most capitalistic nation on earth, strays measurably from the ideal. For example, federal, state, and local governments operate some potentially profitable activities (parks, power companies, and the Post Office come to mind). Many markets in the U.S. are not very competitive, as they are dominated by large monopolies or oligopolies (and here, the list is endless). Finally, various levels of government regulate the economy, purchase goods and services from private concerns, extend many lucrative benefits to favored businesses, and maintain markets abroad. Still, the ideal construct of capitalism allows us to compare and contrast the economic systems of various societies to this definition or compare the American economy to itself over time.

Bureaucracy

Weber was concerned with the operation and expansion of large-scale enterprises in modern society's public and private sectors. Weber believed that bureaucracy is a particular case of rationalization applied to human organizations. Bureaucratic coordination of human action is the distinctive mark of modern social structures. To study these organizations, both historically and in contemporary society, Weber ([1921] 1968, pp. 220-221) developed the characteristics of an ideal-type bureaucracy: 1) Hierarchy of authority; 2) Impersonality; 3) Written rules of conduct; 4) Promotion based on achievement; 5) Specialized division of labor; and 6) Efficiency. According to Weber, bureaucracies are efficient, goal-oriented organizations designed according to rational principles. Offices are ranked in a hierarchical order, with information flowing up the chain of command and directives flowing down. The organizations' operations are characterized by impersonal rules that state duties, responsibilities, standardized procedures, and conduct of office holders. Offices are highly specialized. Appointments to offices are made according to the specialized qualifications of the applicants rather than their class, race, sex, or family background.

> The decisive reason for advancing bureaucratic organization has always been its purely technical superiority over any other form of organization. The fully developed bureaucratic mechanism compares with other organizations exactly as does the machine with the non-mechanical modes of production.

> Precision, speed, unambiguity, knowledge of the files, continuity, discretion, unity, strict subordination, reduction of friction and material and personal costs—these are raised to the optimum point in the strictly bureaucratic administration [...] And as far as complicated tasks are concerned, paid bureaucratic work is not only more precise but, in the last analysis, it is often cheaper than even formally unremunerated honorific service (Weber [1946] 1958, 214).

> When fully developed, bureaucracy stands [...] under the principle of *sine ira ac studio* (without bias or favor). Its specific nature, which is welcomed by capitalism, develops the more perfectly the bureaucracy is 'dehumanized,' the more completely it succeeds in eliminating from official business love, hatred, and all purely personal, irrational, and emotional elements that escape calculation. This is the specific nature of bureaucracy, and it is appraised as its special virtue (215-216).

These ideal characteristics are intended to promote the efficient attainment of the organization's goals.

Some have seriously misinterpreted Weber and have claimed that he liked bureaucracy or that he believed that bureaucracy was an "ideal" organization. Others have pronounced Weber "wrong" because bureaucracies do not live up to his "ideals." Others have even claimed that Weber "invented" bureaucratic organization. Nevertheless, Weber described bureaucracy as an "ideal type," not an ideal social institution in the colloquial sense of the term. Again, the ideal bureaucracy is a measuring rod to compare actual bureaucracies. While Weber recognized bureaucracy's technical efficiency, he also recognized its corrosive nature on humans and traditional societies, as this quote makes clear. "No machinery in the world functions so precisely as this apparatus of men and, moreover, so cheaply [...] Rational calculation [...] reduces every worker to a cog in this bureaucratic machine and, seeing himself in this light, he will merely ask how to transform himself into a somewhat bigger cog [...] The passion for bureaucratization drives us to despair" (Weber, [1921] 1968, p. ix).

Weber's studies of bureaucracy still form the core of organizational sociology. The bureaucratic coordination of the actions of large numbers of people has become the dominant structural feature of modern societies.

> From a purely technical point of view, a bureaucracy is capable of attaining the highest degree of efficiency and is in this sense formally the most rational known means of exercising authority over human beings. It is superior to any other form in precision, in stability, in the stringency of its discipline, and in its reliability. It thus makes possible a particularly high degree of calculability of results for the heads of the organization and for those acting in relation to it. It is finally superior both in intensive efficiency and in the scope of its operations and is formally capable of application to all kinds of administrative tasks [...] The needs of mass administration make it today completely indispensable. The choice is only between bureaucracy and dilettantism in the field of administration (pp. 223–224).

It is only through this organizational device that large-scale planning and coordination, both for the modern state and economy, become possible. The consequences of the growth in the power and scope of these organizations are central to understanding the modern world.

Authority

Weber's discussion of authority relations also provides insight into what is happening in the modern world. On what basis do men and women claim authority over others? Why do men and women give obedience to authority figures? Again, he uses the ideal type to begin to address these questions. "All ruling powers, profane and religious, political and apolitical, may be considered as variations of, or approximations to, certain pure types. These types are constructed by searching for the basis of legitimacy, which the ruling power claims" (Weber [1946] 1958, p. 294). Weber distinguished three main types of authority: (1) Traditional, (2) Rational-legal, and (3) Charismatic.

Rational legal authority is anchored in impersonal rules that have been legally established. "The state is a human community that (successfully) claims the monopoly of the legitimate use of force within a given territory" (Weber, [1946] 1958, p. 78). This rational-legal authority characterizes modern states and other social relations in modern societies. "Our modern 'associations,' above all the political ones, are of the type of 'legal' authority. That is, the legitimacy of the powerholder to give commands rests upon rules that are rationally established by enactment, by agreement, or by imposition. The legitimation for establishing these rules rests, in turn, upon a rationally enacted or interpreted 'constitution.' Orders are given in the name of impersonal norm, rather than in the name of a personal authority; and even the giving of a command constitutes obedience toward a norm rather than an arbitrary freedom, favor, or privilege" (pp. 294-295). Weber asserts that although rational-legal authority can be found in the remote past, "in its full development, all this is specifically modern" (p. 295).

Traditional authority often dominates pre-modern societies. It is based on the belief in the sanctity of tradition, of "the eternal yesterday." Because of the shift in human motivation, modern students often struggle to conceive of tradition's hold in pre-modern societies. Unlike rational-legal authority, traditional authority is not codified in impersonal rules but is usually invested in a hereditary line or a particular office by a higher power (Weber, [1921] 1968, p. 227). "Patriarchalism" is an important example; it is the type of authority exercised by the father, the rule of the master over the serf, or the monarch over her subjects (p. 231).

Finally, charismatic authority rests on the appeal of leaders who claim allegiance because of the force of their extraordinary personalities.

> 'Charismatic authority' [...] shall refer to a rule over men, whether predominantly external or internal, to which the governed submit because of their belief in the extraordinary quality of the specific person. The magical sorcerer, the prophet, the leader of hunting and booty expeditions, the warrior chieftain, the so-called 'Caesarist' ruler, and under certain conditions, the personal head of a party are such types of rulers for their disciples, followings, enlisted troops, parties, et cetera. The legitimacy of their rule rests on the belief in and the devotion to the extraordinary, which is valued because it goes beyond the normal human qualities and was originally valued as supernatural. The legitimacy of charismatic rule thus rests upon the belief in magical powers, revelations and hero worship (Weber [1946] 1958, 295-296).

Again, Weber describes an ideal type; he was aware that mixtures would be found in legitimizing authority. The appeal of Jesus Christ, one of the critical charismatic figures in history, was also partly based on tradition. State leaders, such as Reagan and Kennedy, often have some charismatic appeal in addition to their rational-legal and traditional bases of authority.

Causality

Weber firmly believed in the multi-causality of social phenomenon, though he expressed this causality in probabilities (Coser, [1971] 1977, p. 224). Weber's notion of probability derives from his recognition of the system character of human societies and, therefore, the impossibility of making exhaustive predictions. Prediction becomes possible, Weber believed, only within a system that focuses concern on a few social forces out of the wealth of forces and their interactions that make up empirical reality (Freund, 1968, pp. 7-8). Within such constraints, causal certainty in social research is not attainable (nor is it attainable outside the laboratory in natural sciences). The best that social scientists can do is focus theories on the most important relationships between social forces and forecast from that theory in terms of probabilities.

In this connection, it is often said that Weber was in a running dialogue with the ghost of Karl Marx. However, contrary to many interpretations, Weber did not attempt to refute Marx; he believed Marx contributed significantly to understanding human societies. However, he did disagree with Marx's assertion of the absolute primacy of material conditions in determining human behavior. Weber's system invokes ideas and material factors as interactive components in the social evolutionary process. "He was most respectful of Marx's contributions, yet believed, in tune with his own methodology, that Marx had unduly emphasized one particular causal chain, the one leading from the economic infrastructure to the cultural superstructure" (Coser, [1971] 1977, p. 228). Weber believed this could not adequately consider the complex web of causation linking social structures and ideas.

Weber attempted to show that the relations between ideas and social structures were multiple and varied, and those causal connections went in both directions. While Weber agreed with Marx that economic factors were central to understanding the social system, he emphasized the influence and interaction of ideas and values on sociocultural evolution. Gerth and Mills (1946, p. 63) summarized Weber's posited relationship between material conditions and ideas in the following passage: "There is no pre-established correspondence between the content of an idea and the interests of those who follow from the first hour. But, in time, ideas are discredited in the face of history unless they point in the direction of conduct that various interests promote. Ideas, selected and reinterpreted from the original doctrine, do gain an affinity with the interests of certain members of special strata; if they do not gain such an affinity, they are abandoned." It is in this light that *The Protestant Ethic and the Spirit of Capitalism* must be read.

The Protestant Ethic

Weber's concern with the meaning people give to their actions allowed him to understand the drift of historical change. He believed that rational action within a system of rational-legal authority is at the heart of modern society. His sociology was primarily an attempt to explore and explain this shift from traditional to rational action. What was it about the West, he asks, that is causing this shift? To understand these causes, Weber examined many civilizations' religious and economic systems.

Weber came to believe that the rationalization of action can only be realized when traditional ways of life are abandoned. Because of its erosion, modern people may need help realizing the hold of tradition over pre-industrial peoples. Weber's task was to uncover the forces in the West that caused people to abandon their traditional religious value orientation and encouraged them to develop a desire to acquire goods and wealth (Coser, [1971] 1977, pp. 227-228). "A man does not 'by nature' wish to earn more and more money, but simply to live as he is accustomed to live and to earn as much as is necessary for that purpose. Wherever modern capitalism has begun its work of increasing the productivity of human labour by increasing its intensity, it has encountered the immensely stubborn resistance of this leading trait of pre-capitalistic labour" (Weber, [1904] 1958, p. 60). After careful study, Weber concluded that the Protestant ethic broke the hold of tradition while it encouraged men to apply themselves rationally to their work.

> Waste of time is thus the first and in principle the deadliest of sins. The span of human life is infinitely short and precious to make sure of one's own election. Loss of time through sociability, idle talk, luxury, even more sleep than is necessary for health […] is worthy of absolute moral condemnation […] Time is infinitely valuable because every hour lost is lost to labour for the glory of God. Thus, inactive contemplation is also valueless, or even directly reprehensible if it is at the expense of one's daily work. For it is less pleasing to God than the active performance of His will in a calling (pp. 157-158).

Calvinism, he found, had developed a set of beliefs around predestination. Calvin's followers believed that one could not do good works or perform acts of faith to ensure their place in heaven. They believed that you were either among the "elect" or were not among them and lost. However, wealth was taken as a sign (by you and your neighbors) that you were one of God's elect, encouraging people to acquire wealth. For the Calvinist, Weber writes, "The world exists to serve the glorification of God and for that purpose alone. The elected Christian is in the world only to increase this glory of God by fulfilling His commandments to the best of his ability. But God requires social achievement of the Christian because He wills that social life shall be organized according to His commandments, in accordance with that purpose" (p. 108). The Protestant ethic, therefore, provided religious sanctions that fostered a spirit of rigorous discipline, encouraging men to apply themselves rationally to acquire wealth.

Weber studied non-Western cultures as well. He found that several societies had the technological infrastructure and other necessary preconditions to begin capitalism and economic expansion. However, capitalism failed to emerge. The only forces missing were the positive sanctions to abandon traditional ways. Through comparative analysis, Weber attempted to identify "not only the necessary but the sufficient" conditions that fostered capitalism (Gerth and Mills, [1946] 1958, p. 61). "We have no intention whatever of maintaining such a foolish and doctrinaire thesis as that the spirit of capitalism [...] could only have arisen as the result of certain effects of the Reformation, or even that capitalism as an economic system is a creation of the Reformation [...] On the contrary, we only wish to ascertain whether and to what extent religious forces have taken part in the qualitative formation and the quantitative expansion of that spirit over the world" (Weber, [1904] 1958, p. 91).

While Weber does not believe that the Protestant ethic was the *only* cause of the rise of capitalism, he believed it to be a powerful force in fostering its emergence. "The religious valuation of restless, continuous, systematic work in a worldly calling, as the highest means of asceticism, and at the same time the surest and most evident proof of rebirth and genuine faith, must have been the most powerful conceivable lever for the expansion of that attitude toward life which we have here called the spirit of capitalism" (p. 172). Having contributed to the emergence of capitalism, these religious motivations (wertrational) become undermined by the new economic system.

> The Puritans wanted to work in a calling; we are forced to do so. For when asceticism was carried out of monastic cells into everyday life, and began to dominate worldly morality, it did its part in building the tremendous cosmos of the modern economic order. This order is now bound to the technical and economic conditions of machine production which today determine the lives of all the individuals who are born into this mechanism, not only those directly concerned with economic acquisition, with irresistible force. Perhaps it will so determine them until the last ton of fossilized coal is burnt. In Baxter's view [a religious writer], the care for external goods should only lie on the shoulders of the "saint like a light cloak, which can be thrown aside at any moment." But fate decreed that the cloak should become an iron cage.

> Since asceticism undertook to remodel the world and to work out its ideals in the world, material goods have gained an increasing and finally an inexorable power over the lives of men as at no previous period in history. Today the spirit of religious asceticism—whether finally, who knows? —has escaped from the cage. But victorious capitalism, since it rests on mechanical foundations, needs its support no longer. The rosy blush of its laughing heir, the Enlightenment, also seems to be irretrievably fading, and the idea of duty in one's calling prowls about in our lives like the ghost of dead religious beliefs (pp. 181-182).

Success is stripped of all ethical and religious meanings and centers on accumulating material possessions and wealth as an end. "In the field of its highest development, in the United States, the pursuit of wealth, stripped of its religious and ethical meaning, tends to become associated with purely mundane passions, which often actually give it the character of sport" (p. 182). The economic system thus becomes one that is increasingly based on the rational calculation of means to achieve success, on zweckrational.

Of all of Weber's work, *The Protestant Ethic* is probably the most widely known but arguably most misunderstood. Gerth and Mills, who not only wrote about Weber but borrowed heavily from him in their analyses, cite the Protestant Ethic as only one strand among many in the causal order that led to the transition from feudalism to capitalism. They point out that Weber gave more weight to material factors in his latter essays ([1946] 1958, pp. 63-65). Lenski (2005, pp. 180-181) also sees the Protestant Ethic as a weak, secondary force in the transition. Collins (1980) also minimizes the view that Weber considered the Protestant Ethic a significant factor in the rise of capitalism. He points out that this analysis was performed early in Weber's career and that Weber later gave the nation-state a much more significant role in the rise of capitalism in later writings. Throughout the agrarian era, the nation-state took steps to rationalize law, making it less subject to the arbitrary whim of local rulers. The state also took steps to standardize taxation and currencies and laid the institutional foundations for banking, finance, investment, and the enforcement of contracts. All these, Weber maintained, are necessary structures promoting capitalist development (see also Elwell, 2013, pp. 50-52). This Weberian analysis of the rise of capitalism rather than the Protestant Ethic has strongly influenced Sanderson and Lenski. The main point of Weber's *Protestant Ethic*, these theorists maintain, was to round out Marx's economic determinism, assert that ideas and ideologies matter, and have a role—although secondary—in determining the speed and character of sociocultural change.

Oligarchy

Weber noted the dysfunctions of bureaucracy in terms of its impact on individuals. Its significant advantage, efficiency in attaining goals, makes dealing with individual cases unwieldy. The impersonality, crucial in attaining the organization's efficiency, is dehumanizing. By its very nature, bureaucracy generates an enormous degree of unregulated and often unperceived social power. Because of bureaucracy's superiority over other forms of organization, it has proliferated and now dominates modern societies. Weber warned that those who control these organizations control the quality of our lives and are mainly self-appointed leaders. Bureaucracy tends to result in an oligarchy or rule by the few officials at the organization's top. "The principles of office hierarchy and of levels of graded authority mean a firmly ordered system of super- and subordination in which there is a supervision of the lower offices by the higher ones" (Weber [1946] 1958, p. 197). In a society dominated by large formal organizations, there is a danger that social, political, and economic power will become concentrated in the hands of the few who hold high positions in the most influential organizations.

The issue was first raised by Weber, but Robert Michels, a sociologist and student of Weber, more fully explored it. Michels was a socialist and was disturbed to find that the socialist parties of Europe, despite their democratic ideology and provisions for mass participation, seemed to be dominated by their leaders, just as the traditional conservative parties. He concluded that the problem lay in the very nature of organizations. Michels (1915) formulated the 'Iron Law of Oligarchy. The iron law states, "It is organization which gives birth to the dominion of the elected over the electors…of the delegates over the delegators. Who says organization, says oligarchy" (p. 365). According to the "iron law," democracy and large-scale organization are incompatible. Any large organization, Michels pointed out, is faced with coordination problems that can be solved only by creating a bureaucracy. A bureaucracy, by design, is hierarchically organized to achieve efficiency—large numbers of people cannot make decisions that must be made every day efficiently. The effective functioning of an organization requires the concentration of much power in the hands of a few people.

Specific characteristics of leaders and members of organizations reinforce the organizational characteristics promoting oligarchy. People achieve leadership positions precisely because they have unique political skills; they are adept at getting their way and persuading others of the correctness of their views. Once they hold high office, their power and prestige are further increased. Leaders have access and control over information and facilities unavailable to the rank-and-file. They control the information that flows down the channels of communication. Leaders are also motivated to persuade the organization of the rightness of their views and use all their skills, power, and authority to do so. The organization's design makes the rank-and-file less informed than their "superiors." Finally, from birth, we are taught to obey those in positions of authority. "Such compliance has been conditioned into the officials, on the one hand, and, on the other hand, into the governed" (Weber, [1946] 1958, p. 229). Therefore, the rank-and-file looks to the leaders for policy directives and is generally prepared to allow leaders to exercise their judgment on most matters. So strong is this tendency that Weber states that it does not matter who oversees the organization. "The objective indispensability of the once-existing apparatus, with its peculiar, 'impersonal' character, means that the mechanism [that is, the bureaucracy]—in contrast to feudal orders based upon personal piety—is easily made to work for anybody who knows how to gain control over it. A rationally ordered system of officials continues to function smoothly after the enemy has occupied the area: he merely needs to change the top officials" (p. 229). Leaders also control potent negative and positive sanctions to promote their desired behavior or discourage behavior they find harmful to their interests. They can grant or deny raises, assign workloads, fire, demote, and, most gratifying of all sanctions, the power to promote.

Most importantly, they promote junior officials who share their opinions, making the oligarchy self-perpetuating. Therefore, the very nature of large-scale organizations makes oligarchy within these organizations inevitable. Bureaucracy, by design, promotes the centralization of power in the hands of those at the top of the organization.

Societal Oligarchy

However, the concern over bureaucracy's threat to a particular organization's members has overshadowed its effects on the larger society. Weber was genuinely concerned about rationalization and bureaucratization's impact on sociocultural systems. While it is easy to see oligarchy within formal organizations as we experience it almost daily, Weber's views on the inevitability of oligarchy within whole societies are subtler. Bureaucracy has come to dominate the social structure of modern society. Bureaucracies are necessary to provide the coordination and control so desperately needed by our complex society (and huge populations).

Nevertheless, while modern societies depend on formal organization, bureaucracy eventually undermines human freedom and democracy. "We must remember this fact—which we have encountered several times and which we shall have to discuss repeatedly: that 'democracy' as such is opposed to the 'rule' of bureaucracy, in spite and perhaps because of its unavoidable yet unintended promotion of bureaucratization" (p. 231). While government departments are theoretically responsible to the electorate, this responsibility is almost entirely fictional. The electorate (and even Congress) often do not know what these bureaucracies are doing. Government departments have grown so numerous and complex that they cannot be supervised effectively.

The modern era is one of interest-group politics, in which the degree of participation of the ordinary citizen in the forging of political positions is limited. Our impact on political decision-making depends, to a large extent, on our membership in organizational structures. The power of these groups depends on organizational characteristics such as membership size, commitment to the organization's goals, and wealth. However, it is through organizations that we lose control of the decision-making process.

Those on top of bureaucratic hierarchies can command vast resources to pursue their interests. This power is often unseen and unregulated, which gives the elite at the top of these hierarchies vast social, economic, and political power. Massive economic bureaucracies that impact our lives, which we have little control over, further compound the problem. Not only do these corporations affect us directly, but they also affect our government organizations designed to regulate them.

Rationalization

The rationalization process is the practical application of knowledge to achieve the desired end. It leads to efficiency, coordination, and control over the physical and social environment. It is a product of "scientific specialization and technical differentiation" characteristic of Western culture (Freund, 1968, p. 18). It is the guiding principle behind bureaucracy and the increasing division of labor. It has led to unprecedented increases in the production and distribution of goods and services. It is also associated with secularization, depersonalization, and oppressive routines. Increasingly, according to Weber, human behavior is guided by observation, experiment, and reason (zweckrational) to master the natural and social environment to achieve the desired end, the factory being one optimal example:

> No special proof is necessary to show that military discipline is the ideal model for the modern capitalist factory, as it was for the ancient plantation. However, organizational discipline in the factory has an entirely rational basis. With the help of suitable measurement methods, the optimum profitability of the individual worker is calculated like that of any material means of production. On that basis, the American system of "scientific management" triumphantly proceeds with its rational conditioning and training of work performances, thus drawing the ultimate conclusions from the mechanization and discipline of the plant. The psycho-physical apparatus of man is completely adjusted to the demands of the outer world, the tools, the machines—in short, it is functionalized, and the individual is shorn of his natural rhythm as determined by his organism; in line with the demands of the work procedure, he is attuned to a new rhythm through the functional specialization of muscles and through the creation of an optimal economy of physical effort. This whole process of rationalization in the factory and elsewhere, and especially in the bureaucratic state machine, parallels the centralization of the material implements of organization in the hands of the master. Thus, discipline inexorably takes over ever larger areas as the satisfaction of political and economic needs is increasingly rationalized. This universal phenomenon more and more restricts the importance of charisma and of individually differentiated conduct (Weber, [1921] 1968, p. 1156).

Freund (1968) defines rationalization as "the organization of life through a division and coordination of activities on the basis of exact study of men's relations with each other, with their tools and their environment, for the purpose of achieving greater efficiency and productivity" (p. 18). Weber's general theory of rationalization (of which bureaucratization is but a particular case) refers to increasing human mastery over the natural and social environment. In turn, these changes in social structure have changed human character through changing values, philosophies, and beliefs. The bureaucratization process has encouraged superstructural norms and values such as individualism, efficiency, self-discipline, materialism, and calculability (all of which are subsumed under Weber's concept of zweckrational). Bureaucracy and rationalization were rapidly replacing all other forms of organization and thought. They formed a stranglehold on all sectors of Western society. "The decisive reason for the advance of bureaucratic organization has always been its purely technical superiority over any other kind of organization. The fully developed bureaucratic mechanism compares with other organizations exactly as does the machine with the non-mechanical modes of organization" (Weber [1946] 1958, p. 214). Rationalization is the most general element of Weber's theory. He identifies rationalization with an increasing division of labor, bureaucracy, and mechanization. Weber also associates it with depersonalization, oppressive routine, rising secularism, and being destructive of individual freedom.

Since modern societies are so pervasively dominated by bureaucracy, it is crucial to understand why this enormous power is often used for ends that counter the interests and needs of people. Why is it that "as rationalization increases, the irrational grows in intensity"? (Freund, 1968, p. 25). The rationalization process is the increasing dominance of *Formal Rationality* (zweckrational) over rational action within the context of human values, traditions, and emotions (*Substantive Rationality*). Substantive rationality involves the assessment of goals and means in terms of ultimate human values such as social justice, peace, customs, and human happiness.

Weber maintained that even though a bureaucracy is highly rational in the formal sense of technical efficiency, it does not follow that it is also rational in the moral acceptability of its goals, or the means used to achieve them. Nor does an exclusive focus on the organization's goals necessarily coincide with the broader goals of society. It often happens that the single-minded pursuit of practical goals can undermine the foundations of the social order; in Weber's words, "the existence of those fundamental elements of irrationality—a conflict between formal and substantive rationality of the sort which sociology so often encounters" (Weber, [1921] 1968, p.

225). What is suitable for the bureaucracy is not always good for society as a whole—and often, in the long term, it is not suitable for the bureaucracy.

An extreme case of rationalization was the extermination camps of Nazi Germany. The goal was to kill as many people as possible most efficiently. The result was the ultimate dehumanization--the murder of millions of men, women, and children. The men and women who ran the extermination camps were, in large part, ordinary human beings. They were not particularly evil people. Most went to church on Sundays; most had children and loved animals and life. William Shirer (1960) comments on business firms that collaborated in the building and running of the camps: "There had been, the records show, some lively competition among German businessmen to procure orders for building these death and disposal contraptions and for furnishing the lethal blue crystals. The firm of I. A. Topf and Sons of Erfurt, heating equipment manufacturers, won out in its bid for the crematoria at Auschwitz. The story of its business enterprise was revealed in a voluminous correspondence found in the records of the camp. A letter from the firm dated February 12, 1943, gives the tenor:

To: The Central Construction Office of the S.S. and Police, Auschwitz

Subject: Crematoria 2 and 3 for the camp.

We acknowledge receipt of your order for five triple furnaces, including two electric elevators for raising corpses and one emergency elevator. A practical installation for stoking coal was also ordered and one for transporting ashes (Shirer, 1960, p. 971).

The "lethal blue crystals" of Zyklon-B used in the gas chambers were supplied by two German firms that had acquired the patent from I. G. Farben. Their product could do the most effective job for the least possible cost, so they got the contract. Shirer summarizes the organization of evil. "Before the postwar trials in Germany, it had been generally believed that the mass killings were exclusively the work of a relatively few fanatical S.S. leaders. But the records of the courts leave no doubt of the complicity of several German businessmen, not only the Krupps and the directors of I.G. Farben chemical trust but smaller entrepreneurs who outwardly must have seemed to be the most prosaic and decent of men, pillars—like good businessmen everywhere—of their communities" (pp. 972-973). In sum, the extermination camps and their suppliers were models of bureaucratic efficiency using the most efficient means available at that time to accomplish the goals of the Nazi government.

However, German corporations went beyond supplying the government with the machinery of death; some actively participated in the killing process. "This should occasion neither surprise nor shock. I.G. Farben was one of the first great corporate conglomerates. Its executives merely carried the logic of corporate rationality to its ultimate conclusion...the perfect labor force for a corporation that seeks fully to minimize costs and maximize profits is slave labor in a death camp. Among the great German corporations who utilized slave labor were AEG (German General Electric), Wanderer-Autounion (Audi), Krupp, Rheinmetall Borsig, Siemens-Schuckert and Telefunken" (Rubenstein, 1975, p. 58). I.G. Farben's synthetic rubber (Buna) plants at Auschwitz are an excellent example of the relationship between corporate profits and Nazi goals. I.G. Farben's investment in the plant at Auschwitz was considerable—over $1,000,000,000 in 1970s American dollars. The construction required 170 contractors and subcontractors; housing had to be built for the corporate personnel and barracks for the workers. S.S. guards supplied by the state would administer punishment when rules were broken. The workers at the plants were treated like all other camp inmates. The only exception was one of diet; workers in the plants would receive an extra ration of "Buna soup" to maintain "a precisely calculated level of productivity" (p. 58). Nor was any of this hidden from corporate executives; they were total participants in the horror. With an almost inexhaustible supply of workers, the corporation worked their slave laborers to death.

The fact that individual officials have specialized and limited responsibility and authority within the organization means they are unlikely to raise fundamental questions regarding the moral implications of the organization's overall operation. Under the rule of specialization, society becomes more intricate and interdependent but with a less common purpose. The community disintegrates because it loses its common bond. The emphasis in bureaucracies is on getting the job done in the most efficient manner possible. Considering the impact organizational behavior might have on society, the environment, or the consumer does not enter the calculation. The problem is further compounded by the decline of many traditional institutions, such as the family, community, and religion, which served to bind pre-industrial man to the group's interests. Rationalization causes the weakening of traditional and religious moral authority (secularization); the values of efficiency and calculability predominate. In an advanced industrial-bureaucratic society, everything, including human beings, becomes a component of the expanding machine.

The result is a seeming paradox—bureaucracies, the epitome of rationalization, acting in very irrational ways. Thus, we have economic bureaucracies in pursuit of profit that deplete and pollute the environment upon which they are based. We have political bureaucracies set up to protect our civil liberties that violate them with impunity. Agricultural bureaucracies (educational, government, and business), initially set up to help the farmer, end up putting millions of these same farmers out of business. Service bureaucracies were initially designed to care for and protect the elderly but now routinely deny service and engage in abuse. Weber called this formal rationalization as opposed to substantive rationality (the ability to anchor rational actions in consideration of the whole). It can also be called the irrationality of rationalization or, more generally, the irrationality factor. This irrationality of bureaucratic institutions is a significant factor in understanding contemporary society.

Weber and Marx

Weber believed that the alienation documented by Marx had little to do with the ownership of the mode of production but was a consequence of bureaucracy and the rationalization of social life. Marx asserted that capitalism has led to the "expropriation" of the worker from the mode of production. He believed that the modern worker is not in control of their fate and is forced to sell his labor (and thus the self) to private capitalists. Weber countered that loss of control at work was an inevitable result of any system of rationally coordinated production (Coser, [1971] 1977, pp. 230-232). Weber argued that men could only engage in socially significant action if they joined a large-scale organization. "When those subject to bureaucratic control seek to escape the influence of existing bureaucratic apparatus, this is normally possible only by creating an organization of their own which is equally subject to the process of bureaucratization" (Weber [1921] 1968, p. 224). In joining organizations, they would have to sacrifice their personal desires and goals for the organization's impersonal goals and procedures. By doing so, they would be cut off from a part of themselves and become alienated. "Weber's views about the inescapable rationalization and bureaucratization of the world have some obvious similarities to Marx's notion of alienation," Lewis Coser writes, "Both men agree that modern methods of organization have tremendously increased the effectiveness and efficiency of production and organization and have allowed an unprecedented domination of man over the world of nature. They also agree that the new world of rationalized efficiency has turned into a monster that threatens to dehumanize its creators. But Weber disagrees with Marx's claim that alienation is only a transitional stage on the road to man's true emancipation" ([1971] 1977, p. 232).

Socialism and capitalism are economic systems based on industrialization—the rational application of science, observation, and reason to produce goods and services. Both capitalism and socialism are forms of a rational organization of economic life to control and coordinate this production. Moreover, the production of goods is becoming central to social life. Socialism is predicated on government ownership of the economy to provide the coordination to meet the needs of people within society. If anything, Weber ([1921] 1968, pp. 224-225) maintained that socialism would be more rationalized and bureaucratic than capitalism. Thus, socialism would also be more alienating to human beings (Gerth and Mills [1946] 1958, p. 49).

Social Evolution

According to Weber, because bureaucracy is a form of organization superior to all others, further bureaucratization and rationalization may be an inescapable fate. "The bureaucratic structure is everywhere a late product of development. The further back we trace our steps, the more typical is the absence of bureaucracy and officialdom in the structure of domination. Bureaucracy has a 'rational' character: rules, means, ends, and matter-of-factness dominate its bearing. Everywhere its origin and its diffusion have therefore had 'revolutionary' results…This is the same influence which the advance of *rationalism* in general has had" (Weber [1946] 1958, 244). Weber feared that our probable future would be even more rationalized and bureaucratic, an iron cage that limits individual human potential rather than a technological utopia that sets us free. In his essay "Politics as a Vocation," Weber (1918) seems almost resigned to a dystopia, "Not summer's bloom lies ahead of us, but rather a polar night of icy darkness and hardness, no matter which group may triumph externally now" (p. 128). Though he still has hope:

> Politics is a strong and slow boring of hard boards. It takes both passion and perspective. Certainly, all historical experience confirms the truth—that man would not have attained the possible unless time and again he had reached out for the impossible. But to do that a man must be a leader, not only a leader but a hero, in a very sober sense of the world. And even those who are neither leaders nor heroes must arm themselves with that steadfastness of heart which can brave even the crumbling of all hopes. This is necessary right now, or else men will not be able to attain even that which is possible today. Only he has the calling for politics who is sure that he shall not crumble when the world from his point of view is too stupid or too base for what he wants to offer. Only he who in the face of all this can say 'In spite of all!' has the calling for politics (p. 128).

While Weber had a foreboding of an "iron cage" of bureaucracy and rationality, he also makes clear that he recognized that human beings are not mere subjects molded by sociocultural forces.

We are both creatures and creators of sociocultural systems. Furthermore, there are other possibilities, even in a sociocultural system that increasingly institutionalizes and rewards goal-oriented rational behavior in pursuit of wealth and material status symbols. New prophets or a rebirth of older ideals and traditions may yet arise. "No one knows who will live in this cage in the future," he writes, "or whether at the end of this tremendous development entirely new prophets will arise, or there will be a great rebirth of old ideas and ideals or, if neither, mechanized petrification embellished with a sort of convulsive self-importance. For of the last stage of this cultural development, it might well be truly said: 'Specialists without spirit, sensualists without heart; this nullity imagines that it has obtained a level of civilization never before achieved'" (Weber [1904] 1958, p. 182).

Weber's Legacy

While many of Weber's insights have been integrated into sociology, few practiced historical-comparative macrosociology in the latter half of the 20th century, and fewer still would call themselves Weberian. One such practitioner, C. Wright Mills (1916-1962), deserves special note. Mills' work is about bureaucracy and rationalization. Rationalization, you will recall, is the practical application of knowledge to achieve the desired end. Its goal is efficiency; its means are total coordination and control over the social processes needed to attain whatever goal is set. It is the guiding principle behind bureaucracy and the increasing division of labor.

According to Mills, the rise of white-collar work is rooted in occupational change due to recent growth in bureaucracies, technological change, and the increasing need to market the goods of an industrial society. The central characteristic regarding white-collar workers in modern industrial societies is that they are unorganized and depend upon large bureaucracies for their existence. Through their mass existence and dependence, they have changed the character and feel of American life. Jobs, Mills observed, are broken up into simple, functional tasks. Standards are set in terms of pace and output. Where economically viable, machines are employed. Where automation is impossible, the tasks are parceled out to the unskilled. Policy-making and executive functions are centralized and moved up the hierarchy. With the automation of the office and growth in the division of labor, the number of routine jobs is increased, and authority and job autonomy become attributes of only the top positions. There is a more significant distinction between managers and staff regarding power, prestige, and income (Mills [1951] 1973, p. 205).

The routinized worker is discouraged from using her independent judgment; her decision-making is following strict rules handed down by others. She becomes alienated from her intellectual capacities, and work becomes an enforced activity (p. 141). Independent thought on the job is discouraged as workers are rewarded for following the bureaucratic rules and routines handed down from above. There is also a shift in the exercise of power in such bureaucratic societies, from the brutal and overt power of authority based on force to the softer forms of power founded upon manipulation (p. 110). This form of power disguises the oppositional nature of the relationship, disguising the oppressor and removing all checks on exploitation (p. 349).

As bureaucracies are centralized and enlarged, the circle of those who run these organizations has narrowed. However, the consequences of their decisions have become enormous (Mills [1956] 1970, p. 23). According to Mills, the power elite are the key people in the three major institutions of modern society: 1) the economy, 2) the Government, and 3) the Military. All other institutions have diminished in scope and power. They have been either pushed to the side of modern history or made subordinate to the big three (p. 6). State, corporations, and military bureaucracies have become enlarged and centralized, a means of power never equaled in human history. These hierarchies of power are the key to understanding modern industrial societies. Power is rooted in authority, an attribute of social organizations, not of individuals. He argues that it is not a conspiracy of evil men but a social structure that has enlarged and centralized the decision-making process and placed this authority in the hands of men of similar social backgrounds and outlooks (pp. 7-9). Their similar social backgrounds provide one of the significant sources of unity among the elite. Most of the elite, Mills asserted, come from the upper third of the income and occupational pyramids. They are born of the same upper class. They attend the same preparatory schools and Ivy League universities. They join the same exclusive gentleman's clubs and belong to the same organizations. They are closely linked through intermarriage (p. 19).

The coordination of elites also comes from the interchange of personnel between the three elite hierarchies. Mills asserts that the closeness of business and government officials can be seen by the ease and frequency with which men pass from one hierarchy to another. Mills also asserted that much coordination comes from the growing structural integration of dominant institutions. As each of the elite domains becomes larger, more centralized, and more consequential in its activities, its integration with the other spheres becomes more pronounced (pp. 7-8).

Mills claims that the corporate sector is the most powerful of the three sectors of institutional power. However, the power elite cannot be understood as a mere reflection of economic elites; instead, it is the alliance of economic, political, and military power. Mills saw two other levels of power in American society below the power elite. At the bottom are the great masses of people. Largely unorganized, ill-informed, and virtually powerless, they are controlled and manipulated from above. The masses are economically dependent; they are economically and politically exploited. Because they are disorganized, the masses are far removed from the classic democratic public in which voluntary organizations hold the key to power (pp. 28-29).

Mills saw a middle level of power between the masses and the elite. Composed of local opinion leaders and special interest groups, they neither represent the masses nor have any real effect on the elite. Mills saw the American Congress and political parties reflect this middle power level. Although Congress and political parties' debate and decide on some minor issues, the power elite ensures that no serious challenge to its authority and control is tolerated in the political arena. The privileged positions allow them to transcend the ordinary environments of men and women. The elite has access to levers of power that make their decisions (as well as their failure to act) consequential (p. 36).

By 1958, Mills seemed more concerned with the rise of militarism among the elites than with the hypothesis that many elites were military men. According to Mills, the rise of the military state serves the interests of the elite of industrial societies. For politicians, the projection of military power serves as a cover for their lack of vision and innovative leadership. For corporate elites, the preparations for war and the projection of military power underwrite their research and development and guarantee stable profits through corporate subsidies. This militarism is inculcated in the population through schoolroom and pulpit patriotism, manipulation, and control of the news through the cultivation of opinion leaders and unofficial ideology. "It is not the number of victims or the degree of cruelty that is distinctive; it is the fact that the acts committed and the acts that nobody protests are split from the consciousness of men in an uncanny, even a schizophrenic manner. The atrocities of our time are done by men as "functions" of social machinery—men possessed by an abstracted view that hides from them the human beings who are their victims and, as well, their own humanity. They are inhuman acts because they are impersonal. They are not sadistic but merely businesslike; they are not aggressive but merely efficient; they are not emotional at all but technically clean-cut" (Mills, 1958, pp. 83-84). The control of powerful bureaucracies makes elite decisions very consequential in the modern age. Because those at the top of these hierarchies act in their self-interests with few checks on their power, they act irresponsibly and lead the nation and the world to disaster.

Like Weber before, Mills cautions that a society dominated by rational social organization is not based on reason, intelligence, and goodwill toward all. It is through rational social organization that modern-day tyrants (as well as more mundane bureaucratic managers) exercise their authority and manipulation, often denying the opportunity to their subjects to exercise their judgment.

> Given these effects of the ascendant trend of rationalization, the individual 'does the best he can.' He gears his aspirations and work to the situation he is in, and from which he can find no way out. In due course, he does not seek a way out; he adapts. That part of his life which is left over from work, he uses to play, to consume, 'to have fun.' Yet this sphere of consumption is also being rationalized. Alienated from production, from work, he is also alienated from consumption, from genuine leisure. This adaptation of the individual and its effects upon his milieux and self-results not only in the loss of his chance and, in due course, of his capacity and will to reason; it also affects his chances and his capacity to act as a free man. Indeed. Neither the value of freedom nor of reason, it would seem, are known to him [...] There is then rationality without reason. Such rationality is not commensurate with freedom but the destroyer of it (Mills [1959] 1976, 170).

Social scientists' task is to make clear how these social structure changes affect human values and behaviors and to bring reason to bear on human affairs.

Two other macro-sociologists strongly influenced by Max Weber are Norbert Elias, a German sociologist who studied under Weber's brother, Alfred, and George Ritzer, perhaps the most famous American sociologist writing at this time. These sociologists focus on changes in the social structure—the enlargement and centralization of bureaucratic organization—and how these changes impact human behavior. Elias's work centers on the "civilizing process" in the latter Middle Ages. At the same time, Ritzer looks at what he calls "McDonaldization," an update of Weber's rationalization process that looks at the fast-food restaurant as the ideal type of bureaucracy in the modern world. Roderick Seidenberg may or may not have been directly influenced by Weber, but his two books on the growing rationalization of society are certainly in line with Weber's rationalization theory.

Chapter 9: The Sociology of C. Wright Mills[1]

C. Wright Mills is well-known as a social critic, but sociologists rarely give him credit as a social theorist. However, Mills was very much rooted in classical social theory as it informed his social criticism throughout his life. One can see Karl Marx's influence when Mills writes of capitalism and its interrelations with the state. Emile Durkheim's impact is apparent when Mills writes of the cash nexus replacing societies' social bonds. When Mills writes of the cultural hegemony of elites, expressed in religion, myth, folklore, and popular culture, you can hear echoes of Antonio Gramsci and Thorstein Veblen, as well as the work of Robert Michels and his assertion of the rule of oligarchy. However, it is readily apparent that Max Weber is the dominant theoretical influence on Mills' worldview. Weber's views on bureaucracy, power, authority, and rationalization theories undergird Mills' criticism of the American class structure, the power elite, and Cold War relations. Nevertheless, more than synthesizing relevant insights from classical theory, Mills believed that, like the classics, contemporary social scientists must focus on the critical issues of their time; they should "take it big" (Aronowitz, 2012). This belief animated Mills' criticism of the social sciences and the intellectuals of his time.

Mills (1959) writes that the focus of the classics is substantive problems. "I believe that what may be called classic social analysis is a definable and usable set of traditions; that its essential feature is the concern with historical social structures; and that its problems are of direct relevance to urgent public issues and insistent human troubles." According to Mills, classical theorists tied their concepts and methods to investigate issues that threatened the widely held values of freedom and reason. Marx's sociology focused on capitalism's problems, its origins, growth, and impact on world societies, workers, capitalists themselves, and the environment. Weber's sociology repeatedly returns to the social and personal problems caused by the growth of rationalization, born of the necessity to coordinate and control ever-larger populations and complex production processes carried by both private and public bureaucracies. Mills' sociology

[1]From "The Sociology of C. Wright Mills" by Frank W. Elwell. From The Routlege International Handbook of C. Wright Mills Studies edited by Jon Frauley. Reproduced by permission of Taylor & Francis Group.

builds on these foundations and is primarily concerned with late capitalist-bureaucratic society, the continuing diminution of human freedom, and the role of reason in governing political life.

Social Psychology

Traditional social psychology has focused on the nature of social interaction in determining the individual's psychology and character. Gerth and Mills' *Character and Social Structure* (1953) argues that the major societal institutions—economic, political, military, religious, and kinship—determine the forms of these social interactions within sociocultural systems. As these institutions undergo historical transformations, the dominant character and personalities of those living in these societies also change. "In interpreting contemporary social change, we have found ourselves more and more interested in those roles and technologies that involve violence and which involve economic production. Like many other observers we believe that revolutions in these orders are now crucial to the course of world history" (p. 404).

Mills views human nature as malleable, formed by its interaction with historical and contemporary social structures. Human nature is formed by society's production methods, political domination, and international anarchy, in sum by the "unruly forces of contemporary society itself" (Mills, 1959, p. 13). Sociocultural systems determine the types of men and women who inhabit society; the individual cannot be understood apart from the historical, social structures where they interact with others, thus forming their character (p. 162). In pre-modern times, primary and intermediate groups molded the individual. In the modern world, in contemporary times, the nation-state has become the "history-making unit," the forge upon which modern humans are formed (p. 158). Through socialization, aspects of human personality are encouraged or repressed, developing human beings' character and defining the varieties of men and women who make up society.

The economic-political system of societies is an incredibly influential force in creating human character. The ongoing struggles between democracy and fascism, or capitalism and socialism, are between different economic-political systems and over what types of human beings will prevail in the future (p. 158). Historical transformations within societies—such as the decline of agricultural jobs, the increase in white-collar and sales work, the rise of bureaucracies, and the decline in the functions of family and community—all affect the predominant character of the men and women who inhabit the society. By "predominant character," Mills means their values, ideologies, beliefs, and expectations. The structural characteristics of a society determine its norms, values, and belief systems, which motivate character formation. Socialization from infancy to adulthood is an essential factor in explaining the biography and character of the individual. "Adequate understanding requires that we grasp the interplay of these intimate settings with their larger structural framework, and that we take into account the transformations of this framework, and the consequent effects upon milieu. When we understand the social structures and structural changes as they bear upon more intimate scenes and experiences, we are able to understand the causes of individual conduct and feelings of which men in specific milieu are themselves unaware" (p. 162).

Gerth and Mills (1953) conclude that humans are unique in the animal kingdom because they are historical beings. They define the individual in terms of historical and social development so that no single theory will fit society for all time and place. "He creates his own destiny as he responds to his experienced situation, and both his situation and experiences of it are the complicated products of the historical epoch which he enacts" (p. 480). Men and women are members of society, and through their social interactions, they create their destiny. Mills (1956) argues that structural changes are coming ever more rapidly in modern societies. As institutions become more prominent, embracing, centralized, and interconnected, the pace of structural change increases (pp. 20–21). With this enlargement and centralization, the circle of those who control these organizations becomes narrower and more consequential, making a mockery of democratic processes and human freedoms.

Alienation

Like Karl Marx, Mills attributed alienation to the detailed division of labor. However, he also attributed much of it to bureaucratic rationality promoted by capitalism's drive to efficiently produce goods and services to maximize profit (Mills, 1951, pp. 224-28). While Marx focused on manufacturing labor, Mills asserted that alienation was also true of modern-day white-collar and professional work. The centralization of decision-making merges with the "formal rationality" of bureaucracy to remove autonomy from such jobs and destroy the white-collar worker's freedom. This destruction, Mills says, goes beyond Marx's ownership concerns, as "rationality itself has been expropriated from work and any total view and understanding of its process" (p. 226). It is not just capitalism and the world market that is the alien power over men that Marx wrote about, though that remains a factor in Mills' worldview; it is Max Weber's bureaucratic rationality. Work has increasingly come under the control of mechanization, with the detailed division of labor on the one hand and centralized management on the other. For Mills, alienation is primarily due to these factors, which are a part of the bureaucratization and rationalization process accelerated by capitalism's growth and rule.

Mills views the detailed division of labor as a characteristic of work in the modern world, based on the shift from an agriculturally based mode of production to one based on manufacturing, sales, and services. In mature industrial societies, he writes, many employees are dependent upon large bureaucracies in which working conditions have allowed alienation to spread far beyond working-class occupations (p. 224). Most white-collar workers have little power to make decisions on the job and little freedom or control over work processes or products. He argues that industrialism subjugates the worker's entire self to the work process, not just their physical motions. All of the features of wage work have come to characterize white-collar work. In many respects, it is worse. White-collar workers must sell themselves in the personality market, which may be even more alienating than just selling their physical labor (pp. 225-227).

In early-stage capitalism, when production was below the demand for goods and services, salesmanship was knowing the product and providing the necessary information to the potential buyer. However, when capitalism develops the potential to produce far more than the consumer is likely to buy (a principal contradiction of capital, according to Marx), marketing and salesmanship become an essential branch of any industry. The power of capitalist production requires a salesforce steeped in the psychology of persuading people to consume. One's entire personality then becomes part of the forces of production. Mills calls this the "personality market" and believes it "underlies the all-pervasive distrust and self-alienation" characteristic of modern society. Echoing Durkheim, Mills asserts that contemporary society no longer has shared values and mutual trust as the foundation of social solidarity. Only the cash nexus binds us together (p. 188). We live within a web of superficial contacts permeating all areas of social life. Our work requires that we pretend to be interested in one another to manipulate and sell products, services, or even the self. "In the course of time, and as this ethic spreads, it is got on to. Still, it is conformed to as part of one's job and one's style of life, but now with a winking eye, for one knows that manipulation is inherent in every human contact. Men are estranged from one another as each secretly tries to make an instrument of the other, and in time a full circle is made: one makes an instrument of himself, and is estranged from It also" (pp. 188).

Power & Authority

Mills identifies three forms of power in modern society: 1) coercion or physical force; 2) authority, which is attached to positions that others believe are justified by tradition or rationality; and 3) manipulative power that is often wielded without the conscious knowledge of those subject to it (1958, p. 41). Ultimately, the police and military power of the state undergird all forms of state authority. Nevertheless, human organizations that depend on constant force and coercion to keep members in line are inefficient and ultimately ineffective. A system based solely on the continuous use of force must expend much energy policing its members; it stifles initiative and provides an obvious target for rallying opposition (1951, p. 110). Laws and administrative rules are expressions of authority. Fines and loss of freedom are the formal sanctions for disobedience. However, most do not disobey. Most are socialized to obey power and come to believe in the legitimacy of the authority above them.

Authority based on bureaucratic rationality provides an inviting target for opposition from employees and unions. Symbols of legitimation serve to either justify or oppose existing arrangements of power and authority. Such symbols are among the essential areas of study for social scientists. Most governments do not merely rely upon the governeds' consent but rather manufacture that consent through manipulation (pp. 109-111). Before the modern era, the government's power and authority were apparent and personal, often producing fear and obedience in the governed. If the administration became too abusive or its force too weak to keep the people obedient, its legitimacy could quickly become the target of revolt.

The loss of employment and wages undergird the power of government and economic institutions over their employees. However, such economic coercion is insufficient in engendering white-collar workers' commitment and loyalty. Bureaucratic work does not merely need the conforming behavior of the men and women under its sway but their commitment to the organization's goals (p. 110). The bureaucracy aims to efficiently attain its goals through written rules of authority and conduct for all employees. Individuals within the hierarchy have well-defined status and relationships with others. In time, Mills writes, employees internalize the enterprise's purpose and authority relationships. Following the organization's rules provides them safety from those above and authority over those below. Their careers, wages, and the possibility of promotion depend on following the rules and pleasing those above. "In due course, their very self-images, what they do and what they are, are derived from the enterprise" (p. 109).

However, manipulative power is hidden from the oppressed; it effectively removes the check of reason and conscience of the obedient. Large, centralized bureaucracies exercise this manipulative power and amplify its spread through mass communication (p. 110). Since Mills' writing, social media have further spread its corrosive influence on human thought and behavior. Manipulation has become the dominant form of power in such organizations, shifting from direct authority relationships to more subtle manipulation to secure loyalty and obedience (1951, p. 106). The goal is to have workers internalize organizational goals and directives without their awareness that they are not their own. Authority in the mid-twentieth century shifted from coercion and legitimated authority to manipulation. Exploitation moves from overt to covert, from obvious to subtle, from control over peoples' bodies to control over their minds.

These same techniques, augmented by mass media and surveillance technologies, are also becoming more prevalent in government. "In the amorphous twentieth-century world, where manipulation replaces authority, the victim does not recognize his status. The formal aim, implemented by the latest psychological equipment, is to have men internalize what the managerial cadres would have them do, without their knowing their own motives, but nevertheless having them. Many whips are inside men, who do not know how they got there, or indeed that they are there" (1951, p. 110). Accordingly, bureaucracies increasingly manipulate their workers, clients, and customers. Bureaucracies employ this manipulative power through ever more sophisticated methods of control. These methods are provided by science, including social science, in the form of propaganda and surveillance technologies, now vastly augmented through the internet and "Big Data" analysis.

The new technologies of mass communication, surveillance technologies, and advances in the behavioral and social sciences enable the shift to rule by manipulation. However, Mills writes that these technological advances merely allow change to occur; the shift's cause is the centralization and enlargement of political and economic power. Impersonal manipulation replaces explicit authority. In authority relations, there is a need to justify power to secure obedience and loyalty. With manipulation, there is no need for justification. Manipulation occurs when centralized institutions cannot justify their authority through reason (1951, p. 349). The goal of manipulation is to have men and women—employees or citizens—internalize directives, unaware that these are not their motives. The coercion of the past has not miraculously transformed into the democratic ideal of "the consent of the governed." The fact is that elites now manufacture the governeds' consent through manipulation (1951, p. 110).

Like Marx before him, Mills critiques social scientists who focus exclusively on ideas and ideologies as prime movers in men's and women's actions. These "value orientations and normative structures" are open to manipulation by powerful groups within the social order that use symbols to justify or oppose existing power relations. One should not confuse the causes of government with its legitimations (1959, p. 37). Institutional rulers, he writes, have the means to monopolize and manipulate society's master symbols. He notes that the means of power now have the capabilities of manufacturing consent. "That we do not know the limits of such power--and that we hope it does have limits--does not remove the fact that such power today is successfully employed without the sanction of the reason or the conscience of the obedient" (1959, pp. 40-41). Further, he writes that the power structure can flourish even when the ruler and the ruled lack all intellectual conviction and belief, that is, an utter lack of legitimation for government actions and widespread apathy among the population (1959, p. 41). This is an observation that seems even more salient in our era.

"Moral insensibility" is Mills' term for the mass indifference brought about by continually seeing atrocities in news and entertainment programs. With such overexposure, horrors no longer reach individuals on a human level; they become devoid of meaning and reality. The continuous viewing of such cruelties affects the observer and normalizes the viciousness in social life. Increasingly, men functioning on the orders of organizations commit the atrocities of our time, "men possessed by an abstracted view that hides from them the human beings who are their victims and, as well, their own humanity. They are inhuman acts because they are impersonal. They are not sadistic but merely businesslike; they are not aggressive but merely efficient; they are not emotional at all but technically clean-cut" (1958, pp. 88-89).

In sum, Mills sees coercion as the last resort of authority, the "final form of power." However, he adds, it rarely has to be exercised. Power justified by the beliefs of the obedient (authority) and manipulative power (exercised below conscious thought of the powerless) are also critical factors. "In fact, the three types must constantly be sorted out when we think about the nature of power" (1959, p. 41).

215

Bureaucracy

C. Wright Mills bases his theories on bureaucracy on the writings of Max Weber. His breakthrough work, co-authored with Hans Gerth, was the seminal book *From Max Weber* (1946), still widely read and cited as an accessible source of Weber's theories. Most critics ascribe most of the heavy theoretical lifting to Gerth, but there is little doubt that Mills integrated Weber into his worldview. Aronowitz (2012) writes, "Crucial to Gerth and Mills' understanding of how modern institutions work was Weber's theories of bureaucracy as inimical to democratic decision making in corporations and labor unions as much as in government" (p. 16). Arnowitz writes that Mills came to see bureaucratic institutions along Robert Michels' lines, as oligarchical institutions dominating social life. In the modern age, bureaucratic authority has become enlarged and centralized.

While most people in feudal society were peasants, they became workers in private companies and government bureaucracies in modernity. The nation-state has developed from a loose collection of kings and nobles, self-equipped knights and peasant armies to powerful government bureaucracies, standing armies, and sophisticated military machines (1958, p. 24). In America, the connections between government and business have grown so close that they are virtually indistinguishable. "Under American conditions the growth of executive government does not mean merely the 'enlargement of government' as some kind of autonomous bureaucracy; it means the ascendancy of the corporation men into political eminence" (p. 30). According to Mills, a few hundred corporations now dominate the American economy. The economy has become a permanent war economy dominated by private corporations. Corporate interests dominate the state; militarism now dominates the thinking of politicians and people.

With the centralization and enlargement of bureaucracies, Mills noted the growth in administrators and managers. These positions require a set of role expectations that Mills labeled the "managerial demiurge." The demiurge is an elaborate game of manipulation based on bureaucratic and political skills. With such a large number of people holding administrative positions, this demiurge has profound consequences for society (1951, p. 81).

Power Elite

Mills borrows the emphasis on capitalism as a primary power center from Marx and Engels, and the focus on the rational-legal power of bureaucracy from Weber in his explorations of the power elite in American society. Mills saw the social structure's bureaucratization as an ongoing process that threatened to replace a loosely integrated democracy with a more managed "corporate-like society" (Mills, 1951, p. 78). This corporatization is accelerated in wartime but continues during times of peace as well. In the past, transportation, communication, and the means of violence limited capitalist and state power. Nevertheless, as these technologies advance and the degree of bureaucratic organization enlarges and concentrates, the limits of power and authority have also expanded (Mills, 1956, p. 23). Those who control the bureaucracies that dominate modern capitalist-industrial society are far more powerful than the Caesars or even the early 20th-century dictators. "That the facilities of power are enormously enlarged and decisively centralized means that the decisions of small groups are now more consequential" (p. 23).

According to Mills, American society has an elite in command of the resources of vast bureaucratic organizations that dominate the social order (1956, pp. 3–4). As the bureaucracies continue to centralize and enlarge, the circle of those who run these organizations narrows, and the consequences of their decisions become enormous (p. 7). According to Mills, the power elite are the key people in modern society's three major institutions: the government, the corporations, and the military. Each of these three institutions has become larger, more powerful, and centralized in its decision-making in the twentieth century. In a society dominated by large bureaucratic organizations, the top of these three dominant institutions have acquired an enormous degree of social, economic, military, and political power (p. 9).

Mills identifies bureaucratic hierarchies as the source of elite power. Thus, power and authority in American life are rooted in social organization, not individuals. Personal wealth or family connections give individuals greater access to these positions of control, but the real power is rooted in these bureaucratic hierarchies of state, corporations, and military. Thus, these hierarchies are crucial to understanding modern American society, for they are the basis of power, wealth, and prestige in modern times.

According to Mills, the corporate structure has enlarged and concentrated into a handful of significant financial and manufacturing institutions. The government has also broadened its power and scope. Mills does not claim it is a conspiracy of evil men manipulating and controlling everyone. Instead, it is a social structure with an inordinate degree of power and authority vested in just a few offices. "For they are in command of the major hierarchies and organizations of modern society. They rule the big corporations. They run the machinery of the state and claim its prerogatives. They run the military establishment. They occupy the strategic command posts of the social structure, in which are now centered the effective means of the power and the wealth and the celebrity which they enjoy" (pp. 3-4). Significant national power, Mills claims, is now almost exclusively in the upper hierarchies of economic, government, and military bureaucracies. Men of similar social class backgrounds and outlooks fill these leadership positions (pp. 7-9).

Other social institutions, such as family, education, labor, and religion, have been diminished in scope and made subordinate to these dominant institutions. Schools have become training grounds for corporations and governments, sorting young people for their future positions in the hierarchy and inculcating obedience to authority, the glories of capitalism, and the American way of life along the way. "Families and churches and schools adapt to modern life; governments and armies and corporations shape it; and, as they do so, they turn these lesser institutions into means for their ends" (p. 6). Mills gives examples of chaplains in the military to improve morale, schools, and universities training students for specialized jobs in government, corporations, or the military. Industrial society has broken the back of the extended family through geographic and social mobility, and the army, with its endless wars, furthers the decline. The purpose of these "lesser" institutions is to legitimate the authority and the decisions of the "big three" (p. 6). Through socialization, the individual internalizes the legitimations of the status quo—the hierarchies of power and authority become the norm, what is right and natural.

According to Mills, the elite of these three hierarchies come from similar social class backgrounds, go to the same prep schools and Ivy League universities, and belong to the same clubs. The majority come from the upper third of the wealth pyramid in America and tend to marry within their caste. Non-upper-class elite members consist of hired corporate managers, experts, and corporate lawyers—competent technocrats who have risen through the ranks and are subsequently sponsored by the elite and the organizations they control.

Mills' power elite thesis is not a claim for all nations, and for all times, his focus is on American society (p. 20). Nor is he claiming that elite power is omnipotent—the power and unity of the elite have varied over time, as has the degree of their foresight and control of the state's machinery. "The idea of the power elite does not mean that the estimations and calculated risks upon which decisions are made are not often wrong and that the consequences are sometimes, indeed often, not those intended. Often those who make decisions are trapped by their own inadequacies and blinded by their own errors" (pp. 21-22).

Their typical social class, education, experiences, and the expectations of their positions in the hierarchy produce men of similar values and outlook. However, Mills does not claim that this is all that unifies the elite. There is increasing coordination between the three sectors, particularly during wartime. This coordination did not fulfill some master plan, nor was it the primary source of their unity. "But it is to say that as the institutional mechanics of our time have opened up avenues to men pursuing their several interests, many of them have come to see that these several interests could be realized more easily if they worked together, in informal as well as in more formal ways, and accordingly they have done so" (p. 20). Mills contends that coordination between government and corporations depends on membership on corporate boards and private clubs. Some of the coordination also comes from the interchange of personnel between the three elite hierarchies. One can see the closeness of business and government officials by the ease and frequency with which men pass from one order to another (p. 83). The interlocking directorates among corporations and the revolving door between industry, government, and the military reinforce their power. These means of coordination are even stronger today.

Mills writes of the growing structural integration of elite domains. As these dominant institutions become more centralized and consequential in their actions, the coordination and integration with the other spheres of power and authority become more pronounced. Voters judge the executive branch's competence by the economy's performance. Economic health highly depends on foreign relations, military spending, monetary policy, and regulatory activities. The executive branch makes all such decisions regarding the economy's performance. Mills asserts there is an ever-growing convergence of interest between the three centers of power and authority. The decisions made in corporate boardrooms have a bearing on the military establishment. Military decisions affect the political domain, and decisions made there affect economic activities and military operations. "There is no longer, on the one hand, an economy, and, on the other hand, a political order containing a military establishment unimportant to politics and to money-making. There is a political economy linked, in a thousand ways, with military institutions and decisions. On each side of the world-split running through central Europe and around the Asiatic rimlands, there is an ever-increasing interlocking of economic, military, and political structures. If there is government intervention in the corporate economy, so is there corporate intervention in the governmental process. In the structural sense, this triangle of power is the source of the interlocking directorate that is most important for the historical structure of the present" (pp. 7-8).

Mills claims that the corporate sector is the most powerful of the three sectors of institutional power. Its interests are in a military establishment armed and ready for war on a moment's notice and a private corporate economy unfettered by democracy (1958, pp. 30-31). Nevertheless, Mills did not understand the power elite as a mere reflection of economic elites; instead, it is the alliance of economic, political, and military power. He bases this power on functionally rational bureaucracies and asserts that their power and authority are increasing (1959, pp. 115-116).

According to Mills, the masses at the bottom of American society primarily depend on government and corporate bureaucracies and are unorganized, ill-informed, and easily manipulated from above. Mills asserted that a people's belief system, values, and political outlook on a whole range of issues are a function of their contact with others and, increasingly, their exposure to media. In this, the mass media is decisive. The media have become the common denominator of consciousness, part of America's self-image reaching directly into the home and molding the consciousness of children, adolescents, and adults. His main concern was not with the media's explicit political content, which is but a small part of media programming (in his time). Instead, he focused on the rapidly growing entertainment fare that diverted attention from social issues. He remarked upon the emerging media world of entertainment, sports, and leisure. "These competing worlds, which in their modern scale are only 30 years old, divert attention from politics by providing a set of continuing interests in mythical figures and fast-moving stereotypes [...] And their effects run deep: popular culture is not tagged as 'propaganda' but as entertainment; people are often exposed to it when most relaxed of mind and tired of body; and its characters offer easy targets of identification, easy answers to stereotyped personal problems" (1951, p. 336). The mass marketing of consumer products, which sponsors these attractions, is also a recent phenomenon that profoundly impacts men's and women's consciousness. Echoing Durkheim, Mills asserts that local communities and informal groups no longer serve to moderate and protect people from the reach of central governments or corporations. Subject to the constant media barrage of infotainment, commercials, and propaganda, the classic democratic public in which voluntary organizations hold the key to power is undermined (1956, pp. 28–29).

Mills asserts that the new and powerful force of mass media is shaping modern consciousness. Contradicting Marx, he states that "if the consciousness of men does not determine their existence, neither does their material existence determine their consciousness. Between consciousness and existence stand communication, which influence such consciousness as men have of their existence" (1951, pp. 332-33). Mills notes that media was not so pervasive in Marx's day when only books, newspapers, and pamphlets with competing political-social views vied for public support (some few were published by Marx). However, in modern times, mass media plays a more decisive role in forming the population's political and consumer consciousness. This role of the media is particularly true in Western democracies. Such media (now along with social media) are pervasive, invading every aspect of social life and providing government and corporations (and now foreign entities) with the means for manufacturing consent.

Mills also outlines a middle level of power between the elite and the masses. This intermediate level comprises special interest groups, opinion leaders, professional organizations, public intellectuals, and celebrities. Most of these groups are economically dependent on economic and government bureaucracies; most do not have labor unions' economic power to balance this dependence. However, this level has some organization and resources and limited capacity to affect minor issues through its representation in Congress and political parties. Nevertheless, they neither represent the masses nor significantly impact the elite. The power elite ensures no serious challenge to its interests is allowed in the political arena (Mills, 1958, p. 36).

The liberal theory of government resulting from a moving balance of forces depends upon an assumption of truly independent units of roughly equal power. According to Mills, this assumption rested upon the existence of a large and self-determining middle class. However, the old middle class declined with the small businessman, the true independent professional, and the family farm. A new type of white-collar worker and quasi-professional dependent upon large corporate, government, and military bureaucracies has replaced this old middle class. The new middle class is in the same economic position as the wage worker, dependent upon large organizations for their livelihood. Politically, they are in worse condition, for few are in labor unions (p. 36).

The clash between competing interests occurs at the middle level of power, but it is mainly a conflict over a slice of the existing pie. Political commentators and political scientists write about this struggle, but it is removed from any debate over fundamental policy. Even here, Mills asserted, the conflict among competing interests becomes muted as these interests increasingly become integrated into the apparatus of the state. Bureaucratic administration replaces politics, and the maneuvering of cliques replaces the open clash of parties.

Integrating previously autonomous political forces (such as labor, professional organizations, and farmers) into the modern state is overt in contemporary totalitarianism. Under such regimes, independent organizations are co-opted and integrated as appendages of the nation-state. In formal democracies, the process is much less advanced and explicit, yet it is still well underway. These interest groups increasingly maneuver within and between the state's political parties and organizations seeking to become a part of the state. Their chief desire is to maintain their organizations and secure their members' maximum economic advantage (pp. 39–41). Thus, the middle level of power does not question the elite's rule, nor does it seek any benefit for the great masses of men and women outside of their organizations.

In societies where power is diffused and decentralized, history results from innumerable decisions by numerous men. All contribute to eventual changes in the social structure. No individual or small group has much control in such societies, and history moves "behind men's backs." However, Mills asserts that in social systems where the means of power have become enlarged and centralized, those who control the dominant bureaucracies modify the structural conditions in which most people live. They have the means of affecting history (p. 22). The positions of the elite allow them to transcend the environments of ordinary men and women. The elite have access to levers of power that make their decisions and actions consequential. In a society where structural institutions have become enlarged, centralized, and all-encompassing, who controls these institutions becomes the central issue. One principal consequence of this fact, Mills writes, is that modern nation-state leaders can exert much more coordination and control over the state's actions.

To date, Mills feared these leaders were acting (or failing to act) irresponsibly, thus leading the state and its citizens to disaster. However, this does not mean that it always must be so. The immense structural change that has enlarged the means and extent of power and concentrated it in so few hands now makes it imperative to hold these men responsible for the events (p. 100). With the publication of *The Causes of World War III* in 1958, Mills seemed more concerned with the rise of militarism among the elite than with the hypothesis that many elites were military men. According to Mills, the rise of the military state serves the interests of corporate and government elites. For politicians, the projection of military power covers a lack of vision and innovative leadership. For corporate elites, the preparations for war and military action underwrite their research and development and guarantee stable profits through corporate subsidies (p. 87). This militarism is inculcated in the population through schoolroom and pulpit patriotism, through manipulation and control of the news, the cultivation of opinion leaders, propaganda, and nationalistic ideology.

Mills asserts that it is not just the existence of a power elite that has allowed this manufactured militarism to dominate. The apathy and moral insensibility of the masses and the political inactivity of intellectuals in communist and capitalist countries enable militarism. Most intellectual, scientific, and religious leaders echo the elaborate confusions of the elite. They refuse to question elite policies; they refuse to offer alternatives. They have abdicated their role, allowing the elite to rule unhindered (Mills, 1958, pp. 88–89).

Capitalism

Mills' view of capitalism is influenced by Weber's and Marx's macrosocial theories. According to Marx, the class that owns or controls the mode of production (the combined forces and relations of production) is, by definition, the ruling class. "What else does the history of ideas prove, than that intellectual production changes its character in proportion as material production is changed? The ruling ideas of each age have ever been the ideas of its ruling class" (Marx & Engels, 1848, p. 19). Marx reasserted that the capitalist class exerted a controlling interest in the English government in Volume 1 of Capital. These ruling ideas emphasize maintaining the status quo and promoting ideas that enhance already powerful positions. Because the capitalist class controls the forces of production, the class can also dominate non-economic institutions. The ruling class's viewpoints become the widely accepted view of society through influence or outright control over critical institutions such as media, government, foundations, and higher education. The United States began as a nation of small capitalists, but the economy has been transforming into one dominated by large corporations since the Civil War. The growth of government and military power matches this enlargement and centralization of the economy.

However, Mills does not restrict himself to capitalists alone in asserting his power elite hypothesis. The power of the ruling classes in mature capitalist societies, according to Mills, is rooted in the economic, government, and military bureaucracies. These organizations give the elite the authority to make (or often not to make) consequential decisions. Their power is based on their command of the significant bureaucracies in American society. They run the corporations, the levers of government, and the military establishment. "They occupy the strategic command posts of the social structure, in which are now centered the effective means of power and wealth and the celebrity that they enjoy" (1956, pp. 3-4).

One of the most significant contradictions of capitalism that Marx writes about is production's tendency to overrun consumption, glutting the market with goods and services that it cannot sell, thus causing periodic economic crises of recession and depression. Capital seeks to address this contradiction by continually seeking new markets for its goods and services. Mills writes of the importance of consumerism in American life. To create new markets, corporations must relentlessly sell their products. Mills writes that this continuous selling has turned America into a "Big Bazaar," central to understanding the family and the factory. The Bazaar feeds, clothes, amuses, supplies all life wants and necessities, and creates new needs and wants! "What factory is geared so deep and direct with what people want and what they are becoming? Measured by space or measured by money, it is the greatest emporium in the world; it is a world—dedicated to commodities" (1951, p. 167). According to Mills, consuming has become a new religion, becoming, for many, the meaning of life itself.

Mills asserts that nation-states are not homogenous units; they do not possess the will, intellect, interests, or honor. The nation-state merely refers to a defined territory organized under the authority of a government. It is a dominating apparatus that monopolizes the legitimate use of force and authority within that territory. "'Legitimate means more or less generally acquiesced in by publics and masses, for reasons in which they believe. In the case of the nation-state these reasons are the symbols and ideologies of nationalism" (1958, p. 53). In the "superstates," the power and authority are concentrated in the hands of economic, military, and political institutions. This small elite makes the internal and international decisions that affect all (p. 54).

In 1951, Mills described a robust welfare system that actively alleviates inequalities and offers some protection to lower-income classes. "Not so much free labor markets as the power of pressure groups now shape the class positions and privileges of various strata in the United States" (1951, p. 299). He describes a welfare system that attempts to manage class relations without modifying the class structure. He writes that the welfare system limits the exploitation of those most exposed to the free market's vagaries so that the victims do not revolt. It is in this analysis of the American welfare state where Mills seems the most dated. Over the last 40 years, the American elite has dismantled large parts of the welfare system, seeing it only as a drain on their hard-earned wealth rather than a mechanism of alleviating class antagonisms and possible revolt. Mills also recognized that the welfare state served the middle levels of power. Labor unions, trade associations, industry groups, and agricultural interests vie for political favors.

They lobby for tax breaks, subsidies, transfer payments, and government contracts. Increasingly, Mills writes, the state determines the privileges and wealth of these organized interest groups (1951, p. 299).

Rationalization

According to Mills, the increased application of technological rationality is a permanent feature of modern industrial societies. The continuing industrial revolution is "the master trend of our time" (1958, p. 74); in the name of efficiency, both the means of production and consumption become exploitive and alienating. Mills notes that the political economy—the combination of private capital and the political establishment—controls the avenues to wealth, income, access to consumer goods, and the power over productive capital (1956, p. 10). Therefore, social life is increasingly subject to the manipulations of private and public bureaucracies. The theme of his main body of work is on the enlargement and centralization of bureaucratic coordination. Like Weber before him, he examines this bureaucratization's effects on the individual's freedom and autonomy, alienation, and moral compass. Mills was concerned about the social order, as bureaucratization threatened democracy and reason in the guidance of human affairs.

According to Weber, public and private bureaucracies increasingly centralize and broaden their scope in advanced industrial societies. Bureaucracies are human organizations specifically designed to efficiently achieve the organization's goals, whatever those goals may be. Public bureaucracies are organized around such purposes as the administration of justice, collecting taxes, or providing education. Corporate bureaucracies seek to maximize their capital through winning public contracts, foreign trade, or marketing goods and services to the consumer economy.

Max Weber wrote of two broad types of rationality. The first, "formal rationality," is goal-oriented action based on observation and logic; the individual or the organization has a goal, for example, to increase capital, and they take logical steps to achieve that goal. The individual bases these steps on pure rationality—tradition, values, and emotions do not enter the equation. Formal rationality contrasts with "substantive rationality," or goal-oriented behavior pursued within a wholistic context of human values, emotions, and traditions. Population growth and the growing complexity of production and marketing necessitate the development of bureaucratization of the social structure for coordination. As societies become more bureaucratic, Weber writes, formal rationality becomes a dominant motivator of human actions; substantive rationality becomes less of a factor. Formal rationality becomes a habit of thought, the *modus operandi* of behavior, and the primary way of judging individuals, institutions, and the world around us. Weber calls this the "rationalization process."

However, Weber warns that just because an action is rational in achieving a short-term goal does not mean it is rational in terms of the wider society or even the bureaucracy's long-term goals. It often happens that the single-minded pursuit of practical goals can undermine the foundations of the social order, a situation that Weber described as "the existence of those fundamental elements of irrationality—a conflict between formal and substantive rationality of the sort which sociology so often encounters" (Weber [1921] 1968, 225). What is good for the bureaucracy is not always good for society as a whole—and often, in the long term, it is not good for the bureaucracy either.

Mills echoes these concerns regarding the irrationality of rationalization. He is primarily concerned with rationalization's threat to such traditional values as freedom and democracy. In the past, there was a positive relationship between rationality and freedom, as formal rationality became an increasingly prominent motivator to human action; it freed the individual from the bonds of tradition, superstition, and ignorance. Nevertheless, borrowing heavily from Weber, Mills asserts it was not to last. Rather than rationality being seated in the individual, formal rationality is increasingly taking form in bureaucratic organizations. Bureaucracies have usurped "both freedom and rationality" from the individual through its rules, planning, measurement, and monitoring. "The calculating hierarchies of department store and industrial corporation, of rationalized office and government bureau, lay out the gray ways of work and stereotype the permitted initiatives. And in all this bureaucratic usurpation of freedom and of rationality, the white-collar people are the interchangeable parts of the big chains of authority that bind the society together" (1951, p. xvii).

In *White Collar*, Mills (1951) writes about the rationalization process of Americans' work life. Rationality is taking on a new form, to be increasingly seated in the big-scale large organizations ruled by bureaucracy. A prime example, he writes, concerns the professions. Rather than the independent professional of the nineteenth and early twentieth centuries, in which broad knowledge of a field was cultivated and valued, most professionals today work for large organizations. In such organizations, professionals have become managers overseeing junior professionals, semi-professionals, and assistants performing routine, though often highly specialized, tasks. "So decisive have such shifts been, in some areas, that it is as if rationality itself has been expropriated from the individual and been located, as a new form of brain power, in the ingenious bureaucracy itself" (p. 112).

Mills applies Weber's insight into his analyses of twentieth-century American society, though using somewhat different terminology. Mills calls it "rationality without reason," and in reference to elites engaged in the Cold War, "crackpot realism" (1958, p. 175). Bureaucratic rationality, he writes, is not merely a reflection of the will and reason of the individuals who make up the organization—the bureaucracy usurps the individual's capacity to reason as well as their freedom. "In fact, often they are a means of tyranny and manipulation, a means of expropriating the very chance to reason, the very capacity to act as a free man" (1959, p. 169).

Social Studies

The bureaucratic ethos extends to using social science methods of abstract empiricism by public and private bureaucracies for such diverse activities as selling deodorant and candidates. "As it is practiced in business—especially in the communication adjuncts of advertising—in the armed forces, and increasingly in universities as well, 'the new social science' has come to serve whatever ends its bureaucratic clients may have in view" (p. 101). Rather than be focused on traditional social problems and issues, social science in bureaucracies' service adopts the client's political, military, or business perspective. It seeks to increase the efficiency and effectiveness of bureaucratic domination in modern society (pp. 115-116).

Abstract empiricism is a style of doing sociology that Mills maintained tended to obscure thought rather than increase people's understanding of human social behavior. It consists of reifying empiricism and research methods above substance—substituting statistical significance for substantive significance. According to Mills, sociologists have become experts in surveys and collecting facts rather than developing expertise in social phenomena. In misguided attempts to ape the physical sciences in sophisticated methodology, it leads to "thin and uninteresting" results (p. 205). One can get a feel of why his contemporaries so disliked him in the following passage.

> Those in the grip of methodological inhibitions often refuse to say anything about modern society unless it has been through the fine little mill of The Statistical Ritual [...] Moreover, as for 'importance,' surely it is important when some of the most energetic minds among us use themselves up in the study of details because The Method to which they are dogmatically committed does not allow them to study anything else. Much of such work, I am now convinced, has become the mere following of ritual—which happens to have gained commercial and foundation

value—rather than, in the words of its spokesmen, a 'commitment to the hard demands of science' (pp. 71-72).

According to Mills, a mystique has grown up around methodology and statistics that is primarily misplaced. While it provides valuable exercises for students and gives employment to unimaginative social scientists, it does not often advance the discipline or our understanding of the social order (p. 205). Empirical research should aim to discipline ideas and theories; it should not be an end in itself (p. 71).

Mills is even more scornful of the social sciences' tendency toward what he called "grand theory" (pp. 25-49). Such theory was a tendency that was perhaps not as widespread as Mills thought, and somewhat short-lived. His critique may have been more of a personal one toward Talcott Parsons' work rather than a general tendency in the field.

Like classic social analysis, Mills believed that social studies should be multidisciplinary, rooted in history, and focused upon substantive problems of urgent public interest. He further thought that the classical tradition helps understand and analyze contemporary issues and human troubles. Mills advocated a type of social studies that focused on significant problems of the era using methods and conceptions from several disciplines. A social scientist needs not master all the "materials and perspectives" of the various fields to bring clarity to critical social issues. Specialization should occur around social problems rather than the traditional disciplines (p. 142). Moreover, Mills adds that any social study worthy of the name is historical; quoting Paul Sweezy, he asserts that sociology should attempt to write "the present as history" (p. 146). However, Mills saw impediments to this tradition fulfilling its promise, obstacles from within the discipline and their academic and political settings.

C. Wright Mills asserts that the sociological imagination is characteristic of traditional social analysts—singling out Emile Durkheim, Karl Marx, and Max Weber, among others, in this regard (p. 6). He writes that such classical theorists, whatever particular problem they are writing about, focus upon three broad themes. First, they analyze society's structure and its components, asking how the various parts relate to one another and the whole. A functionalist is a systems theorist; they examine how the different elements interact with one another and to the whole. This interaction includes contributions to maintenance as well as to change in society.

Second, one who practices the sociological imagination, like the classical theorists, is concerned with historical analysis. What are the master historical trends by which society is changing? How does the historical period in which it exists affect the various parts and the whole sociocultural system? What are the essential features of the historical period? How do these features differ from what has come before or after? Who or what is capable of making history in this historical era? Who has the power to get their way despite the opposition of others? "Every social science—or better, every well-considered social study—requires an historical scope of conception and a full use of historical materials" (p. 145). The interactions of men and women, Mills writes, are only intelligible to themselves and the social scientist in the context of the social and historical structures that pattern and circumscribe their perceptions, motivations, and life chances (1951, p. xx). Change in these structures will often scramble the prevailing attitudes, beliefs, and motivations, causing confusion and stress among the population.

The third characteristic of the classical theorists, and those who practice the sociological imagination, focuses on people. "What varieties of men and women now prevail in this society and in this period? And what varieties are coming to prevail? In what ways are they selected and formed, liberated and repressed, made sensitive and blunted?" (1959, p. 7). One can see this in Marx's analysis of capitalism's structure and dynamic and its effects on the bourgeoisie and proletariat. It is apparent in Durkheim's focus on population growth and the division of labor, the impact of these forces on social cohesion, and the resulting anomie of individual members of the society. Finally, it is evident in Max Weber's analysis of the effects of bureaucracy's growth and the consequent rationalization in modern society. Mills borrows heavily from these traditions in his studies of American social order and change.

Very often, changing social structures cause problems experienced by men and women in their daily lives. Further, as society becomes more interconnected and complex, the pace of social change increases and becomes more encompassing. Therefore, we must look beyond the individuals involved to understand such personal troubles. Our time's significant problems, Mills argues, require social scientists with imagination, those who can look beyond narrow disciplinary boundaries and bring all of the tools, concepts, theories, and methods to bear in clarifying the significant problems plaguing our world. "It is in terms of such topical 'problems,' rather than in accordance with academic boundaries, that specialization ought to occur" (p. 142). The topical problem that Mills investigates in his major works is the intensifying application of rationality to producing and selling goods and services and the resulting bureaucratization of social organization, ultimately undermining human reason itself.

Conclusions

In 1957, Mills wrote a letter to the editor of Commentary discussing his Marxian influence. "Let me say explicitly: I happen never to have been what is called 'a Marxist,' but I believe Karl Marx one of the most astute students of society modern civilization has produced; his work is now essential equipment of any adequately trained social scientist as well as of any properly educated person. Those who say they hear Marxian echoes in my work are saying that I have trained myself well. That they do not intend this testifies to their own lack of proper education" (Mills, K. & Mills, P., 2000, p. 237). One indeed hears echoes of Marx in his work. Marx's influence is evident in Mills' emphasis on alienation and capitalism's centrality in determining the sociocultural system's dominant character.

Nevertheless, capitalism is characterized above all by Weber's concept of rationalization utilized to maximize profit. This rationalization is evident in capital's intensifying production technology, the ever more detailed division of labor, automation, rational distribution systems, and the application of science and communications technology to market its goods and services. Rationalization is the master trend, and capital's private bureaucracies continuously strive to maximize surplus value (profit). Mills sees capitalism as a political-economic system that merges with governments to exploit labor and consumers. The intensification of the industrial mode of production increases government bureaucracies' power and authority in coordinating the conditions (infrastructural, legal, monetary, and administrative) for industrial growth. As an arm of economic power, the state uses its military forces to secure additional foreign markets and resources and favorable trade arrangements. All of which promote the development of the rationalization of social life.

Mills writes that the key to power is in the technological development of the means of production and consumption; both are exploitive and leave people open to the impersonal manipulations of corporate and government bureaucracies (1958, p. 26). Mills identifies the corporate sector as the dominant bureaucracy. "Above all, the privately incorporated economy must be made over into a publicly responsible economy. I am aware of the magnitude of this task, but either we take democracy seriously or we do not. This corporate economy, as it is now constituted, is an undemocratic growth within the formal democracy of the United States" (1958, pp. 123-124).

Chapter 10: The Sociology of Norbert Elias

Norbert Elias (1897-1990) is difficult to classify. While the contemporary theorists covered in this volume have each been strongly influenced by some part of the classical tradition, the extent and nature of that influence have been variable. On one extreme, there is Braverman, who was strongly influenced by Marx to the exclusion of other theorists, rarely writing anything that contradicted Marx himself. Most other contemporary theorists based their vision on a more diverse heritage; for example, while Merton is undoubtedly influenced heavily by Durkheim, one can also find flashes of Weber and Marx among his writings. Finally, there are a few theorists who are challenging to classify. While the classical tradition influences them, the influence comes from so many diverse sources that it is *almost* arbitrary to single out a dominant strain. Examples of such synthesizers in this volume are Gerhard Lenski (to be covered later) and Norbert Elias.

However, by basing classification on the "prime mover," "change agent," or "engine of history" within the theory, the categorization of which school a theorist belongs to—Marx, Durkheim, Weber, or Malthus—becomes based on firmer criteria. While many theorists influenced Mills, for example, the prime mover of his theory is rationalization; thus, his theory is well within the tradition of Weber. Wallerstein's engine is capitalism; thus, his theory aligns with Marx and Engels. Norbert Elias is also a synthesizer, though one in the Weberian tradition.

Why classify Elias's theory as being within the Weberian tradition? First, like Weber, Elias attempts to bridge the gap between macro and micro sociology, focusing on how structural and individual personalities interact in social change. Second, Elias's "civilization process" has much in common with Weber's concept of rationalization, having similar origins in the changing character of interactions between social structure and individual personality. Indeed, the civilization process is Elias's attempt to subsume rationalization in a much broader trend that includes the ever stricter control of impulses, drives, and emotions, an advance in personal shame and embarrassment regarding our animal nature (our bodies, elimination, and sexuality), and putting such "animalic" activities behind the scenes of social life (Elias, [1939] 2000, p. 414). Third, the underlying engine of change within Elias's theory is the "monopoly mechanism," based on the enlargement and centralization of administrative structures that parallel Weber's bureaucratization process. Fourth, and finally, Elias, like Weber, advocates value-free sociology. He criticizes many 19th-century theorists for failing to keep their ideology, hopes, and class interests out of their sociology. He is also a critic of his contemporaries on this score.

This is not to say that Elias has no other influences or slavishly follows Weber's every lead. He has a strong independent streak and is free with his criticisms, rejections, and revisions of Weber's work. Elias has also been influenced by other theoretical traditions, notably Auguste Comte and Emile Durkheim, focusing on the importance of the division of labor and growing mutual dependence in social life. Nevertheless, Weber is the dominant influence on Elias's theory.

Like other theorists in this volume, Elias remarks that contemporary sociologists have strayed from the discipline's roots. He says that nineteenth-century theorists primarily focused on the long-term social change process, while most twentieth-century theorists seem fascinated with stability and equilibrium (Elias, [1968] 2000, p. 458). Much of this is due, Elias reports, to the tendency of the discipline's founders to mix their political opinions and ideologies into their sociology. People of the nineteenth century strongly believed in the ideal of progress. Social scientists often mixed this belief with their factual descriptions and predictions, thus shifting their focus from what is to what "ought to be" (p. 468). Twentieth-century sociologists strongly rejected the idea of progress; subsequent generations of social scientists had access to far more accurate historical and empirical data that failed to support many of the assertions of the founders (p. 458). Rather than revise classical theories or choose what is useful and supported by valid and reliable evidence, most social theorists reject the traditional macro-theory concerned with long-term social change. Instead, they turned to a vision of society as a static entity. Elias says that part of this was an overreaction to the ideal of progress embodied in much of nineteenth-century social theory. However, part of the rejection is also based on the values and beliefs of contemporary theorists.

The belief in progress by nineteenth-century sociologists was not due to simple advances in science and technology in the nineteenth century. The advance was insignificant compared to the twentieth century, and there is little relationship between such advances in standard of living, health, life expectancy, and modern comforts and faith in progress (p. 462). Elias asserts that if such a relationship existed, numerous scientific revolutions since World War II would have made us all true believers. Instead, Elias contends that many nineteenth-century sociologists were part of the rising industrial classes—the middle or working classes. They sought confirmation in their theories that the future was theirs and that their ideals and class interests would be achieved through social development (p. 461). Twentieth-century sociologists lost this faith in progress despite advances in science and technology because of this same technology's association with world wars and the real threat of nuclear or other technical annihilation (p. 462).

Nevertheless, Elias discerns another reason for this loss of faith. Sociologists in the West are now predominantly of established classes in mature industrial societies. While not in decline, these societies no longer dominate the world as they once did (p. 464). Moreover, the economic and political equality trends of former colonies and dependent nation-states to these former dominant powers are not reversing. "Theories which reflect the ideals of rising classes in expanding industrial societies have been replaced by theories dominated by the ideals of more or less established classes in highly developed societies whose growth has reached or passed its peak" (p. 466).

The result is that the social theory of the 20th century has a very conservative caste derived from observation and measurement of present-day democratic industrial societies of the West. Such societies are highly centralized, with a high division of labor and less inequality than societies at earlier stages of development. With such an exclusive focus on a particular social type, Elias asks, how can sociologists develop general social theories that successfully model slave or feudal states of the past or even authoritarian states of the present? Societies are so vastly different from Western democracies, Elias adds, that "not even the same laws, let alone the same norms and values, apply to all people" (pp. 467-468).

Because of these problems, Elias argues for a historical sociology that embraces the idea of long-term social processes. However, unlike many 19th-century thinkers, a value-free sociology does not confuse sociological description and prediction with the investigator's ideology, beliefs, or wishes. Elias believes that by continuing the scientific enterprise, the social sciences can develop more realistic ideas about human societies and behavior, slowly discrediting fantasy and ideology and thus making a real contribution to social practice (p. 468).

Individual and Society

The idea behind Elias's key concept of "the civilizing process" is essentially Weberian. Personality and social structure are closely interrelated—as social structure changes, so does the individual personality structure, which causes a further change in social structure. Humans are oriented by nature and nurture (social learning through informal socialization, education, and socially created reciprocal need) to exist only in interdependent relationships with others (pp. 481-482). It is through these interdependencies (or "figurations") that individuals define the self and the world. They satisfy their needs and orient their thoughts and actions. As these figurations change, individual personality structure necessarily changes as well. Like a dance, Elias writes, the figuration is independent of the individuals who make it up at any time; its character and form largely orient them to one another. However, the character and form of the dance depend on historical and contemporary individuals who make up the figuration (p. 482). The individual and society (figurations) are, therefore, inseparable. They are parts of a single whole, incapable of being understood as separate phenomena (p. 469).

To support this assertion of the interrelationship and interdependence of social and individual structures, Elias looks at changes in the habitus (personal habits such as eating, sleeping, sex, natural body functions, and bathing) of people from the Middle Ages through the 1930s by examining etiquette books. He finds the change in prohibition and recommendation in a specific direction across generations, without any conscious coordination or control by individuals or social structures. This change includes the ever-stricter control of impulse and emotion, first in public and then in private as well; an advance in personal shame and embarrassment regarding our animal nature (our bodies, waste elimination, sleep, and sexuality); and putting such "animalic" activities behind the scenes (privacy in bedrooms, bathrooms, kitchens) of social life. He roots these changes in concurrent social structure changes, an enlargement and centralization of authority structures (the state), with its monopoly on force and taxation, and the consequent growth of interdependence fostered by the increasing division of labor. However, we will first explore the specific nature of the changes.

Elias contends that socially instilled conduct is part of a person's whole way of life and that the prescribed conduct for activities such as eating reflects people's relation to one another and their whole social world (Elias, [1939] 2000, p. 39). In the Middle Ages, people ate from a common dish, taking meat with their fingers, drinking from a common goblet, and spooning soup from the same pot. Elias asserts that this sharing of utensils and dishes should not be interpreted as a lack of civilization on the part of medieval people but rather as a reflection of their relationship with one another. These people were not emotionally separated from one another to the same degree as individuals in our own time. They were not socialized into relationships and behaviors that separate "one human body and another," but rather to a social world in which individuals were more a part of a homogenous whole. Consequently, medieval people lacked the instilled affective reaction against coming into contact with food that might have touched someone else's mouth, had little shame or embarrassment in observing others engaging in bodily functions such as waste elimination or bathing, or exposing themselves thus engaged to the sight of others (p. 60).

The pattern of the civilization process is similar across behaviors. In medieval societies, behaviors accepted as normal or only mildly prohibited gradually became proscribed, more strictly controlled, or taboo. At first, Elias states, the prohibitions were given their force through appeals not to offend others, on purely social grounds; as we approach modernity, the restraints became a part of the socialization of children and therefore internalized and functioning even when the individual is alone (p. 117). Such behaviors became invested with learned feelings of shame and embarrassment on the part of individuals as they internalized the social proscriptions of their society (p. 118).

This process can be demonstrated by examining etiquette books on the socially approved ways to perform such natural functions as eliminating gas, excrement, and urine. Early works of etiquette enjoined their readers not to greet someone who is defecating or urinating (1530), to not relieve oneself in front of ladies like a "rustic" (1570), and to "not foul the staircases, corridors or closets with urine or other filth" (1589) (pp. 110-112). On passing gas (either from above or below), early advice was to do it without noise, if possible, "but it is better that it be emitted with a noise than that it be held back," or cover it with a cough (1530). As we approach modern times, Elias points out, such prohibitions and instructions on bodily functions could no longer be openly written about, nor were they needed. While feelings of shame and embarrassment over these issues were absent in the Middle Ages, the gradual development of these feelings prevented their discussion as we approach modern times (p. 114). Elias says this delicacy in discussing such issues is now [the 1930s] being relaxed, particularly compared to the nineteenth century. People can now more freely talk about natural functions without the "forced smile" or embarrassment of the past. This lack of embarrassment is because the individual has so thoroughly internalized the control of the behavior that such discussion does not jeopardize it. "It is a relaxation within the framework of an already established standard" (p. 119). However, like all impulse control, in the late Middle Ages, such proscriptions had to be openly discussed in books and taught to members of the upper class at court; only with the rise of the middle classes did the family become the institution responsible for the internalization of such drive control (pp. 116-117).

Another aspect of the civilizing process discussed by Elias is the prohibitions and prescriptions regarding sexuality. Again, the process runs the familiar course, lightly prohibited at first, gradually taking on social condemnation, the violation of prohibitions and prescribed behavior then taking on feelings of shame and embarrassment. While monogamous marriage has long been the ideal in the West and has long been buttressed by the Church, "the actual control and molding of sexual relations" has changed over time (p. 154). Monogamy only became binding on both sexes late in Western history when the sexual drive had come under firm social control, and individuals have internalized socially approved expression. It is only in recent times that extramarital relations have become "really ostracized socially" and "subjected to absolute secrecy" (p. 154). The civilization of the sex drive does not seek to eliminate sexuality, only control, restrict, channel, and hide it from public view. Over time, the drive is invested with shame and embarrassment; people become more reserved in discussing it. From within the family, the individual is taught "habitual self-restraint," as well as the proper expression and prohibitions of the drive. Other socialization agents and institutions—indeed the very "structure of social life"— reinforce the civilized drive, which becomes internalized and part of the self (p. 158).

Other aspects of the civilizing process can be illustrated by examining Elias's discussion of the ever-stricter personal control of emotions. Again, Elias considers the Middle Ages his standard, conceding that the transformation probably began well before this age. Elaborating on the expression of aggression and cruelty in war as an example, Elias states that while not as uninhibited as they once were in ancient times, cruelty and torture were given freer rein on medieval battlefields than on modern ones (p. 162). In earlier times, warriors were free (and often encouraged) to take pleasure in killing and torturing others, while now they are increasingly restricted through laws, rules of engagement, and threats of punishment, as well as a learned sense of shame and repugnance to such activity. In modern times, these behaviors are expressed in soldiers only when social control breaks down (p. 162). Modern warfare is conducted far more impersonally, directed by faceless leaders against a usually invisible enemy. "And immense social upheaval and urgency, heightened by carefully concerted propaganda, are needed to reawake and legitimize in large masses of people the socially outlawed drives, the joy in killing and destruction that have been repressed from everyday civilized life" (p. 170). Elias recognizes that there are short-term reversals of the civilizing process—say, torture again becoming acceptable to a government (if not a people) after it has long been banned. However, despite these reversals, the long-term trend is clear.

Elias also writes that these "pleasures" gradually take on an indirect and "refined" form. Again, this transition of emotional life follows the familiar pattern: the free expression of aggression and hostility gradually being prohibited and channeled by rational rules as we approach modernity; the exercise of force and aggression being delegated to a few (police, soldiers), rules of engagement formulated and enforced, expressions of hostility pushed behind the scenes in modern life. The outlet for aggressive drives and urges on the part of the broader population is channeled into socially approved forms of spectator sports, movies, and literature (pp. 170-171).

According to Elias, outbursts of such emotions as joy, anger, cruelty, hatred, and celebration were much closer to the surface in medieval social life. People acted more in line with their affective drives and feelings in these times—more "easily," "freely," "spontaneously," "directly," "quickly," and "openly" than in modern times (pp. 162-163; p. 180). Elias again attributes this to the structure of social and personal life. People lived without physical security in a society where death from violence, accidents, and disease was a daily occurrence; neither life nor property was safe from confiscation by others. No central authority could keep order; it could force people to keep the peace or "exercise restraint" in dealing with one another (p. 169). Such a situation gives strong encouragement to live fully for the moment. Consequently, there was minimal self-control or social restraint on the free expression of one's emotional life (pp. 169-170).

It is important to note that Elias does not believe the civilizing process follows a linear development path. There are reversals, countertrends, and sudden and rapid changes in either direction. However, over the long term, the direction of change is unmistakable (p. 157). Moreover, that change can be characterized as more significant self-control of affective behavior (human drives and emotions). The fact that the change in the civilizing process *is* directional and occurs across generations without the conscious control of institutions or individuals is remarkable and begs for explanation. Furthermore, Elias has one.

Centralization and State Formation

There is a parallel structural process at work that, beginning in the Middle Ages, led to the formation of states and the eventual monopoly of these states over the means of violence and taxation. The rise of the state brings about a dramatic change in the social structure that has far-reaching consequences on social life. Before the state, the individual had to be constantly fearful of physical attack, destruction, or confiscation of property. With a stable monopoly of force and taxation, life becomes more predictable for the individual and more amenable to planning, deferred gratification, and rational conduct.

Elias believes that the rise of the monetary economy gives kings and princes a gradually growing advantage in their struggles to wrest power from petty feudal lords. Moreover, this gradual centralization, bringing increased territory, wealth, and power to an increasing absolutist monarchy, eventually transformed the West, bringing about the rise of civilization (p. 188).

Under feudal conditions, the upper class consisted of independent warrior knights on their estates who owed but loose allegiance to any central authority. Over time, these independent warriors in manors and estates gradually lost their independence and were reduced to dependent courtiers. That this was a structural process and not the result of a historical accident is attested to by the fact that it occurred across Europe roughly simultaneously; that we speak of the "age of absolutism" (p. 188). Nor is it a coincidence, Elias says, that it parallels the civilization process itself, which was closely "linked to the formation of the hierarchical social order with the absolute ruler and, more broadly, his court at its head" (p. 188). The formation of the absolutist court demanded a change in the behavior, drives, and emotions of former warrior nobility; to retain standing, the nobility had to civilize their behavior to come into line with their dependence on the central ruler.

> How did this increased constraint and dependence come about? How was an upper class of relatively independent warriors or knights supplanted by a more or less pacified upper class of courtiers? Why was the influence of the estates progressively reduced in the course of the Middle Ages and the early modern period, and why, sooner or later, was the dictatorial "absolute" rule of a single figure, and with it, the compulsion of courtly etiquette, the pacification of large or smaller territories from a single centre, established for a greater or lesser period of time in all the countries of Europe? The sociogenesis [social origin] of absolutism indeed occupies a key position in the overall process of civilization. The civilizing of conduct and the corresponding transformation of the structure of mental and emotional life cannot be understood without tracing the process of state-formation, and within it the advancing centralization of society which first found particularly visible expression in the absolutist form of rule (p. 191).

Like a true Weberian, Elias believes that there are several factors behind the rise of the state. Primarily, he believes the rise of the money economy at the expense of barter is the most crucial factor. Money weakened the feudal lords on fixed rents and strengthened the middle-class merchants and artisans who produced and traded wealth and the central ruler whose tax system gave him a share in the growing economy (p. 192).

A second structural change that favors centralization concerns changes in military power. Under feudalism, vassals (including the nobility) were obligated to give the central ruler military service in return for their estates. As the economy grew, central rulers had funds to raise, equip, and maintain armies, growing less and less dependent upon the services of their feudal warriors (p. 192). At the same time, there were changes in military techniques that changed the character of warfare and further devalued the services of the nobility. These techniques included the development of mass infantry, which again was advantageous to the central ruler (pp. 192-193). Elias reports that the nobility lost their monopoly on weapons and soldiering, which passed into a single ruler's hands (p. 193).

In addition to these structural developments that promoted the state's rise, Elias believes one other is important enough to describe in detail. This is the rise of the bourgeois classes. The wealth and power of these classes were also dependent upon the rise of the money economy. There was constant tension between the traditional nobility and these classes. While the tensions and conflicts varied between societies and over time, centralized rulers quickly learned to exploit these tensions and interest groups, supporting one for a time and then the other to neutralize and prevent either from gaining too much power and becoming a true rival to the ruler and the absolute state (p. 194).

In addition to these structural changes, several technological developments also promoted centralization and the rise of the state. These technological changes included the slow development of firearms that gave massed infantry advantage over a few nobles fighting on horseback (p. 192); advances in bureaucratic organization that enabled efficient rule (p. 239); and advances in communication and transportation which allowed the centralized authority to effectively rule over ever larger areas (pp. 238-239).

Another way of looking at these technological and structural factors that promoted the rise of the state is to look at them as factors that change the balance between the forces of centralization and decentralization. The rise of the monetary economy promotes centralization by replacing land ownership as the dominant form of wealth. As long as land is wealth, processes of centralization and decentralization (feudalization) alternate: military competition among small estates in a given region for dominance (more land, wealth, and power), eventual supremacy by one lord who then dominates many warriors, and then a wave of decentralization as that lord and his descendants allocate estates to their supporters and warriors to start the process anew (p. 313). The rise of a monetary economy and the creation of wealth from manufacturing and trade break this cycle. The development of firearms and mass armies, bureaucracy, transportation, and communication have a similar effect on the forces of centralization versus decentralization, allowing kingdoms and states to grow ever more extensive and powerful. The monopoly mechanism is the engine of social change that has been operating throughout history but has been unleashed by this change in the balance of forces between centralization and decentralization.

The Monopoly Mechanism

To grasp the general monopoly mechanism, readers should consider the discussion of state formation appearing above or the formation of economic monopolies under capitalism. As previously stated, with the evolution of modernity, the nation-state has achieved a monopoly on tax monies and the use of force within a given area. The modern state can be defined as a monopoly over a given area (p. 268). The formation of the state with its monopoly on force makes possible restricted economic competition within its area of control, which makes the operation of the monopoly mechanism among economic units inevitable (p. 277; pp. 303-304). Though the resulting competition is constrained and excludes the use of force, the mechanism works similarly.

The mechanism of monopoly, according to Elias, operates whenever there are several social units of roughly equal social power competing for scarce resources—usually, Elias adds, the means of production. In such a competitive situation, there will inevitably be winners and losers. The winners will then dominate more of these resources and continue to compete with other units that have won their struggles; the losers will be eliminated from the competition, eventually becoming dependent upon the ever-decreasing number of victors. Eventually, as the struggle continues, there will be a single winner or unit upon which all others become dependent. A system of free competition will have been replaced by a monopoly, which then allocates all opportunities and resources (p. 269).

Now, Elias continues, in this movement, the monopoly mechanism transforms relatively independent social positions into highly dependent positions—free knights and warriors into courtiers, or independent merchants into employees [or, in the case of Wal-Mart, associates] (p. 270). These people's personalities and affect structure—their emotions, drives, attitudes, and beliefs—are also transformed in this process. (Mills ([1951] 1973, pp. x-xiii) also makes this point regarding the transition of professionals and independent merchants to employees quite

240

forcefully). The attitudes, emotions, beliefs, skills, and drives that make a knight successful in medieval society are far different from those of a courtier. Rather than physical strength and combat skills, his success depends on resources and opportunities to be dispensed from the prince; he must now practice restraint and subordinate his desires and needs to his lords. "The means of struggle have been refined or sublimated. The restraint of the effects imposed on the individual by his dependence on the monopoly ruler has increased" (p. 274). The civilizing process has been advanced.

Moreover, this is true for those who dominate and have become dependent (p. 270). The monopoly mechanism does not stop here. It is not the case that the monopoly evolves to absolute rule by a single unit or individual, and all change ceases to operate. As the number of dependent individuals rises, their power vis-à-vis the monopolist increases. This change in power relations occurs because of their sheer numbers and because the monopolist must employ people to help fully exploit their monopoly position. "The more comprehensive the monopolized power potential, the larger the web of functionaries administering it and the greater the division of labor among them; in short, the more people on whose work or function the monopoly is in any way dependent, the more strongly does this whole field controlled by the monopolist assert its own weight and its own inner regularities" (pp. 270-271).

As the monopoly continues to develop over the centuries, there is a concurrent increase in the division of labor, and the monopolist comes to coordinate the actions of many functionaries; they become almost as dependent on these other functionaries as they are on the monopolist. Over time, resources are increasingly distributed more equally to these functionaries—first, say, to administrators, then to lower strata functionaries of the organization. The private monopoly becomes one that serves a far broader social stratum (p. 271). Moreover, this movement, Elias claims, "[…] is nothing other than a function of social interdependence" (p. 273). A monopoly with a high division of labor, he believes, will inevitably move toward a state of equilibrium in which income and advantages from the monopoly will have to be distributed on a more equitable basis than to just those at the top—even to the "advantage" of the whole figuration. Again, this is true of the state and economic monopolies; Elias does not detail any limits to the process. Restricted conflict and competition over the distribution of resources within the monopoly occur. Sometimes, the process is reversed for a time, but the long-term process is toward an equitable distribution of resources for all (pp. 273-274).

This egalitarian shift can be seen, Elias says, with the state and its passage from the rule of absolute monarchs to democracy, as well as the evolution of single-owner economic concerns and their passage to corporate structures that allocate their resources now to numerous groups of stockholders, corporate officers, administrators, employed professionals, and eventually to skilled and unskilled workers. Within a monopoly, distribution changes from a private affair in which most resources of the figuration go to the monopolist to a public monopoly in which resources are allocated to the figuration as a whole. Elias adds that this can only fully develop in societies with a high division of labor (p. 276).

Socialization

Elias details changes in the institutions by which the civilizing process is accomplished. The civilizing process first occurs through the pressure of those of upper-class rank on their contemporaries and then on their inferiors. In this stage, basic conduct rules were often written in etiquette books or repeated in aphorisms and doggerels, becoming a conscious part of court society. The rules of conduct were transmitted from above to the classes below. With the rise of the middle classes, this courtly behavior lost some of its force, and some of the behavior patterns of the bourgeoisie (particularly those involving money and sex) were merged with courtly behavior codes to become the new standard (p. 440).

As the middle and industrial classes gained ascendancy, the civilization process was accomplished through gradual changes in the socialization of youth that would instill a sense of personal shame and embarrassment regarding socially proscribed behavior (pp. 116-117). It is not until this second stage, when the family becomes the dominant institution responsible for civilizing the child that such rules of conduct are internalized early, often thought of (if at all) as "second nature."

However, Elias states that the socialization process itself was not changed. The family was and remains the primary socialization agent for children, and the supervision of youth has become no more rigorous as we approach modern times. Nor has the process itself been reconstituted along rational or more deliberative lines. It is still accomplished in the same haphazard manner, where the parents' socially patterned habits and rules are passed early on to the children, with only slight modification over the generations (p. 159). Nevertheless, through the years, the civilized rules and behaviors instilled through the socialization of children incrementally changed to incorporate the new standards of behavior and the feelings of shame, embarrassment, satisfaction, and pleasure associated with these standards (p. 109).

Elias is ignoring the role of the school here. Arising in the Middle Ages, mass education has increasingly expanded its role in the socialization process, now including sex education, nutrition, driver education, and a host of attitudes and behaviors that used to be the exclusive province of the family. As the family is a very conservative institution highly resistant to change, and the schools are very responsive to government regulation and other formal institutions that make up the structure of any society, one would expect the civilizing process to advance rapidly in the years ahead.

Elias remarks that an enormous gulf exists between adults and children's behavior because the civilizing process is now accomplished through childhood socialization. This gulf did not exist in medieval times. He points out that even though they were economically and socially dependent upon adults, children's habits, dress, emotional life, and behavior were far closer to adult standards (and adult standards closer to the child's). Further, adults did not try to protect children from the world's ways to the same degree. In keeping with the state of the civilizing process itself, sex, violence, and intimacy were more freely expressed and thus more open for children to see (pp. 147-148). Consequently, as the civilizing process changes social structures, it becomes internalized in individuals through consequent socialization. A growing gap exists between adults and children's behavior and affects (emotions) through time. There is an increasing segregation and a lengthening of childhood as well. Recognition of these changes is critical in understanding earlier personality structures and those in our own time (p. 148). Individuals have not developed in the same manner throughout history; the socialization process varies across societies and through time (pp. 153-154).

As we approach modernity, more of the civilizing process is given to early childhood socialization. Consequently, children must internalize complex behavior standards within a brief time. Their drives and urges must be channeled into the socially approved forms of expression; their behavior molded, shame and revulsion associated with their ability to uphold these standards (as well as the ability of those around them) and made part of the self. "In this the parents are only the (often inadequate) instruments, the primary agents of conditioning; through them and thousands of other instruments it is always society as a whole, the entire figuration of human beings, that exerts its pressure on the new generation, forming them more or less perfectly" (p.

119). It is through this process that the distance between the behavior of adults and children is increased, to the point that "only children were still allowed…to behave as adults did in the Middle Ages" (p. 124).

The primary mechanism for molding the child is fear. As the source of fear within a society changes, it changes the code of conduct demanded of its members (pp. 441-442). The dominant fear in Western societies was of one person for another. As the state gains a monopoly on physical violence, this fear diminishes, and "indirect or internalized fears increase proportionately" (p. 442). Elias claims that not only does the type of fear change, but also the frequency, oscillation, and intensity of that fear.

> Here, as everywhere, the structure of fears and anxieties is nothing other than the psychological counterpart of the constraints people exert on one another through the intertwining of their activities. Fears form one of the channels—and one of the most important—through which the structure of society is transmitted to individual psychological functions. The driving force underlying the change in drive economy, in the structure of fears and anxieties, is a very specific change in the social constraints acting on the individual, a specific transformation of the whole web of relationships, above all the organization of force (p. 442).

Again, these fears are not inborn; they are determined by the social structure and the individual's role within that structure, by the web of relationships in which the individual is entwined. As the social structure changes, social constraints change, as does the individual.

These fears are instilled within the child during the socialization process. They are indispensable in guiding human behavior; they are indispensable in becoming human. Once instilled in childhood, they are internalized and function automatically (pp. 442-443). Children come into the world as malleable, and their personalities and behaviors are molded through fear to conform to prevailing social standards. "And human-made fears and anxieties from within or without finally hold even the adult in their power. Shame, fear of war and fear of God, guilt, fear of punishment or of loss of social prestige, man's fear of himself, of being overcome by his own affective impulses, all these are directly or indirectly induced in a person by other people. Their strength, their form and the role they play in the individual's personality depend on the structure of his society and his or her fate within it" (p. 443).

Future

The civilizing process is ongoing, and the direction is set by state formation, economic concentration, and the consequent division of labor. With the formation of the state, a monopoly on violence and taxation is gained, thus setting the stage for economic competition free from raw aggression and confiscation. Economic competition leads to concentration and eventual monopoly, causing the masses to depend on enormous organizations for their livelihoods. The skills, attitudes, and behavior needed to succeed become refined and restrained. Economic and political monopoly leads to the growth in the division of labor and greater dependence of individuals upon one another. "As more and more people must attune their conduct to that of others, the web of action must be organized more and more strictly and accurately, if each individual action is to fulfill its social function. Individuals are compelled to regulate their conduct in an increasingly differentiated, more even and more stable manner" (p. 367). For this reason, social control becomes internalized, surrounded by shame and fear (pp. 367-368). The structural changes of political and economic concentration combine to cause a complete change in the character of the men and women who inhabit the society, a change in drive structure and emotions, and a change in the whole personality.

The competition among states and economic units within states continues to fuel the monopoly mechanism, with the division of labor a consequence of organizational growth. Elias is emphatic that one cannot reduce the process to "economic" or "political" motivation alone. Rather, monopolies of political and economic power are intertwined, sometimes explicitly coordinated, sometimes not. Elias rejects the Marxist interpretation that all can be reduced to economic infrastructure, but he does not believe it is purely political either. The same monopoly mechanism is transforming economic and political organizations; the growth of these monopolies is transforming social structures and, thus, social life (p. 437).

Merchants and corporations are driven to expand their enterprises for economic gain, fearing that competing firms will grow larger and eventually put them out of business. Similarly, Elias claims that competing states are driven to expand their power and influence despite many individuals' goodwill and yearning for peace (p. 437). "The competitive tension between states, given the pressures which our social structure brings with it, can be resolved only after a long series of violent or non-violent trials of strength have established monopolies of force, and central organizations for larger dominions, within which many smaller ones, 'states', can grow together in a more balanced unit. Here, indeed, the compelling forces of social interweaving have led the transformation of Western society in one and the same direction from the time of utmost feudal disintegration to the present" (p. 438). Moreover, it shows no sign of stopping soon.

However, the monopoly mechanism does not stop with establishing a monopoly. While the monopoly begins by granting all benefits to a few based on hereditary connections, this allocation of resources creates tensions and pressures for a more equitable redistribution of monopoly benefits. Monopolies also bring in their wake a more refined division of labor; functionaries and professionals are needed to administer and coordinate the activities. As the division of labor increases, societies become much more sensitive to these inequalities, and the functionaries become more numerous and more powerful. Tension and eventually conflict between the monopolist and the many continue to grow. These tensions can only be resolved by breaking the monopolist's control in the name of the many (p. 439). Moreover, this, according to Elias, is true for both political (states) and economic monopolies.

Monopoly formation will continue well into the foreseeable future. States will continue to engage in wars to establish monopolies of force over more extensive areas of the earth (p. 445). The process will continue until the struggle is for establishing a global monopoly of force, a single world government (pp. 445-446). Then, the process continues as the struggle for state monopoly benefits shifts from the arena of physical force to the more controlled and refined competition of the civilized. Furthermore, the same holds for the economic order. Economic monopolies will continue to enlarge and centralize; struggles for their benefits will escalate between functionaries within these organizations and between the rest of society and the organization itself. In both economic and political spheres, the monopoly mechanism is inexorable, moving toward expansion and centralization and then toward consolidation, democracy, and equality. "What cannot be decided in advance, however, is how long the ensuing struggle will take" (p. 439).

About Elias

Norbert Elias was born in Breslau, Germany (now Wroclaw in Poland) on June 22, 1897 (Information for this brief biography was obtained from Goudsblom and Mennel, 1998, Salerno, 2004, and Mennel, 2007). His father, Herman Elias, was a businessman in the textile industry, and his mother, Sophie, was a homemaker. His family lived among extended family in the Polish section of the city. Although he was Jewish, his family attended synagogue only several times a year. He finished his secondary education in 1916, receiving a solid foundation in science, mathematics, classics, languages, and literature. Upon graduation, he joined the German army, serving in the signal corps during World War I. His unit's task was to maintain telegraph lines on the Western Front; it was here that Elias experienced firsthand the horrors of war.

At the war's end, Elias began studies at Breslau University in medicine. He completed his preclinical work in medicine but was not comfortable with the medical surgery of the day and consequently turned exclusively to philosophy for his doctorate. He completed his dissertation in July 1922. However, the degree was not conferred until January 1924 because of a conflict between Elias and his dissertation supervisor, the neo-Kantian philosopher Richard Honigswald (1875-1947). "Elias's objection," writes biographer Stephen Mennell, "concerned Kant's contention that certain categories of thought—Newtonian space, time, causality, and some fundamental moral principles—are not derived from experience but are inherent, eternal, and universal in the human mind. *His rejection of that assumption is fundamental to all his subsequent work.* Its immediate effect was to lead Elias out of philosophy and into sociology, particularly the historically oriented sociology then dominant in Heidelberg, where Elias went in 1925 to pursue his further studies" (Goudsblom and Mennel 1998, pp. 5-6, emphasis added).

At Heidelberg, he studied under Alfred Weber, Max's younger brother, and was welcomed into the intellectual salon society of Marianne Weber, Max's widow. Here, Elias immersed himself in the study of both Weber and Marx. It was also at Heidelberg where he became good friends with Karl Mannheim, who brought Elias with him as his assistant upon appointment as chair of Sociology at Frankfurt in 1929. However, when the Nazis came to power in 1933, Elias barely had time to finish his thesis before fleeing the country for first France and then, two years later, England. Despite his urgings, his parents remained in Germany and died during the war; his father died at Breslau, and his mother at Auschwitz.

The Civilizing Process, a work widely considered his masterpiece, was written in this refugee period when Elias had few friends, no steady work, and few prospects. A small grant from a Jewish refugee organization allowed him to complete the project. He lived in a small, rented room, spending his days in the library of the British Museum. The book was published in Switzerland in 1939 and remained largely unread and unknown for thirty years.

Elias then picked up odd jobs at English universities—a research fellow at the London School of Economics and a guest lecturer at Cambridge. Finally, in 1954, he obtained a full-time faculty position at Leicester University. With Ilya Neustadt, they set up a successful sociology program with a strong emphasis on comparative-historical sociology (p. 85). After six years as a lecturer, Elias was promoted to Reader, a post he held till his formal retirement in 1962. Elias was a committed and prolific scholar throughout his time at Leicester till the end of his life. But it was not until 1969, with the republication of the original German text of *Uber den Prozess der Zivilisation* and the subsequent translations of the work into English, Elias became widely recognized as a significant sociological theorist, some believing he was the equal of Durkheim or even Weber.

Chapter 11: George Ritzer's Rationalization of Consumption

As is evident from the opening paragraphs of *The McDonaldization of Society (1993)*, George Ritzer's (b. 1940) analysis of contemporary society is influenced by Max Weber's rationalization theory. Ritzer did not coin the term "McDonaldization" because there was a need for new terminology to describe goal-oriented rationality's growing role in modern society. Weber developed an adequate vocabulary to describe the process eighty years ago with terms like rationalization, zweckrational, and formal vs. substantive rationality. Instead, Ritzer coined the term "McDonaldization" to describe rationalization—the exact process extensively described by Weber—because modern audiences could better identify with fast food restaurants and students could more easily relate to them (1993, p. xii). Weber, Ritzer says, viewed bureaucracy as the archetype of a rational human organization; Ritzer now views the fast-food restaurant as the prime example of rational social organization in the modern era (p. xi).

However, renaming the rationalization process after your primary example is a double-edged sword. While it resonates with people today, it does not add anything to rationalization theory. Calling the process "McDonaldization" implies that the fast-food industry represents a distinctively different type of organization than has existed in the past. Using the term implies that the fast-food industry is the prime mover in the process and is directly or indirectly related to all rationalizing institutions (p. xiii). However, Ritzer is not claiming that McDonald's represents a distinctively new form of social organization, only that it refined and applied the principles of rationalization to fast food. Nor is Ritzer claiming that the rationalization in the fast-food industry has directly or indirectly affected all other rationalizing institutions—though he sometimes comes close (p. xiii). His pivotal point in this book is that fast food is one of many institutions undergoing the rationalization process in contemporary society, albeit one that has carried the process further than most. For these reasons, this chapter will use the terminology developed by Weber to describe the rationalization process.

In addition to Weber, Karl Marx influenced Ritzer, though this influence was felt in his later writings. While Marx is scarcely mentioned in Ritzer's first book of theoretically based social criticism, *The McDonaldization of Society* (1993), Marx's theories of capitalism and exploitation become increasingly prominent in Ritzer's later works (2004, p. xvii). For example, his concept of the "means of consumption," developed in *Enchanting a Disenchanted World* (2005) is influenced by Marx, as is his identification of capitalism as one of the primary forces (along with rationalization) transforming the contemporary world in the *Globalization of Nothing* (2004). In addition to Weber and Marx, the influence of C. Wright Mills can be discerned in Ritzer's penchant for writing for a general intellectual audience and for using sociological theory to inform his social criticism. As will become apparent as this chapter develops, Ritzer's actual critique of American society also owes much to Mills. The influence of Mills should come as no surprise as Mills was also a student of Weber and Marx. Ritzer's work over the last twenty years has increasingly focused on the impact of three overarching social forces rapidly transforming sociocultural systems worldwide. These three forces are rationalization, capital development, and Americanization. Ritzer's sociology addresses three crucial questions: What are the characteristics of these social forces? What are their dynamics, and why are they gathering strength and expanding globally? Furthermore, how has their continued growth affected their experience and quality of life?

Rationalization, Capitalism, and Americanization

Rationalization is the application of logic, observation, and science to achieve desired ends. According to Ritzer, the significant characteristics of the process are efficiency, predictability, calculability, and control. Weber saw bureaucracy as a prime example of the rationalization process applied to human organizations. These organizations are hierarchical, controlled through directives from the topmost offices, and written rules define the responsibilities and authority of each office within the hierarchy. There is a well-defined (and often detailed) division of labor. Staffing and promotion within the organization are done through objective criteria such as educational attainment, skill, and competence rather than ascribed characteristics such as family, race, or gender. Measuring these qualities in staff is one of the most frustrating and time-consuming procedures carried out within bureaucracies. How does one objectively measure competence within a bureaucratic organization? Most bureaucracies, of course, attempt to quantify such measures. Bureaucracies are often bureaucratizing—refining rules and regulations, adjusting the division of labor, and monitoring employees for greater compliance with the organization's rules—to attain the organization's goals more efficiently and effectively. Of course, those in the topmost offices are also responsible for setting the organization's goals, and those in intermediate and subordinate positions are structurally constrained to carry out these directives.

While Ritzer sees bureaucracy as continuing today, he believes McDonald's is a more effective model of the rationalization process applied to human organizations (1993, pp. 18-19). Again, Ritzer did not use the term "McDonaldization" to describe a new process, only to reach a broader audience and illustrate the rationalization process more effectively. He readily admits that the fast-food restaurant is part of a conglomerate and is organized in a bureaucratic manner. In addition to many of the characteristics of a bureaucracy, Ritzer notes, the fast-food restaurant has borrowed from the assembly line and Frederick Taylor's "scientific management" to bring more predictability and control to the production of hamburgers and other fast foods. The assembly line and scientific management can be subsumed under the rationalization process, as mentioned by Weber ([1921] 1968, p. 1156) himself. For an extended discussion of Taylorism or scientific management, see the chapter on Harry Braverman.

What are the rational characteristics of a fast-food restaurant? There are many. They have an incredibly detailed division of labor. Unlike traditional restaurants that rely on chefs, cooks, or short-order cooks, fast food restaurants rely on unskilled laborers who are assigned a simple task that is endlessly repeated. They can do this because these restaurants have a limited menu. Much of the food preparation is done in factories away from the restaurant. The hamburger patties and chicken nuggets are formed, the fries are pre-cut, and the buns are baked and shipped to the restaurants for final cooking and assembly. Food preparation on site is broken down into simple steps, and the restaurant employs technology to take the variability and guesswork out of its preparation. Rather than servers, the restaurant employs counter people and gives them cash registers with pictures instead of prices. Rather than bussers, the restaurant encourages customers to clear their tables. To move customers quickly through the dining experience, restaurants provide finger foods that can be rapidly eaten and uncomfortable seating that discourages lingering over the meal. A recent innovation that has made it even more efficient has been the "drive-through," where the customer is not even given a table and is required to remove the waste from the premises.

Ritzer points out that there are many attractions for consumers to fast-food restaurants (and other rationalizing institutions). They are fast, particularly if the customer is willing to take items directly off the menu. Their efficiency, combined with the volume of their business, allows them to give more food for the money (p. 62). They offer very predictable fares. The food has been designed to appeal to a broad audience. While no one will anticipate a gourmet feast, they can avoid spoiled or bad-tasting food or outrageous prices. By design, the Big Mac you buy in San Francisco will be identical to the one purchased in Tulsa and identical to the one you buy in New York next week (2005, p. 78). This predictability is ensured through centralized control, written rules, regulations, procedures, and technology. Another attraction of fast-food restaurants (and fast food in general) is that the innovation fits modern lifestyles. The growth of fast food also coincides with (1) the rise of the automobile culture, (2) the increase in women working outside the home, (3) the increased pace of modern life, and (4) the decline of the family meal (of which fast food is both a cause and an effect) (1993, p. 150).

The second force sweeping the world, according to Ritzer, is capitalism. Ritzer agrees with Weber that capital is a powerful social force that influences individual actions in ways consistent with the market, pushing them to acquire marketable skills, work, and consume. Weber wrote:

> The capitalist economy of the present day is an immense cosmos into which the individual is born and presents itself to him, at least as an individual, as an unalterable order of things in which he must live. It forces the individual, in so far as he is involved in the system of market relationships, to conform to capitalist rules of action. The manufacturer, who in the long run acts counter to these norms, will just as inevitably be eliminated from the economic scene as the worker who cannot or will not adapt himself to them will be thrown into the streets without a job (Weber, [1904] 1950, pp. 54-55).

In addition, Weber and Ritzer see capital as providing much of the driving force behind the rationalization process. The profit motive becomes readily apparent in Ritzer's discussion of the contributions of Ray Kroc, founder of the McDonald's franchise, to the modern consumer economy. Kroc, he reports, invented little that was new. He just applied the McDonald brothers' rationalization techniques to his chain of restaurants (Ritzer, 1993, pp. 31-32). His single innovation was in developing the franchise system. Ritzer points out that earlier franchises granted franchises by region, often creating influential franchisees who acted independently of the licensing company. These earlier franchises also charged higher initial fees—their actual product was the selling of the franchises themselves. After the sale, they had little interest in the success or failure of the individual franchisees. "Kroc maximized central control and thereby uniformity throughout the system by granting franchises one at a time and rarely granting more than one franchise to a specific individual. Another of Kroc's innovations was to set the fee for a franchise at a rock-bottom $950." "At McDonald's, profits did not come from high initial fees, but from the 1.9 percent of store sales that it demanded of its franchisees. Thus, the success of Kroc and his organization depended on the prosperity of the franchisees" (p. 32). Kroc's innovations gave greater authority and control to the corporate structure (a form of centralization) and a direct interest in the success of all its restaurants. Furthermore, continuing rationalization could best serve this interest, particularly in a highly competitive market.

As pointed out by Marx and the hundreds who followed, capitalism is committed to growth. The object of capitalism is to maximize the rate of profit as quickly and efficiently as possible. Therefore, economic growth achieves the capitalists' and their managers' goals and drives. We measure the health of individual corporations by measures of growth--increases in sales, productivity, and profitability are considered the corporate priority. This need for growth is driven by a "confluence of interests" among manufacturers, stockbrokers, managers, bankers, politicians, and consumers (Ritzer, 2005, p. 27).

In a society dominated by capitalism, more than just individual corporations have this commitment to growth; economic expansion becomes society's commitment. The success or failure of government depends on the performance of state and national economies, particularly during election years, which in America occur every two years. In addition, in an age that prohibits government increases in taxation, economic growth becomes one of the few avenues for growth in tax revenue. Finally, economic growth enriches economic elites further and protects their wealth from the threat of redistribution, and these elites can exercise tremendous power to achieve their ends. The demands of the lower classes for income increases have traditionally been met in American society by increasing economic output. Economic growth has long been a way of "painlessly" addressing the needs of the poor and the working classes. Without economic growth, only open class warfare could address these demands. Through economic growth, the state can increase the living standards of the masses without addressing inequality—something essential for capitalism itself.

Although the forces of rationalization and capitalism are separate, Ritzer writes, they are also very much intertwined. As Harry Braverman and others pointed out, profit motivates millions of entrepreneurs (and wannabees) to adopt technologies and techniques that can lower the costs of producing, delivering, or selling the product or the service to the customer. Chief among these techniques is the detailed division of labor, which breaks jobs up into simple steps, the replacement of labor with technology, and close monitoring of the performance of employees—all of which are part of the rationalization process. The rationalization of the economy is in the interests of capitalists, and capitalism provides much of the drive (not all) for the rationalization process.

Ritzer also points out that our cultural value system drives rationalization and is seen as a valued end (Ritzer, 1993, p. 38, pp. 147-149). This calls to mind Weber's comments about rationalization becoming a habit of thought that we bring to bear on more and more areas of social life. "The whole process of rationalization in the factory and elsewhere, and especially in the bureaucratic state machine, parallels the centralization of the material implements of organization in the hands of the master. Thus, discipline inexorably takes over ever larger areas as the satisfaction of political and economic needs is increasingly rationalized" (Weber, [1921] 1968, p. 1156). Besides corporate capitalism, Ritzer briefly points to other institutions undergoing significant rationalization in the last 50 years. Chief among them are medicine, higher education, and agriculture. Each of these sectors is increasingly becoming integrated into the corporate economy, but each has other factors involved with its rationalization (Ritzer, 1993, pp. 53-54, p. 75, pp. 102-103; 2004, p. 33).

Unfortunately, Ritzer fails to detail the importance of competition in the relationship between capitalism and rationalization. The goal of capitalist enterprises is to maximize the rate of profit, and this drive is often expressed without competition through uneven quality and exorbitant prices. However, in sectors subject to the spur of competition, the profit motive can best be satisfied through tighter controls on production costs, thus lowering the price charged to consumers and producing products and services of higher quality than your competitors. It is interesting that Ritzer's paragon of rationalization, McDonald's, is in the highly competitive fast-food market. Another excellent example of a rationalized enterprise often used in the literature is Wal-Mart, also in a highly competitive field. While much of its success is due to its marketing strategy of small-town and suburban stores, low overhead, tight control of labor costs, and volume buying, other factors are behind its success. For example, its advanced computer tracking system directly ties its inventory to ordering from manufacturers. The company has also developed state-of-the-art systems for managing the flow of goods from the stockroom to the floor, saving millions in interest expense on its inventory. Through these and other steps rationalizing the retail industry, Wal-Mart went from a small regional retailer in the 1970s to the world's largest by the 1980s.

However, all sectors of American capitalism are less competitive than retail. After World War II, many sectors of the American economy were dominated by oligopolies in which four or fewer firms controlled fifty percent or more of a given market. As a result, innovation and productivity declined in American industry in the post-war years. It was only with the introduction of foreign competition in many markets in the mid-1970s that American industry began to apply the principles of rationalization with seriousness again to regain its competitive edge. These rationalizing principles included 1) tightening coordination and control, 2) squeezing wages, 3) applying computer and information technology to boost productivity, 4) outsourcing and moving production facilities overseas, and 4) downsizing (Elwell, 1999, pp. 75-83). As a result of these rationalizing trends, American capitalism is doing quite well—though many American workers are not. Capitalism can be said to be an incredibly effective carrier of rationalization in highly competitive markets.

Rationalization also exists in not-for-profit organizations, as demonstrated by Weber's "ideal type" of human organization, bureaucracy. Bureaucracies, and thus rationalization, exist in both capitalist and public enterprises. For Weber, the state was the primary carrier of rationalization, though he considered capitalism a close second. Weber writes, "As mentioned before, the bureaucratic tendency has chiefly been influenced by needs arising from the creation of standing armies as determined by power politics and by the development of public finance connected with the military establishment. In the modern state, the increasing demands for administration rest on the increasing complexity of civilization and push towards bureaucratization" ([1946] 1958, p. 212). Although the goals of public bureaucracies are not often related to profitability, they are formal rational organizations. Such non-profits pursue rationalization because it can lead to lower costs. Many such organizations must exist within tight state budgets or seek to control costs to expand their operations (Ritzer, 1993, p. 148).

The third force transforming the world, Americanization, can be defined as the spread of American cultural elements—products, lifestyles, customs, institutions, and ideologies—around the globe. Ritzer (2004) sees this as a "unidirectional process" that tends to overwhelm local cultural elements (p. 85). Much of this spread appears to be due to American economic and military dominance. American companies, for example, locate production facilities and consumer outlets or market their goods and services overseas. Selling products involves advertising and often establishing Americanized stores and outlets in these foreign locales. Also important is the American production of mass media content (particularly movies) and American military dominance worldwide.

Much of Americanization, Ritzer readily admits, is due to either capitalism or rationalization. The establishment of American markets overseas, for example, owes a great deal to the necessity of the capitalist enterprise to expand profits, as does much of American foreign policy, including the use of its military (p. 81). However, Ritzer claims Americanization is not simply reducible to rationalization or capitalism (p. 92). All three forces are separate though intertwined; the strength of their role varies by country and the process being analyzed. Ritzer believes there is great value in keeping them analytically separate. Because of American hegemony, there is undoubtedly some truth in Ritzer's argument. There is an intrinsic attraction in much of the world to things American. However, much of the spread of American values, customs, and lifestyles is simply because the processes of rationalization and capital development are more advanced in America than in the rest of the world (at least, so far). Moreover, these processes have changed American values, customs, and lifestyles significantly. For both reasons, the spread of capitalism and rationalization worldwide currently has an American flavor.

The continuing development of capitalism, rationalization, and Americanization has created a culture of "hyper consumption" in America (p. 88). So important has consumption become, Ritzer argues, that America is now "better characterized by consumption than production" (2005, p. 26). With the expansion of capitalism, the rapid spread of consumer society threatens to overwhelm indigenous cultures worldwide (p. 38).

The Cathedrals of Consumption

"Cathedrals of consumption" is a term Ritzer uses to describe the "new means of consumption" developed since the 1950s in American society. If you have not yet guessed, Ritzer is fond of coining terms. In this chapter, I will report on truly useful terms. "Cathedrals of Consumption" is useful in collectively describing many of the malls, superstores, casinos, hotels, and other consumption sites described by Ritzer. The architecture, interior design, and product placement are intended to inspire awe and promote consumerism among customers, as are the spectacles many of these places provide. However, there are problems using the term to refer to fast-food restaurants and small chain stores, which are far more functionally designed. Perhaps these could be referred to as "parish churches of consumption"? Walmart and the warehouse stores also do not fit the image of soaring architecture and spectacular displays. Other than offering various goods piled higher and deeper, they are designed almost exclusively along rational lines.

Ritzer argues that this new means of consumption is distinctly American and consists of institutions such as malls, superstores, Internet stores (such as Amazon.com), warehouse stores, theme parks, cruise lines, mega-malls, and casinos (pp. 9-20). Ritzer calls them "cathedrals" because they have a religious feel about them. "These settings are more frequently described as cathedrals of consumption in these pages, pointing up the quasi-religious, and 'enchanted' nature of such new settings. They have become locales to which we make 'pilgrimages' in order to practice our consumer religion" (2005, p. x).

Capitalism increasingly employs rationalization in marketing mass-produced goods and services as it develops. Capitalism develops efficient marketing tools for these goods and services by applying logic, observation, and science (mainly social science). The central problem of capitalism is no longer production, using the techniques of rationalization and managerial manipulation, the system has created abundance. The problem is getting people to buy and consume the goods and services produced. "In 20th-century capitalism, the focus shifted increasingly from production to consumption, resulting in a parallel shift from control and exploitation of workers to consumers" (p. 51).

Institutions built along rational lines to sell goods and services leave little room for mystery, surprise, or awe (p. 91). Mass-produced products, entertainment, and services have also become commonplace. According to Weber (and Ritzer), rationalization ultimately leads to disenchantment.

The fate of our times is characterized by rationalization and intellectualization and, above all, by the 'disenchantment of the world.' Precisely, the ultimate and most sublime values have retreated from public life either into the transcendental realm of mystic life or into the brotherliness of direct and personal human relations.

It is not accidental that our greatest art is intimate and not monumental, (nor is it accidental that today it is only within the small, intimate circle that there is something that corresponds to the prophetic spirit), which in former times swept through the great communities like a firebrand, welding them together. If we attempt to force and to 'invent' a monumental style in art, such miserable monstrosities are produced as the many new monuments of the last twenty years. If one tries intellectually to construe new religions without a new and genuine prophecy, then, [such a creation] will create only fanatical sects but never a genuine community ([1946] 1958, p. 155).

257

While rationalization was necessary to remake the old general store and farmers' markets into efficient "selling machines" adept at manipulating many people to buy the available goods and services, such efficiency alone tends to be cold and machinelike (p. 46). To counter the disenchanting aspects of rationalization, the cathedrals of consumption have employed spectacle—stunning visual displays of goods, soaring architecture, simulation of experience, and entertainment—to attract customers (p. 94).

Nevertheless, it takes work, Ritzer says (in agreement with Weber), to mass-produce magic and enchantment, and it is incredibly challenging to sustain the illusion over time (pp. 87-88). Through the years, there has been an arms race among various corporations controlling the means of consumption to produce more fabulous spectacles to attract customers. When successful, the cathedrals must further rationalize to serve the growing crowds; when they do, the enchantment dims (p. xi). Yesterday's spectacle became commonplace. The following display must continually be improved; spectacle becomes incessant and everywhere (p. 94). This competition in terms of spectacle is nowhere more apparent, claims Ritzer, than in Las Vegas (pp. 97-104). (Recent adventure movies also come to mind—sequels to *Spiderman* and *Pirates of the Caribbean*, as well as Batman, pile the villains and the violence higher and higher in a futile attempt to continue to awe audiences.) These new cathedrals and advertising have rapidly spread a new culture of consumerism worldwide.

The transformation of the means of consumption into selling machines, plus the rise in the ubiquity and effectiveness of advertising, has changed the consumption habits of Americans. Citing the work of Juliet Schor, Ritzer reports that Americans spend about 3 to 4 more time shopping than Western Europeans and that the average American consumes almost twice as much as they did forty years ago (p. 32). Shopping malls are increasingly marketing entertainment along with goods. (Mills' "big bazaar" comes to mind.) The mega-malls, such as the Edmonton Mall and the Mall of the Americas, are among the most prominent tourist attractions in their countries, the latter drawing 40 million visitors in 2003 (p. 120). Ritzer terms this "hyper consumption," a condition in which people spend most of their resources to consume (p. 135). Moreover, not just traditional shopping and tourist venues pattern themselves after malls; one can see the same techniques used to stimulate consumption in museums, sports stadiums, hospitals, and university campuses (pp. 20-23). Increasingly, we live in a world that is constantly pushing us to consume.

Credit cards are of interest to Ritzer because they allow merchants and consumers easy access to the future earnings of potential consumers to buy products or services. The credit card industry has grown tremendously in the last 40 years as Americans increasingly purchase on credit (p. 135). "Banks have, to a large degree, shifted from the business of inducing people to save to luring them into debt. Americans receive about 5 billion mail solicitations, up from about 3 billion in 1997, imploring them to sign up for a credit card. The profits from servicing debt, especially credit card debt, are much higher than those derived from savings. Easy and extensive credit has played a key role in making America's modern mass consumer society possible and that, especially in the form of credit cards, is being exported to many parts of the world" (p. 33). As a result, Americans have become a nation of spenders and debtors, consuming well beyond our means (Ritzer, 1995, p. 5).

Globalization

Ritzer sees the process of globalization as one in which the world is becoming increasingly more capitalistic, rationalized, and Americanized. He contrasts this vision with the more optimistic vision of globalization theorists who see the world growing more diverse, heterogeneous, and free (2004, pp. 79-80). According to Ritzer, the intertwined processes of capitalism, rationalization, and Americanization rapidly overwhelm local products, entertainment, and markets.

Globalization has been caused by the rapid expansion of capitalism, its industrial capacity, marketing ability, and tremendous technological and organizational advances (pp. 110-111). Under technological advance, Ritzer lists industrial machinery that increases productivity, communications, and transportation. Under organizational advance, Ritzer includes such things as the modern franchise system and the location of production and consumption facilities around the globe. Rationalization means that globally marketed products will be competitively priced with local manufacturers. The economies of scale mean mass production must be accompanied by mass marketing, and there is no bigger market than the world itself (pp. 103-104). A second factor behind the growth of globalization is the growth in the reach and power of mass media, allowing goods and services to be more effectively marketed (p. 111).

The fact that globalization is driven by capitalism does not bode well for those who see it as a liberating, heterogeneous process. Capitalism is based on exploiting workers and, increasingly, consumers (Ritzer, 2005, p. 42). The system is driven to rationalize production and consumption to increase profitability. Rationalization—creating rules and regulations, an ever more detailed division of labor, hierarchies of authority, assembly lines, and bureaucrats—is not conducive to human freedom, personal initiative, or values. In place of such human values and yearnings, modern marketing has substituted the desire for consumption, things, entertainment, and comfort. In the process, traditional human institutions and values have been weakened or eliminated, first in America and now worldwide.

Form over Substance

The spread of capitalism and rationalization throughout the world created consumer culture. Ritzer also critiques the products of these rationalized organizations. He devises a continuum from "nothing" to "something" and claims that modern products and services tend to fall on the "nothing" end of the spectrum. "The social world, particularly in the realm of consumption, is increasingly characterized by nothing. In this case, 'nothing' refers to a social form that is generally centrally conceived, controlled, and comparatively devoid of distinctive substantive content" (Ritzer, 2004, p. 3). He says that products and services with a quality of "something" can be characterized by being unique, tied to specific times or places, humanized, and often enchanted. Products and services with the quality of "nothing" tend to be characterized by the opposite—they tend to be generic, lacking in ties to time or place, dehumanized, and disenchanted (p. 20).

Ritzer writes, "This definition carries with it no judgment about the desirability or undesirability of such a social form or about its increasing prevalence," which is disingenuous at best. The use of the term "nothing" is a pejorative made abundantly clear by his descriptions and by his dedication at the front of the book ("To Sue, who is really something"). In addition, all products of capitalist enterprises are defined as "nothing" by his very definition ("centrally conceived, controlled"). Finally, in his list of characteristics of nothing and something, Ritzer has included "disenchantment" and "dehumanization," both characteristics of rationalization. For these reasons, I am not overly fond of Ritzer's nothing-something terminology. However, he has made some valid distinctions between the products of local producers and large, centralized corporations.

Ritzer best illustrates the difference between locally and globally produced goods and services by comparing franchised Mexican food restaurants and independently owned Chinese restaurants. Chinese restaurants "are shaped by loose cultural models," some central office do not dictate their design, menu, and décor but are the product of individual decisions guided by these models (pp. 108-109). The food has undoubtedly been adapted to American taste, but the adaptations have great individuality and variety. There is also great variety in food quality in such restaurants, as well as their atmosphere, sanitation, and prices.

Ritzer compares this variety to Taco Bell franchises in the same locales. Rather than coming from a loose cultural model, the restaurants are based on the structural model of Mexican restaurants imposed from corporate headquarters. Such franchises are centrally conceived, tightly coordinated, and controlled (like McDonald's). The buildings are designed along similar lines, décor and menus are identical, and ingredients, preparation, and packaging are identical. The food has also been processed to appeal to a mass audience; consequently, ingredients that might offend some segments are eliminated. The resulting fare bears little resemblance to authentic Mexican food (pp. 108-109). Nevertheless, it is predictable, relatively inexpensive, and designed to appeal to American tastes.

Ritzer concludes that globalization has not been caused by the loose cultural models that inspire the spread of Chinese restaurants worldwide but rather by the tight, structural models of corporate capitalism that have produced fast foods (p. 109). Consequently, globalization is likely to lead to the creation of a vast, homogenous consumer culture centered upon an abundance of mediocre goods and services designed and marketed to enhance the bottom line of corporations.

Irrationality of Rationalization

Like Weber, Ritzer is also concerned with the irrationality of rationalization. In such rational systems, Ritzer says, humans are often denied the opportunity to exercise their reason (1993, p. 12). "Most specifically, irrationality means that rational systems are unreasonable systems—they serve to deny the basic humanity, the human reason, of the people who work in them or are served by them. In other words, rationality and reason are often used interchangeably in other contexts; here they are employed to mean antithetical phenomena" (p. 121). This quote could have been taken from C. Wright Mills, who defined the problem as institutional rationality denying individual reason ([1959] 1976, p. 170). It is also the essence of Weber's formal versus substantive rationality.

Ritzer claims that we mainly think of such institutions as irrational because they are dehumanizing (p. 130). Workers cannot develop their skills or exercise judgment (p. 131). He claims this is irrational for the worker and the employer because such treatment of workers leads to "job dissatisfaction, alienation, absenteeism, and turnover" (p. 130). Ritzer is technically correct—this is seemingly irrational for employers. However, this seeming irrationality is more than offset by the minimum wages paid to unskilled workers, which are broadly addressed as the "problem of management" (as discussed by Braverman) and considered one of the costs of doing business. However, employee discontent is a real problem in the fast-food industry. "In fact, the fast-food industry has the highest turnover rate—approximately 300 percent per year—of any industry in the United States. That means that the average worker lasts only about four months at a fast-food restaurant; the entire workforce of the fast-food industry turns over three times a year" (1993, p. 132).

Nevertheless, these organizations are designed for the efficient attainment of the goals of the enterprise; personal ties and human connections between customer and provider are discouraged. Modern fast-food restaurants and other consumption centers are not designed to serve a small, stable clientele but to sell significant quantities of food to many strangers. Such organizations are dehumanizing places to work, shop, eat, be entertained, or be served (p. 22).

In addition, though a bureaucratic organization is highly rational in the formal sense of technical efficiency, it does not necessarily follow that it is also rational in its goals. Rational social organizations are structured to attain the organization's goals. These goals are quantitative, so rarely do they involve the assessment of either the means or the goals of the organization in terms of such human values as social justice, peace, community, health, or human happiness. Such factors are not likely to enter the calculation unless forced from the outside. Most officials within the organization do not know of the decisions and actions of other offices. Besides, these officials have specialized knowledge and limited authority, prohibiting them from action. Such officials are unlikely to question the moral implications of organizational goals or the means used to attain them.

This lack of responsibility for bureaucratic decisions was best illustrated by Tom Lehrer, a singer/songwriter who wrote parodies in the nineteen sixties and seventies. Lehrer did a song about Werner Von Braun, a German rocket scientist during World War II who was instrumental in developing the V-2 Rocket that devastated parts of London. After the war, he was brought to the U.S. to work for the National Aeronautics and Space Administration (NASA). One of the lines of the song speaks of the relationship between specialization and morality: "Once the rockets go up, who cares where they come down? That's not my department, says Werner Von Braun." Moreover, again: "In German and English, I know how to count down, and I'm learning Chinese, says Werner Von Braun." Von Braun's willingness to work for the Nazis and then the Americans—first at war and then at space exploration—illustrates how the dictates of rational social organization trump individual values and convictions.

For Ritzer, the central irrationality of the continuing rationalization of consumption is the process's impact on indigenous cultures. It leads all it touches to a homogenous consumer culture in which the human variety is stifled. There is a sameness to American cities and towns, with their landscapes dominated by fast food outlets, malls, and superstores. There is sameness from one mall to another—the stores may vary in placement, but the major chains are all represented, and the products are virtually identical. This sameness, Ritzer writes, is rapidly spreading around the world. Cultures, with their diversity of values, folkways, and cuisine—a whole way of life that has evolved over centuries—are rapidly being abandoned and replaced by a culture centered around the needs, values, and products of corporate capitalism.

Another irrationality Ritzer mentions in passing is consumer culture's impact on the global environment (2005, p. 38). With about 20 percent of the world's population, hyper-production and consumption in the developed world alone have already dramatically impacted environments regarding resource availability and pollution. Can the world genuinely sustain the globalization of such a culture?

Nevertheless, the ultimate in irrationality, Ritzer writes, is Weber's "iron cage." In a society dominated by rational social organizations, the rules and regulations of these organizations increasingly proscribe our behavior. Ritzer, like Weber, feels that with the proliferation in the growth and power of rational organizations, people spend an increasing amount of their time in rational social organizations. "Thus, people would move from rationalized educational systems to rationalized workplaces and from rationalized recreational setting to rationalized homes" (1993, pp. 22-23). Such organizations are dehumanizing and structured to dictate our decision-making and behaviors (Ritzer, 2005, p. 85). Working within such settings means an individual must cut herself off from personal beliefs, sentiments, and values; the rules designed to attain the organization's goals efficiently are her guide. Being served by such organizations means being more efficiently manipulated to consume products, services, and entertainments that are not our free choice. Moreover, these same techniques have been adopted by our political system as well. Weber's iron cage is a vision of the end of reason in human affairs, the ceding of our freedom and reason to rational social organizations.

About Ritzer

George Ritzer was born in upper Manhattan in 1940 to working-class parents. His father was a taxi driver, and his mother was a secretary. (Information for this brief biography was obtained from Ritzer, 2007 and Dandaneau and Dodsworth, 2007.) While the family had to struggle economically, it was the same struggle other families in his neighborhood faced. "I suppose the key event in my life was going to the Bronx High School of Science, which at the time was the preeminent public high school in New York, maybe in the country, and maybe it still is" (Dandaneau and Dodsworth 2007, para 3). He graduated from the Bronx High School of Science in 1958. He drifted into college because "that was what people are doing," deciding to attend City College of New York in upper Manhattan because it was close to his home and free. He describes himself as a marginal student, first studying business and then transferring to psychology when this proved not to his liking. He received a B.A. from City College of New York in 1962 and, still in apparent drift, decided to pursue an M.B.A. from the University of Michigan in 1964. "I decided I wanted to go back in the direction of business, and I don't know that I can explain to you why that happened, but it did. So, I applied to the M.B.A. program at the University of Michigan. I never had good grades, but I always did well on standardized tests. I forgot what Michigan used, probably the GRE. I did well on it, got admitted, and I received at least a partial scholarship" (2007).

Upon graduation from Michigan, he took a management job at Ford Motor Company, which quickly proved a mistake. He found the job at Ford meaningless and routinized: the company stifled his creativity or initiative. In addition, relations within the factory were strained. "We would spend hours wandering around the factory watching people work. I came from a working-class background; I was sensitive to what the workers were looking at when they looked at me looking at them. And they were hostile to us, as well they should have been. Added to that was a kind of class warfare going on within management, which had to do with the younger people like me, who came with advanced degrees and who thought of themselves as hotshots, and our bosses and even their bosses, most of whom had worked their way up in the ranks" (2007).

Within a few weeks, Ritzer says, he decided that life at Ford was not for him. He, therefore, began the Ph.D. program in Labor and Industrial Relations at Cornell University in 1965. His studies in the program focused on organizational behavior, with a minor in sociology. Having never taken a sociology course before, his minor advisor, Gordon Streib, started him off on an introductory text; he studied under such sociologists as Robin Williams and Margaret Cussler. Upon graduation, he became an assistant professor at Tulane University. In 1970, he became an associate professor at the University of Kansas. In 1974, on the strength of *Sociology: a Multiple Paradigm Science*, he became a full professor at the University of Maryland, where he remains.

Throughout his career, Professor Ritzer has received many honors and awards, including being named a Distinguished University Professor at the University of Maryland in 2001, the first Fulbright Chair at York University in Canada, and the American Sociological Association's (A.S.A.) Distinguished Contributions to Teaching Award in 2000. Ritzer has also been active in the A.S.A. and the Eastern and Southern Sociological Society, holding many elected and appointed offices throughout his career.

Ritzer is a one-person publishing phenomenon. His publications include monographs, advanced theory texts, undergraduate theory texts, journal articles, book reviews, and encyclopedia entries. "I basically trained myself as a social theorist, and so I had to learn it all as I went. Consequently, I never wanted to read other peoples' summaries of what classical theorists had to say. I would read it myself. I would very often just teach a seminar. If I wanted to get a better handle on Parsons, I would teach a graduate seminar on Parsons. I have learned much social theory that way and continue to learn much social theory that way" (2007). The fact that Ritzer does not want to read other people's summaries is interesting because much of his scholarly output consists of such summaries. However, I understand the point. I have purposely avoided summaries and critiques of the modern theorists covered in this volume because I wanted to read them fresh and with an open mind. However, regarding classical theorists, my understanding has been greatly enhanced by secondary literature (including Ritzer's work). Nevertheless, such secondary sources must be selected with care.

His various theory texts, many of which have gone through multiple editions, were written to clarify abstract theory for students and himself. He continues to revise them and add to them today. "For example, I have just finished a new chapter for the next edition of my Classical Sociological Theory text on Tocqueville. It was a real revelation reading his work systematically (as well as secondary sources on it). His work is underappreciated; there is an important grand theory in it on the relationship between equality, centralization, and freedom [...] Writing those texts has helped me learn a lot about theory. In addition, writing and revising such texts is not divorced from scholarly work—I have had many ideas as a result of work on those textbooks that led to scholarly papers" (2007). Many of his works have been translated; McDonaldization to about 16 different languages. In addition, Ritzer has edited *The Encyclopedia of Sociology* and *The Blackwell Encyclopedia of Sociology*, as well as several volumes of readings, and has performed similar services for journals and publishers. Finally, he has also presented papers extensively at professional meetings and guest lectures. He has often been interviewed in the popular media and given speeches and talks to a more general audience.

Chapter 12: Roderick Seidenberg[2]

Seidenberg begins by pointing out that we are a species dominated by organization. Since the beginning of our history, it is apparent that there has been a trend towards ever more explicit, consciously calculated rules and procedures guiding human action and thought. The trend of social organization is growing in its reach over more aspects of social life and its depth of control. It is currently sweeping through societies, whether authoritarian, democratic, or somewhere in between. Organization affects every aspect of life, from the most mundane to the highly specialized. It is integral to our international production processes, which require immense coordination among various financial, mining, production, distribution, and consumption systems. International, national, regional, and local governments are all in the mix, as are educational institutions, correctional institutions, military, communications, and transportation industries. There is a clear trend toward ever more explicit, consciously formalized relationships among people within these organizations as well as the relations between these entities.

The function of social organizations is to coordinate the actions of individuals in an ever-closer mesh of institutionalized processes and procedures to achieve the desired ends of the organization more efficiently. While many complain of bureaucracy's red tape and inefficiencies, the complaint is often one of it not being efficient enough. Interestingly, the proposed solution usually furthers its rules and procedures to broaden its reach (or to put the organization in more competent hands). According to Seidenberg, the only critics of the trend toward greater organization are the anarchists, "whose number is inconsequential, and whose influence is nil" (1950, p. 3). Seidenberg is wrong on this point, as anarchist numbers and influence have increased as the influence of social organization over the individual has escalated dramatically in recent years.

---

[2] This essay is to be published in the Journal of Big History.

Seidenberg relates the increasing specialization of the labor market and the motivation toward globalization (he calls it "internationalism") as stemming from the same principle of organization. We rarely question the principle; it has become axiomatic in our social life. "This bland and unquestioning acceptance is a measure of its momentum—the promise of a mounting trend toward further organization" (p. 4). Seidenberg asks what causes this increasing organization and why it seems to accelerate in modern society. What effect will this all-encompassing principle have on our future? Are we compelled to accept its dictates for all our social activities? Finally, what does this mean for democracy, individual freedom, and the concept of free will?

Seidenberg conceives social organization as a process of consciously contrived and defined relationships in service to the ever-more efficient achievement of a desired end. As the organization is consciously contrived, it is clearly the product of intelligence, constantly assessing and refining procedures to eliminate friction between the various parts of the organization. The organization's smooth operation demands consistency, standardization, clearly defined rules and procedures, and thus, the elimination of variation and spontaneity in the various parts of the organization.

The organizational imperative is most apparent in political-economic sectors of society. Governments of all stripes and levels are expanding their power and scope, and economic institutions are enlarging and centralizing. Planning has replaced haphazard development, science, logic, and reason, and the increasing reliance on expertise, experience, and data are replacing intuition and laissez-faire development.

We now have an engineering approach to all physical, social, economic, and political problems. For example, educational programs, after-school activities, counseling, and social work address delinquency problems. If that fails, there is the criminal justice system and its legions of juvenile courts, drug rehabilitation organizations, and reform schools. Pollution problems are monitored through science and dealt with through law and tax policy (however imperfectly to date). Moreover, who doubts that any effective response to global climate change must be even more intensive and organized by national and international organizations across governments and corporations?

The trend throughout history has been the increasing application of organization, as evidenced by engineering works, articulated legal systems, religious institutions, military organizations, and imperial bureaucracy. However, in the recent past, the principle of rational organization has come to dominate societies, extending and deepening its reach into all areas of social life. This deepening includes the socialization of children, education, the production and consumption of goods and services, communications and transportation, and social welfare. Seidenberg believes the principle of organization is rooted in our behavior as rational human beings, a rationality or technique that seems ingrained into our very being that "we follow rather than invent" (p. XX).

However, he asserts, rational organization's dynamic nature is a recent phenomenon in the long evolutionary line of our species, as early sapiens exhibited little planned organization, living under instinct and tradition. Seidenberg maintains that the social group firmly integrated early sapiens and that their actions and beliefs were within narrow limits of fixed patterns of norms, customs, and habits. This form of organization, he asserts, is far different than what modern people experience, with our explicitly codified rules, procedures, laws, and agreements. We live in a social world where traditions and customs are constantly questioned based on the efficient attainment of goals and readily abandoned or reinterpreted if the situation demands it. A world where social order is deliberate, consciously constructed, and constantly expanded.

Humankind is unique, Seidenberg argues, in that we are subject to two forms of evolutionary change. First, as an animal, Homo Sapiens have been the beneficiaries of biological evolution, equipping us with advances in brain capacity as well as our social nature. Second, social evolution is based on the accumulation of material culture and the transmission of accumulated knowledge. This second type of evolution has far exceeded the speed and scope of natural evolution.

However, this social evolutionary process did not operate in early humans, for early humans did not have a history. Seidenberg posits that there was a long prehistory before humans acquired written records or oral traditions. In *Anatomy of the Future*, Seidenberg argues that humans entered their historical period only after an extended development period. The historical period only encompasses five or six millenniums, while the prehistoric period lasted "at least a thousand millenniums of slow biological evolution" (1961, p. 128). Given humankind's animalism, there must have been eons of time in which instincts ruled human behavior. Moreover, their divergence from this animalistic nature entailed humankind entering a new and increasingly conscious thought in addressing the problems of living.

According to Seidenberg, intelligence first rises as a complement to instinct, coming to the fore as a directive force when the stresses of living overwhelmed the person or novel situations arose in which instinct could not provide guidance. Societies' accumulated knowledge of the natural and social world and social evolution—changes in the relationship between societies and nature—resulted in better tools, plant lore, and agriculture over hundreds of thousands of years. This intensification of production, which entails ever more complexity and enlargement, caused a rise in population and the need for a more intensive social organization of labor, production, distribution, and government based on criteria over and above simple kinship ties.

Seidenberg posits that history marks the struggle between instinct and intelligence as the guiding force in human affairs. Throughout the historical process, the force of conscious intelligence accumulated more experience, precision, and success in navigating the physical and social worlds and became ever more prominent. The pressure of increasingly rational thought forces older forms, habits, and customs to shed and be replaced by new insights, ideas, and experiences. The old ways based on long-standing customs and traditions are reinterpreted and converted in their structure and function into the "rationalized and purposive institutions of civilized society" (1950, p. 23).

Seidenberg quickly points out that through the extended period of human history, it was not as if intelligence and organization replaced instinct, for, in his view, there is a biological priority throughout the historical process. "For the primary ends of life, however elaborated, are reducible to instinctual urges, which intelligence seeks to satisfy to its own means" (p. 37). Our instincts long for wealth, sex, and social prestige, and intelligence tells us how to achieve these goals. Seidenberg posits that instincts had priority throughout the early part of history, but intelligence began to dominate over time as knowledge accumulated.

The transition, Seidenberg states, must have taken place over many generations in fits and starts, pushed by a developing consciousness, learned experiences, and contact with other groups that instigated change in long-established traditions and ingrained habits. The tempo of change accelerated when humans became aware of the change over time. They stepped onto the stage of history and became historic beings fully conscious, entering a "world of choice, or consciousness of direction" (p. 21).

He writes that fashioning tools and using fires in early prehistory set the evolutionary trajectory. Nevertheless, the transition must have been unimaginably slow, with early humans guided by instincts within the biological order "to a position of increasing imbalance under the cumulative pressure of emerging intelligence" (p. 50). However, the decisive steps were the adoption of agriculture and the Scientific Revolution. With the adoption of agriculture, humankind learned to supplement nature's bounty by domesticating plants and animals (p. 41). Though domestication began as an unconscious process, observation and intelligence soon supplemented nature to increase yields.

Seidenberg credits the 16th and 17th centuries Scientific Revolution as the second great intensifier of the shift from instinct to intelligence. The key to this revolution was not the discovery of new ways of thinking but the peeling off and abandoning of old ideas based on the ancients, traditions, faith, and emotions, instead relying upon observation and rational and logical reasoning. Through science, societies accumulate and organize knowledge and eventually apply it to order, control, and adapt to natural and social environments. Furthermore, the accumulating successes of the scientific enterprise carry us ever more swiftly to a post-historic future.

Seidenberg recognizes that social evolution has long eclipsed organic evolution in speed and its accumulation of adaptations. Organic evolution is a slow process, dependent upon random change, environmental fit, and passing successful genes to future generations. On the other hand, social evolution depends upon experience and learning and is thus far faster and more responsive to adaptation to different natural and social environments. It is doubtful, Seidenberg concludes, that modern humans are more intelligent than their recent forebears, but they have the advantage of a highly developed culture; the mind is, from the first, a social product (p. 43).

Seidenberg asserts that what we know as history is simply the shift of direction in societies' social structure from instinct to intelligence. The first is marked by society as an organic whole, tradition-bound by the habits of the eternal yesterday. The second is marked by the explicit organization of society, one coordinated by rationality, observation, and cumulative knowledge. Seidenberg's definition of organization closely matches Max Weber's take on bureaucracy and the rationalization of society. Seidenberg points out that organization primarily relies on predictability, which requires further organization and order in all contiguous system parts. Seidenberg writes that an organization needs predictability and precision, which calls forth the application of the measurement of all things, a tremendous asset for integrating the various parts of the system and achieving order (p. 53).

Seidenberg considers the machine a crystal that, once introduced into the system, brought about changes in all it touches. The machine performs its functions through the pure organization of parts working together with minimum friction and the highest possible efficiency for a predetermined goal—whether pumping water from coal mines or flying an airplane. Seidenberg asserts through the machine that "the incipient drift toward organization has been broadened into an obligatory and all-pervasive principle, encompassing in its sweep the whole of life" (p. 150). The mechanized world demands adherence to its rhythms as a price for its bounty. Expanding complexities of production and distribution systems, and the sheer number and variety of goods and services demand further coordination and control, as does the rise in the human population (pp. 133-134). An insistent, ever-more restrictive organization of social life must necessarily condition human thought, behavior, values, and emotions.

Knowledge and experience are cumulative and rapidly increasing. An increasing tempo in the rate of change marks the shift between instinct and intelligence. Throughout history, the growing dominance of formal organizations marks intelligence's increasing role in human affairs. "The mounting flow of historic events reveals an ever-accelerating movement from the virtually unchanging vistas of primitive man to the ceaseless changes of today." Seidenberg asserts that, with this transition to organization, humans changed "from a pre-conscious to an ever more purposive and conscious phase," and societies changed from organic and tradition-bound entities to organizational patterns consciously designed to achieve specific goals (p. 50).

Seidenberg also notes that communication technology plays a critical role in the speed of social evolution, citing first the invention of the alphabet and later the printing press as accelerants of development. He predicts that instant communication in his day, both universal and subject to further development, will appreciably speed up social change until it reaches its natural limits.

There is a difference between the organic societies of the past and future societies structured along rational lines. One difference that Seidenberg notes is in their "temporal awareness." In organic societies where instincts dominate, it is unsurprising that such people would consider the past natural, binding themselves to tradition. In rationalized societies, people live with endemic change and thus look toward the future yet to be realized.

Seidenberg foresees increasing organization and technological progress, though he is aware of limits. It is certain, he states, that limitless development challenges common sense itself. Quoting Goethe's observation that trees never reach the sky, Seidenberg points out that the second law of thermodynamics argues against such hubris, as does any critical understanding of evolutionary theory or even the law of diminishing returns. Humankind could never keep up with an accelerating pace of change. However, he avers that we have not reached such limits as technological and organizational development, which are continuing to advance. "The momentum

272

of change has perhaps not even reached its apogee, and life may witness new revelations beside which the surprises of the past may fade into insignificance. But even such a state of affairs is a far cry from an unending progression, a vista of indefinite advance" (p. 66).

Cultural knowledge has accumulated even faster in the seventy-plus years since Seidenberg wrote his first jeremiad, as has the enlargement and centralization of social organizations. Furthermore, as this change quickens, the form and structure of society necessarily change as well. He believes the changes are all-inclusive and irreversible. Going back to his crystallization analogy, Seidenberg likens it to a change of phase in the chemical world, a historically determined fate (p. 131 & p. 172).

This drift is not always in a straight line, and Seidenberg maintains that history is full of contradictions, reversals, and advances, as are the people who make it. Some intellectuals may warn of the drift, while others deny or obscure it. As it continues, many will rebel against the loss of freedom, the loss of traditional belief systems, the mutation of values, and the constraints on behavior. However, such warnings and rebellions are transitory and have little long-term effect. The direction is unmistakable throughout human history; through the rise and fall of villages, city-states, empires, and nation-states, it is toward ever more organized societies along rational lines. The transition, Seidenberg asserts, is not one of choice but fate, inherent and inescapable as part of the social evolutionary process (p. 55 & p. 172). He asks, "Where is it taking us?" His answer is to a static, unchanging condition, a frozen state of permanence that may last as long as prehistory.

Post-History

Seidenberg predicts an ever-growing need to maintain coordination, control, and order, responding to the dictates of our complex economies, growing populations, and environmental and social impacts. Social organizations will necessarily continue to enlarge and centralize. The web of "societal relationships will be drawn ever finer and more firmly," ensnaring the individual ever more tightly under their coordination and control, restricting freedom of action and thought and subjecting individuals to their dictates (p. 176). Drawing analogies to the social insects, Seidenberg asserts that the objective of social organization is to seek ever more perfect adjustments of the organism to the physical and social environment, or "the demands of life through a collective rather than an individual technique of adaptations" (p. 182).

Under such conditions, the individual's consciousness will atrophy, gradually disappearing in the post-historic period. Seidenberg views human consciousness as a historical artifact resulting from the moving tension between animalistic instinct and social intelligence as the prime movers of human thought and action. He views history as a passing phase between prehistory and our post-historic future. It is not the triumph of individual intelligence over instinct that is the prime mover here; Seidenberg is writing about social intelligence or the cumulative nature of social experience embodied by social structures and institutions. The individual organism is stationary in mental capacities throughout Sapiens' prehistoric and historic times, but social organization accumulates ever more knowledge, experience, and wisdom. The social evolutionary process thus reduces the individual to a "limited, vicarious, and partial share in the ever-widening panorama or societal enterprises and relationships" (p. 190).

Freedom of action is also an artifact of history. Seidenberg points out that individual freedom is impossible in a world activated by instinct and is "destined to evaporate" in the post-historic future (p. 236). Toward that future, the tempo of social change will also gradually slow over many generations, culminating in a period of unchanging continuity. It will be the end of history and the beginning of a post-historic age (p. 237).

Seidenberg is a reluctant pessimist, and he ends his jeremiad with the observation that social development has forced humankind to give up some of our most cherished myths. First, we gave up our belief in animism, then the earth-centered universe. In our age, we are giving up believing in the dignity of the individual and our exceptional worth. Even giving up our beliefs in a God "whose attributes, under the impact of man's rationalistic scrutiny, became ever more abstract until He vanished in the metaphysical concept of the Whole" (pp. 237-38). He claims these illusions were "inestimable," but their loss is merely a stage in our journey to the "icy fixity" of the post-historic age (p. 238).

Anatomy of the Future

Roderick Seidenberg published *Anatomy of the Future* in 1961, 11 years after the *Post-Historic Man*. He again points out the ever-accelerating speed of change in all aspects of the sociocultural system. Seidenberg asks whether this change is merely continuing along the path set from the Renaissance, or is something new afoot? Foretelling the future, or prognostication through looking at the entrails of animals, is a lost art, he writes. All we must go on are forecasts based on some theory of history, either explicitly stated or assumed. Seidenberg points to several historians who have concerned themselves with writing about prospects for the future, particularly the cyclical theories of Arnold Toynbee and his treatise on *The World and the West.*

Seidenberg sees little merit in cyclical theories, even when it comes to the rise and fall of empires. He asserts that such empires "are neither related in a direct linear progression nor repeat precisely some inherent cycle of rise and fall" (1961, p. 6). However, his main criticism of such theories is their failure to recognize the "space-time continuum of history as a whole" (p. 5). He writes that they fail to consider the cumulative nature of social evolution, the increase and widespread dissemination of knowledge, instantaneous global communication, the exponential rise in population, and the ever-increasing complexity of production and distribution processes. These and other changes have led to the impending formation of a dominant world culture, a phenomenon that is unanticipated and unacknowledged by cyclical theories.

Two difficulties in identifying laws or even historical trends are that history is a brief and incredibly complex period. Nevertheless, cumulative aspects of history can be readily identified; this includes the gradual increase and dissemination of knowledge, the increase in the rate of change, and the increase in the size and scope of social units. This increase in size holds for entire societies and the social organizations within societies. Out of the great profusion of history, we are beginning to discern a meaningful pattern. The social world is rapidly evolving into "a single, homogenous, universal pattern of life," one dominated by social organizations, the profusion of knowledge, and rapid social change (pp. 6-7).

Many argue that social predictability is impossible because of individual free will. Seidenberg responds that this impossibility ignores the sense of continuity that individuals and all societies rely upon in their daily activities. "Hence we may say there is a reciprocal, if inverse relationship between freedom and predictability; to argue that individual freedom precludes the possibility of social prediction is not only to run counter to experience, but to carry the logic of the situation to a reductio ad absurdum. In the void create by this barren logic, all social planning, indeed all social enterprise, would be implicitly restricted to a mincing and inert sterility" (p. 10).

Seidenberg writes that the growth and dissemination of knowledge, the increasing rate of change, and the increase in the size and scope of social units are tangible social trends. To deny the existence of such historical forces "is to separate the fabric of history into a meaningless series of isolated and unrelated facts," as well as deny social reality (p. 12). Such historical trends cannot tell us the precise outlines of the future. However, they can help us focus on their probable trajectories and their impact on the fundamental structures of human societies, that is, on the anatomy of the future (p. 13).

Seidenberg returns to his hypotheses of dynamic tensions between unconscious instinctual drives as part of humankind's biological endowment and conscious social intelligence's increasing role in addressing life's problems. Human brain development and communication ability first distinguish humans from the biological world. Once consciousness develops, it increasingly supplements instinctual drives—sometimes devising new adaptations to satisfy these drives, sometimes denying immediate gratification in hopes of later rewards. Others often learn these adaptations and, when successful, become a part of social order. The balance between instinct and intelligence moves increasingly toward intelligence, as exemplified by the rise of conscious social organization throughout human history. The interplay of these two motivating forces of human action comprises the operating force of history (p. 14).

While some maintain that humans stand alone as problem-solving animals, Seidenberg disagrees, pointing out that all life forms share this adaptability to some degree if they are to survive. Citing Flinders Petrie, Seidenberg defines humans "as an organism that seeks always to undo its adjustments" (p. 14) or a problem-raising animal. Constantly seeking better methods or ways, this faculty of perpetual dissatisfaction is the prime mover of social evolution. This constant seeking may not be accurate for the tradition-bound history of peoples of the distant past, but it has undoubtedly been confirmed after the Scientific Revolution. Since that revolution, humankind has been continually undoing its adjustment, constantly searching for new and better ways of manipulating its environment and organizing social life.

The Scientific Revolution augured an increasingly rational approach to understanding nature and using the knowledge gained to manipulate natural and social environments (p. 15). Seidenberg argues that the Scientific Revolution is similar to previous historical transformative events, such as the agricultural revolution or the invention of writing. Like them, it was followed by an increase in population and changes in the structures of society. However, the Scientific Revolution also stands apart. It is different in that it is not focused on a specific change in technologies or customs but marks a fundamental change in the manner of thinking, specifically, the consistent application of "rational faculties" (p.18). This change was achieved by adding rationality to the toolkit of apprehension and discovery of knowledge and stripping away the fog of tradition, superstition, authority, and emotions, leaving rationality and observation as their core. Seidenberg asserts that this revolution in thought is irreversible, sustained, and continuous, "whose trajectory into the future promises to augment our deviation from the past in ways beyond our reckoning" (pp. 18-19).

Science, coupled with engineering, has produced breathtaking achievements. Seidenberg anticipates that humankind will soon have control over the evolution of our kind as well as all other life on Earth, a period of unprecedented power but also responsibility. Nevertheless, the wonders science has produced to date, he writes, "support our sense of a great watershed" between our past and future. This watershed changes everything, from our material life to the very meaning of what it is to be human (p. 19).

Moreover, the "one-sided emphasis upon the rational component of the human psyche" is not just oriented toward the future but also the past. Earlier modes of apprehension and understanding are increasingly undermined by advances in science, destroying for many the long-understood realities of life propagated by religion, spirituality, philosophies, traditions, and emotions. (pp. 19-20).

It begins with early humans diverging mentally from other animal life in the early part of human evolution. While early humans were unaware of this divergence between instinct and intelligence, over time, humans became conscious. Gradually, an awareness developed that set humankind apart from the rest of the animal kingdom. Seidenberg writes that we attempt to synthesize our instinctual responses through culture and cultural change with our increasing bent toward "rational procedure." Nevertheless, the synthesis is never achieved; it is unceasing, and the dilemma remains at the core of the human animal (p. 21). With the scientific revolution's accumulation of knowledge, rationality took an ever-greater role in human affairs, and it would soon exert a dominant influence on the challenges of social life.

Seidenberg seeks to clarify his distinction between the two polarities of instinct and intelligence. Instincts, he writes, are the intuitive and emotional sensibilities of the mind—more concerned with ends that endow life with values. On the other hand, intelligence is focused on the conscious means to attain these ends. In describing intelligence, he uses such terms as "rational, analytical, deliberate, and purposive aspects of the mind" (p. 23). As unprecedented technological and organizational developments in the last hundred years or so take an ever-increasing role in human affairs, we progressively control the means of life. However, this rapid increase and perfection of mundane means have completely "dissipated and obscured" our more intangible aims and goals (p. 26).

However, it is not a straight-line, unilinear development. "Even today, the methodical rationalism to which we seem wholly dedicated has called forth a dark and countervailing irrationalism" (p. 23). Seidenberg points to the rise of fascism in politics and philosophy, existentialism's appeal, and modern art's rise. In our day, many reject science; there is a renewed attraction to fascism, a rise of fundamentalist religions, and a fascination with the occult and Eastern mysticism. Seidenberg identifies rationalism as a "world movement" and the opposition to that movement as a rejection of its aims based upon "intuitive and emotional" responses to the loss of traditional ways of life (p. 27). The dominant institutions of societies are structured "to enhance the welfare of the community rather than that of the individual" (p. 27). That is to say that the means of life are socially determined, while the individual has the burden of determining the meaning of life.

Seidenberg's analysis of modern art is of particular interest. He points out that the right and left dictatorships consistently condemn modern art. They see it as a revolt against a rationalized, bureaucratic life—of mass conformity and obedience to the state's authority—an affirmation of human freedom and spirit. "Thus, the artist and poet, alienated under the persistent affirmation of pragmatic values and consciously oriented objectives, are merely prophets crying in the wilderness of a rationalized world. The revolt in the art world turns out to be a revolt in the name of art against a mechanized, collectivized world of blank conformity" (p. 31). As an architect, Seidenberg has the opposite opinion of traditional compared to modern architecture. Our world is one of box-like skyscrapers, in seemingly active hostility to anything that is not purely functional and efficient. In comparing Madison Avenue with St. Patrick's Cathedral, he points out that we live in a world quite different from traditional societies—a world devoted to efficiency and purpose, to things rather than people. The architecture of our time reflects our shallow lives, of a people cut off from tradition and spiritual values, unaware of the more mysterious aspects of life (p. 32).

Traditional societies resemble organisms, held together through cultural bonds of love and affection, of shared beliefs and values. Modern societies have all the character and charm of an organization. Nevertheless, it is an organization that is increasingly necessary for our complex society. It is an organization growing more complex and intricate with instant communication, rapid transportation of people and goods, and growing political, economic, and social globalization. Even though we are confronted with increasing organization in every aspect of our daily lives, we have convinced ourselves that "where there is no alternative, there is also no problem" (p.35). However, there is, indeed, a problem. Even though organization is necessary and on a path toward ever further expansion and centralization, it has a decisive impact on human freedoms, individual control over life choices, and democracy.

The reasons for organizational growth are easy to identify. An organizational imperative is "organization demands further organization" (p. 36). To deal with an organization, say a corporation, on a (somewhat) equal footing, workers must organize to achieve fair wages and benefits. Individuals organize into parties, interest groups, or social movements to achieve political goals and influence government tax policies and programs. Seidenberg asserts that the efficient operation of any social group requires the organization to function effectively. He also identifies more systemic reasons for the growth of organizations, including the complexity and intensifying speed of production processes, the rapid growth of population, the expansion of scientific knowledge and its application in technology, the speed of modern communications, and the need to expand the exploitation of natural resources, particularly the growth and distribution of food. He clarifies that energy is vital to future growth, a resource upon which all others depend.

He foresees a time when nuclear energy will be called upon to replace fossil fuels, but it "will demand a very high degree of organization if it is to become effectively available in amounts commensurate with the scope of the problem" (p. 38). Seidenberg writes that the exponential population growth will also necessitate organizational forms worldwide to ameliorate the impact on the natural environment and the conservation of natural resources. "The problem arising out of man's primary instincts will either have to be abandoned to the cruel checks and balances of nature or resolved under the deliberate and conscious direction of human intelligence" (p. 39). Seidenberg predicts that as our numbers and technologies continue to proliferate, the need for further coordination and control will become even more compelling. To obtain maximum efficiency and predictability, the human element is increasingly being integrated into social organizations as producers and consumers—an integration that is slowly changing human nature.

This increasing organization is the historical struggle first detailed in *Post-Historic Man*, in which Seidenberg proposes that early humans transitioned from pre-conscious instinctive behavior to consciousness. Seidenberg posits that the transition from instinct to consciousness occurred over millennia and entails ever greater rationality in social institutions and procedures. Modernity has brought a rapid increase in human production and consumption capacities, expanding populations, advances in science and technology, the exponential growth of knowledge, instantaneous communication, rapid transportation, and a dizzying rate of social change. All these trends combine to create a world increasingly vulnerable to disruption, instability, and disorder (p. 40).

As the disorder mounts, the drift toward further organization becomes inevitable, not so much as a conscious decision—though rational planning and bureaucracy are almost ingrained reactions to social problems for most people. Instead, "it arises out of the implicit necessities of the situation, out of the constantly greater need for integration and coordination in the functioning of our highly complex civilization" (p. 40). Seidenberg asserts that the drift is not the province of totalitarian regimes but democracies as well. It will continue despite reactions against the rationalizations of life by anarchists and other irrational movements.

We are caught up in a significant shift from individual control by instinct to the social control of rational social organizations. By its inevitable expansion, the principle of rational social organization continues to transform the social structures of society—the institutions, procedures, and activities. This expansion of formal structure affects the character of the men and women who inhabit and are formed by that society. Organization, Seidenberg asserts, must necessarily move toward universality and thus humankind toward a collectivized society in which atomized individuals are subsumed in a vast organizational web. As social organizations become more rationalized and bureaucratic, they become ever more dominant in human affairs, and the very nature of human beings—consciousness, locus of control, introspection—will shift as well. Seidenberg sees the present as a "climatic turning point in this metamorphosis," we are rapidly moving into a future that is quite different from our past (p. 41).

Since the Scientific Revolution, human society's advances have been confined to material and social structural concerns rather than spiritual and ethical values, focusing on the means of life rather than its ends. The accelerating technological developments play havoc with societies, upsetting traditional institutions, customs, norms, and values, which prove inadequate for maintaining social cohesion and order. Traditional institutions and norms are progressively replaced "in favor of deliberate control and administration, of planned management and direction" (p. 44).

Since the 18th century, there has been an insistent demand for yet further rational social organization to provide the coordination and control needed by massive and growing populations, complicated production techniques, extensive supply chains, the detailed division of labor, and massive inequalities within and between societies. These are just a few of the coordination demands on modern social structures. There are numerous groups and organizations whose actions must be coordinated domestically and globally. All these organizations interact with one another and continue to change because of these interactions and further technological innovations. Formal social organizations increasingly coordinate "every phase and aspect of contemporary life," whether economic, political, or social. This rational order has not evolved slowly like prehistoric societies' rituals, norms, and values. They are "intentionally contrived and consciously integrated" and rapidly adopted into the structure of sociocultural systems, thus contributing to the tempo of social change and the need for further regulation. "For we live in a world that is moving, irreversibly it would seem, towards a condition of total organization" (p. 44).

Seidenberg asserts that we confront rationalized institutions focusing us on means rather than ends everywhere. Society markets higher education to the young as a means to a decent job and a comfortable lifestyle rather than for citizenship or the love of learning. Religion is marketed as the key to wealth and success rather than spiritual guidance and transcendence. Medicine is corporatized and monetized rather than caring for the sick and elderly. Agriculture focuses on finance and production rather than care for the land.

This rationalization is not only valid for authoritarian societies, where traditional structures and norms are often eliminated through coercion and force. Formal organizations of both government and corporate variety taking over the functions of informal institutions of family and community are also proceeding in democratic societies despite the cultural lag of tradition. Seidenberg adds that this is true for representative democracies and oligarchies disguised behind such democratic facades (p. 45). The drift toward total organization does not result from some political, economic, or social ideology. It is not the result of a conspiracy of evil men—such as the capitalist class, communist conspiracists, wannabe dictators, or the plans of the Illuminati. It does not need military conquest, missionaries, or even propaganda to spread control. Instead, the rationalization process provides the needed control and coordinating function "of all other means in the milieu of modern life" (p. 46).

Because rational social organization is ubiquitous and integral to modern life, we fail to grasp its direction and potential in weakening primary groups and its impact on individual human attitudes, values, and behaviors. Few question its nature, and fewer still posit that its growth is the dominant social force determining the future of human societies (p. 47). Rational social organizations are built like machines, with the various human parts serving specific functions in their contributions to the organization's goals. Seidenberg points out that it is a fitting metaphor, as machines and bureaucracies are consciously designed along similar lines. The rise of political, social, and economic organizations, along with machine technology, created the Industrial Revolution. "The growth of modern technology and the improvement of machine design, contingent upon the phenomenal advances in science and the ingenuity of engineers, demanded in turn the development of appropriate social accommodations to ensure their smooth and fruitful functioning" (p. 48).

A technological society requires a corresponding increase in rational organization, not only in the core industrial countries but also in areas supplying raw materials, cheap labor, and markets for industrial goods and services. Globalization is not just a recent phenomenon. Seidenberg recognizes the existence of worldwide distribution systems allocating raw materials to core countries and industrial products domestically and around the globe. He writes of the necessity of communication and transportation systems for these complex and far-flung operations. All such activities require coordination, synchronization, control, and conformity. The need has intensified in the 60 years since Seidenberg wrote his opus.

While Seidenberg identifies the development of machine technology as the initiator of the need for the increased coordination provided by rational organizations, its recent expansion is also due to the sociocultural system's needs. "Organization breeds organization," Seidenberg writes, comparing it to the actions of "crystallization," always seeking the integration of whatever it touches into its systems, eliminating chaos and promoting predictability, calculability, and order. He writes that expansion is "global in scope" as humankind moves in unison under the impetus of rationalization (p. 51).

There is, of course, opposition to the rationalization process. Nevertheless, even this opposition must be organized to be even partially effective. Seidenberg illustrates this by pointing to the collapse of nineteenth-century anarchism, the one philosophy that explicitly opposed rational organization in all its forms and advocated its destruction. Now the province of cranks and terrorists, it was once a movement that rivaled Marx's communism. To illustrate the "inherent necessity" of organization even in the pursuit of irrational goals, Seidenberg points to Nazi Germany. The anti-rationalism of Germany's "descent into the past" was accomplished through military and industrial technology and ever-tighter organization and coordination by the fascist state.

The irrationality of Nazi Germany occurred in one of the most advanced civilizations of its time. Their "blood-and soil revolt," the mass murder of millions of misfits, Jews, Romani, Slavs, and homosexuals, were accomplished "with characteristic Teutonic zeal and passion, to the organizational procedures of a world directed towards the future rather than the past" (p. 52). Seidenberg predicts that these irrational eruptions will continue in the future, as they are a reaction against the ever-growing rationalization of social structures. He believes they are reactionary movements "fought with the technological means and organizational procedures of the very system they aim to destroy" (p. 126). As such, they tend to reinforce rather than undermine the organizational structure of the social system.

The growing successes of science and industrial technologies have engendered much faith in their power and efficacy. While these successes create social change that creates problems, such as population growth and environmental destruction, mitigating these threats will undoubtedly involve more rationalization. Seidenberg points to the inevitable increase in global programs to deal with the problem of regulating population growth, organizations of far greater range and scope than in the past. He also points to the growing mechanization of agriculture, both in response to a growing population and other social forces such as technological innovation, an organizational imperative, and corporate farming (p. 55).

Seidenberg asserts that the social structure of future societies will be one of universal rational organizations. The drift, he writes, is deepening, reaching downward into ever more personal relationships and outward into all manner of social, political, and economic activities. He then asks what the effect of this future on the individual will be. "What influence will the form and structure of society under the dominant sway of organization exert upon the means and ends, the ways and values of life?" (p. 56). Can freedom exist in a society that reduces the individual to a mere cog in the social mass?

Seidenberg is not predicting a slide into totalitarianism as exemplified by twentieth-century dictatorships or in such novels as *1984*. Such authoritarian regimes may serve as a transitional phase. However, if the system's foundation is cruelty, terror, and domination of the masses, they will inevitably become the target for revolt. Instead, in line with the modern democracies of the West, he forecasts an evolutionary trajectory in which the individual is absorbed into the multitude of organizations that make up the sociocultural system. He predicts a system that increasingly manipulates information and manufactures opinions. Individual consciousness will slowly erode, "along with its spiritual implications," and in the long millenniums, the total integration of humankind into "a stable, unchanging, and unchallenged unity" (pp. 57-58). Like many social scientists, he believes human beings are sufficiently plastic in human "nature" and sufficiently adept at technology and rationalized social organization that humans could adjust both their environment to their needs and their needs to their environment (p. 58).

The complexity of modern social structures—the myriad of government and corporate organizations and their interrelationships—all drive social structures to higher levels of order, systematization, coordination, standardization, regimentation, and conformity. Rational social organization demands order and, therefore, the elimination of chaos and uncertainty (p. 59). Modern societies are thus driven to consciously contrived laws, rules, and regulations rather than relying upon internalized traditional norms, customs, and values.

Rational organizations increasingly dominate social structures, replacing traditional organizations' functions. Organization necessarily diminishes the individual's role and integrity in the process. However, it is not a smooth and unobstructed evolutionary process. Culture is necessarily rooted in the past, with traditional values promoting individual liberty and the sacredness of human life. Traditional culture is incompatible with the new ethos of rationalization with its increasing disregard for traditions and values. Such traditions slow down, though not arrest, the spread of modernity (p. 60). However, Seidenberg avers that individual freedom is only viable in the transitional phase we call history. Humans were ruled by instincts in prehistory and will be ruled by rational social organization in post-history (p. 63).

Seidenberg recognized more than sixty years ago, well before the development of big data and internet surveillance and manipulation, that organizations would mine our personal data for purposes of coordination and control:

> To that end, we are classified and indexed, tabulated, and numbered, not as persons but as irreducible fragments of the social whole, in the name of increased efficiency and further expansion, of increased order and standardization. Our births, deaths, marriages, income and occupations, habits, tastes, and predilections are being analyzed and correlated in a critical search for social control and predictability […]The commonly accepted notion that the freedom of the individual will be preserved, if not enhanced, as society itself becomes increasingly organized betrays our homage to nineteenth-century liberalism; today, the problem of the conflict between freedom and organization is emerging in all its desperate implications as the dominant challenge of the future (pp. 61-62).

With the development of electronic communications and more powerful surveillance techniques in the twenty-first century, the old faith in nineteenth-century liberalism that freedom and privacy will be preserved may be waning! Moreover, Seidenberg postulated that in the distant future, the individual would diminish in importance, be ever more open to surveillance and manipulation by rational social organizations, and finally lose all status, becoming an atom in the social whole of a "mass-directed civilization" (p. 64).

Contemporary individuals are without direction from the internal dictates and binding mores of primitive societies. Nevertheless, many are stripped of guidance from religious institutions, community bonds, and traditions. Finding themselves isolated, they are reduced to a small, insignificant role in the functioning of vast, impersonal, bureaucratic organizations that continuously monitor and regulate their actions. Thus alienated, the individual is subject to the external constraints of laws and regulations of the whole society and the rules of their immediate organization. At the same time, they are subjected "to a continuous barrage of manufactured opinion, propaganda, and mass manipulation" to enforce conformity and loyalty to the system (p. 64).

The character and speed of the transformation have engendered a backlash of opposition. Some engage in violence against the system, lashing out in often irrational anger and hatred toward those perceived as collaborators, hastening the new order (p. 65). Others go through the motions apathetically, drop out of mainstream culture, and exist on the margins. Nevertheless, the fate of the opposition is evident, for it is part of the long evolutionary process that began when humans first attained consciousness, was hurried along by the rise of science and industrial technology and continued in the social dominance of rational social organization. "[I]n view of the inescapable nature of our course, the one supreme question that remains to be asked is whether mankind, aware of the ultimate sterility of the present trends, can preserve the humanizing traditions of its vanishing past" (p. 65).

Seidenberg views individualism as a transitional stage, "arising out of a welter of changing modes of social cohesion," as the balance between instinctual and rational modes of operation shifts in dominance (p. 72). With this shifting dominance, life's challenges have become so complex, interrelated, and urgent that they can only be met with equally complex and interrelated organizational procedures planned along rational lines. According to Seidenberg, the course is set;

humankind cannot "live half in the future and half in the past by revitalizing the simplicities of an earlier dispensation" (74).

He argues that intelligence is different from knowledge, understanding, or wisdom. Intelligence is "directionless, a neutral agency of the mind concerned above all with the mutual relationships of presented facts and given data." Knowledge is the accumulation of these factual relationships. As knowledge accumulates, it serves "as a moving fulcrum," increasing the power of intelligence "in the growing complexity of human affairs." As modern society accumulates more precise and accurate information and knowledge about the material and social world, intelligence becomes indispensable (p. 79).

Therefore, material and organizational development depend on the accumulation of knowledge; their interaction has produced the technological and organizational advances of the past few centuries. This lack of a storehouse of knowledge helps explain the long-delayed historical development of the systematic application of rational intelligence to the material (technology and the manipulation and control of things) and social world (organization, coordination, and control of people). Seidenberg claims this delay points to a critical limitation of intelligence as knowledge can continue to grow without bounds. In contrast, intelligence, or our ability to synthesize and integrate this knowledge meaningfully, has definite limits (p. 81). Here again, Seidenberg may be in error, as general artificial intelligence may soon exceed human intelligence by many orders of magnitude. Nevertheless, regardless of any limitations, we are following a course of ever-increasing complexity in a social world that is already so complex and intricately connected that it is beyond our individual capacities of understanding (p. 93).

The development of technology and formal social organization has resulted in a highly detailed division of labor. In the modern era, the individual is increasingly circumscribed, a mere cog "on the edge of ever vaster, socially sustained enterprises" (p. 84). Rules and regulations constrain personnel actions and decisions within these organizations. These rules are based on standardization and consistency, all designed to promote productivity and efficiency in achieving the organization's goals. These organizations dwarf the individual, and their actions are often beyond their comprehension or control. In societies increasingly dominated by rational organizations, the individual becomes an "unthinking beneficiary" of a system designed by social intelligence that increasingly eliminates individual intelligence (p. 85). With the development of surveillance and social manipulation technology, the social system progressively constrains individual behavior and thought. The organization reaches its ideal efficiency to the degree of reducing individuality to its minimum in serving "the demands of human automatons" (p. 85). Thus, the need for a social system for ever-increasing organization, coordination, and control, no matter the type of political-economic system—dictatorship or representative democracy, capitalism, or socialism.

Seidenberg stresses the transition humankind is undergoing: a change in social structure toward rational social organization in response to specific challenges of living. Our initial successes with science and technology encouraged us to extend the range and influence of rational procedures to all aspects of social life. We extend the system's benefits "little inclined to question its bearing or ultimate direction" in area after area of social life previously untouched by its reach (p. 100). One can see this drift since Seidenberg's day in expanding educational systems, daycare, welfare agencies, and old-age institutions.

This drift has human consequences: psychological problems, rage against the system, widespread alienation, apathy, drug abuse, meaninglessness, and social dropouts. These problems are addressed, naturally enough, through social organizations aimed at promoting conforming behavior. While the techniques of terror, fear, confinement, and other uses of force are prominent today, Seidenberg believes these are ineffective and require too many resources to be efficient. He writes that they will gradually be supplanted by rationalized and more invasive "modes of indoctrination" (p. 102). Even dictatorships, he predicts, may be replaced by more enduring and stable methods of control based on science and technology.

The most severe and sustained opposition to organizational drift is our traditions and the philosophy of humanism. "The entire tradition of humanist values based upon the spiritual primacy of the self, is now at stake" (p. 104). As rational social organization transforms the social structure of society, it continuously confronts our sense of values. Rational social organizations have focused all our critical intelligence on the means of life and left the individual to find meaning. These values and ideals, at least for now, are a countervailing influence on the drift toward rational social organization, but their power over human thought and behavior is in decline.

Seidenberg, writing amid the Cold War and burgeoning environmental awareness of Americans, recognizes specific problems of nuclear war, population growth, and the rapid exhaustion of natural resources. He also recognizes that there is extreme poverty in three-quarters of the world. Addressing these problems, Seidenberg argues, can only be successfully approached through further social organization. He argues that our social organization has caused these problems and, despite its limitations, will have to be resolved through rational intelligence (p. 125). There is a worldwide acceptance of rationalization as the solution to our problems. It has become integral to how we perceive the world, a habit of thought of individuals and entire societies (p. 127).

Consciousness, Seidenberg insists, is a product of our dichotomous make-up of instinct and intelligence. The intelligence of historical humans has created the high cultural attainments of science, religion, arts, and the humanities, as well as the proliferation of complex rational social organizations. These attainments, he argues, constitute "a dramatic emergence of a new dimension of life," and consciousness will change in interaction with this new dimension (p. 128). The "organizational network of modern life demands, and in turn promotes, increased predictability in every phase and aspect of our complex civilization" (p. 138). He projects that "consciousness will gradually fade out" as rational social organization becomes the controlling feature of human thought and action and eventually achieves a stable condition in which change slowly recedes. The social order solidifies ("crystallizes" is his term). In sum, his theory is that human history is a period of rapid and accumulating change in which individuals reach the height of a conscious phase, only to lose that consciousness as social organization and technological change slows and eventually stops in future millennia (pp. 129-130). Increasingly, the means of life have become confused with their ends; no longer concerned with transcendence, human life focuses on itself in the routine of daily living (p. 139).

The prime function of rational social organization is to make ever-finer adjustments to the natural and social environments or, conversely, adjust the individual to the needs of the social and natural environments. Social animals, insects, and mammals have only one approach to survival: "life becomes encased in an endless cycle of rigidly established routines. Like an inward-sweeping spiral, intelligence moves, not toward greater freedom, but towards the elimination of all freedom" (p. 152).

In this conception, the historical era of humankind is but a brief period of cumulative change and consciousness between the two much more extended periods of pre- and post-history in which human life is unchanging and fully adjusted to its natural and social environments. He avers that this future may seem improbable, but it is the fate of many life forms on Earth, and we are clearly moving in that direction (pp. 143-144). Seidenberg asserts "that our rationality is in the service of an encompassing irrationality...the world has become subtly mad beneath the façade of its rationality (pp. 144-145).

Many perceive the nonconforming individual as an anti-social deviant. "In the present stage of our development, the locus of the conflicts is to be found in the depths of our spiritual, and perhaps even more, our psychological maladjustments" (pp. 146-147). To hasten the smoother functioning of society, we have developed modern techniques to promote the adaptation of the individual to the social system. These techniques run the gamut from more effective forms of advanced persuasion and advertising to the use of psychoactive drugs in democracies to the more immersive indoctrination of propaganda, force, cruelty, and coercion of the more authoritarian regimes (p. 143).

Seidenberg already maintains that there is a rising protest of humanists arguing against organizational drift and the consequent dehumanization. Nevertheless, the process continues. Past values are rapidly being transformed and reinterpreted into different forms of organized religion, education, and loyalty to corporations and nation-states. "The transformation of the world into an ever more organized, rationally directed systems of living constitutes the dominant characteristic of our passage into the future" (p. 142). In the process, we are losing the "depth-dimension of life" as rational social organization expands into all areas of social life, appearing ever more "necessary, meaningful, and inevitable" (pp. 142-143). Thus, "the circle of protest and understanding narrows as the system itself expands, and there with the potentially creative focus of life become ever more diluted, ineffectual, and impotent" (pp. 147-148).

Even if humankind manages to escape this fate, Seidenberg argues, we will confront mounting social problems caused by society's "tragic imbalance between the high achievement of its technology and the static if not regressive capacities of its individuals" (p. 149). Seidenberg gives short shrift to forecasts of superabundance or the creation of a material paradise, pointing out that the hoarding characteristics of the rich know no bounds. He considers nuclear war a clear possibility, leading to the collapse of civilization, pointing out that his speculation is "on an as if basis, on the assumption, however dubious, that humanity will spare itself the desperate ignominy of suicide" (p. 171). However, another fate awaits if we get through this threat of civilization collapse and destruction. "In the long perspective of the future there is reason to believe, certainly, that the seeming divergencies of our world will be absorbed and forgotten in an all-inclusive rationalization of life" (p. 171).

About Seidenberg

Not much is known about the early life of Roderick Seidenberg. Sources report that he was born in Heidelberg, Germany, on October 20, 1889, though some accounts had it in 1890. When he came to America is still unknown—was it as a child with his family or as an adult? He studied architecture at Columbia University from 1906 to 1910, with enthusiasm for using architecture and leftist ideas to improve the lot of humanity, at least according to some of his friends (Clayton, 1998, p. 41). Around 1917, his friend, Carl Zigrosser, introduced him to Mabel Dwight (Mabel Williamson Higgens), a graphic artist. She had recently separated from her husband of ten years, rebelling against a domestic role that kept her from her artistic career. Although she was some 14 years older than Seidenberg, they soon moved in together into his apartment.

In late 1917, as a United States citizen, he was drafted for World War I. He declared himself an "absolute conscientious objector," meaning he would not contribute directly or indirectly to the war effort. He is imprisoned first at Camp Upton on Long Island, court marshaled for refusing to clean a parade ground and sentenced to 20 years in prison. The army sent him first to Fort Leavenworth and eventually transferred him to Fort Riley before releasing him in 1920 after serving about a year and a half of his sentence. While imprisoned, he wrote passionate letters in which he asserted the depth of his love for Mabel, the monotony of prison life, his heartfelt conscientious objection to war, and the abuse and torture endured by him and his compatriots. He wrote of his imprisonment in a 1932 article for H.L. Menken's *Mercury* titled "I Refuse to Serve" but only mentioned the abuse he and his fellow absolute conscientious objectors endured in passing. Instead, he focuses on the prison's hellish conditions and how nonviolent demonstrations improve conditions. However, his friend, Karl Zigrosser, details some of the abuse Seidenberg initially received at Leavenworth. This torture included prolonged solitary confinement in dark cells, a bread and water diet, and being manacled nine hours of the day "with his arms out even with his shoulders" (Traxel, 1980, p. 107; Antliff, 2001, p. 161).

After his release from prison in 1920, he and Mable lived in Greenwich Village. She continued developing her artistic reputation, and he became an associate with the New York architecture firm of Sugarman & Berger. With that firm, he designed the exterior of the New Yorker Hotel and the Garment Center Building (New York Times, Obituary 1973). Sometime in the mid to late 1920s, he met and fell in love with his future wife, Catherine Howard, and became estranged from Mabel Dwight.

Starting in the 1920s and into the 1930s, Seidenberg began authoring occasional essays for literary magazines. He published pieces in journals like *The Freeman*, the *New Republic*, and *The Nation*. Hirch (2003) characterizes these pieces as rather "avant-garde artistic experiments," with a clear indication "that he saw culture and politics as interrelated" and that he "had a secular, left-of-center, cosmopolitan, and pluralist view of the world" (p. 71). Hirsch writes that "Seidenberg was markedly reticent about his past" (p. 71).

In 1935, Seidenberg became the national editor of *Architecture and Art* for the Federal Writers Project (FWP), a New Deal Works Progress Administration (WPA) to relieve mass unemployment. At the national level, the FWP set itself the task of creating a comprehensive guidebook on every state in the nation, detailing its artistic, cultural, and historical attributes. The national office authorized each state to hire a few professional writers, but most state workers had to qualify for relief before joining the FWP. Some performed well; some were ill-suited to their tasks. On the other hand, the national office comprised professionals with a broad knowledge of American culture and deep expertise in their fields. Hirsch credits Seidenberg as responsible for the "markedly superior in style and content" of the Guidebook essays under his editorship" (p. 72). "From the tourist's point of view, Seidenberg thought adequate treatment of architecture necessary to any guidebook venture; but beyond that, he contended, the guides offered an opportunity to instruct American taste and to help ordinary Americans know and appreciate the built environment. There was an opportunity 'to clarify [...] a broader conception of architecture as an expression of historical (and social forces)—as a resolution, in visible form, of the trends and tendencies of our civilization'" (p. 73).

In 1937, Seidenberg moved to Bucks County, Pennsylvania, where he continued in architecture, altering old houses and turning to writing. In his personal life, when Mabel Dwight became chronically ill and destitute, he and his wife, Catherine, took her in and cared for her throughout her life. In 1950, Seidenberg published *Post-Historic Man* (sometimes referred to as *Posthistoric Man;* both are acceptable, but I will go with the hyphen), following it up eleven years later with *Anatomy of the Future*. Both books were well-reviewed then and forgotten by all except a few. In this paper, we reviewed the original works as an in-depth illustration of the rationalization process and the increasing dominance of social organization in coordinating and controlling human behavior.

Part 4: Population, Production, & Evolution

Macro Social Theory encompasses a rich tapestry of ideas that shed light on the complex interplay between population, production, the environment, and social structures. T. Robert Malthus, a pioneering figure in sociology and demography, contributed seminal insights into the relationship between population growth, resource scarcity, and its impact on social change. This introductory essay focuses on a section of Macro Social Theory, examining the works of four significant theorists—T. Robert Malthus, Marvin Harris, Gerhard Lenski, and Stephen Sanderson. By delving into their theories, we aim to unveil the commonalities shared between these recent thinkers and Malthus, particularly in exploring the intricate connections between population dynamics, production systems, the environment, and their influence on social structures and change. Through this exploration, we illuminate the lasting influence of Malthusian ideas and their relevance in contemporary macrosocial theory.

T. Robert Malthus, in his seminal work, highlighted the potential conflict between population growth and limited resources, emphasizing the potential for environmental and social consequences. Malthus argued that the population tends to grow geometrically. At the same time, food production increases arithmetically, leading to inevitable and constant checks on population growth, such as famine, disease, and war (positive checks), abstinence, vice, and loosening moral behavior (preventive checks). His ideas challenged the prevailing optimistic views of progress and warned about the potential negative impacts of population pressures on social stability.

Marvin Harris, a notable anthropologist in the last half of the 2nd century, drew inspiration from Malthusian and Marian insights and expanded them through his theory of cultural materialism. Harris examined the relationship between population dynamics, technology, and social structures by emphasizing the importance of material and environmental factors in shaping social behavior. His approach highlighted the role of subsistence strategies, resource availability, and ecological constraints in driving societal organization and change. Harris, like Malthus, recognized the importance of understanding how population and production systems interact with the environment, influencing social structures and cultural practices.

Gerhard Lenski, a prominent sociologist who also wrote in the latter half of the 20th century, furthered Malthusian perspectives through his theory of sociocultural evolution. Lenski examined the impact of population growth and technology on the development of societies, particularly in terms of the transformation of social structures and institutions. He argued that as populations grow and technological advancements occur, societies change their production systems, social hierarchies, and modes of social organization. Lenski's work aligns with Malthusian ideas by emphasizing the critical role of population dynamics and production capacities in shaping social structures and societal evolution.

Stephen Sanderson, an evolutionary sociologist, built upon Malthusian foundations in his analysis of social change and adaptation. By drawing from evolutionary theory, Sanderson explored the relationship between population growth, resource competition, and social structures. He argued that as populations expand and resources become scarce, societies experience adaptive changes, such as the emergence of social complexity, hierarchical systems, or technological innovations. Sanderson, like Malthus, recognized the significance of population pressures in shaping the dynamics of social structures and the trajectory of social change.

As you explore the theories of Marvin Harris, Gerhard Lenski, and Stephen Sanderson alongside T. Robert Malthus's foundational insights, we witness the enduring influence of Malthusian ideas in contemporary macro social theory. These thinkers, each situated within different disciplines and time periods, draw upon Malthus's understanding of the intricate relationships between population, production, the environment, and social structures. Their shared emphasis on the impact of population dynamics on social change,

As we explore the theories of Marvin Harris, Gerhard Lenski, and Stephen Sanderson alongside T. Robert Malthus's seminal contributions, we unveil the enduring commonalities that link these recent thinkers to Malthusian perspectives. Their investigations into the intricate interplay between population, production, the environment, and social structures echo Malthus's concerns about the implications of population growth against the backdrop of limited resources. These theorists shed light on the complex dynamics that underlie societal development, resource allocation, and social change, emphasizing the significance of understanding the population-environment nexus in comprehending the challenges and possibilities that shape our social world. Through their collective insights, we gain a deeper appreciation for the continued relevance of Malthusian perspectives in Macro Social Theory, inspiring us to navigate the complex interplay between population dynamics, production systems, and social structures with heightened clarity and insight.

Chapter 13: T. Robert Malthus's Social Theory

Thomas Robert Malthus (1766-1834) is given only passing mention in social theory texts and monographs and is hardly mentioned in our introductory sociology texts. While he is widely considered the founder of social demography, his work is rarely recognized as theory, read, or taken seriously. All that is known about Malthus by modern-day social scientists comes through writings about Malthus—and many of these writings rely heavily on hostile critics who have grossly oversimplified his writings. If mentioned at all in works of social theory, it is often to dismiss his supposed prediction of eventual population explosion and collapse. Many social scientists conclude that Malthus is only of historical interest—an example of an early Cassandra predicting a future population explosion that has been proven wrong by subsequent events. Reading the original *Essay on Population*, however, and his subsequent works quickly expose this view as quite mistaken. Because of the prevalence of misinformation about Malthus, two points need to be stressed: (1) Preconceived notions strongly influence a person's interpretation of a text, and (2) Never trust secondary sources unless they are heavily documented and footnoted! This chapter will be heavily footnoted, closely tying interpretations of Malthus with the original Essay.

A few scholars, however, have taken Malthus seriously. Several social scientists focus heavily on the centrality of the relations between human populations and their environment to understand all other aspects of sociocultural stability and change. Many of them have identified Malthus as a founder of the evolutionary paradigm. This social evolutionary tradition runs from Malthus to Herbert Spencer, William Graham Sumner, V. Gordon Childe, Leslie White, and Julian Steward. Modern-day practitioners include Marvin Harris, who advocated such an ecological-evolutionary strategy for anthropology, and Gerhard Lenski, who advocated a similar strategy for sociology. Malthus's focus on the relationships between population and food production—and the effects of this interaction on other parts of the social system—forms the foundation for the theories of Gerhard Lenski and Marvin Harris. Other modern practitioners within this tradition include Mark Cohen, Ester Boserup, Robert Carneiro, Patrick Nolan, and Stephen K. Sanderson. The evolutionary tradition's influence, directly or indirectly from Malthus, can also be seen in the work of famous writers such as Jared Diamond. The failure to include Malthus in our theory texts leaves little foundation for modern-day social evolutionary theory. Consequently, students are left with the impression that contemporary ecological-evolutionary theory has little root in the social sciences but instead has been borrowed from the "hard" science of biology. However, as Charles Darwin and Alfred Wallace acknowledged, Malthus's population theory has also profoundly affected biology. A passage in Darwin's autobiography states that some fifteen months after beginning his inquiry, he read Malthus on population for amusement. "It at once struck me that under these circumstances favorable variations would tend to be preserved, and unfavorable ones to be destroyed. The results of this would be the formation of a new species. Here, then I had at last got a theory by which to work" ([1876] 1958, p. 42). Wallace reports in his autobiography that "perhaps the most important book I read was Malthus' *Principle of Population*...its main principles remained with me as a permanent possession, and twenty years later gave me the long-sought clue of the effective agent in the evolution of organic species" (1905, 232).

Malthus has other attributes that make him a suitable candidate for inclusion in the social science canon. His writing style is surprisingly readable, his prose is lively, and his arguments and examples connect with modern readers. He pioneered empirical data in the inductive/deductive process of theory building, a necessary discipline lacking in many of the early practitioners of the social sciences (see, for example, Malthus [1798] 2001, p. 130 & p. 206). In addition, as part of his "social system" orientation, much of his analysis pre-figures the functional analysis of contemporary sociologists and anthropologists (see, for example, pp. 283-284). It is time to recognize Malthus's contribution to social thought and time to make him a part of the social science canon.

Malthus's *Essay on Population* begins by pointing out that our ability to produce children will always outstrip our ability to provide energy for their survival. This imbalance, Malthus says, is a condition of our biological existence. Therefore, he continues, the population must be kept in line with what society can produce in sustenance. Finally, he states that every way available to keep the population in check—preventive and positive—has negative consequences for individuals and

296

societies. Because of this simple fact, Malthus argues, we can never achieve the just and equitable society anticipated by believers in material and spiritual progress—poverty, pain, vice, and misery will always be the lot of some.

The 1798 Theory

Malthus' *Essay* addressed two essential works of the day. Marquis de Condorcet had recently published *Outline of the Intellectual Progress of Mankind* (1795), in which he took the Enlightenment-inspired position that societies pass through stages. Each stage represents the progressive emancipation of man's reason from superstition and ignorance (much of Condorcet's vision gets passed on to his French successor—Auguste Comte). William Godwin published *Enquiry Concerning Political Justice* (1793), which made similar claims regarding the perfectibility of society. In his Essay, Godwin claimed that corrupt institutions repressed man's natural goodness. These institutions would be gradually replaced by the spread of reason and greater social equality (Winch, 1987, p. 26). As evidenced by Condorcet and Godwin, the idea of social progress was even more widespread in Malthus's day than in our own. Both attribute the lower classes' vice and misery to problems in society's social structure—basically, government and economic institutions. For them, the solution to widespread misery was to reform elements of the social structure to conform to the enlightened principles of equality and justice. Society must be reformed so that resources can be fairly allocated to all. To this claim, Malthus responds that structural reform can make some improvements. However, he maintains that "no possible form of society could prevent the almost constant action of misery upon a great part of mankind" (Malthus, p. 222, pp. 245-246, quote on p. 246).

Malthus claims that the problems of human societies are not primarily due to flaws in the social structure (pp. 212-213). Instead, the problems are of a "nature that we can never hope to overcome"; they are the consequences of an imbalance between our ability to produce food and our ability to produce children (p. 274). We are far better at making babies than finding food for their survival. Malthus writes that this problem exists in all past and present societies and must exist in any future society. Because of this natural law of imbalance between population and production, Malthus asserts, inequality is built into the very structure of human societies. Creating a technological or enlightened society where resources are fairly and equitably distributed to all is impossible (pp. 245-246).

Malthus' basic theory can be summarized as follows: Humankind has two basic needs: food and sex—one leading to the production of food and the other to the reproduction of children. However, the power of reproduction is "indefinitely greater" than the power of production. If unchecked, Malthus maintained, population levels would double in size about every 25 years (pp. 135-136). His estimate of population doubling time, it turns out, is a perfectly accurate estimate according to current demographic theory. Malthus based this estimate on observations of substantial population growth in the New World, where resources were abundant for the small population of European immigrants. In such an environment, the population proliferates. However, this growth can only be a temporary phenomenon. Once the population reaches the productive level of the land, it must be checked. The population will grow again if productive capacity suddenly increases because of the introduction of innovative technologies. However, potential population growth must be continually checked because productive capacity can never maintain this growth rate for long—double every 25 years.

These checks are of two basic types: (1) *preventive* checks, in which people attempt to prevent births in some manner, and (2) *positive* checks, in which the life span of an existing human being is shortened in some way. "Positive" is used here because the check is characterized by actions that terminate life—not in the colloquial sense that it is good or desirable. Malthus labels these "positive" checks because they actively cut down the existing population by reducing the human life span.

A posited cyclical relationship between production and reproduction is central to Malthus' theory. An increase in productivity will lower food costs, thus making it cheaper for a family to have children. More children would live (or be allowed to live); fewer efforts would be made to prevent conception. Eventually, the rise in population would increase the demand for food, driving prices up and leading to challenging times for the poor. The population would be leveled off through the more efficient operation of positive and preventive checks. The high price of provision, plus the lower wages for labor (because of the surplus of workers), would induce farmers to increase productivity by hiring more workers, putting more land under the plow, and using technology to increase productivity. This increase in productivity would loosen the constraints (the checks) to reproduction—it would continue the cycle (pp. 143-144). Malthus recognized that the cycle is not steady paced. Wars, disease, economic cycles, technological breakthroughs, the lag between changes in the price of food and money wages, and government action can all temporarily disrupt or spur the cycle (Winch, 1987, p. 22). The "oscillation" between the growth of subsistence and population, and the misery that it causes, has not been noted in the histories of humankind, Malthus writes because these are histories of the higher classes (Malthus, [1798] 2001, p. 144). Nonetheless, he maintains that a continuing cycle between population and production necessitates the operation of stringent checks on population growth.

Malthus illustrates the unequal growth in production and reproduction with the oft-quoted model—a comparison of arithmetic and geometric (or exponential) growth. This model is often considered Malthus's basic principle of population in both the popular press and secondary literature. It is not his theory of population but merely a thought experiment illustrating the power of unchecked population growth. Starting with a billion people (in the British style, "a thousand million"), Malthus points out that if allowed to double in size every 25 years, the human population would increase in the following manner: 1, 2, 4, 8, 16, 32, 64, 128, 256, 512. Subsistence, however, does not necessarily grow at an exponential rate. Assuming an initial quantity of 1 unit and adding an additional unit every 25 years, subsistence would increase as 1, 2, 3, 4, 5, 6, 7, 8, 9, 10, and so on. In 225 years, Malthus says, the population would be at 512 billion—511 billion more than at time 1. However, in that same period, the means of subsistence would only have increased by 10. In 2000 years, Malthus adds, the difference between population and production would be incalculable (pp. 142-144).

Malthus is not predicting that the human population will grow in these numbers, for that would be impossible in his system of constantly acting checks on the population. He is not saying that the production of subsistence must only grow arithmetically. He is saying that subsistence could never keep up with unchecked population growth; the powers of growth are too unequal! Population growth must be continually checked. He remarks in the *Essay* that he is aware that such a disparity between production and population in the model could never exist:

> I am sufficiently aware that the redundant twenty-eight millions, or seventy-seven millions, that I have mentioned, could never have existed. It is a perfectly just observation of Mr. Godwin, that, *'There is a principle in human society, by which population is perpetually kept down to the level of the means of subsistence.'* The sole question is, what is this principle? Is it some obscure and occult cause? Is it some mysterious interference of heaven which, at a certain period, strikes the men with impotence, and the women with barrenness? Or is it a cause, open to our researches, within our view, a cause, which has constantly been observed to operate, though with varied force, in every state in which man has been placed? *Is it not a degree of misery, the necessary and inevitable result of the laws of nature,*

which human institutions, so far from aggravating, have tended considerably to mitigate, though they never can remove? (pp. 212-213, emphasis added).

He was not predicting a future population calamity as is often misinterpreted; he was merely using a mathematical model to illustrate the unequal powers of our ability to produce food and children. Malthus demonstrates the impossibility of unchecked population growth by extrapolating what would happen without checks on population. So ingrained is the view that Malthus predicted a population collapse far into the future that readers continually gloss over this critical point. That Malthus is not predicting the "overshoot and collapse" of the population will be emphasized repeatedly in this chapter.

Much of the literature on Malthus misses this critical point and interprets this model as illustrating an inevitable population "overshoot" of the resource base (some would also claim a collapse). Nevertheless, the checks are responsive to the relations of production and population; it is not like an expanding balloon that pops when it reaches some absolute limit. The difference between Malthus and his mis-interpreters lies in viewing the possibility of "overshoot" somewhere in the future. For Malthus, population growth is always running against the available resources to support it; checks are present in every human society to prevent population collapse. To repeat: population growth almost always exceeds the means of subsistence, but checks on this growth constantly occur, which rarely leads to collapse (p. 195). Societies are free from overshooting only when they first settle in new lands, are recovering from severe depopulation due to natural disasters or plague or are in the immediate aftermath of introducing innovative technology that significantly expands food production. In all other situations, there is more population than can be supported by existing production and distribution systems—this portion of the population is usually called "the poor." As a result, people experiencing poverty suffer higher mortality rates than the rest of the population. Remove this check, Malthus argues, through technological innovation that increases yield per acre or the discovery of new lands, and fertility rates increase until population level again reaches the new production and distribution limits, and the check again takes effect.

The model is not a prediction of the future of population growth or the speed of technological development—it is a model of the relationship between the two. While Malthus' illustrative model was based on steady arithmetic growth of productive capacity, slow or moderate growth is not central to his theory. An increase in agricultural production—even if it were exponential—would only increase the birth rates of the poor (recall, the price of food will decline, and more children will reach maturity). Thus, it eventually necessitates the operation of checks on the population when the population again exceeds productive capacity. It is only by assuming productive capacity as doubling at least every 25 years at a steady pace and potentially limitless (in other words, conceiving the power of production as equal to that of reproduction) that the checks will not need to be a part of the system. Malthus is unwilling to make this assumption—to do so flies in the face of observation and logic.

It is also counter to experience since Malthus authored the Essay as well. While it is commonplace in the secondary literature to claim that productivity more than matched population growth since Malthus, this is decidedly not the case. Estimates are that there were one billion people on earth when Malthus drafted the original *Essay.* Assuming the estimated 25-year doubling time for unchecked population, today's population would now be up to 256 billion. It is not nearly so high (8.2 billion in 2025). All along, there have been stringent checks on the population. At the same time, food production has increased substantially but not at the same rate as unchecked population growth (consistent with Malthus's assumption). Instead, in accordance with Malthus's theory, the rise in productivity in the last 200-plus years has been met by a substantial rise in population (a genuinely exponential rise, though far less than potential unchecked growth). The poor are still among us. There is great poverty and misery in the world. Checks on the population are still in operation—checks aimed at preventing conception and positive checks of increased mortality due to disease and malnutrition. A just, equitable, and enlightened society is still beyond our grasp.

Population Checks

The necessity of checks on population growth is based on our biological nature. The checks, Malthus argues, are necessary to keep the population in line with subsistence from the environment. Malthus asserts that animal and plant species are impelled by instinct to reproduce. There is only one type of check on wild plant and animal life—the lack of room or nourishment for offspring. That is the "positive check" of premature death (pp. 142-143). These positive checks would include famine and disease in human populations, leading to high infant and child mortality rates (p. 161). One of the most widely used positive checks, Malthus suggests, has been infanticide committed throughout human history (p. 156). In addition, Malthus saw a good portion of the human population carried off by war, disease, unwholesome occupations, hard labor, misery, and vice (pp. 188-189). These positive checks operate on the poor and powerless much more so than the well-to-do and the elite—for the poor themselves were the "excess" population—the part of the population that current production and distribution practices cannot adequately support (p. 161).

However, checks on the human population are not confined to the positive checks of nature. For humans, reason intervenes. In an equal state, Malthus argues, the only question is whether subsistence can be provided to offspring. In the real world, however, where inequality is the rule, "other considerations occur." In this world, potential parents will ask questions like: Will having children lower my standard of living? Will I have to work much harder to support my children? Will I have to see my children hungry and miserable despite my best efforts? Will I lose a significant amount of independence and be forced to accept the handout of charity to support my children? (pp. 142-143). If a couple decides not to have children, they must prevent conception. These preventive checks are accomplished through individuals' many independent cost-benefit decisions regarding children and work (pp. 142-143, p. 176).

Preventive checks, Malthus recognized, come in many varieties. The ideal for Malthus was to practice celibacy before marriage and to delay marriage until children could be supported. However, he asserts that this forces individuals to deny a basic human need—a "dictate of nature" (pp. 142-143). Recall that one of Malthus's main postulates is that the "passion between the sexes is necessary" and constant (p. 135). Therefore, this necessary restraint produces misery for those who practice celibacy and marry late (pp. 175-176). For those who cannot practice such ideal discipline (most human beings, Malthus implies), the constraints on population growth necessarily led to "vice" (pp. 142-143).

Under the category of vice, Malthus includes such practices as frequenting prostitutes, "unnatural acts" (non-procreative sex), and the use of birth control. There are several problems caused by vice. First, vice serves to increase the sum of unhappiness in both men and women. (p. 195). Second, vice often leads to shortened life spans by increasing exposure to disease and drugs (pp. 188-189). Finally, the acceptance or approval of widespread non-procreative sexuality will "destroy that virtue and purity of manners"—the very goal of those who profess the perfectibility of society (p. 195). Malthus argues that vice is a necessary consequence of constraints on population growth.

Malthus' definition of vice includes the practice of birth control—even birth control confined within marriage. Some birth control practices were prevalent in his day—mainly using sponges.

Malthus alludes to these practices several times (in the language of his day). What is clear from the *Essay* is that he considered birth control practices an effective preventive check (just as he considered other more traditional forms of vice effective in preventing population increase). However, Malthus believed the widespread use of contraception would change the moral behavior of men and women and inevitably affect family and community life (p. 195). Therefore, he did not consider birth control—even in marriage—an ideal solution to limiting population growth. This failure to explicitly consider birth control a viable and now socially acceptable preventive check on population growth has puzzled and angered many. Some urged Malthus during his lifetime to explicitly promote the use of birth control in subsequent editions of the Essay. He ignored such pleas (Winch, 1987, p. 53).

Social movements arose in the 19th century—many calling themselves "Malthusian"—that warned of out-of-control population growth and advocated the distribution of various birth control devices. Many today perceive a population crisis and advocate contraception as a viable solution. Malthus also makes clear that, although he was genuinely concerned about the effects of vice on society, of the two types of checks on population (positive and preventive), he much preferred the preventive (Malthus, [1798] 2001, p. 168). Indeed, birth control within marriage would be second only to abstinence as the least objectionable preventive check in Malthus' system. In addition, as Malthus knew well, birth control (even within marriage) could be a solution for many individuals who could not practice the ideal of celibacy. Still, he never became an advocate and never thought of birth control as a viable solution to the population problem. Part of this reluctance to embrace birth control undoubtedly lies in reaffirming a social ideal—in this case, the traditional ideal of celibacy before a late marriage—that people can aspire to (even though it is honored more in the breach). Malthus, who married at 38, believed in the rightness of the prevailing mores of his time and attempted to live by their dictates.

Nevertheless, much of his reluctance to sanction birth control as a viable solution to the population problem is also rooted in his social theory. Malthus's system points to difficulties relying on preventive checks to control population levels. The availability of contraception alone cannot stabilize a population, Malthus argues, because people also must have a perceived interest in preventing births. For many, in Malthus' day as well as our own, there is no such interest—in fact, the cost/benefit analysis of having children often favors large families among people experiencing poverty. Children are assets in many families; the individual cost/benefit analysis likely favors high birth rates for poor parents and lower birth rates for better-off people (p. 138, pp. 142-143). Children are economic assets in pre-industrial and early industrial societies, where they can contribute directly to economic production activities. In such societies, they are also a form of social security in the parent's old age. In such a situation, the poorer the parents, the greater the economic incentive to have children. In addition to this direct economic incentive, there is also the fact that in societies with high infant mortality, having many children is a sound strategy for ensuring that a few will survive to adulthood. Wealthier prospective parents, with access to better nutrition, less hard labor for their children, and better living conditions, could be more confident that the children they did have would survive to adulthood. Thus, making birth control available will not significantly impact the birth rate if it is not perceived to be in the immediate material interests of the parents.

A second reason that preventive checks are not a viable solution, Malthus asserts, is that people experiencing poverty often lack the foresight, opportunity, and discipline to use contraception or to put off marriage. Such preventive checks are far more likely to be taken by the most educated and wealthy classes, not the poor and uneducated, who feel the full brunt of the positive checks (p. 159). This reluctance to use birth control on the part of the poor is not due to a lack of intelligence but rather their lack of education and resources. This means that many children are born with no corresponding increase in sustenance. Nature accomplishes what must be done in the form of hunger, disease, and other afflictions that shorten the poor's life span. The *Essay* systematically explores the effects of these necessary checks—both positive and preventive—on the entire sociocultural system. For these reasons, birth control, as well as other methods of preventive checks, operates with "varied" force among the different classes of society—the poor are checked more often by the positive checks of rising mortality—and, Malthus believes, it will always be so (p. 161).

This same cost-benefit calculation Malthus wrote about is responsible for the demographic transition. With the transition to industrialism, particularly with the prohibition of child labor and social security, children lose their productive value; they no longer contribute to the family's economic well-being. Malthus recognized that increasing a family's wealth and education would lead to the use of more preventive checks and smaller families, which is one reason he became a strong advocate for universal education in his later years. Nevertheless, he maintains that education cannot solve the population problem. Some will always be poor. Having larger families will be in their interest (cost/benefit). Currently, population growth around the world is leveling off. This leveling is accomplished by spreading preventive checks (because of changes in the cost-benefit analysis for individuals, the spread of education, or government compulsion) and through higher mortality rates among people experiencing poverty. It is also interesting that world population growth is slowing down along with agricultural production. The dynamics between population and food production are the material foundation of all societies, and we now turn to this foundation. With improved birth control technology and the increasing levels of education, income, and empowerment of women, the mix between positive and preventive checks to control population has changed dramatically since Malthus's day, with preventive checks being far more prevalent even among people experiencing poverty. However, the positive and preventive checks still act with varying force among the different income groups within and between societies. They are still a significant factor in population and production relationships.

Inequality

Malthus asserts that a working class is essential to every society—labor will always be necessary to wrest subsistence from nature. Malthus saw society as a system; consequently, the various parts of that system contributed to the social whole. The *Essay* is highly compatible with a functional perspective. He further views the institution of private property and the self-interest of individuals as motivating human thought and action (p. 250). People are motivated to act through the spur of necessity—to avoid poverty or obtain riches. Unequal rewards for industry and idleness are the "master spring" of human activity (p. 283, & pp. 193-194). The desire for riches, or the fear of poverty, also motivates humans to regulate the number of their offspring.

Again, Malthus' main point is that there is an imbalance between our ability to produce food and our tendency to produce children. In a state of equality where resources are shared equally, the necessity of checks on the population would fall on all. However, those with better access to resources (following their self-interests) will not put themselves and their families at such risk. Therefore, the fundamental self-interest of the elite in their immediate families is that inequality is established and maintained. Consequently, food and other resources are unequal in any human society (p. 146). This fundamental inequality means people experiencing poverty must pay the "positive check" in lowered life expectancy. Therefore, poverty is due to the imbalance between our ability to produce food and our tendency to reproduce the species (p. 216).

Because the population tends to outstrip available food supplies, the mass of people must be subjected to physical distress (lack of food and other necessities) to limit population increase (either through preventive checks or, failing those, positive checks). Because of this imbalance, "millions and millions of human existences have been repressed" (p. 189). Malthus asserts that the necessity to repress population existed in every society in the past, exists in the present, and will "forever continue to exist" (p. 195). The necessity to repress many potential offspring is due to our physical nature—our reliance on food and the necessity of sexuality.

Malthus consistently demonstrates the necessity of workers and proprietors in all societies beyond hunting and gathering levels (pp. 193-194, p. 222, & p. 242). Labor is the only property owned by people experiencing poverty, which they sell in exchange for money to purchase the necessities of life. "The only way that a poor man has of supporting himself in independence is by the exertion of his bodily strength" (p. 250). Nevertheless, unlike the latter "Social Darwinists," Malthus does not see poverty as a consequence of moral worth or fitness to survive. He does not believe that the poor are necessarily responsible for their condition; instead, they "are the unhappy persons who, in the great lottery of life, have drawn a blank" (p. 216). He does not attempt to justify the "present great inequality of property" (p. 250). Malthus views severe inequality with horror and asserts that it is not necessary or beneficial to the bulk of humanity. He further argues that we are morally obligated to alleviate the plight of people experiencing poverty—though we must recognize that we can never entirely do so (p. 171, & p. 250). Malthus asserts that to attain the greatest good for the greatest number of people; *institutional reform must be made in recognition of the laws of nature*. Social Darwinism came later in the 19th century and significantly differed from Malthus' theory. A close reading of the *Essay* reveals a position more akin to that of American conservatives (both Republican and Democrat) in the latter half of the 20th century. Many of their arguments over welfare reform were anticipated and voiced by Malthus in the debates over the "Poor Laws" of England.

Welfare

The "Poor Laws" provided some public assistance to people experiencing poverty in England from the 16th century until the early 20th century. They consisted of several Acts of Parliament over this period and many amendments to these Acts. They intended to provide minimal relief to the poor and suppress vagrancy and begging. Because many felt that poverty resulted from an unwillingness to work on the part of the poor, relief was often minimal. Malthus's critique of the British Poor

Laws stems from three distinct sources: (a) his functional analysis of poverty, welfare, and population growth; (b) the high value Malthus places on achieving the greatest good for the greatest number of people; and (c) the high value he places on human liberty. Malthus analyzes the functions and dysfunctions (though he does not use functionalist terminology) of welfare and concludes that it does not significantly alleviate the misery of people experiencing poverty. He asserts that eventually, it necessarily increases the number of people who become dependent on the charity of others. This dependence does not promote the happiness of the greatest number of people. Finally, such welfare provisions serve to limit human freedom and promote tyranny.

Malthus claims that the Poor Laws were instituted through two primary human motivations. First, he asserts that elites use Poor Laws to reduce labor costs. The laws interfere with the labor market by putting a cap on wages, stimulating higher birthrates among the laboring classes—thus lowering the cost of labor for both manufacturing and national armies (pp. 187-188). The second motivating factor behind welfare—or the attempt to alleviate the plight of the poor—is human benevolence and a desire for social justice (p. 253). Sometimes, elite self-interest is cloaked in the language of compassion. At other times, the laws are motivated purely by benevolence (pp. 169-170 & pp. 187-188). Regardless of motivation—whether conceived purposefully to hold down labor costs or conceived out of compassion to alleviate distress—the provision of welfare removes the necessity of some population checks on people experiencing poverty.

The result of removing some of the population checks is that the population rises; the labor market becomes flooded with new laborers and those willing to work longer and harder to support their increased number of offspring (p. 254). The fatal flaw of the poor laws, at least in Malthus' view (though it would not be a flaw in the view of elites), is that they encourage population growth without increasing provisions to support that growth (pp. 165-166, pp. 169-170, & p. 188). Under the law of supply and demand, poor laws will "raise the price of provisions and lower the real price of labour" (pp. 166-167). Labor is the only commodity the poor have to sell to obtain provisions. Thus, available provisions must be spread over more people, and distress becomes more widespread and severe (pp. 169-170).

Malthus's harsh criticisms of welfare laws seem based on his desire to promote the greatest good for the greatest number of people. Poor laws soften the fear of poverty, diminish the poor's power to save (through lowering the price of labor), and weaken the incentive to work. Worse, the laws remove one of the significant checks (fear of poverty) to early marriage and having children (pp. 167-168). The only valid basis for an increase in population, Malthus argues, is an increase in the means of subsistence (p. 186). If subsistence does not increase, but the population does, available provisions must be spread over a more considerable number of people. Thus, a higher proportion of the next generation will live in poverty (p. 169 & p. 188). However noble in intentions, Malthus argues, poor laws will always subvert their purpose. He acknowledges that it may appear hard in individual circumstances, but holding dependent poverty as disgraceful allows the preventive checks on the population to operate. Malthus does not advocate for positive checks—he seeks to minimize their operation. The spread of preventative checks will promote the greatest good for the greatest number (p. 166).

Malthus is also concerned with the loss of human freedom when welfare systems are established. One of his "principal objections" is that welfare subjects people experiencing poverty to "tyrannical laws" that are inconsistent with individual liberties (pp. 168-169). Malthus asserts that with aid to people experiencing poverty, authority must be given to a specific class who will manage the necessary institutions to provide relief. These institutions will be charged with formulating rules to discriminate between those who are worthy of aid and those who are unworthy. Thus, this class will exercise power over the life affairs of all forced to ask for support. He cites frequent complaints from the poor regarding such administrators. He observes (sociologically) that: "the fault does not lie so much in these persons, who probably before they were in power, were not worse than other people, but in the nature of all such institutions" (p. 169). Malthus believes that a government that attempts to "repress inequality of fortunes" through welfare mechanisms will be "destructive of human liberty itself." He also fears concentrating so much power in the hands of the state—as absolute power corrupts absolutely (p. 25 & p. 252).

Finally, Malthus is also concerned with the effect of dependence on the poor themselves. Hard labor, he concedes, is evil, but dependence is far worse. In feudal society, serfs depended on the bounty of the great lords of the manor. Basic human dignity and liberty for the masses were non-existent. Only with the introduction of manufacture and trade did the poor have something to exchange for their provision—their labor. This independence from the elite has contributed significantly to the civil liberties of Western society. By fostering a population dependent for their subsistence on others, the Poor Laws serve to weaken the foundation of these civil liberties (p. 252).

No matter how much is collected for poor relief, the distress of poverty cannot be removed (p. 162). Preventing poverty's misery and distress is beyond social institutions' powers. In our attempts to alleviate the plight of the poor through welfare laws, we sacrifice the liberties and freedom of the poor, subjecting them to "tyrannical regulations" in exchange for promises of relief. However, society cannot fulfill its part of the bargain—cannot eliminate poverty's distress without removing necessary checks on population—thus creating more poor people. The poor are forced to sacrifice their liberty and get little in return (pp. 169-171). Malthus concludes that the increase in the number of people living in poverty, despite proportionately more resources devoted to welfare, is compelling evidence that welfare laws only worsen the conditions of people experiencing poverty (p. 263).

Further, Malthus points out that the poverty rate was worsening despite the significant increase in the nation's wealth in the century before Malthus authored his *Essay*. National wealth had been "rapidly advancing" through industrialization (pp. 260-261 & p. 263). Why was not a sizable portion of this great wealth used to benefit the ordinary person? Malthus addresses the problem by reiterating that the only proper foundation for the population is the provision produced from the land (p. 258). An increase in the stock of provisions must accompany any rise in the wages of laborers. Otherwise, the nominal rise in the cost of labor will be followed by increased costs of available food and other necessities of life (p. 254).

In Malthus' time, the increase in manufacturing had not been accompanied by a comparable increase in land productivity. Thus, early industrialization had a negligible impact on bettering the condition of the poor. Malthus asserts that industrialization has crowded people with low incomes in slums. These environments are conducive to disease and the breakdown of moral behavior— thus increasing the operation of positive checks on the poor (pp. 259-261 & p. 263). Neither welfare nor industrial manufacturing alleviates the plight of people experiencing poverty because neither serves to increase the stock of provisions. Therefore, welfare and manufacturing lead to lowering the cost of labor—the only commodity people experiencing poverty have to exchange for their provisions.

The Limits of Reform

This analysis of welfare does not lead Malthus to advocate that the poor should be left to their plight. Instead, he suggests some institutional reforms—reforms consistent with the law of population—that will make a more just, equitable society. Malthus's suggested reforms are not intended to eliminate poverty, for the law of population makes that impossible. Rather, Malthus's reforms are intended to promote the greatest good for the greatest number of people within the constraints of natural law. His proposals attempt to tie population growth to increases in land production. First, he advocated the abolition of all parish laws by which the poor could only get aid through their local parish church. This abolition, he asserts, will give freedom of movement to the peasantry so that they can move to areas where work is plentiful. The abolition of parish laws would allow the operation of a free market for labor, the lack of which is often responsible for preventing the rise in laborer's wages following supply and demand (p. 170).

Second, Malthus advocates incentives for tilling new lands and "encouragements held out to agriculture above manufactures, and to tillage above grazing" (p. 170). Agricultural labor must be paid on par with labor in manufacturing and trade. This encouragement of agriculture, Malthus maintains, would furnish the economy with "an increasing quantity of healthy work" and contribute to the land's produce. This increase in produce would provide the necessary foundation for population growth among people experiencing poverty. Without the prospect of "parish assistance," the laborer would have the necessary incentive to better their condition (p. 170).

Third, Malthus advocates the establishment of "county workhouses" supported by general taxation. These workhouses were intended to provide a place "where any person, native or foreigner, might do a day's work at all times and receive the market price for it" (pp. 170-171). The "market price" would keep relief at the prevailing wage, thus providing people experiencing poverty with equitable treatment with men and women privately employed, not providing incentives for workers to go on relief, and not undermining local labor markets. The fare should be challenging; capable people would be obliged to work for the prevailing wage. Malthus advocates establishing these workhouses to eliminate the most severe distress while maintaining the necessary incentive for human industry and the operation of preventive checks on the population.

Finally, Malthus states that human benevolence and compassion must augment these social policies (pp. 170-171). For Malthus, "the proper office of benevolence" softens the "partial evils" arising from people acting in self-interest. Nevertheless, compassion and benevolence can never replace self-interest as the mainspring of human action (p. 253). Malthus asserts that while we cannot eliminate poverty, our moral obligation is to minimize inequalities as much as the laws of nature will allow. Malthus is no believer in evolution as progress and is therefore clearly at odds with the later Social Darwinists over the proper role of government.

At several points in the *Essay*, he points out that while inequality is essential to motivate human beings to be active and productive, inequality does not need to be as great as it existed in his society. While he criticized welfare, his critique was of welfare's relationship with population growth. Malthus did not criticize welfare on the basis that people experiencing poverty should not receive help because of some alleged unfitness—recall that he thought them merely "unlucky." Welfare, Malthus wrote, would temporarily remove the necessity of population checks among the poor without a corresponding increase in productivity. He stated this was self-defeating—the numbers of the poor would increase, production (mainly food) would not, and the poor's share in a stable output would decrease.

Malthus' reform proposals put him at odds with the later Social Darwinists. In later writings, he also advocated universal education and a rise in the price of labor in hopes of promoting the widespread use of preventive checks among the lower classes (Winch, 1987, p. 65). Petersen (1990, p. 283) also reports that Malthus advocated many other reforms, including extending suffrage, free medical care for people experiencing poverty, state assistance to emigrants, and direct relief (of a temporary nature) to the poor. By many accounts, Malthus was an honest and benevolent "reformer, committed to the betterment of society and all the people in it." Still, he maintained that there would always be a lower class, and this class would always suffer from deprivation of the necessities of life. These deprivations must lead to preventive and positive checks on the population.

Many others, it must be reported, maintain that he was mean-spirited and seemed to revel in making life miserable for people experiencing poverty. Dickens, for example, clearly based his Scrooge character on his reading of Malthus's characterization of the poor. When asked to contribute money to help the poor, Scrooge responded: "'I don't make merry myself at Christmas and I can't afford to make idle people merry. I help to support the establishments I have mentioned [the Workhouses and Prisons] they cost enough: and those who are badly off must go there.' 'Many can't go there; and many would rather die.' 'If they would rather die,' said Scrooge, 'they had better do it, and decrease the surplus population.'" While this passage from Dickens is based on Malthus's writings, it is a mischaracterization of both the letter and spirit of those writings.

Still, others have a different view. John Bellamy Foster, a modern-day Marxist and thus a strong critic of Malthusian theory, furthers the characterization. "In expert testimony before a Parliamentary Committee on Emigration in 1827, Malthus advocated reforms in the Poor Laws that would create an even harsher environment for those seeking parish relief and urged the committee to refuse relief to all children who were born two years after his reforms had been instituted. He also commended landlords "who pulled down cottages the moment they became vacant and argued against the construction of new cottages since he believed that a shortage of housing would discourage early marriage" (1999, p. 61). It is harsh indeed, but ultimately consistent with his insistence that individuals having children must feel the full consequences for bringing children into the world. Otherwise, preventive checks would not be exercised, the problem would worsen through the generations, and more positive checks would inevitably come into play. It is doubtful that any person could truly revel in advocating such a harsh judgment that goes against conventional morality; instead, it is a realist's position consistent with what he considers natural law. Taking the *Essay* as a whole, Malthus seeks to minimize inequality whenever such an action would serve the greater good and the long-term interests of the greatest number of people. One need not agree with Malthus's policy pronouncements to appreciate his theory.

That Foster is hostile to Malthus is evidenced by the following passage: "Nowhere were Malthus's narrow parsonic values more evident than in his view of women's indiscretions. Thus he sought to justify the double standard imposed on women who were 'driven out of society for an offense ['a breach of chastity' outside of marriage, especially if resulting in illegitimate birth] which men commit nearly with impunity' on the grounds that it was 'the most obvious and effectual method of preventing the frequent recurrence of a serious inconvenience to the community'" (Foster, 2000, p. 100). A reading of the complete passage (p. 216) reveals a different picture. Malthus does not seek to "justify" the practice, he seeks to explain it. He points out that the double standard is a breach of "natural justice," that the custom originated because of a necessity to limit population growth to what the environment could provide (through the work of two parents). Malthus is engaging in what has become known as a functional analysis of the double standard; he is not advocating that it is right or just, only that the belief system is functional for a society intent on limiting its population. One would expect this double standard to change in a society where birth control is widely available and encouraged, as it has in Western societies.

Taking Malthus's word, he does not consider inequality a good thing. However, he considers it necessary, rooted in the two unequal powers of reproduction and production. He also repeatedly states that it need not be as great as it was in the England of his time. He sees the system's injustice and considers it a partial evil—but he also sees some inequality as essential for the total social system. Malthus's *Essay* was designed to demonstrate the impossibility of a social utopia—but he insisted that although eliminating inequality was not possible, we could (indeed, should) reduce social and economic inequality through structural reform.

Malthus's Legacy

According to historians of social theory, the legacy of Malthus is most keenly felt in evolutionary theory—social and biological—both directly and indirectly. Most importantly, Malthus profoundly influenced Herbert Spencer (1820-1903) in his formulation of social evolutionary theory. In a series of papers beginning in 1842, this evolutionary theory became fully explicit in Spencer's first major work, *Social Statics*, in 1850:

> Nature, in its infinite complexity, is ever growing to a new development. Each successive result becomes the parent of an additional influence, destined in some degree to modify all future results […] As we turn over the leaves of the earth's primeval history—as we interpret the hieroglyphics in which are recorded the events of the unknown past, we find this same ever-beginning, never-ceasing change. We see it alike in the organic and the inorganic—in the decompositions and the recombinations of matter, and in the constantly-varying forms of animal and vegetable life […] With an altering atmosphere, and a decreasing temperature, land and sea perpetually bring forth fresh races of insects, plants, and animals. All things are metamorphosed […] Strange indeed would it be, if, in the midst of this universal mutation, man alone were constant, unchangeable. But it is not so. He also obeys the law of indefinite variation. His circumstances are ever changing, and he is ever adapting himself to them (Spencer [1950] 1883, 45-46).

As previously mentioned, in their formulation of biological evolutionary principles, Charles Darwin and Alfred Wallace were also influenced by Malthus, both directly and indirectly, through Spencer. Again, the original influence was from social science to biology and not from biology to social science as is commonly believed.

Nevertheless, Spencer and the biologists turned Malthus on his head. They used the principle of the struggle for survival and reproductive success within a population to demonstrate the inevitability of improvements in a species. This improvement was accomplished, according to Spencer, through "adaptation"—those who exhibited more fitness to survive a given environment inevitably enjoyed substantial reproductive success and passed on these adaptations to their progeny.

> Those to whom this increasing difficulty of getting a living which excess of fertility entails, does not stimulate improvements in production—that is, to greater mental activity—are on the high road to extinction; and must ultimately be supplanted by those who the pressure does so stimulate […] And here, indeed, without further illustration, it will be seen that premature death under all its forms, and from all its causes, cannot fail to work in the same direction. For those prematurely carried off must, in the average of cases, be those in whom the power of self-preservation is the least, it unavoidably follows that those left behind to continue the race are those in whom the power of self-preservation is the greatest—are the select of their generation. So that, whether the dangers to existence be the kind produced by excess of fertility, or of any other kind, it is clear, that by the ceaseless exercise of the faculties needed to contend with them, and by the death of all men who fail to contend with them successfully, there is ensured a constant progress towards a higher degree of skill, intelligence, and self-regulation—a better coordination of actions—a more complete life (Spencer, 1852, pp. 459-460).

Moreover, it is through the gradual improvement of the species that human societies "progress."

> Progress, therefore, is not an accident, but a necessity. Instead of civilization being artificial, it is part of nature, all of a piece with the development of the embryo or the unfolding of a flower. The modifications mankind have undergone, and are still undergoing, result from a law underlying the whole organic creation; and provided the human race continues, and the constitution of things remains the same, those modifications must end in completeness [...] So surely must the things we call evil and immorality disappear; so surely must man become perfect (Spencer, 1883, p. 80).

In time, Spencer saw the social evolutionary process as one of increasing complexity—growing populations, an increasing division of labor, and greater integration of this increasing heterogeneity through social organization. Other social evolutionists of the latter half of the 19th century included Edward Tylor and Lewis Henry Morgan. For assorted reasons, social evolution fell out of favor in the social sciences in the first half of the nineteenth century, carried forward in the 1940s through the 1950s single-handedly by the work of Leslie White, later joined by Julian Steward. Then, in 1959, the centennial year of Darwin's publication of *The Origin of Species*, the interest of social scientists was reawakened, and social evolution again became a widespread theory in the social sciences (Carneiro, 2003, pp. 122-123).

Modern ecological-evolutionary theory is stripped of notions such as the inevitability of "progress" and the perfectibility of man. It has focused on the Malthusian notion of the

314

interrelationships between population and production and their effects on other parts of the sociocultural system. If any notion of "direction" remains in modern ecological-evolutionary theory, it is with Spencer's proposition that societies evolve toward greater complexity. Ecological-evolutionary theory has also widened its focus on the environment from Malthus's narrow (though fundamental) focus on agricultural productivity.

Although addressing herself against the neo-Malthusians, Ester Boserup (1910-1999) is consistent with Malthus and current ecological-evolutionary theory. She was born in Copenhagen in 1910 and graduated from the University of Copenhagen in 1935. Her degree was in theoretical economics, and she has a broad social science background. Her research in economic development began with a decade at the UN and its agencies in the late 1940s. She spent the remainder of her career as a consultant and independent researcher. She died in 1999.

Boserup (1965) states two basic views on the relationship between population growth and food supply. One can look at how changes in food production affect population growth, or one can look at how population change affects agriculture. She asserts that Malthus and his followers believed that the food supply could only grow slowly and that food supply was the main factor governing the population growth rate. Population growth is, therefore, seen as the result of previous changes in agricultural productivity. Changes in the availability of arable land, agricultural innovation, invention, or other changes that increase agricultural production will lead to population increases.

"In other words, for those who view the relationship between agriculture and population in essentially Malthusian perspective there is at any given time in any given community a warranted rate of population increase with which the actual growth of population tends to conform" (p. 11). Boserup approaches the problem from the opposite direction. She demonstrates that population growth is the primary stimulus to agricultural development and productivity. In sum, agricultural development is caused by previous population growth rather than vice versa. As we have seen, this is only partially true. Malthus recognized the reciprocal relationships between food supply and population well; the speed of the growth in food supply was not an essential factor in his theory, for Malthus posited that this growth could not long keep pace with unchecked population growth. However, neo-Malthusians, those who took Malthus's theory as a prediction of population overshoot and subsequent collapse, may be accused of viewing food production as relatively inelastic.

Boserup believes that classical economists such as Malthus were misled because they were writing at the time of European settlers' expansion of agriculture in the Americas. Because of this, they distinguished between two ways to raise agricultural output: expansion into new land by creating new fields and more intensive cultivation. However, this distinction is not suitable; primitive agriculture does not make use of permanent fields. It shifts cultivation from plot to plot, allowing a fallow period to give the land time to regenerate. "[I]n primitive agriculture there is no sharp distinction between cultivated and uncultivated land, and it is impossible to distinguish clearly between the creation of new fields and the change of methods in existing fields" (pp. 12-13).

The accurate measure of the intensification of agriculture, according to Boserup, is the *frequency of cropping*. "Once the time-honored distinction between cultivated and uncultivated land is replaced by the concept of frequency of cropping, the economic theory of agricultural development becomes compatible with the theories of changing landscape propounded by natural scientists" (p. 13). Soil fertility is not simply a gift of nature, a quality that never changes; soil fertility is highly variable and strongly associated with agricultural methods.

Boserup groups land use into five distinct types in order of increasing intensity. The first is *forest-fallow*, where land plots are cleared in the forest and planted for a year or two. The land is left fallow for the forest to regenerate from 20 to 25 years. The fallow period is only six to ten years, with *bush-fallow* when the land is covered in bushes and small trees. "The periods of uninterrupted cultivation under bush-fallow systems varies considerably. It may be as short as one to two years (similar to conditions under forest fallow) and it may be as long as the fallow period, i.e., six to eight years." *Short fallow* is a system in which the fallow is one or two years. In the fallow period, the land is invaded by wild grasses. With *annual cropping*, the land is left uncultivated for only several months between harvest and planting. Within this group, Boserup also includes crop rotation systems. Finally, *multi-cropping* occurs when the same plot of land bears two or more crops yearly; such a system has no fallow period.

Boserup does not mean that land-use typology should be a classification scheme only; rather, it is meant to broadly characterize the main stages of the evolution of agriculture from prehistoric times to the present. "Even if we cannot be sure that systems of extensive land use have preceded the intensive ones in every part of the world, there seems to be little reason to doubt that the typical sequence of development of agriculture has been a gradual change—more rapid in some regions than in others—from extensive to intensive types of land use" (pp. 17-18).

Once "frequency of cropping" is used to measure intensification, theories of the economic development of agriculture can be linked with changes in the local landscape, flora, and fauna. For example, as people shorten the fallow period, forests deteriorate, and bushes take over the land. Further intensification will bring wild grasses. "The invasion of forest and bush by grass is most likely to happen when an increasing population of long-fallow cultivators cultivate the land with more and more frequent intervals" (p. 20). In this way, many forest and bush areas gradually became savannahs due to the intensification of agriculture. Many believe that a large share of the open grasslands of the world originated in this way. These new grasslands provide food for cattle, horses, and other animals suitable for domestication. Such a view contradicts the traditional theory of the origins of herding societies. The traditional theory held that nomadic tribes turned to agriculture only when their herds could no longer support their population. "The sequence is now supposed to be the reverse: tribes which previously cultivated short-lived plots in the forest and bush land have come to rely on the grazing of animals only after they cultivated forest plots for a very long period ending in the transformation of the forest into grassland" (pp. 20-21). Other tribes, according to Boserup, used the animals attracted to the new grasslands to help cultivate and fertilize the fields.

Boserup also insists that attention must be focused on its being an agricultural system. As population increases, most land brought under more frequent cultivation in each area was already used for fallow, hunting grounds, or grazing areas. "It follows that when a given area of land comes to be cropped more frequently than before, the purpose for which it was hitherto used must be taken care of in a new way, and this may create additional activities for which new tools and other investments are required" (pp. 13-14). Thus, population changes often have direct effects on agricultural technology. For this reason, Boserup claims that even primitive agricultural output can be increased significantly by additional labor inputs—far more than neo-Malthusian authors assume.

The traditional view is that the primary cultivation tool is the chief criterion for classifying primitive agricultural systems. Thus, we have Simple Horticulture (digging stick), Advanced Horticulture (hoe and irrigation), and Agrarian societies (plow and animal power). This view places undue emphasis on technological advances (through either innovation or contact). "This theory is apt to mislead because it ignores the fact that the kind of agricultural tool needed in a given context depends upon the system of land use: some technical changes can materialize only if the system of land use is modified at the same time, and some changes in land use can come about only if they are accompanied by the introduction of new tools" (p. 23).

In forest fallow cultivation, the burning of undergrowth frees the land of weeds, and hoeing is entirely unnecessary. When the fallow is shortened, bushes and weeds take root; burning is not an effective method of clearing the land, so the hoe is needed. As the fallow shortens, grass takes root, which is difficult to remove through hoeing; thus, the plow becomes necessary. Not only that but with the disappearance of the roots of bushes and trees, the plow also becomes possible. Finally, Boserup adds that as grasslands replace forests with the shortening of fallow, nomads often invade them to feed their herds. Thus, animals suitable for cultivation and fertilization appear "around the time when the local cultivators need them and become able to use them" (p. 25).

With the shortening of fallow, new methods of regaining fertility must also be developed and employed. 1) Forest fallow—ashes left after burning natural vegetation; 2) Bush fallow—ashes and organic materials brought from surrounding lands; 3) Short fallow—manure from animals and humans; and 4) More intensive systems—a variety of techniques, including compost, silt, manure, household waste. Both the methods of cultivation and fertilization become more labor intensive with the shortening of fallow. While such methods produce more crops per acre, they also require far more human labor to produce these yields—and the increases in yield are not commensurate with the effort. More work is needed to produce food; with population increasing, a household must work harder to maintain its standard of living. The short-term effect of intensification, Boserup maintains, is necessary to lower output per person-hour. "But sustained growth of total population and of total output in a given area has secondary effects which—at least in some cases—can set off a genuine process of economic growth" (p. 118). These secondary effects of intensification include a compulsion to work harder and more regularly, changing work habits, and raising overall productivity. Intensification facilitates the division of labor and the spread of urbanization, communication, education, and population and urban growth, stimulating the further intensification of agriculture.

Thus intensification, Boserup maintains, could only occur in response to population pressures within a given area. Even when people have access to more intensive techniques and tools, the investments in labor are so significant that they are not likely to be made unless a population increase makes them necessary. Unless population pressures are keenly felt, people may reject more intensive cultivation methods as a bad bargain—far more work for only marginally more food (p. 41).

Another significant contribution to the literature on social evolution made by Boserup was her book *Woman's Role in Economic Development* (1970). In this book, Boserup clarified that gender is one of the main criteria for the division of labor in all societies. However, there is great diversity in this division of labor between the sexes across societies. She finds that the primary factors related to work and the subsequent status of women are population density and the availability of land. This division of labor in farming systems also carries over into non-farm activities.

Boserup also directly addresses the neo-Malthusians who insist that population growth destroys the land's natural fertility. It cannot be denied, Boserup says, that the food potential of many of the world's areas was diminished or destroyed by over-grazing and more intensive forms of agriculture. Some think cutting down forests for agriculture has led to drier climates and the spread of deserts, while others point to erosion brought on by intensive cultivation and grazing (p. 22). However, this is only part of the story. Many tribes also irrigated the dried-up lands, developed terracing to prevent erosion, or improved soil fertility and yield through animal manure and cultivation.

> It is true that some regions which previously supported a more or less dense population are barren today, but it is equally true that regions which previously, under forest fallow, could support only a couple of families per square kilometer, today support hundreds of families by means of intensive cultivation. Growing populations may in the past have destroyed more land than they improved, but it makes little sense to project past trends into the future, since we know more and more about methods of land preservation and are able, by means of modern methods, to reclaim much land, which our ancestors have made sterile (p. 22).

Boserup does not so much refute Malthus as to round him out by providing a complete picture of the multitude of relationships between population, agricultural production, and the environment. While Malthus focused on the necessity to keep human numbers in line with the food that could be produced, Boserup focused on how the amount of food that can be produced depends upon human numbers. Both recognize that the production of food can be intensified. Boserup demonstrates that primitive agricultural production is quite responsive to increased labor. On the other hand, Malthus also recognized that food production could be increased, but he asserted that such intensification could only equal natural population growth for an abbreviated time. Boserup did not dispute this; she did document that a growing population often stimulates agricultural production. Malthus made similar assertions in his *Essay on Population* as well. For Malthus, the principle of population "keeps the inhabitants of the earth always fully up to the level of the means of subsistence; and is constantly acting upon man as a powerful stimulus, urging him to the further cultivation of the earth, and to enable it, consequently, to support a more extended population" (Malthus, [1798] 2001, p. 281). Boserup's contribution is that she clearly elaborated the relationships between population growth and agricultural production and empirically verified the relationships throughout the social evolutionary process. Boserup posits that the relationships between population growth and the intensification of production influenced ecological-evolutionary theory in anthropology and sociology. For example, Marvin Harris, Gerhard Lenski, and Mark Cohen use Boserup's primary argument to link population pressure to the original agricultural revolution in which hunters and gatherers transitioned to agriculture in response to population pressure forcing a change in their way of life.

Most modern-day social evolutionary theorists trace their roots back to Spencer, Morgan, Tylor, or even Darwin, their opinion of Malthus being biased by the secondary literature. While I have no desire to downplay the significance of these early evolutionary theorists on contemporary ecological-evolutionary theories, Malthus deserves a significant amount of credit as well. Gerhard Lenski, Marvin Harris, and Stephen K. Sanderson are two modern practitioners of ecological-evolutionary theory—a theory in which the relationships between population and production play a significant role. Like most, Harris, Lenski, and Sanderson have been influenced by other theorists, but Malthus and Spencer heavily influenced their overarching theoretical systems. Both place the relationships between population and production at center stage in determining sociocultural stability and change. We now turn to Lenski's Ecological-Evolutionary theory.

Chapter 14: Gerhard Lenski's Ecological-Evolutionary Theory[3]

Gerhard Lenski's (1924-2015) theory begins with the insights of T. Robert Malthus. From Malthus, Lenski borrows the observation that human societies are part of the world of nature and are subject to natural law. Sociocultural systems can only be fully understood as being responsive to the interactions of populations with their environments (Lenski & Lenski, 1987, p. 55). Like Malthus's theory, the relationship between population and production lies at the base of Lenski's perspective. Like many life forms, humans have a reproductive capacity that substantially exceeds the necessary environmental subsistence resources. Thus, Lenski concludes that human populations tend to grow until they come up against the limits of food production and are checked (p. 32). The checks consist of the positive and preventive checks that Malthus first explored in 1798. Lenski asserts that the capacity for population growth has been a "profoundly destabilizing force throughout human history and may well be the ultimate source of most social and cultural change" (p. 32). Lenski posits that the relationships between population, production, and environment drive the evolution of sociocultural systems.

The influence of Malthus is also clearly apparent when Lenski discusses the nature of social inequality. Like Malthus, he asserts that we are social animals obliged to cooperate in producing a living (Lenski, 1966, p. 24). Also, like Malthus, he claims that humans are strongly motivated by self-interest. Lenski believes that this self-interest is rooted in our species' genetic heritage. Because our behavior and attitude formation depend on learning and individual experience—and because no two humans can be exposed to identical learning and experiential processes—humans develop differences and a sense of individual identity. These quickly lead to the formation of self-interest (Lenski, 2005, pp. 37-38). Therefore, Lenski (1966) states, "*when men are confronted with important decisions where they are obliged to choose between their own, or their group's, interests and the interests of others, they nearly always choose the former*—though often seeking to hide this fact from themselves and others" (p. 30; emphasis in the original).

---

[3] An earlier version of this chapter appeared in *Macrosociology: Four Modern Theorists*, 2006, Colorado: Paradigm Publishers. Reprinted by permission.

Since most of the resources needed for survival are in short supply, he continues, a struggle for rewards will be present in every human society. Individuals are born with various innate abilities and circumstances; thus, social inequality is rooted in our nature. Some minimal distribution of wealth is necessary to ensure the survival of "others whose actions are necessary" to themselves, but any surplus (goods and services over and above the minimum required to keep necessary workers alive and productive) will be distributed unequally (pp. 44-45).

In the earlier stages of sociocultural evolution, resources are allocated based on personal characteristics—hunting skills or plant-gathering productivity. With the development of a more complex division of labor, these inequalities become institutionalized in class, caste, race, sex, and ethnic systems. Thus, like Malthus before him, Lenski concludes that inequality is inevitable in any complex sociocultural system (complex as measured by a division of labor). However, the degree of inequality varies across societies and through time (p. 442).

While it begins with Malthus, Lenski's perspective is also an integrating device. According to his report, his other major theoretical influences have been Herbert Spencer, Charles Darwin, Karl Marx, Friedrich Engels, Max Weber, Robert Michels, and Thorstein Veblen. Contemporary influences include C. Wright Mills, Leslie White, and Marvin Harris (Lenski, Lenski, and Nolan, 1991, p. xviii). One can see the influence of Weber in Lenski's discussion of power and the multidimensional nature of stratification; the influence of Veblen as Lenski writes on the importance of status and status striving; the influence of Mills as Lenski discusses power, authority, and manipulation; and the influence of White on Lenski's discussion of the importance of technological change. Finally, one can certainly see the influence of Harris in Lenski's growing focus in later editions of *Human Societies* on the importance of environmental, technological, and population variables, as well as the existence of feedback from social structures and cultural superstructures in determining the direction of sociocultural change.

Sociocultural Evolution

Like evolutionary theory in biology, Lenski puts ecological-evolutionary social theory as an all-encompassing sociological paradigm that can serve as a viable framework to bring order and research focus to the discipline. However, it is essential to remember the differences and the parallels between natural and social evolution for practitioners within biology and those in the social sciences. While drawing false parallels between growing complexity (sometimes labeled "progress") in sociocultural and natural systems, many biologists misled themselves and the general public into believing that life naturally progresses toward complexity. At the same time, social observers have also been misled by faulty analogies between social and biological evolution. The misapplication of biological evolution by the "Social Darwinists," 19th-century social scientists who characterized nature's struggle as bloody and brutish and used this faulty biological model to justify the inequality around them, still haunts social evolutionary theory today.

Like Spencer, Lenski insists that sociocultural evolution is a particular case of the general evolutionary process. "Viewed from the perspective of the new science of genetics, it is clear that far more than analogy is involved. Both sociocultural and organic evolution are processes by which populations have been formed and transformed in response to changes in the stores of heritable or transferable information they possess. In organic evolution, the entire population of living things, human and nonhuman, has been formed and transformed; in sociocultural evolution, it is the human population alone. Thus, organic and social evolution may be defined as cumulating heritable or transferable information within populations and its attendant consequences (Lenski, 2005, p. 43). Human populations, Lenski points out, are subject to environmental and biological influences just as animal populations are. Rather than relying on genetic change to adapt to changes in the external environment, human populations have evolved culture. The process of evolution—inorganic-organic-social—is cumulative and evolving (p. 121). Lenski's ecological-evolutionary theory of sociocultural systems begins with and remains rooted in the basic biological paradigm.

True to its subject matter and development method, Lenski's theory has evolved over the years as it examined more evidence and read more widely in the historical, anthropological, and sociological literature. *Power and Privilege* (1966) primarily presents an ecological theory of inequality. While the book examines a succession of societal types based on subsistence strategies, there is little theoretical development explaining changes in these technologies. The various editions of *Human Societies* (1970-2015), on the other hand, look at the relationships of sociocultural systems to their natural and social environments and evolutionary change both within and between societal types. The first of these was written by Lenski alone in 1970. The 6th edition, which I refer to often in this chapter, was published in 1991. I use this because it presents a more mature version of ecological-evolutionary theory and one of the last in which Gerhard was the first author. It is also the latest edition on my bookshelf at this time. *Ecological-Evolutionary Theory* (2005) is a summation of his life's work.

In this chapter, I will summarize Lenski's ecological-evolutionary theory using these three works as my primary sources. He begins, as most theorists do, by making a simple assertion about the nature of man. Human beings are a part of nature, and nature profoundly affects social life. By nature, we are social beings required to live with others in social groupings or societies. Only through our association with our kind can we harvest resources from the earth. Only in association with others can we satisfy our many needs and desires. Our physical needs and drives must be met by nature—food, clothing, sexual expression, affection, and shelter. Also, by our nature as human beings, we have an immense capacity for learning; our behavior is therefore guided by what we have learned rather than upon instinct. However, another human genetic trait related to our capacity for learning is our ability to create and use symbolic systems. Human nature causes us to form sociocultural systems to satisfy our physical wants and desires. Our reliance on learning and using symbols means these systems profoundly influence our personalities, beliefs, values, attitudes, and characters (1966, pp. 25-26).

Social life—cooperation with others—is necessary for both the species' survival and the "maximum satisfaction of human needs and desires" (p. 26). Human needs and desires include everyday basic physical needs across all societies, such as food, drink, sex, play, and personal survival. These basic physical needs are rooted in our genetic heritage (2005, p. 46). Humans seek to maximize pleasure and minimize pain.

Also, since we are by nature social beings, the society into which we are born has a strong effect on shaping many of these basic needs and desires as well as creating "derivative" or secondary needs and desires (1966, pp. 25-26; 2005, p. 47). In this list, Lenski includes such drives as the need for love and affection, respect and prestige from our fellows, and some meaning and order in life. Since societies differ radically, the "nature and intensity" of these needs vary. Since individual experience within a particular society differs radically, the "nature and intensity" of these needs vary among individuals *within* the same society (1991, p. 23).

Lenski notes that survival is given the highest priority of all human needs and desires by most human beings (1966, p. 37). This fact means that the threat of physical violence is a powerful deterrent in human affairs. It also means that resources necessary for survival (food and water and the resources needed to procure them) are highly valued. Other widespread goals are health, prestige or social honor, salvation, physical comfort, and love and affection. Still, other goals are sought, Lenski posits, because they help us attain things such as money, office or position within an organization, or education and training (1966, pp. 37-40).

In addition to human needs and desires, humans share a variety of constants across all societies. Lenski notes that humans everywhere have similar physiological and mental capabilities; we have an excellent capacity for learning and devising languages, symbol systems, and cultures (1991, pp. 23-25). These constants serve as resources to meet our primary and secondary needs. In addition, Lenski adds, humans have a highly developed consciousness and a sense of the individual self; we are often ruled by powerful emotions and appetites (1991, p. 25). These constants, Lenski makes clear, lead to the "antagonistic" character of social life. These two constants motivate humans to put their own needs and desires ahead of others and are primarily responsible for the conflict and tension characteristic of human societies (1991, p. 26; 2005, pp. 38-39).

Again, like Malthus before him, Lenski notes that our reproductive capacity exceeds our productive capacity. This reproductive drive is a regular feature of nature, which widely scatters the seeds of life but is comparatively miserly in providing food and sustenance for this life. It is inevitable, both men remark, that many will die premature deaths, and others will live close to the edge of starvation (1966, p. 31; Malthus, [1798] 2001, p. 136). Lenski remarks that, to "some extent," at any rate, humans have freed themselves from these constraints by learning to increase their food supply through cultivation and control of their reproduction through social practices and technologies (1966, p. 31). Malthus devoted a whole book (which also went through numerous editions), demonstrating that this "freedom" from nature's constraint was illusionary. Instead of freedom, Malthus insists, human populations must constantly adjust to the availability of resources through positive checks (shortening of life span) and preventive checks (social practices and birth control technology) on population growth. These continuous and necessary checks profoundly impact the rest of the sociocultural system. Lenski reaches the same conclusion in his later writings (1991, p. 54; 2005, pp. 57-58). Population-level, growth, and subsistence technology become prime causal agents in Lenski's general ecological-evolutionary theory.

Another point Lenski makes about the scarcity of goods and resources in his 1966 book is also relevant to other aspects of sociocultural systems and their impact on human behavior. Lenski asserts that humans have an insatiable appetite for goods and services. "This is true chiefly because the goods and services have a status value as well as a utilitarian value" (1966, 31). Prestige or social honor is one of the chief needs or goals that Lenski identifies as universal. However, as a secondary or derivative goal, what goods and services bring social honor vary across societies and over time. What social actions are accorded high prestige and social honor also vary? Granting social honor (or scorn) is one of several ways society shapes the individual.

The struggle for resources within a sociocultural system is not necessarily violent. The struggle is often carried out within economic and political rules. However, even in the absence of violence, the struggle is serious for the men and women involved. Human beings are unequally endowed with physical abilities to compete in this struggle. However, this is not the chief reason for the inequalities in human societies we see throughout history, though it is worthy of note (1966, pp. 31-32).

Human societies are rooted in the environment, part of the world of nature (1991, pp.6-8). As such, the environment profoundly influences its social structure and culture. Lenski goes as far as to assert that all a society's characteristics are ultimately due to just three things: the influence of the environment (both biophysical and sociocultural), the influence of our species' genetic heritage, and the influence of prior sociocultural experience itself (1991, pp. 17-18; 2005, p. 76).

Sociocultural systems are the primary ways humans adapt to their biological, physical, and social environments. A society's sociocultural environment involves communication and contact with other sociocultural systems. Adaptations to biophysical and sociocultural environments, Lenski asserts, are critical. The welfare of societal members and their survival depends on how well their society adapts to these environments (1991, p. 10). As we will see, adaptation to changing biological, physical, and social environments is the engine of sociocultural evolution.

Sociocultural Systems

Like most sociologists, Lenski asserts that society is a system; however, he continues that it is an imperfect system at best (2205, p. 16). Analogies between societies and biological organisms or mechanical systems can be misleading, for such analogy calls to mind perfect coordination and integration of the various parts of the system. This perfection is not the case with sociocultural systems, where the parts have varying degrees of autonomy and independence from the overall system (1966, p. 34; 1991, p. 20). The fact that society is imperfect means that not all parts function to strengthen the entire system. Many patterns and behaviors contribute nothing to the general welfare of society but serve the interests and needs of individuals or constituent groups. The fact that society is imperfect also means that conflict is a regular feature of all societies, not an abnormal condition, as posited by many functionalists. However, it is a sociocultural *system*, and as such, there must be enough cooperation among the members of the society so that the system can maintain itself (1966, p. 34).

Lenski asserts that societies have two primary goals: (a) the maintenance of the political status quo within the society and (b) the maximization of production (1966, pp. 41-42). By maintaining the political status quo, Lenski means that societies strive to minimize political change through laws and the machinery of state, police, military, and other agencies of social control. Societies also maintain themselves by fostering political ideologies that justify and celebrate the state. Production maximization is achieved through promoting technological change or wars of conquest. Not all societies give these goals an equal priority. A society's preference depends on its degree of stratification. Lenski posits that highly stratified societies with powerful elites tend to emphasize political stability, while those less stratified favor maximizing production (1966, p. 42).

Economic goods and services are not distributed equally to all society members—some get more than others. Lenski believes that the distribution of goods and services (as well as prestige) is primarily determined by power. Taking his cue from Weber, Lenski defines power as the ability of a person or group to achieve their goals even when opposed by others (1966, 45). Also consistent with Weber, Lenski asserts that stratification is a "multidimensional phenomenon"; populations are ranked along various dimensions such as occupation, education, property, racial-ethnic status, age, and gender. Lenski refers to each of these dimensions as a "class system." Class systems are "a hierarchy of classes ranked in terms of a single criterion" (1966, pp. 74-80, quote on p. 79). Thus, "African American" is a particular class within the American racial-ethnic class system, while "working class" is a particular class within the American occupational class system.

An individual's position in each of the relevant hierarchies (which vary by society) determines their class. Their class will often affect their access to goods and services and the prestige accorded to them by others. The members of each class share material interests with one another, and these interests are often the basis for class consciousness (or awareness of common position and interests) and "hostility toward other classes" (1966, p. 76).

"One of the great advantages of a conscious recognition of class systems as a distinct level of organization is that we are led to see that the struggle for power and privilege involves not only struggles between individuals and classes, it also involves struggles between class systems, and thus between different principles of distribution" (1966, p. 81). Lenski points out that the Civil

Rights movement in the United States can be appropriately viewed as a struggle to reduce the importance of the racial-ethnic class system as a basis of distribution. Class systems differ in complexity, the degree of mobility possible within the system, the system's importance in the distribution of goods and services, and the degree of hostility between the classes within the system. "Viewed in their totality, distributive systems resemble a system of wheels within wheels. The complexity of these systems varies considerably and seems to be largely a function of the societies' level of technology" (1966, pp. 82-84, quote on p. 84).

There are two primary "laws" of distribution. While they are somewhat contradictory, both are consistent with Lenski's postulates on the nature of man and society. According to Lenski, humans are social animals who must cooperate to achieve their needs efficiently. This need to cooperate leads him to posit that "enlightened self-interest" will lead humans to "share the product of their labors to the extent required to ensure the survival and continued productivity of those others whose actions are necessary or beneficial to themselves" (1966, p. 44). However, Lenski also states that human beings are primarily motivated by self-interest. Human self-interest leads him to posit that goods above the minimum needed to keep most producers alive and productive will be distributed based on power. This self-interest has enormous consequences for the degree of inequality within societies.

Force is a very inefficient and expensive way to maintain order. "Though force is the most effective instrument for seizing power in a society, and though it always remains the foundation of any system of inequality, it is not the most effective instrument for retaining and exploiting a position of power and deriving the maximum benefit from it" (1966, p. 51). Thus, those who seize power will soon move to "legitimize" their rule and transform force into authority. Power is legitimated through three significant institutions. First, of course, is through the rule of law. Lenski notes that laws are often written to benefit positions of power. Since they appear to embody "abstract principles of justice," they are pretty effective in gaining widespread acceptance and compliance from most people (1966, p. 52).

A second method of legitimation employed by elites involves shaping public opinion through educational and religious institutions, as well as the media. Many of those who work in these institutions are beholden to elite owners or donors; if not directly dependent on elites, they are exposed to their threats or blandishments. Lenski points out that consensus and coercion are far more closely related than many appreciate. Like Mills, he points out, "coercive power can often be used to create a new consensus" (1966, p. 53).

Lenski notes that the press of daily events in most people's lives facilitates the legitimation process. Most are engaged full-time in making a living; they have neither the time nor the financial resources to become involved in the political arena for long. While it is possible to arouse the majority in times of crisis or political revolution, the necessity of work, family, and private life continually reasserts itself. Consequently, the elite or their officers usually handle the affairs of the state (1966, p. 54).

As force shifts to authority and manipulation, some critical changes occur in the distribution of goods and services that have far-reaching effects on the degree of inequality within societies. Thus, elites are caught in the rules of their own game. With the rule of law, some of their actions must be consistent with prevailing conceptions of justice and morality. To act otherwise would be to jeopardize their legitimation. Secondly, there is a shift in the personality and character of the elite from those comfortable with the use of force and power to those more comfortable with "cunning," manipulation, and diplomacy.

In addition, Lenski asserts that a shift of power from force to manipulation and authority also involves institutionalizing authority. By this, Lenski means the rise of bureaucracy, where authority becomes a socially acceptable form of power in the office rather than the individual. Officers who enjoy such authority rule based on their office rather than their characteristics, and the rule becomes impersonal and not easily challenged. In addition, Lenski writes that such institutionalized power is likely to be far more decentralized than the centralized rule of founding elites. Competing power centers can develop if they remain subject to the rule of law (1966, p. 56).

In this transition period from force to authority, retainers and the middle class arise. This middle stratum consists of public officials, priests, soldiers, artisans, merchants, and others who serve as overseers and technicians in the service of elites. The chief function of this middle stratum is to separate the surplus from the producers (1966, pp. 62-63). Over time, Lenski posits that the relations between the political elite and this middle stratum change as these classes acquire some of the power and privileges of the elite. "This is not difficult since it is their normal function to act on behalf of the elite. Powers delegated often become powers lost; once lost they are not easily recovered" (1966, p. 63).

According to Lenski, the cumulative effect of these changes on the governance of sociocultural systems is marked. The movement from force to authority, the rise of manipulation and cunning as power techniques, and the rise of a middle stratum that begins to appropriate some power and privileges to itself all strengthen a move toward constitutional government. As defined by Lenski, constitutional government is a system in which the political elite makes some concessions in the distribution of resources in return for the legitimation and consent of the governed.

Societies can be remarkably stable over time. Hunting and gathering societies existed with little technological, population, or structural change for thousands (if not millions) of years. Ancient civilizations that depended upon river irrigation for their agriculture were also remarkably stable. These stable societies can be characterized as successful attempts to balance energy consumption and their finite biological and physical environments. In other words, one of the primary reasons for the stability of many social and cultural elements in many societies is their adaptive value to the sociocultural system (1991, p. 48).

Nevertheless, other causes exist for the remarkable stability in many sociocultural systems. As is often remarked, humans are creatures of habit, which means we are reluctant to change. In addition, tradition or custom—the "eternal yesteryear" of Weber—has a compelling hold on individuals within a society. Tradition and habit cause men and women to accept existing institutional arrangements and distribution systems as "right and natural," no matter the fairness to themselves or others (1966, p. 32). Through socialization, we have all been taught the culture's values, norms, morality, attitudes, beliefs, and ideologies. Through this process, such norms and values take on an almost "sacred" character, thus becoming extremely resistant to change (1991, p. 50).

Another essential impediment to sociocultural change is the need for some standardization. This resistance to change is because most sociocultural change is built upon or added to existing structures and institutions. While newer innovations may offer many advantages, past adaptations of society may prohibit the widespread adaptation of these innovations. Lenski mentions driving on the right side of the road as an example (1991, p. 48).

Another reason for sociocultural stability over time is the systemic character of the society itself. Most of the elements of a sociocultural system are linked to others. Change in one element often causes a change in many others (in a system, as the ecologists are fond of telling us, you cannot change *one* thing). An example of innovation causing extensive system change is the recent movement of married women to the outside labor force, which then caused extensive adjustments in all major institutions (family, government, distribution systems) and many of our cultural values and ideologies. Due to the systemic character of society, members and organized groups often resist such innovations (as the recent struggles over women's liberation attest) (1991, p. 50).

Other causes of sociocultural continuity mentioned by Lenski are related to the ones already given: adaptation, tradition and habit, standardization, and the systemic character of society. For example, Lenski mentions costs (both monetary and psychic) as a significant impediment to the adaptation of innovation. In this connection, he offers as an example the costs of dollars, time, and energy for Americans to change to the metric system (1991, p. 49). However, the resistance to metrics on the part of Americans is also clearly related to tradition, personal habits, systemic character, and standardization. Rather than an impediment to change, the cost is better conceived of as a primary factor in the individual decision-making process of adaptation. When confronted with innovation, the individual performs a cost/benefit analysis to reveal if the costs of adapting the innovation are worth the anticipated benefits (Harris, 1979, p. 61). Lenski places the individual members of society as the prime actors in adaptation; cost-benefit is the calculus they use in making their decisions (1991, p. 58; 2005, p. 64).

Societies evolve in response to changes in their natural or social environments. Sociocultural change is of two types: innovation and extinction. The first involves adding new elements such as technologies, social practices, institutions, or beliefs to the system. The second type of change, of course, is eliminating old elements in the system. While extinction indeed occurs, sociocultural evolution is cumulative; change and innovation are added far more to the system than older elements eliminated. This cumulative process, Lenski adds, is one reason sociocultural systems have grown more complex over time (1991, p. 48).

It is also important to note that sociocultural innovation is based on altering existing structures and behavior patterns. Lenski states there are ultimately only three major factors determining the characteristics of sociocultural systems: (1) human genetic heritage; (2) the biological, physical, and social environment; and (3) "the influence of prior social and cultural characteristics of society itself" (1991, pp. 17-18). Therefore, the force of historical experience played a significant role in shaping social institutions and thought.

The rate of innovation and change dramatically varies across different societies. Lenski identifies several factors that influence this rate. The first is "the amount of information a society already possesses" (1991, pp. 54-55). A society with a larger store of cultural information often combines innovation with older cultural elements, thus amplifying and propagating innovation throughout the sociocultural system. One need only think of the recent innovation of the internet and its myriad uses by governments, educational institutions, research labs, corporations, and a host of other entities and individuals. Thus, the rate of change is accelerated in advanced industrial societies, and as the store of technical information increases, it speeds up the potential for change even further (2005, p. 66).

A second factor that varies the innovation rate is population size. Here, Lenski refers to the simple fact that the more people within a population there are, the more potential innovators there are, and the greater the number of people searching for solutions to a particular problem. However, he also refers to the fact that large populations are highly organized, have access to more varied information, and face more complex problems that demand technological or social change (1991, p. 55).

A third factor affecting a society's rate of change and innovation is the stability of the physical and biological environment. "The greater the rate of environmental change, the greater the pressure for change in culture and social organization" (1991, p. 55). Changes in the physical and biological environment can be due to natural processes (such as climate change during the interglacial period some 11,000 years ago) or occasioned by the actions of sociocultural systems themselves (such as desertification which has occurred throughout human history, or the global warming of today).

One of the most critical factors that affect the rate of change within a society "is the extent of that society's contact with other societies" (1991, p. 55). Isolated societies, or those with minimal contact with others, experience very slow rates of innovation" (1991, p. 68). While environmental necessity is the key to understanding "pristine" change—a change that occurs in isolation from contact with other societies—the rapid adoption of most technologies and social practices are done through borrowing technologies and practices from other societies, or cultural diffusion (1991, p. 51).

A fifth factor in determining the rate of innovation is the character of the physical and biological environment. Some environments, such as the Arctic or desert regions, cannot support innovations like agriculture. However, the environment has more subtle effects: "The absence of vital resources, such as adequate water supply or accessible metallic ores, can also hinder innovation, as can endemic diseases and parasites that deplete people's energy. Topography has played an important role in shaping patterns of intersocietal communications. Oceans, deserts, and mountain ranges have all prevented or seriously impeded the flow of information between societies, while navigable rivers and open plains have facilitated it. Considering the importance of diffusion, enormous differences in the rate of innovation can be explained by this factor alone" (1991, p. 56).

Lenski also notes that "fundamental" innovations affect the overall rate of innovation within a society. By fundamental, Lenski refers to innovations like plant cultivation, writing, the plow, or the invention of the steam engine. Adapting such fundamental innovations causes rapid and often revolutionary changes in many other areas of the sociocultural system (1991, pp. 56-57).

The seventh factor affecting the rate of innovation noted by Lenski is society's attitudes and ideologies toward change and innovation. These ideologies and attitudes vary by a society's prior experience with change and the society's dominant ideology (or the elite's ideology). Lenski notes that a society dominated by capitalist ideology is far more supportive of innovation and change than societies dominated by Confucianism or Islamic fundamentalism (1991, pp. 57-62).

Finally, Lenski notes that technological innovation itself tends to occur at an accelerating rate (1991, p. 57). This acceleration is because technical information, like other cultural information, can often be recombined to produce novel inventions. In addition, technological innovation is related to several other factors affecting the rate of innovation discussed above: population growth, environmental and biological change, and increasing cultural contact, as well as affecting the attitudes and ideologies of societies regarding change.

Sociocultural change occurs due to individual members adapting to their natural and social environments. Of course, not all people have equal power in decision-making; "who decides" often depends on the nature of the choice and one's position in the stratification system. Consequently, a few make many important decisions, and these few may choose alternatives that enhance or bolster their interests rather than the interests of the whole society. It is an imperfect social system (1991, pp. 58-59). Structural elites acting in their interests provide positive and negative reinforcement for the adoption or extinction of technological and social change. This feedback can often be decisive in determining whether change is propagated throughout the sociocultural system or whether it is extinguished.

Technology and Population

Changes in subsistence technology and population have far-ranging consequences for human organization, cultural beliefs, and values. Two types of change are of tremendous importance: changes in essential subsistence technologies and changes in population levels (1991, p. 54). Technology and population, of course, are closely intertwined. Consistent with Malthus, Lenski asserts that an increase in food production and more children can be allowed to live (1966, p. 64). Especially in pre-industrial societies where children are economic assets, subsistence production increases inevitably lead to population increases (1991, pp. 172-173). Better methods and technologies of contraception allow individuals to apply preventive checks on their fertility (1991, p. 54). On the other hand, population level and growth put pressure on the biological and physical environments and provide a more direct stimulus for further technological development. Population and subsistence technology are linked, substantially impacting the rest of the sociocultural system.

Lenski uses Goldschmidt's classification of subsistence throughout human history, beginning with Hunter and Gatherer and then to Horticulture, Agrarian, and Industrial. Social scientists may use different classification schemes, and other types of societies not included in this chart could be identified. However, not as widespread, pastoral, fishing, and maritime societies have adapted to specific environments. Interestingly, most social scientists and lay people favor some such scheme of classifying societies based on their mode of production. In discussing international relations, it is helpful to identify whether a society is industrial or agrarian and how developed it is within either of the categories. By referring to societies as such, there is an implicit recognition that subsistence technology is central to understanding the institutions, attitudes, and beliefs within those societies.

This classification scheme of different modes of production (which can be further broken down into "simple" and "advanced") is based on technology. Social practices draw subsistence and other primary resources from the environment, such as metallurgy, plow use, iron, and fossil fuel.

Figure 4.1: Criteria for Classifying Primary Types of Human Societies (1991, 71)

Type:	Cultivate	Metal	Plow	Iron	Fossil Fuel	Hi-Tech
H & G	−	−	−	−	−	−
S. Horticulture	+	−	−	−	−	−
Horticulture	+	+	−	−	−	−
S. Agrarian	+	+	+	−	−	−
Agrarian	+	+	+	+	−	−
Industrial	+	+	+	+	+	−
Hyper industrial	+	+	+	+	+	+

I added the "Hyper Industrial" type along with the "Hi-Tech criteria to Lenski's original table. I picked it up from Harris 1998, who, in reaction to the popular term "post-industrial," began using it. It denotes a societal condition in which virtually all social institutions (government, family, education) have adapted to the demands of the industrial economy. Many scholars favor *hyper-industrialism* over *post-industrial society* to refer to complex industrial societies such as Canada and the U.S. The prefix *hyper-* denotes "over and above," even to the point of "abnormal excess." To describe contemporary North America as "hyper-industrial" is to stress its continuity with the past and its rapidly changing nature—even to abnormal excess.

Technology and population combined set firm limits on widespread organizational characteristics, ideas, and ideologies. These limits include maximum community size and complexity, the division of labor, the degree of inequality, the degree of military power that the society can project, the complexity of stratification systems, and the overall wealth of the society (1966, pp. 47-48; 1991, p. 71). Advances in subsistence technology are also significant because they are often related to improvements in other technologies, such as transportation and communications, which lead to more remarkable societal growth and complexity. The population's demographics, over and above sheer size, can also dramatically impact the rest of the sociocultural system. Such demographic properties as age and sex composition, birth and death rates, density, and migration patterns all have the potential for far-reaching impacts on social structure and cultural beliefs and values (1991, p. 29). Consider the changes that have occurred in hyper-industrial societies with population aging. The aged have become a powerful interest group and created a welfare state catering to their needs.

Lenski considers population and subsistence production critical in understanding sociocultural systems because these two variables are the principal means by which society regulates energy flow from its environment. Increases in the food supply made possible by innovations in subsistence technology are necessary for high population levels, both of which are preconditions for significant increases in the complexity of a society. The resulting complexity creates many unfamiliar problems for sociocultural systems, all of which call for further technological, social, and cultural change (1991, pp. 60-62).

Inequality

Lenski asserts that goods and services are distributed within a society based on need and power. The enlightened self-interests of humans lead them to equitably distribute goods and services to productive classes to ensure their survival and continued productivity. However, Lenski posits that any surplus is likely to be divided following self-interests, that is, based on social power. *Power and Privilege*'s central focus was developing an ecological theory of stratification. His first hypothesis in this theory predicts "[…] that in the simplest societies, or those which are technologically the most primitive, the goods and services available will be distributed on the basis of need" (1966, p. 46).

As technology and productivity increase, Lenski goes on, a portion of the new goods and services will go toward necessary population growth and feeding a larger population. However, with technological development and subsequent increases in productivity, a more significant surplus of goods and services will also be produced. Lenski's second hypothesis predicts "that with technological advance, an increasing proportion of goods and services available to a society will be distributed on the basis of power" (1966, p. 46). If true, when examining sociocultural systems, we should see that the greater the technological advance (as measured by productivity), the greater the inequality in the distribution of goods and services within society.

Lenski offers several caveats before going on to test his basic theory. Several factors may lead to "secondary variation" in the degree of inequality within a society. Technological development is not the only factor related to productivity and creating surplus goods and services within a society. Since the physical environment also affects productivity, he predicts that environments would also affect inequality. Specifically, an environment with a more extraordinary endowment of natural resources will enable society to achieve more significant surpluses, thus increasing the amount of inequality within society. According to Lenski, another factor that may also affect the degree of inequality is "the military participation ratio." He asserts that the higher the proportion of males serving in the military, the less inequality (1966, pp. 48-49). The political cycle is a definitive source of secondary variation in the degree of inequality within a given societal type. In societies where elites have sought legitimation through constitutional government, some lessening of inequality can be predicted (1966, pp. 49-50). Lenski summarizes his inequality theory: "Though this theory predicts that variations in technology are the most important single determinant of variations in distribution, it does not hypothesize that they are the only determinant. Three others are specifically singled out: (1) environmental differences, (2) variations in the military participation ratio, and (3) variations in the degree of constitutionalism. In addition, since this is not a closed theory, it is assumed that other factors also exercise an influence" (1966, p. 90).

Lenski tests this class inequality theory by examining societies' ethnographies and histories based on different subsistence techniques of ascending technological efficiency: Hunting and Gathering, Simple Horticultural, Advanced Horticultural, Agrarian, and Industrial societies. Lenski's theory becomes more evolutionary and broader in focus in *Human Societies.* Then, it is continually tested and refined over succeeding editions by examining these same societal types. In *Power and Privilege*, Lenski finds increasing degrees of inequality, including in early industrial society. At this stage in development, he finds the degree of inequality at its peak and then begins to lessen as industrial societies mature.

There is an incredible concentration of wealth and power in agrarian societies because, in such societies, the state is seen as the private property of the rulers and a small governing class. This allows them to use the state's powers to expropriate the economic surplus from most of the population. Lenski (1966) reports that up to 50 percent of all the income in agrarian societies was collected by the top one or two percent of the population. This represents far greater inequality than his estimated "15.5 percent" of income that the top two percent of the American population receives annually (1966, pp. 309-310). He adds that *income* inequality appears even less in the former Soviet Union, where there were limitations on how much annual income elites could earn. In succeeding editions of *Human Societies,* Lenski continues to monitor inequalities in industrial societies. In 1993, he estimated that the top ten percent of income earners in Western democracies appear to receive 20 to 30 percent of all income (1991, p. 336). In sum, in mature industrial societies, the lower social classes materially benefit more than in agrarian societies, both in absolute and relative terms. Elites appear to receive far less of the nation's income. Lenski concludes that mature industrial societies thus represent a reversal of a long-standing evolutionary trend in which inequality increased with technological development (1966, p. 308). As a graduate student, I was very impressed. Before reading Lenski's *Power and Privilege*, I had never encountered a book where the evidence rejected the author's central hypothesis. He then goes on to thoroughly explore the reasons behind this rejection. I am still impressed.

Lenski attributes this lessening of inequality to factors not directly anticipated in his original hypothesis (1966, pp. 313-325). The first and perhaps most important is the necessity of a large administrative and technical structure to coordinate the sophisticated technology, significant numbers of people, and elements of the increasingly complex culture (1966, pp. 313-314). Because of their knowledge and expertise, higher administrative and technical positions must be given a degree of latitude in performing their duties. ("Powers delegated often become powers lost" (1966, p. 6). They also demand a larger share of the surplus.

Lenski points to a second factor related to the rapidly growing surplus itself. The elite can buy worker allegiance and commitment by allocating a more significant share to the lower classes, thus promoting further economic growth (1966, pp. 314-315). This may be especially true in an economy that relies heavily upon workers' productivity, whose qualitative output is not so easily measurable. If allocating a greater relative share to the lower and middle classes will still increase the total share of the elite, it may be worth the sacrifice. Lenski also points out that an elite in such an expanding economy may become satiated with material rewards alone—the first billion will mean far more to consumption and lifestyles than the second billion. Such elites may be willing to sacrifice some portion of further rewards for reduced class hostilities, greater economic or political security, or even more leisure time (1966, p. 315).

A third factor behind the lessening of inequality can be attributed to changes in population and production dynamics in mature industrial societies. In the past, except for the surplus drained by the elite (to create what we call civilization), productivity increases were accompanied by increases in the human population. This population increase is because children in traditional societies were productive assets, a way of intensifying production itself. Breaking the link between children and production, the final one being their provision of economic security in old age, changes the dynamic between the two. With the introduction of modern birth control, people can now more efficiently and safely control their numbers; productivity increases can be converted to increases in per capita income. As an additional bonus, a declining birth rate among the lower classes reduces competitive pressures among workers, allowing even the semi-skilled to demand more equitable wages (1966, pp. 315-316).

A fourth factor that Lenski identifies as contributing to growing income equality is the expansion of human knowledge and the concomitant increase in the division of labor. Skilled labor is in a much better bargaining position than the unskilled labor that dominated earlier societies. "Because of the great functional utility of so much of the new knowledge, a host of occupational specialists have appeared who are not interchangeable to any great degree" (p. 318). Such labor can demand a more significant share of the surplus.

The final factor in the lessening inequality of mature industrial societies that Lenski examines is a rise in ideologies that advocate more economic equality. Such ideologies would include the rise of Socialist Parties in Europe and the liberal ideology behind establishing the welfare state in the United States. These ideologies are associated with the rise of constitutional government and democracies in which political power is much more dispersed. As a result, governments have become more representative of the broader population and more active in addressing internal inequalities.

There are several cautions regarding his findings: First, industrial societies were most "equal" (or less unequal) in income. As Lenski notes, inequalities in wealth are far more significant in all societies. Second, a good part of the income equality of industrial societies that Lenski reported occurred in the former Soviet Union. Some of that country's income data was seriously misleading in the 1960s; rubles earned by party leaders were far more valuable than those earned by the average citizen; exclusive access to stores selling foreign goods was assured by membership in the party. Lenski ruefully admits this in his 2005 work in which he remarks on the clever nature of these "golden rubles" in disguising the actual amount of inequality from social scientists (2005, pp. 217-218).

Perhaps more importantly, the Soviet Union is no longer in existence, and along with its collapse, there was a weakening of ideologies favoring income redistribution throughout the world. Third, Lenski's study of the U.S. economy was done in the 1960s, at the tail end of what economists now call the "Great Compression." It was a period when, in response to the speculative excesses of the 1920s and the Great Depression of the 1930s, U.S. incomes were perhaps at their most egalitarian point in history. While trends since this time have given the top income earners an ever more sizable proportion, income inequality is still not as great as in agrarian and early industrial societies. In addition, while Lenski found decreasing income inequality within the U.S. up through the 1960s, he found increasing inequality worldwide. Lenski points out, "*The gap between rich and poor societies has been widening ever since the start of the industrial era*" (1991, p. 337). He contends that this trend is bound to intensify with increasing globalization (and capital growth). Finally, it should be noted that this discussion of inequality has been limited to annual income, and Lenski and others point out that wealth is far more unequally distributed.

About Lenski

Gerhard Lenski was born in Washington D.C. on August 13, 1924, to Gerhard Sr. and Christine (Umhau) Lenski. (This section is based on an correspondence with Gerhard Lenski in 2003.) His father, Gerhard Sr., earned a Ph.D. in History and was a Lutheran minister. His Washington congregation consisted of a mix of members of Congress, people working at foreign embassies (including a few ambassadors), government bureaucrats, clerks, and blue-collar workers. Many of these people and his father's academic friends would be at the family dinner table. Lenski recalls Washington as "[…] a wonderful place to grow up in the 1930s. New Deal Politics were exciting, and my parents and relatives loved discussing and debating the issues of the day."

Lenski's friends from both school and his father's congregation cut across class lines. His interest in stratification, however, really came alive through his experiences at Yale and in the military. He began at Yale in 1941 on scholarship and work-study, working 20 hours a week in the kitchen his first year and in the geology workshop during his sophomore year. In these first two years at Yale, he had a reasonable opportunity to observe "the life of the upper class." In 1943, Lenski left school to serve with the U. S. Army Air Force as an enlistee, eventually earning the rank of sergeant. In the Army, his fellow soldiers and friends were all from working-class or rural families. "It would be hard to exaggerate the contrast between these two worlds, and only a dolt could not be fascinated by the contrast."

His interest in comparative sociology was also rooted in his formative years. An occasional dinner guest in his parent's home was a man who had fought in the Russo-Japanese war and told the young man of the horrors of the experience. Another frequent guest, his father's dissertation advisor, Ernst Correl—a former student of Max Weber's—also stimulated this interest. In addition, there were friends from other places, many with radically diverse ways of viewing the world.

The military also gave him an appreciation of diverse cultures. During his three years with the 8th Air Force, he spent most of his time in England and was briefly stationed in France and the Azores. "While in England, I came to know a number of English people very well and even spent a month billeted with an English family while on assignment with the Royal Air Force, so I had many opportunities to see close up how different our two seemingly similar societies actually were."

As a young man, Lenski began a life-long fascination with the Soviet Union. In particular, he was interested in the contrast between the professed ideals of Soviet communism and the "grim totalitarian reality" of Stalinism—the purges and show trials and the Gulag concentration camps. Lenski was also struck by the brutal treatment of Russian war prisoners upon their return to the Soviet Union after the war. Later, as a sociologist, Lenski made many contacts among Eastern European sociologists and traveled there during the Cold War on several occasions.

There are two other strands of Lenski's sociology to be accounted for in this brief sketch. The first is his obvious bent toward historical sociology. Lenski asserts that he came by this interest as a child in his reading of Genesis. He remembers being frustrated that the Bible had so little to say about life in early times. In high school, he discovered H.G. Wells' *The Outline of History*. Eventually, history was to become one of the foundations of his sociology. The second influence on his sociology, evolution, was initiated in his first-year college course in geology. It was here where Lenski got his "first serious introduction" to evolutionary theory. However, in graduate school, he was discouraged from studying social evolution, as such theory was widely discredited in sociology, and functionalism was hailed as the "coming thing."

After completing his service in the Army in 1945, Lenski returned to Yale on the GI Bill, earning his B.A. in sociology in 1947 and his Ph.D. in sociology in 1950. Lenski was much influenced by A. B. Hollingshead, author of *Elmtown's Youth*, in his graduate studies. Hollingshead became his dissertation director, providing Lenski invaluable advice in Lenski's first major research project focusing on a Connecticut mill town.

Starting as a post-doctoral instructor at the University of Michigan, Lenski became an assistant professor in 1954 and an associate professor in 1959. In 1961, he published *The Religious Factor*, a study of the influence of religion on behavior and attitudes. In 1963, he became a full professor at Michigan before moving to the University of North Carolina at Chapel Hill. In 1966, he published *Power and Privilege*, a study on social stratification, and in 1970, the first edition of

Human Societies. Lenski co-authored the work with his wife, Jean Lenski, beginning with the second edition. In the 6th edition in 1991, they brought in Patrick Nolan as a junior author and a sociologist at the University of South Carolina. Nolan's role in *Human Societies* gradually expanded as Lenski began to retire from academic life. In 1992, shortly after his wife's death, Lenski left Chapel Hill. In 1996, he married Ann Blalock, a policy evaluation researcher. They both lived in Washington State, where he continued work on new editions of *Human Societies* and other writing projects in evolutionary sociology until he died in 2015.

Lenski's sociology developed in conjunction with his teaching. Arriving as a young instructor at the University of Michigan in 1950, Lenski was assigned to teach four introductory sociology courses. "This proved to be an extraordinarily frustrating experience since it was impossible to provide students with a meaningfully integrated and cumulative view of sociology when building on a functionalist foundation." His best students would complain of the fragmentation, the jargon, and the separate elements of the course. After some years of this, he read Walter Goldschmidt's *Man's Way: A Preface to the Understanding of Human Society*. In this book, Goldschmidt, an anthropologist, presented the outlines of a more modern version of a social evolutionary perspective. Unlike the older perspectives of Spencer and Sumner, Goldschmidt focused much more on subsistence technology. This evolutionary perspective suggested ways for Lenski to pull together the disparate pieces of his introductory course "into a coherent and provocative whole." This evolutionary perspective was to lead to *Human Societies* in 1970. Since its initial publication, *Human Societies* has provided this holistic alternative for thousands of sociology students.

Chapter 15: Steven K. Sanderson's Evolutionary Materialism

In these opening paragraphs, I emphasize two characteristics of Stephen K. Sanderson (b. 1945) and his evolutionary materialism. The first is that Sanderson is a synthesizer. While all theorists borrow from those who preceded them to some extent, Sanderson attempts to construct a coherent and consistent theory of social evolution by blending elements of two distinct theoretical traditions: ecological-evolutionary theory, particularly from Gerhard Lenski and Marvin Harris, and the world systems perspective of Immanuel Wallerstein. So taken was Sanderson with the works of these men that he dedicated a significant book, *Social Transformations* (1999), to the three. In explaining the dedication, Sanderson notes that Lenski was the first to point him toward a material evolutionary approach. Harris then showed him how to develop and elaborate this approach systematically. Finally, Sanderson reports that Wallerstein added the critical context of a capitalist world-system in understanding sociocultural evolution in the modern world (Sanderson, 1999, p. xi).

The second characteristic of Sanderson's work that I wish to note in these opening paragraphs is the heavy reliance that Sanderson places on anthropological, historical, and sociological data in testing his theoretical propositions. I will try to capture a basic outline of Sanderson's evolutionary materialism in these pages. I must ignore the wealth of comparative-historical data, and scholarship Sanderson brings to exploring this theory. Sanderson is well-versed in social theory and history; he moves skillfully between the case and the general perspective.

Sanderson's "evolutionary materialism" is an extension of Harris' theory of cultural materialism. Cultural materialism (CM), Sanderson claims, is well suited to explaining sociocultural conditions and changes in pre-modern societies, such as the domestication of plants and animals, the development of chiefdoms and the state, social inequality, and the rise of stratification. However, CM does not do well when dealing with advanced agrarian societies, the transition to modernity, or modern capitalist-industrial societies (1999, p. 1). Sanderson asserts that Harris' CM has not developed concepts or posited relationships that allow for a complete examination of inequality within and between modern nation-states and has not adequately developed a vocabulary or strategy for dealing with such phenomena as corporate capitalism, modern war, or the influence of mass media on political behavior. Starting from a foundation of cultural materialism, Sanderson intends to develop a theory that is more capable of dealing with the origin, maintenance, and evolution of the entire range of human societies—from hunting and gathering through horticultural, agrarian, and modern industrial societies.

As the name implies, evolutionary materialism is primarily focused on social evolution. Rather than view history (or prehistory) as a series of unique and non-recurrent events, social evolutionists see "general and repeatable patterns" of social evolution. These patterns are produced by the cumulated interactions of the sociocultural system with its natural and social environments; these interactions cause societies to change in broadly similar ways. Thus, the domestication of plants and animals occurred in several isolated societies around the globe without the benefit of cultural contact with one another. Cultural contact, however, is part of the social environment of almost all societies, and such contact is often the stimulus that causes evolutionary change. Most societies domesticated plants and animals because of contact with those who had already gone through the process.

It is not the case, Sanderson reminds us, that all elements of sociocultural systems are constantly changing. Social stability (or "stasis") is also very much a part of social evolution (1999, p. 133). Social stability refers to the long-term preservation or maintenance of social institutions, behavioral patterns, and belief systems. Many sociocultural systems are remarkable for their unchanging nature. For example, the ancient Mesopotamians, Egyptians, and Indus peoples created extremely stable civilizations lasting thousands of years (McNeill, 1993, pp. 27-55). However, one does not have to look to prehistory alone for examples of social stability. In general, pre-modern societies also have elements that remained unchanging for centuries. Horticulture, for example, was the primary means of subsistence for thousands of years, with little innovation over the generations. The same may be said for various agrarian civilizations throughout the world. It is only in relatively modern times that the hold of tradition on people's lives begins to loosen; only in modern times does sociocultural change become a far more common phenomenon (Sanderson, 1999, p. 15).

344

In addition to social stasis, "extinction" is another phenomenon that must be accounted for in any evolutionary theory. Extinction is the elimination or collapse of a social system and can occur in several ways. War, disease, natural disaster, or ecological change can sometimes lead to the death of all the members of a social system or to such disruption that the social system collapses. It is also possible, Sanderson maintains, that the growing complexity of society may well lead to collapse. Citing Joseph Tainter's (1988) theory of societal collapse, Sanderson argues that growing complexity leads to higher costs for maintaining administrative bureaucracy. These costs eventually reach a point of diminishing returns, whereby further increases in complexity bring marginal benefit to either elites or the population. Maintaining complexity becomes such a financial drain that society is weakened. Any major shock to the sociocultural system (such as war, disease, or natural disaster) will make it vulnerable to collapse (pp. 127-128, p. 383).

Sanderson notes that many evolutionary theorists in the functionalist tradition maintain that growing differentiation or complexity is the primary adaptive mechanism of sociocultural change. However, Sanderson maintains that increasing complexity is not the only adaptive mechanism. Some evolutionary events are regressive (going back to simpler forms) or are entirely neutral (neither more complex nor regressive) (p. 385). Tainter's societal collapse theory doubts the adaptation qualities of societal complexity. Differentiation, specialization, and growing complexity may be beneficial in the short run (particularly for elites), but it may be a maladaptive strategy in the long term. "The frequency of societal collapse in world history surely provides a reason for having extreme doubt about the allegedly adaptive benefits of social complexity" (p. 131). Having said all this, Sanderson adds in an Afterword that greater complexity seems to be one of the "directional patterns" of social evolution (p. 403).

Should society collapse, surviving members are often absorbed into other social systems, or they adapt earlier (and simpler) social forms to survive, a process known as "devolution" or "regression" (Sanderson & Alderson, 2005, p. 27). Sanderson enumerates several consequences of such collapse. A general breakdown of centralized authority leads to an end of state works such as monumental architecture (pyramids, temples, and palaces), complex irrigation works, the abandonment of storage facilities, and the cessation of food redistribution. This breakdown often leads to severe food shortages and a marked reduction in population size and density; individual or local action must often provide food, shelter, and other needs. Technology and lifestyles thus revert to simpler forms (2005, p. 28). Small political units emerge within the territory of the collapsed state and often contend with one another for power (1999, p. 126).

Like his mentors Harris and Lenski (and thus consistent with Malthus), Sanderson insists that individuals make adaptations, not the sociocultural systems themselves (1999, p. 384; 2005, p. 29). Individuals are strongly motivated to satisfy their own needs and wants because humans are strongly egoistic. We seek to maximize the benefits of our actions and minimize the costs. As individuals seeking to satisfy our needs, we enter relationships and form social structures, institutions, and systems that "are the sum total and product of these socially oriented actions" (1999, pp. 12-13). Changes in the natural or social world (or both) cause some individuals to adapt their social behavior to meet their biological and psychological needs and desires more effectively (1999, p. 10). Specific adaptations on the part of individuals can result from discovery or invention (innovation) on the part of individuals involved or borrowing from other individuals or societies who have already made the innovation (diffusion). While these adaptations may allow the individual to meet their needs or desires better, large numbers of people adapting may have negative consequences for other individuals. In a complex society, particularly in those with high degrees of inequality between groups, adaptations are likely to affect more people positively or negatively in some groups than in others—say by race, class, religious group, or sex (1999, p. 10; 2005, p. 29). Therefore, adaptations on the part of individuals lead to changes in the social environment itself, making further adaptations on the part of others probable.

Therefore, there is no direction to social evolution, no grand historical plan, and history is not unfolding in any predetermined direction. Instead, social evolution is driven by individuals entering and changing social arrangements and institutions to further their interests. However, because many individuals with different interests and unequal power are involved, the continually recreated social structures are not the result of conscious human design but are unintended phenomena that often have unforeseen consequences (1999, p. 13). Therefore, social structure is a product "of human intention but not an intended project" (p. 399). The continuously recreated social system and structures constitute "new sets of constraints within which individually purposive action must operate" (p. 13). Social evolution is the cumulative change of social systems and structures resulting from individuals acting to the best of their abilities and foresight in their self-interests.

Also, like his mentors, Sanderson identifies the "principle causal factors in social evolution" as the "material conditions of human existence" (p. 8-9). Sanderson's ideas of what constitutes these material conditions are consistent with Harris and Lenski in that he includes ecological, technological, and demographic factors. These three factors focus on the infrastructural-environmental interactions of population, production technology, and the environment as they concern the availability of vital resources to sustain population levels with the current form of production. However, Sanderson differs from Harris and Lenski because he also incorporates economic factors within these material conditions. For Sanderson, "economic factors relate to the modes of social organization whereby people produce, distribute, and exchange goods and services; an especially important dimension of economics is the nature of the ownership of the basic means of production" (pp. 8-9).

Like Harris, Sanderson justifies giving material factors causal priority because they are fundamental to life itself; they are essential for survival—how people feed themselves, reproduce, and adapt to and manipulate their environment. If these tasks are not completed, individuals die, and society cannot survive. Therefore, all widespread social practices must be compatible with the infrastructural practices used to adapt to a particular environment (p. 9). These factors operate "probabilistically" for most people over extended periods. Like Harris, he must proceed with caution. Harris abandoned the term "infrastructural determinism" in the 1990s because it too often led to a misinterpretation of the probabilistic nature of his theory. He replaces it with the "principle of the primacy of the infrastructure" (Harris, 1998, p. 142). Sanderson has stuck with "infrastructural determinism." Nevertheless, Sanderson insists, repeatedly to satisfy those too quick to charge "vulgar materialist," that it is emphatically not the case that structural and superstructural factors play no role in sociocultural stability and evolution; there are structural and superstructural feedback mechanisms that often extinguish, slow down, or accelerate infrastructural change (1999, pp. 390-391). Sanderson states that such factors play a causal role in the social evolutionary process, "even if ordinarily in a highly secondary way" (1999, p. 9).

In addition to incorporating economic factors into the infrastructure, Sanderson also differs from Harris and Lenski in that he posits that different material conditions (environment, demography, technology, economy) have different causal priorities and strengths at various stages in the evolutionary process and different historical periods (p. 9). He asserts that determining the precise causal significance of any material factor or combination of factors is a matter for empirical study. He goes on to say that there is no single driving force to social evolution, no one universal cause. "The driving engines of social evolution differ from one social-systemic type (historical epoch, evolutionary stage) to another" (p. 9). Specifically, Sanderson asserts that ecology and demography are dominant infrastructural characteristics in prehistory, explaining hunter and gatherer, horticultural, and pastoral societies. He posits that ecology, demography, technology, and economy are critical for agrarian societies in the historical era before 1500.

Furthermore, he insists that the economy is the most critical infrastructural variable in explaining the modern world after 1500 regarding a society's internal structure and its effects on relations with other sociocultural systems (2005, p. 275). Going further, Sanderson asserts that the ceaseless accumulation of capital is the "driving engine" of social evolution today, an ever-accelerating engine that may lead us to an environmental crisis (1999, pp. 361-362, p. 392). Thus, Sanderson combines Marx with his Malthusian-Evolutionary base: he performs a slightly modified cultural materialist analysis through 1500 and then shifts gears to a Marxist-economic analysis with the transition to capitalism.

For Sanderson, the "economy" encompasses variables internal to individual sociocultural systems and the system's relationships and interactions with other societies. Relying heavily on the work of Immanuel Wallerstein, Sanderson asserts that societies are often enmeshed in large "world systems." Their place in these world systems, whether economically and militarily dominant or subordinate, dramatically affects their consequent evolution (pp. 14-15). "Ever since the work of Immanuel Wallerstein, it has become clear that much social evolution occurs as the result of the effects of large-scale intersocietal networks within which individual societies are located" (p. 400). Any evolutionary analysis of society must consider its role in the prevailing world systems of the time—whether that world-system is a regional empire or the modern capitalist world economy.

Like Harris and Lenski before him, Sanderson also claims that the pace of social evolution varies through history but posits that it appears to be speeding up in modern times (p. 15). He also agrees that the preferred method of evolutionary analysis is the historical comparative method. That is, examining specific sociocultural systems through anthropological, historical, and sociological data and comparing systems within evolutionary stages and historical epochs. Evolutionists are particularly interested in transitions from one sociocultural form to another (pp. 16-17). Moreover, it is in performing comparative historical analysis that Sanderson truly shines; he marshals an incredible amount and variety of social science data to test the power of evolutionary materialism in explaining sociocultural stability and change. This review will briefly focus on two such analyses: the structure and dynamics of agrarian society and the transition to capitalism and industrialism.

The Structure and Dynamics of Agrarian Society

According to Sanderson, five characteristics are shared by all agrarian societies across historical eras. First, as production is based on agricultural produce and livestock, there is a division between an elite or nobility who owns or controls the land and the masses (or peasantry) working the land. This peasantry must pay for access to this land through rent (often a share of the crops produced), taxation, or forced labor services to the nobility (p. 97). A second characteristic all agrarian societies share is the relatively low status accorded merchants engaged in trade. "Indeed, those who dominate production-for-exchange, urban merchants, were typically looked down upon by the aristocracy as money-grubbing individuals who dared to dirty their hands with the soil of commerce" (p. 96). Such individuals might acquire great wealth, but they had little prestige or power within agrarian societies and were often subject to confiscation even of their wealth.

According to Sanderson, the third characteristic common to all agrarian societies is the absence of overt class conflict between nobles and peasants. He asserts there may be sporadic uprisings of the peasantry, but these are rare. Sanderson claims that this is because of the fourth characteristic of such societies. They are held together by an almost monopoly of military force by the landholding elites, who then use this force to dominate and control the peasantry. Thus, these societies are always highly militarized, and the military is always controlled and used to further the material interests of the elite (p. 97). Here, Sanderson overstates the case, claiming that such societies were so wholly dominated by force that there was no ideological or legitimating worldview within these societies; elites and peasantry did not share a consensus on the legitimacy of the social order. This supposition is highly doubtful and ignores the role of religion in most agrarian societies.

The fifth characteristic of agrarian societies cited by Sanderson is that agrarian societies are very stable and unchanging throughout the agrarian era (about 3000 BC to about AD 1500). The "agrarian era" refers to the historical era in which agrarian societies were dominant. They were dominant in technology, military, productivity, and population. Sanderson notes that this characterization must not be taken too literally. The era immediately preceding the agrarian era was transitioning from horticulture to an agrarian society. The invention and diffusion of the plow and the use of animals (draft animals, fertilizer) in the production process significantly increased the productivity of the land, which led to the rapid increase in population, the rise of the state, the creation of a surplus which leads to stratification, urbanization, and technological change. At the end of the agrarian era came the rise of capitalism and the industrial revolution. With such dynamic eras serving as bookends, the agrarian era is bound to look stable and unchanging by comparison. Because agrarian societies were highly stratified, and the elites enjoyed a near monopoly of state and political power, these societies were relatively stable over time. However, Sanderson hastens to add that they were not stagnant have also adopted this view.

Several changes were going on beneath the surface throughout the agrarian era that would slowly grow in importance and eventually lead to social upheaval and change (p. 97). The changes cited by Sanderson that slowly built up force throughout the agrarian era included population growth, increasing the size of political units, change in military and production technology, and economic growth in trade and commodification. Regarding population growth, Sanderson cites Eckhardt (1992) to the effect that the population went from about 14 million people worldwide in 3000 BC to 252 million in 1 AD and 461 million in 1500 AD (1999, p. 103). Such population growth reflects increased agricultural productivity throughout the era.

With the rise in population, there has also been an increase in the size of political units in terms of population and land area under their control. This growth was especially apparent in the latter half of the era for agrarian empires, the largest agrarian political units. Empires are conglomerations of several units conquered by a single unit and forced to pay tribute. Sanderson reports that empires grew in physical size and number dramatically from 3000 BC through 1500 AD (p. 104). Several social, military, transportation, and communications developments enabled the increased size—the first to consider impersonal bureaucracy's development, refinement, and expansion in social technology. In military technology, chariots and horses are used in warfare and greater sophistication in manufacturing weapons. In transportation technology, there is the wheel, improved and more extensive roadways, maps, sea-going vessels, and draft animals. Finally, in communications technology, writing and literacy are developed and spread. "Empires could not become effectively larger until the means were available for controlling and integrating much larger areas" (p. 105).

Sanderson argues that the most significant and far-reaching change in the agrarian era is the slowly accumulating growth in trade and trade networks (p. 113). This trade growth was driven by the material interests of merchants acting to increase their wealth and by simple population growth. As evidence for this growth in trade throughout the agrarian era, Sanderson cites the growth of urbanization from 2250 BC to AD 1500. Reasoning that commerce and trade are the dominant forces behind urbanization, Sanderson cites data to document the growth of urbanization throughout the agrarian era.

There had been phenomenal growth in cities with over 30,000 people and the upper limits of city size. For example, in 650 BC, there were 20 cities worldwide with over 30,000 inhabitants, and the largest city of the time was estimated to have a population of about 120,000. By AD 1000, there were some 70 cities worldwide with a population of 40,000 or more, the largest of which had a population of 450,000. In terms of the estimated population in the largest cities, there is also dramatic growth, going from 894,000 urbanites in BC 650 to 5,629,000 in AD 1000 (p. 112).

As further evidence of the growing importance of trade, Sanderson reviews the work of Andre Gunder Frank (1990), pointing to evidence that trade among agrarian civilizations was a growing factor in the affairs of sociocultural systems since the establishment of the first Mesopotamian state in BC 3000 (1999, pp. 105-111). In addition, Sanderson points to the work of Janet Abu-Lughod (1989), who details a worldwide trade network encompassing societies on the continents of Eurasia and Africa from AD 1250 to 1350. Sanderson argues that the gradual growth of trade and commercialization throughout the agrarian era will eventually become a critical factor in the transition from agrarian to industrial civilization (1999, p. 113). However, it is essential to note that Sanderson does not side with Frank and other "precapitalist world-system theorists" who find evidence for a world trade system beginning thousands of years before capitalism. Frank argues that Wallerstein's capitalist world-system is only the latest manifestation; that capital accumulation within a world trade system has been a driving force of sociocultural evolution beginning with the rise of civilization in Mesopotamia. Sanderson believes that the importance of this precapitalist trade on change in agrarian societies has been dramatically exaggerated (p. 124).

Capitalism and Industrialism

The standard view within sociology, Sanderson notes, is that the industrial revolution is the watershed marking the transition to a modern world. The discipline was born in an attempt to understand and explain the impact of industrialization on traditional structures, values, and ideologies. Nevertheless, Sanderson, like several other recent scholars, believes the origins of modernity are further back in time and are rooted in the transition from feudalism to capitalism in the sixteenth century.

Insisting that the rise of capitalism is the beginning of modernity is intimately wrapped up with Sanderson's placement of the economy in the infrastructure of societies. Capitalism, both the internal relations within a society and the world-capitalist system envisioned by Wallerstein, will become a prime factor in understanding the sociocultural evolution of the modern world. For Sanderson, the rise to dominance of this economic system must mark the beginning of modernity. Harris and Lenski (and this author) view general economic relations and capitalism as structural factors that should be kept separate from material factors (such as production technology and population) when analyzing sociocultural systems. Relegating the economy to the social structure does not necessarily diminish the importance of economic factors in sociocultural evolution. Such structural factors interact intimately with the material factors of the infrastructure and often provide feedback that dampens, quickens or extinguishes their development. We will return to this view in the closing chapter.

It is not that capitalism was suddenly invented in the 16th century; the organized production and sale of goods for profit in markets was probably a part of social life from the domestication of plants and animals (2005, p. 86). Instead, beginning in that century, capitalism began to expand rapidly in some societies. The interests of merchants and those who organized production took on greater weight, their power increased, and many checks on their wealth accumulation were gradually removed (p. 6). Why did capitalism become a dominant force in organizing some sociocultural systems in the sixteenth century? Citing the work of Randall Collins (1980), Sanderson minimizes Weber's analysis of the Protestant Ethic as a significant factor in the rise. Later in his career, Weber gave the nation-state a much more vital role in the rise of capitalism. Throughout the agrarian era, the nation-state took steps to rationalize law, making it less subject to the arbitrary whim of local rulers. The state also took steps to standardize taxation and currencies and laid the institutional foundations for banking, finance, investment, and the enforcement of contracts. All of these, Weber maintained, are necessary structures that promote capitalist development. Sanderson agrees and points to several other factors essential for the rise.

Sanderson's analysis begins with the observation that capitalism did not arise in Europe alone but developed in Japan several hundred years later without significant European contact. What similarities between Western European societies and Japan explain why they rose independently in these two areas of the world? Sanderson enumerates several such similarities: (1) small size; (2) location on oceans; (3) temperate climates; (4) dramatic population growth through the transition; and (5) an actual feudal structure with elevated levels of political decentralization (1999, pp. 161-172). Small size is essential because it minimizes investment in transportation and communication networks within national borders, thus creating an important condition for commercial development. Sanderson posits that location on oceans is crucial because it led to an emphasis on maritime trade instead of overland routes. Population growth—striking in both regions just before capitalist takeoff—leads to a large pool of available urban labor and growing markets for goods (2005, p. 99).

Most importantly, political decentralization meant that large bureaucratic empires could not stifle trade through heavy taxation or the confiscation of the wealth of merchants. "Large centrally organized empires tend to stifle mercantile activity because it is a threat to the mode of surplus extraction used by rulers and the governing classes. The freedom to merchants under the regimes of medieval Europe and Japan was probably the most important precondition that helped push these parts of the world forward as the first states to undergo a capitalist revolution" (pp. 99-100).

These factors, combined with the long-term growth of commercial activity throughout the agrarian era, led to the rise of capitalism in Western Europe and Japan (p. 87 & p. 100). The buildup of trade, particularly in the centuries before 1500, led to the creation of a critical mass, a "density sufficient to trigger a massive capitalist takeoff" (1999, p. 174). Sanderson maintains that the intensity and growth of trade networks would have eventually brought about the rise to power of a capitalist class, even in regions that were hostile to capitalism. However, conditions were particularly favorable in Western Europe and Japan, primarily because of the political decentralization and the consequent competition for power among the nobility, the church, and the merchants (p. 173). The merchant classes of agrarian societies had minor status or social or political power; their wealth was often confiscated, and they were near the bottom of the social order. However, they were indispensable in exchanging goods and services within and between societies. The cities and towns in Europe gradually became dominated by merchants. These merchants gradually came to enjoy considerably more independence, which led them into more significant conflict with the nobility (2005, pp. 88-89). "Gradually their economic power grew, until some 4,500 years after the origins of the first states and quite probably the first genuine merchants, they were able to conquer and subdue the very kind of society that gave them birth" (p. 175).

At this point, Sanderson becomes a world systems theorist with only a few modifications from the basic outline of the perspective developed by Wallerstein. Sanderson maintains that the evolution of the modern world and individual societies that make up that world must be viewed from a world systems perspective. Societies are embedded within a capitalist world system and must be studied within that context (1999, p. 181). Capitalism, Wallerstein maintains (and Sanderson agrees), is born as a world economy; it is not just an individual nation-state phenomenon. It can only be understood as a world-system phenomenon. Once early capitalists gained dominance within several Western European nation-states, these states conducted their internal affairs and relations with other states consistent with the interests of the capitalists within their borders. To understand a society in the modern world, that society must be viewed within the context of its role in the entire world economy (2005, p. 95).

For Wallerstein and Sanderson, capitalism's critical characteristic is the ceaseless accumulation of profit. Just as Marx claimed that capitalism was a system of a few owners of production exploiting the masses for their labor power within a given society, Wallerstein claims that it is also an economic world-system for "surplus expropriation" between nation-states. A world-system is a division of labor in which several societies specialize in various economic activities to meet their needs. This division of labor, or economic specialization, is highly unequal, with some states dominating the labor, markets, and resources of others through economic, political, and military means (pp. 95-97).

According to Sanderson (and Wallerstein), the capitalist world economy contains three principal zones: the core, the semi-periphery, and the periphery. The core consists of the most advanced nation-states, such as the U.S., Japan, Great Britain, and Germany; their economies focus on producing the most highly profitable, technologically sophisticated goods, financial services, and complex manufacturing processes. The economies of the core employ the bulk of the skilled labor, are the most developed, and tend to hold monopolies on many of the goods and services produced. The periphery is the least developed zone and would include such nation-states as Bolivia, Colombia, Kenya, and Pakistan. These nations supply raw materials and labor to the core states, usually at exceptionally low costs. The semi-periphery is an intermediate zone—not as exploited as the periphery, not as technologically sophisticated or powerful as the core; it exhibits characteristics of both.

Capitalists locate manufacturing plants in peripheral societies to produce highly profitable goods. However, they pay little for local labor or materials, often using unsafe or outmoded machinery and abusing the environment and worker health and safety. The profits from these ventures go back to corporate headquarters in the core countries; they are not invested in the periphery. The core uses its economic, political, and military power to exploit peripheral nation-states and regions for their raw materials and cheap labor, make and enforce unfair contracts, and dominate local markets (2005, p. 95).

Nation-states within the core compete for dominance within the world economy. This competition involves economic rivalry and political and military conflict (1999, p. 183). Due to this competition and the striving to develop peripheral and semi-peripheral societies, there is some (albeit limited) movement between the three sectors. Some core states have declined in economic importance and slipped to semi-peripheral status, some former semi-peripheral nation-states have moved up to the core, and some former peripheral nation-states are now semi-peripheral (p. 183).

From the beginning, the capitalist world system has been geographically expanding, so by the early 20th century, it had fully encompassed the globe. At the same time, the capitalist world system has been "deepening." The logic of capitalist relations—the market, production, profit, values, and norms—has been applied to more areas of social life. Sanderson calls this deepening "the chief evolutionary process within the capitalist system" and believes it is responsible for most of the structural changes within the capitalist world system and within the individual nation-states that make up that world system (1999, p. 184).

The "subprocesses" that Sanderson associates with this deepening are all well-known to sociologists and others sensitive to the modern era. These processes include *commodify*ing all goods and services rather than self-production and self-sufficiency. By denigrating "homemade" and making manufactured goods and contractual services natural and desirable, capitalists have expanded their markets (think baby formula or bottled water) into areas undreamed by their forebears. A second subprocess is the *"contractualization"* of social relationships. Services that were once provided to an individual based upon that person's family or friendship ties are being replaced by contractual relations between the individual and a government or private contractor for such services as psychological counseling or childcare. There are several consequences to making this formerly personal service between relatives and friends into a contract between the service provider and client. One example is the interest of family members in marriage counseling is often in keeping the couple together; in a formal counseling relationship, the emphasis is on serving the client.

The sub-processes of deepening also include the *mechanization* of the workplace, now ongoing in manufacturing, the provision of services, and the upper reaches of administration. In addition, Sanderson notes the *proletarianization* or deskilling of the workforce in which the skilled labor of many is replaced by the unskilled labor of the few tending the machines. This deskilling is done in the name of efficiency (as detailed by Adam Smith), and economy, as unskilled labor is far more malleable and less costly than skilled. Finally, there is the process of the *polarization* of rich and poor within nation-states and between the core and the periphery, a process we will examine in more detail in another section (1999, pp. 184-185).

As is evident from his list of subprocesses of the deepening of the capitalist world-economic system (particularly mechanization), Sanderson believes that industrialization is a natural outgrowth of capitalism. He conceives industrialization as a process of "mechanization within capitalism" carried forward because mechanization increases profitability. Sanderson cannot conceive industrialization occurring "outside a highly advanced form of capitalism." He says, "industrialization was built into the evolutionary logic" of capitalist production (1999, p. 257). Natural resources, particularly the availability of coal and water, were critical in determining only where and when it occurred first, Sanderson asserts, but the rise of capitalism itself assured (and essentially explains) the Industrial Revolution. Sanderson doubts that demography or resource shortages played much of a role in the Industrial Revolution. Instead, he asserts that the capitalist profit motive alone pushed technological development to increase productivity and lower the cost of production (2005, p. 108).

Sanderson diverges markedly from Harris's cultural materialism in his analysis of the rise of industrialism. In addition to the stimulus of capitalism, Harris emphasizes population pressures, resource depletion, and the consequent substitution of novel resources in his analysis of the Industrial Revolution, which Sanderson rejects (1999, p. 256). Harris clearly distinguishes between the technology of production and the economic, political, and domestic structures of societies (which includes capitalism). This distinction drives Harris to make a much more detailed analysis of demographic and ecological factors before examining the economy.

According to Sanderson, core nations within the capitalist world system industrialized first, of course, with the periphery and semi-periphery being exploited for their raw materials, markets, and low-cost labor. This initial development allows core states to build a substantial initial lead in accumulating wealth and capital, allowing them to maintain and even increase their wealth relative to the peripheral areas to this day (2005, p. 109).

As with trade and the rise of capitalism, Sanderson maintains that the Industrial Revolution should not be considered a singular event but rather a gradually intensifying technological innovation process that occurs over time. Citing Charles Tilly (1963), Sanderson maintains that "protoindustrialization" begins well before the traditional date of the middle of the 18th century given by most social scientists, some "two or three centuries before (1999, p. 251 & p. 401). Industrialization is, therefore, a process that occurs over many generations down to the present day (1999, pp. 253-254; 2005, p. 107). This dating of protoindustrialization as occurring some 200 to 300 years before the middle 1700s, or around 1500, would seem to argue that industrialization is a process that closely interacts with the rise of capitalist dominance from the beginning. The point is that the Industrial Revolution, while far-reaching and dramatically affecting traditional structures (family, government, economic organization, military) and superstructures (norms, values, traditions), was not as revolutionary as it is often portrayed in terms of its timing and speed (1999, p. 249; 2005, pp. 109-110).

Globalization

His integration of the world systems perspective strongly influences Sanderson's treatment of globalization into evolutionary materialism. Like other world systems theorists, Sanderson points out that globalization is not unprecedented. Capitalism has always been global in scope; it has consistently produced and marketed goods and services through the world system. He points out that the period from 1870 to 1914 had remarkably high rates of international trade that were only matched in the modern world in recent times. This earlier globalization was reversed with World War I, the Great Depression, and World War II. Our recent rise in globalization is truly remarkable only in relation to the period (1914-1970) immediately preceding it—it is not that striking compared to earlier periods (2005, pp. 238-242).

There are three parallel processes to recent globalization: economic, political, and sociocultural. Economic globalization is the most widely written about, and its growth can be easily measured by changes in the ratio of world trade compared to the world's Gross Domestic

Product (GDP). If globalization is becoming a reality, we should find an increasing proportion of goods and services sold on international markets. Citing the World Trade Organization (2001) figures, Sanderson states, "In 1990, the ratio of world trade in goods and services to world GDP was 19 percent. In 2000, just ten years later, it had increased to 29 percent. This means that the ratio of trade to output grew by 52 percent in the decade of the 1990s" (2005, pp. 220-221). This growth in trade relative to GDP is twice as fast as the growth that occurred in the 1980s and three times faster than the rate of growth in the 1970s.

The extent and recent growth of political globalization can be measured through Intergovernmental Organizations' (IGOs) growth. These organizations are designed to encourage governments to cooperate in addressing such issues as trade, defense, finance, and nuclear proliferation, as well as regional and global problems. Examples include the United Nations, NATO (North Atlantic Treaty Organization), the International Monetary Fund, the World Bank, and the North American Free Trade Agreement. Sanderson points out that by joining an IGO, governments must give up some of their autonomy and freedom of action to make collective decisions. He cites data that the average number of IGOs a nation-state belongs to has climbed from 18 in 1960 to 52 by 2000. "The growth of international nongovernment organizations (INGOs)—organizations such as Greenpeace, the International Red Cross, Doctors Without Borders—have been equally explosive" (p. 223).

The growth of sociocultural globalization is much more challenging to measure. It consists of the growing homogenization of taste and the spread of consumer culture worldwide. Such phenomena as the spread of the fast-food restaurant, the centralization and growth of international news and entertainment conglomerates, and the growing amounts of money spent on marketing worldwide are all indications of its growth.

Sanderson maintains that the continued evolution of the capitalist world economy is responsible for the recent growth in all three forms of globalization (p. 235). Sanderson maintains that world capitalism has entered a new phase in which transnational corporations invest in peripheral economies (p. 196). In the past, the peripheral societies were exploited for their raw materials—cheap, unskilled labor was used to mine or harvest their resources and sold for little profit to industries in the core for fashioning into sophisticated manufactured goods. The unskilled labor within these peripheral economies is increasingly used by transnational corporations to manufacture goods, with the bulk of the profits going to corporate headquarters in core countries (p. 221). Sanderson also notes the establishment of free production zones.

> These are geographical areas of counties that are often zoned off from the rest of society by special fences and other devices within which economic activities are carried on with few restrictions on the use of labor [...] Within these zones, sometimes called world market factories because production is destined for the world market, wages are often extremely low and working hours very long, work involves intense levels of concentration, work is often of short duration and thus workers can be subject to sudden unemployment, labor unions are banned, workers have few or no rights, and much work may be dangerous and result in physical harm (p. 230).

This globalization of production (and marketing) is driving political and sociocultural globalization.

Where Sanderson significantly differs from world systems theorists is in his evaluation of capitalism. Although Sanderson recognizes that the relationship between the core and the periphery is still exploitative, the evidence of whether globalization benefits peripheral economies, and their people is mixed (pp. 227-231). He marshals data to show that income, education, and life expectancy are all rising in these peripheral nations while infant mortality is declining. While there are still gross inequalities between nations, peripheral societies are improving. Consequently, Sanderson is much less inclined to condemn capitalism for fostering inequality and more likely to call for reform (p. 254).

One area in which Lenski influences Sanderson is in his treatment of inequality within nation-states. Dealing with wealth and income disparities within core nations, Sanderson admits that "enormous" differences exist between the elite and the rest of the population. However, he notes, there has been a "wide diffusion of economic benefits" to the population (1999, p. 270). He credits this diffusion of income and wealth to the fact that capitalism requires consumers, and because of this fact, wages in the core states have risen (p. 271). Sanderson takes pains here to insist he is not making a functionalist argument. However, he points out that capitalism could not have developed to the extent it has if mass consumption had not co-evolved with it. Sanderson has a natural aversion to functionalist argument, a curious fact for one committed to macro-evolutionary theory. In agreement with Lenski, Sanderson maintains that the primary mechanism that has achieved this diffusion of wealth is parliamentary democracy, which was brought about by universal suffrage and the trade union movement. He also credits the growth of the "organizational society," expanding corporate and government bureaucracies with its managerial classes (pp. 271-272).

Like all world systems theorists, Sanderson is interested in societal inequality and explores why some nation-states have failed to develop economically (2005, p. 183). In answer to this question, he has significant differences from Wallerstein. Sanderson has some doubt that peripheral areas are worse off today than in the past relative to core nations. As reported above, Sanderson does not believe the evidence is conclusive regarding the relative gap between core and periphery—for some measures, he believes the periphery is relatively better off today than it was 20 years ago; on some measures, it is not clear (1999, p. 217 & p. 272; 2005, pp. 228-229). However, Sanderson maintains that the evidence is overwhelming that peripheral areas have improved their economic status in absolute terms. At least some peripheral economies undergo economic development over time (1999, p. 217). On the other hand, Wallerstein maintains that peripheral societies are worse off in absolute and relative terms. The difference between the two has significant implications for world systems theory.

According to world systems theorists, Sanderson reports there was no significant gap between core and periphery societies in the initial stages of the capitalist world economy. However, in later stages, the gap widened considerably (p. 203). The orthodox world systems view is that states that started in the core have been able to use that starting point to increase their economic wealth at the expense of those who began in the periphery of the capitalist world economy (p. 217). This widening gap is because much of the development of the core depends upon the exploitation of the periphery's raw materials, labor, and markets. However, Sanderson maintains that although their economies are primarily dependent upon core nations, many peripheral societies have been able to develop their economies over time (1999, p. 241). This means that the exploitation is not total, and that position in the world system does not explain the differences in economic development between nations.

Peripheral states can use their internal resources to improve their domestic economies despite their dependency upon core nations. Also, citing Lenski, Sanderson notes that societies have a history that precedes their incorporation into the capitalist world economy. "This history is very important [...] in conditioning the way in which a particular precapitalist society will be incorporated into the capitalist system and the results of that incorporation" (2005, p. 199). In general, Sanderson maintains that world systems theorists focus too much on peripheral society's relations with the capitalist world system and not enough on the internal characteristics of society itself. In sum, a second difference between Sanderson and Wallerstein is in the emphasis that Sanderson places upon "endogenous," or a society's internal characteristics in the evolutionary process, versus Wallerstein's almost exclusive focus upon the world system in which individual nation-states are embedded. While Sanderson believes world systems theorists implicitly recognize such internal factors, they rarely incorporate them into their analysis. Sanderson does so far more explicitly (1999, pp. 240-241; 2005, p. 202).

While Sanderson has strayed far from the almost exclusive reliance upon the Malthusian population and production factors in explaining sociocultural phenomenon (as has Lenski, and to a lesser extent Harris), he is still very much within the tradition. The relationship between population and production is still the driving force behind sociocultural evolution, though Sanderson insists that economic factors—especially capitalism—deserve at least equal attention.

About Sanderson

According to Stephen Sanderson, he had about as ordinary an upbringing as possible for a person, let alone a scholar of note, to have. (This section is based on Sanderson, 2007.) He does not claim to have lived in exciting places, known famous politicians, intellectuals, artists, or literary figures, or even travel far from home. On a scale of cultural capital rated from 1 to 10, Sanderson started life as a one and was still a 1 when he began graduate school. After that, things changed, but it took a while.

Sanderson was born in Springfield, Missouri, in 1945, and when he was five, his family moved to a small town on the plains of north central Kansas, where he began school and lived for eleven years. For entertainment, one could visit the baseball field, the swimming pool, or the movie theater, where if you were 12 or under, admission was 14 cents (later raised to 15 cents). Then, the family moved back to Springfield, where Sanderson completed high school and attended Southwest Missouri State College, earning his B.A. in 1967.

Sanderson's father, Waller Eugene Sanderson, was a small businessman who owned and ran a hardware store during the Kansas years and later became an investment salesman. The Sandersons first came to the United States from Scotland in the mid-eighteenth century, settling in Virginia and taking up farming. Later, one branch of the family migrated to Missouri, settling in the small town of Bowling Green, about ninety miles up the Mississippi River from St. Louis. Here J. E. Sanderson's Dry Goods was founded by John Eubank Sanderson (Stephen Sanderson's great-

great-grandfather), a clothing business that remained in the family for four generations. Sanderson's mother, née Marjorie King, grew up in the small town of Greenfield, Missouri, in the southwestern part of the state. Her father was a prominent businessman and engaged in various businesses, particularly a Chevrolet agency and a bank. Sanderson is thus a product of the *petit bourgeoisie* of the rural Midwest, and his fierce independence and self-reliance strongly reflect these class origins.

Sanderson began school in 1950. His first report card is signed by his mother, who wrote to the teacher: "Stephen loves school and talks of nothing else all of the time." Indeed, he loved school from the time he started until he finished his Ph.D. in sociology at the University of Nebraska in 1973. He thus had an intellectual bent from the very beginning. His first great love was science, biology in particular. At about age eleven, he was walking down an alley when he noticed someone had discarded a biology textbook beside an incinerator. Since the book was in good condition, Sanderson picked it up, dusted it off, and took it home. He then devoured it, finding its contents so exciting that he had to stop reading to tell his mother how fascinating it was.

Later, in his sophomore year of high school, Sanderson took a biology course from the most demanding teacher he ever had, Herbert H. Darby, a man who never smiled and who barked out his students' names, always the last name only. The fall semester was devoted to botany, the second to zoology. Sanderson recalls that the first assignment on the first day of class was to memorize the Latin names of forty trees and shrubs and be able to identify them on a field trip later in the week. Later, Sanderson discovered that the textbooks for the course were intermediate college-level biology texts, which were testimony to the rigor of the course.

Because of his love for biology, Sanderson originally planned to become a physician. However, the "*Sturm und Drang*" of adolescence led him into psychology, and he later thought he wanted to become a clinical psychologist. When he registered for his first semester of college, all the psychology courses were filled, so his advisor suggested taking sociology. "What is that"? Sanderson wanted to know. "Take it and find out," replied his advisor. He did and found it fascinating, soon switching his major. His favorite undergraduate course was social theory, a five-credit course that met every day of the week. It started with the Code of Hammurabi and ended with Talcott Parsons. His classmates were mystified that he liked theory and seemed to understand it, and he found it equally mystifying that they did not. The professor was a woman, Oreen Ruedi, who achieved her status long before feminism. She lectured nonstop from the moment she walked into the classroom, and if you dropped your pen, you could be hopelessly behind in your notetaking. On the exams, she took no prisoners. Sanderson loved her, just as he did his equally demanding high school biology teacher.

In graduate school, Sanderson continued his interest in sociological theory, often studying it independently. He specialized in social psychology. He authored his dissertation on the relationship between moral reasoning and religious and political ideologies, using Kohlberg's cognitive-developmental theory as his theoretical foundation. Sanderson expected to make a career publishing this kind of research but was discouraged by editors' rejections of his earliest journal submissions. Then, he discovered the anthropologist Marvin Harris through an interview with Harris in *Psychology Today*. Sanderson started reading Harris's books, beginning with his famous *Cows, Pigs, Wars, and Witches*. Then, in early 1977, he read Harris's magnum opus, *The Rise of Anthropological Theory* (famously known among anthropology students as *The RAT*), and it was a life- and career-changing experience. Harris's materialism struck Sanderson as intuitively correct and extremely powerful, and he noticed striking similarities between what Harris was saying and Gerhard Lenski's evolutionism. In graduate school, Sanderson had been impressed by Lenski's *Power and Privilege* and later by his textbook, *Human Societies*. Sanderson wanted to use this book for his introductory classes, but the required reworking was a deterrent. However, once Sanderson encountered Harris, he decided to face the situation and do it.

He decided to write his text because he disagreed with some features of Lenski's approach, particularly his heavy reliance on technological change as a determinant of long-term social evolution. (Professor Sanderson and I disagree with his assertion that Lenski overly relies upon technological determinants in the evolutionary process; you are urged to read Lenski and Sanderson and judge yourself.) Sanderson began in 1978 and was published in 1988 as *Macrosociology: An Introduction to Human Societies*. Authoring this book was extremely difficult because it required enormous amounts of new learning in anthropology and history. However, it gave him an intellectual foundation, and later books became much easier to write. As remarked in the opening of this chapter, Sanderson's command of history, anthropology, and sociology is impressive.

When sociobiology arrived on the scene in the mid-1970s, Sanderson was immediately attracted. He was interested in the biological foundations of human behavior even as a graduate student. In 1971, he devoted a seminar paper to the relevance of infrahuman animal studies, especially ethology, to understanding human behavior. Given his first great intellectual love, biology, this seemed almost inevitable. When Pierre van den Berghe published *Man in Society: A Biosocial View* in 1975, Sanderson quickly adopted it as one of the textbooks for his introductory course. Along with Lenski and Harris, van den Berghe was a significant influence, as were the evolutionary psychologists when they came along later.

Sanderson taught for thirty-one years at the Indiana University of Pennsylvania, near Pittsburgh. After retiring from full-time teaching in 2006, he moved to Boulder, Colorado, and for a year, was affiliated with the Department of Anthropology at the University of Colorado. He now lives in Riverside, California, and is a visiting scholar at the University of California at Riverside.

Part 5: Summary & Synthesis

In the vast landscape of *Macro Social Theory*, a myriad of voices and perspectives come together to unravel the complexities of society. As we reach the concluding chapter, we are presented with a tapestry woven from the diverse ideas of remarkable theorists. This introduction serves as a testament to the interconnectedness of their theories, revealing the commonalities that transcend disciplinary boundaries and historical contexts. By delving into this rich synthesis of ideas, we gain a deeper appreciation for the enduring themes and shared insights underpinning macrosocial theory.

Throughout the concluding chapter, a recurring theme emerges—the interplay of structure and agency in shaping social phenomena. From the classic sociological works of Emile Durkheim and Max Weber to the contemporary contributions of theorists like Neil Postman and Norbert Elias, a shared emphasis on the reciprocal relationship between social structures and individual actions permeates the discourse. These thinkers recognize that while social structures provide the framework within which individuals operate, individuals, in turn, have the agency to shape and transform these structures. This interplay highlights the dynamic nature of society and the complex processes through which social change unfolds.

Another common thread that weaves through the concluding chapter is the recognition of power dynamics, social inequalities, and stratification. From Karl Marx's exploration of class struggle and the capitalist mode of production to C. Wright Mills' examination of power relations and knowledge production, these theorists expose the mechanisms through which power operates and perpetuates social hierarchies. They shed light on how social, economic, and cultural forces shape societies' distribution of resources, opportunities, and privileges. The analysis of power and inequality underscores the pervasive nature of these issues and the importance of understanding their impact on individuals and communities.

Within the concluding chapter, the significance of culture and identity in shaping social life becomes evident. The contributions of theorists like Gerhard Lenski and Robert Nisbet highlight the multifaceted nature of culture and how it informs our perceptions, beliefs, and behaviors. These thinkers emphasize the role of symbols, meanings, and discourses in constructing social reality and fostering collective identities. They also explore the dynamics of cultural change, hybridity, and the negotiation of identities in a globalized world. The rich exploration of culture and identity underscores the diversity and fluidity of human experiences and the complexities that arise in their intersection.

Finally, the concluding chapter reveals a shared commitment among these theorists to the pursuit of social justice and the critique of oppressive structures, and a collective call for transformative change echoes throughout their works. These theorists emphasize the need to challenge systemic inequalities, dismantle oppressive structures, and foster inclusive societies prioritizing equality, freedom, and dignity.

As we conclude *Macro Social Theory*, we are reminded of the unifying threads that bind these remarkable thinkers. Across social science disciplines, periods, and cultural contexts, they converge on key themes such as the interplay of structure and agency, power dynamics and social stratification, the complexity of culture and identity, and the imperative of social justice. These commonalities reflect the enduring questions, tensions, and aspirations that underpin macro social theory as a vibrant field of study. They remind us of the ongoing relevance and importance of engaging with these ideas as we navigate the complexities of our rapidly changing world.

Chapter 16: Common Ground

The perspectives examined in this book are compatible; as Whitehead said in the introduction, each illuminates' various aspects of a single sociocultural system, leaving the remainder in the background. Each has value, and each misses much significance. This chapter is an argument for synthesis and integration, not eclecticism. Embracing each perspective in full, without priority or weighting, would be to adopt an eclectic perspective. Such practitioners adopt theoretical strategies to fit the problem rather than systematically testing and refining a perspective. Eclecticism has been disastrous for the social sciences. While such a strategy has led to some remarkable insights, it has yet to lead to a holistic, coherent worldview shared by most practitioners. Consequently, has hindered the advancement of the social sciences (for an extensive discussion of this disaster, see Harris 1979, pp. 287-314).

As evolution does for biology, such an explicit and shared worldview offers a beginning framework for organizing the field, informing the researcher what to look for, what needs further testing, clarification, or refinement, and what should be rejected and abandoned. A shared, coherent worldview offers a systematic analytical strategy practitioner, and students can use to guide and prioritize research, order, and interpret new findings and data. Such a worldview offers identity to its practitioners and order to its students. It provides an agreed-upon empirically based alternative explanation to those offered by religion, ideology, or folk wisdom.

The macro social theory presented in these pages has common themes and elements that have heretofore been minimized or ignored. These common attributes include a view that emphasizes the systemic character of societies, a strong materialistic causal order, an explicit evolutionary view of change, and a rich tradition of comparative historical data used to test its generalizations. What is needed is to make these common elements explicit. We will briefly summarize the perspectives of Marx, Weber, and Durkheim concerning their materialism and evolutionism, elements they have in common with an ecological-evolutionary perspective. Marx's materialism is, of course, well-known, and only needs a little elaboration here. The forces and relations of production, that is, production technology and the economic relations based on this technology, are prime movers—though not the only movers—in his conception of sociocultural systems. Engels (1890) summed up the materialist view succinctly in a letter:

> According to the materialist conception of history, the *ultimately* determining element in history is the production and reproduction of real life. Other than this neither Marx nor I have ever asserted. Hence if somebody twists this into saying that the economic element is the *only* determining one, he transforms that proposition into a meaningless, abstract, senseless phrase. The economic situation is the basis, but the various elements of the superstructure — political forms of the class struggle and its results, to wit: constitutions established by the victorious class after a successful battle, etc., juridical forms, and even the reflexes of all these actual struggles in the brains of the participants, political, juristic, philosophical theories, religious views and their further development into systems of dogmas — also exercise their influence upon the course of the historical struggles and in many cases preponderate in determining their *form*. There is an interaction of all these elements in which, amid all the endless host of accidents (that is, of things and events whose inner interconnection is so remote or so impossible of proof that we can regard it as non-existent, as negligible), the economic movement finally asserts itself as necessary. Otherwise, the application of the theory to any period of history would be easier than the solution of a simple equation of the first degree.

In Marx's analyses, these material forces constantly interact with structural and ideological elements of the system, but the material forces are at the heart of the system. Recall that John Bellamy Foster argues forcefully that population and environmental factors were very much a part of Marx's analyses. As expressed by its leading contemporary practitioners, the theory of cultural materialism already incorporates Marx's forces and relations of production as two of the primary determinants of the evolution of sociocultural systems. Cultural materialism considers them prime determinants, along with population and environmental factors, in determining sociocultural stability and change.

The evolutionary character of the Marxian system is not so well known as his materialism, as most commentators focus on his popular calls for revolution. However, as demonstrated in Chapter 1, the evolutionary aspect of Marx's theory is undeniable. Here we will quote from the eulogy for Marx given by Friedrich Engels, his friend and collaborator, which highlights both Marx's materialist and his social evolutionary views:

> Just as Darwin discovered the law of evolution in organic nature, so Marx discovered the law of evolution in human history; he discovered the simple fact...that mankind must first of all eat and drink, have shelter and clothing, before it can pursue politics, science, religion, art, etc., and that therefore the production of the immediate material means of subsistence and consequently the degree of economic development attained by a given people or during a given epoch, form

the foundation upon which the state institutions, the legal conceptions, the art and even the religious ideas of the people concerned have been evolved, and in the light of which these things must therefore be explained (Engels 1883).

While Marx's evolutionary schema of the struggle between economic classes being the engine of social change may be wrong, the conflict seems one-sided, with the exploitive class having almost all the power. Nevertheless, his theory is one of evolution than revolution.

Weber's foundation in materialism has yet to be well known, though many commentators are aware of the evolutionary character of this thought. It is evident in many passages that Weber sees rationalization and bureaucratization as an evolutionary process, engaging in an extensive analysis of the phenomena's causes and consequences (Weber, [1946] 1958, p. 244). However, Weber is widely considered an idealist who places ideas as the prime movers in the evolution of sociocultural systems. At first reading, Weber's "rationalization" might appear to be a theory focused on ideas rather than materialism. However, such appearances can be misleading. Weber used the term "rationalization" to characterize the general evolution of sociocultural systems. The term was applied to general changes in cultural products such as music, science, and the motivators of human behavior. Weber also considered bureaucratization a particular case of rationalization applied to social structures. In this sense, Weber's "rationalization process" can be considered analogous to Spencer's (and later evolutionists') characterization of the evolutionary direction of sociocultural systems as moving toward greater complexity. Rationalization certainly encompasses growing complexity as well as positing a direction to it—the more significant application of observation, science, measurement, logic, and calculation in exploiting the environment through fashioning production strategies, controlling reproduction, coordinating human groups, and downplaying the role of tradition, values, and emotions in human action and promoting the role of goal-oriented rationality. Nevertheless, Weber does not see the rationalization of ideas and cultural products as the prime movers of the process. Instead, he sees the general rationalization process (and the more specific case of bureaucratization) as caused by changes in material conditions.

In viewing Weber as primarily an idealist, many may have been misled by the popularity of Weber's *Protestant Ethic and the Spirit of Capitalism*, where religious ideas were explored as promoting the economic change from feudalism to capitalism in Western Europe. However, as explained in Chapter 8, this work was completed early in Weber's career. *The Protestant Ethic* was intended only to demonstrate that ideas and material forces are part of the sociocultural system. Weber later put far more weight on material factors in his analyses of the rise of capitalism. Moreover, while Weber is well known for his theories of bureaucratization and rationalization, he is much less known for analyzing the causes of these phenomena. The primary function of bureaucracies is to perform administrative tasks efficiently and effectively. Therefore, one of the primary determinants of bureaucratization, Weber states, is the size and scope of the society, "the great state and the mass party are the classic soil for bureaucratization" ([1946] 1958, p. 209). Moreover, again, "It is obvious that technically the great modern state is absolutely dependent upon a bureaucratic basis. The larger the state, and the more it is or the more it becomes a great power state, the more unconditionally is this the case" (p. 211).

However, Weber asserts that it is more than simple bureaucratic growth in response to the sociocultural system's size. "Bureaucratization is occasioned more by intensive and qualitative enlargement and internal deployment of the scope of administrative tasks than by their extensive and quantitative increase" (p. 212). This qualitative enlargement of the bureaucratic administration by the state includes the establishment and administration of public works, taxation, the creation of standing armies and the waging of wars, education, justice, and coordinating and managing the "increasing complexity of civilization" (p. 212). Weber also cites technological factors behind bureaucratic growth, such as the expansion of modern communication and transportation systems which "enter the picture as pacemakers of bureaucratization" (p. 213).

However, perhaps the most significant single factor causing bureaucratization, according to Weber, is the growth in the extent and intensity of the economy:

> The growing demands on culture, in turn, are determined, though to a varying extent, by the growing wealth of the most influential strata in the state. To this extent increasing bureaucratization is a function of the increasing possession of goods used for consumption, and of an increasing sophisticated technique of fashioning external life—a technique which corresponds to the opportunities provided by such wealth. This reacts upon the standard of living and makes for an increasing subjective indispensability of organized, collective, inter-local, and thus bureaucratic, provision for the most varied wants, which previously were either unknown, or were satisfied locally by a private economy (p. 212).

Weber says that capitalism and the state have often acted in alliance, and bureaucracy has been advanced (p. 230). It is now the capitalist market economy, Weber asserts, which exerts the most significant push fueling bureaucratization. Success in business is determined by "…precision, steadiness, and, above all, the speed of operations. This, in turn, is determined by the peculiar nature of the modern means of communications, including, among other things, the news services of the press. The extraordinary increase by which the speed of public announcements, as well as economic and political facts, are transmitted exerts a steady and sharp pressure in the direction of speeding up the tempo of administrative reaction towards various situations. The optimum of such reaction time is normally attained only by a strictly bureaucratic organization" (p. 215). Moreover, as capitalism and the state have grown dependent upon bureaucracy, populations have become more dependent upon capitalism and public administration.

> The ruled, for their part, cannot dispense with or replace the bureaucratic apparatus of authority once it exists. For this bureaucracy rests upon expert training, a functional specialization of work, and an attitude set for habitual and virtuoso-like mastery of single yet methodically integrated functions. If the official stops working, or if his work is forcefully interrupted, chaos results, and it is difficult to improvise replacements from among the governed who are fit to master such chaos. This holds for public administration as well as for private economic management. *More and more the material fate of the masses depends upon the steady and correct functioning of the increasingly bureaucratic organizations of private capitalism.* The idea of eliminating these organizations becomes more and more utopian (p. 229, emphasis added).

Materialism forms the foundation for Weber's rationalization/ bureaucratization process. While the rationalization process is Weber's characterization of the direction of sociocultural evolution, it is clear that he saw this process as caused by changes in material conditions, particularly growth in populations and material production. The intensification of production and population causes bureaucratization and thus promotes the rationalization of the superstructure of human societies; only then do these changes in structure and superstructure react upon material conditions.

Robert L. Carneiro, one of the leading cultural materialists today, puts the relationship between material conditions and ideas thus: "The cultural materialist does not proclaim the independent action of material conditions. That would be absurd. These conditions must somehow be translated into ideas, and these ideas must be funneled into individuals so as to galvanize them into action. The idealist likes to begin the causal analysis with the unquestioned motivating power of ideas. The materialist prefers to begin the analysis one step further back, going behind the ideas to see how they arose in the first place and came to enter people's heads" (2003, p. 216). Recall that Weber's position on the relationships between ideas and material interests is similar. Ideas are adopted, modified, selected, or discredited by people following their material and ideal interests. "Not ideas, but material and ideal interests, directly govern men's conduct. Yet very frequently the 'world images' that have been created by 'ideas' have, like switchmen, determined the tracks along which action has been pushed by the dynamic of interest"(Weber, [1946] 1958, p. 280). Once adopted, or once they enter people's heads, ideas motivate and guide people's actions, reinforcing or opposing the material and ideal interests of statuses and groups within the sociocultural system.

One of Durkheim's primary concerns is the division of labor and its impact on sociocultural systems and individuals. According to Durkheim, such divisions exist within the coordinating bureaucratic organizations of corporations and states and in producing and distributing goods and services. As with Weber, Durkheim's theory of the increasing nature of the division of labor is firmly rooted in materialism and evolutionary theory.

Recall that Durkheim asserted that the increasing division of labor destroys the traditional solidarity of societies and groups based on likenesses and necessitates the development of new methods of integration to bind individuals to the social order. Because of humankind's dual nature— "the one purely individual and rooted in our organisms, the other social and nothing but an extension of society"—the loosening of the social bond would cause rising rates of deviance and disorder (Durkheim, 1914 cited in Mestrovic, [1988] 1993, p. 73). According to Durkheim, the increasing division of labor does not occur on its own or because people are attracted to it to increase productivity or human happiness. Instead, there are material causes for its progress. Durkheim summarizes his position:

> The division of labor varies in direct ratio with the volume and density of societies, and, if it progresses in a continuous manner in the course of social development, it is because societies become regularly denser and generally more voluminous [...] We say, not that the growth and condensation of societies permit, but they necessitate a greater division of labor. It is not an instrument by which the latter is realized; it is its determining cause (Durkheim, [1893] 1960, p. 262).

Durkheim is adamant that population growth and density are a cause rather than an enabler of the division of labor because he sees population growth and density as intensifying the individual's struggle for subsistence. As the population grows and becomes more concentrated, the intensity of the struggle for survival rises, and individuals begin to specialize to avoid competing directly with one another for sustenance. Because of the increasing division of labor, a rising population need not fight with one another over hunting grounds or other scarce resources.

> If work becomes divided more as societies become more voluminous and denser, it is not because of external circumstances are more varied, but because struggle for existence is more acute. Darwin justly observed that the struggle between two organisms is as active as they are analogous. Having the same needs and pursuing the same objects, they are in rivalry everywhere. As long as they have more resources than they need, they can still live side by side, but if their number increases to such proportions that all appetites can no longer be sufficiently satisfied, war breaks out, and it is as violent as this insufficiency is more marked; that is to say, as the number in the struggle increase (p. 266).

The division of labor allows many people to coexist without directly competing for subsistence. It is through the division of labor that a dense population secures the means of survival (p. 270).

Like Spencer, whom he read extensively, Durkheim saw the division of labor as a consequence of the evolutionary process driven by increasing population and density. The division of labor produces a greater volume of goods, services, and variety. Men and women developed new tastes and needs for these goods and services, growing dissatisfied with plain and simple fare. In the process, our intelligence, tastes, needs, and desires develop and become "keener" because we must exercise them more to survive. We specialize to survive and, in the process, evolving "a more intense and more varied culture" (p. 273).

> Civilization is itself the necessary consequence of the changes which are produced in the volume and in the density of societies. If science, art, and economic activity develop, it is in accordance with a necessity which is imposed upon men. It is because there is, for them, no other way of living in the new conditions in which they have been placed. From the time that the number of individuals among whom social relations are established begins to increase, they can maintain themselves only by greater specialization, harder work, and intensification of their faculties. From this general stimulation, there inevitably results a much higher degree of culture. From this point of view, civilization appears, not as an end which moves people by its attractions for them, not as a good foreseen and desired in advance, of which they seek to assure themselves the largest possible part, but as the effect of a cause, as the necessary resultant of a given state. It is not the pole towards which historic development is moving and to which men seek to get nearer in order to be happier or better, for neither happiness nor morality necessarily increases with the intensity of life. They move because they must move, and what determines the speed of this march is the more or less strong pressure which they exercise upon one another, according to their number (pp. 336-337).

While Durkheim concerns himself with the impact of these evolutionary changes on social structure (the division of labor, social solidarity) and on individuals (anomie, suicide), his macro social theory is strongly materialistic and explicitly evolutionary. As with Weber's rationalization process, Durkheim's increasing division of labor is consistent with Spencer's characterization of evolution moving toward ever greater complexity.

In the following section, I will summarize a theoretical perspective that borrows heavily from each of the theoretical traditions reviewed in this book. As a cultural materialist, I have long believed that with minor modification, the ecological-evolutionary perspective could serve as the basis for synthesis for a single macro-sociological perspective. According to Robert Carneiro, while Marvin Harris coined the term "cultural materialism, "it is a perspective that is rooted in the social theories of Malthus, Spencer, and Marx and can trace its history through Leslie White" (Carneiro, 2003, p. 218). I am about to add some Weber and Durkheim to the mix.

A Synthesis

This synthesis begins with the simple assertion that sociocultural systems significantly impact individual character, behavior, drives, and beliefs. Humans are compound beings consisting of two parts: one of egoistic drives centered on satisfaction of our physical needs and desires (food, sex, love, and affection), the other of a moral system that gives us a sense of altruism and responsibility to others that individuals internalize through their participation in a sociocultural system. However, social systems consist of physical human beings and, therefore, must exist within the physical (geographical, chemical, biological) constraints imposed by the natural environment in which they are located. As these physical constraints change—either through the actions of societies or nature—sociocultural systems evolve, inevitably affecting the character and values of those who make up that society.

Universal Model of Sociocultural Systems

Harris created a "universal model" of sociocultural systems intended to display the structure and dynamics of all societies, Hunting and Gathering Societies through the massive Hyper-industrial Societies of today. The table below represents a modified form of Harris's model's structure and superstructural components and some added dynamics.

Table 16.1

I. ENVIRONMENT

Refers to the physical, biological, and chemical constraints to which human action is subject.

II. INFRASTRUCTURE

A. Mode of Production: The technology and practices employed for expanding or limiting essential subsistence production, especially the production of food and other forms of energy. Examples: subsistence technology and technical-environmental relationships.

B. Mode of Reproduction: The technology and practices employed for expanding, limiting, and maintaining population size. Examples: mating patterns, fertility, mortality, infant mortality, contraception, abortion, and infanticide.

III. STRUCTURE

A. Primary Group Structure: Consists of a small number of people interacting intimately. They regulate reproduction, primary production, socialization, education, and enforcing domestic discipline. Examples: family, community, and friendship networks

B. Secondary Group Structure: Consists of large and small groups whose members interact without emotional commitment to one another. They perform many functions, such as regulating production, reproduction, socialization, education, and enforcing social discipline. Examples include government, military, police, corporations, education institutions, service and welfare organizations, and professional and labor organizations.

IV. SUPERSTRUCTURE

A. Cultural Superstructure: Consists of the symbolic processes necessary for the human psyche, such as play, recreation, sports, and aesthetics. Examples include art, music, dance, literature, rituals, sports, games, hobbies, and the cultural knowledge base.

B. Mental Superstructure: Refers to Weber's conscious and unconscious motives for human behavior. Examples include values, emotions, traditions, and zweckrational (goal-oriented rational action).

The table is loosely adapted from Marvin Harris's *Cultural Materialism*, pp. 46-47. For those keeping score, I have retained the broad concepts of Harris's cultural materialism regarding the infrastructure (production and population), structure (human organizations), and cultural superstructure. I have also retained Harris's primary causal focus on the infrastructure's impact on the rest of the sociocultural system. However, I have substantially modified Harris's concept of structure and superstructure to incorporate Weber's concepts of bureaucracy and rationalization. Finally, I related Harris's concept of intensification to bureaucratization and rationalization and emphasized the existence and importance of feedback loops from the structure and superstructure.

Harris's perspective is, in large part, a synthesis of Malthus and Marx. I have modified his original vision by integrating Durkheim and Weber into the strategy to make it a genuinely sociological perspective.

Postulates

The individual theorists presented in this volume show that macrosociology has a pronounced systems orientation. The various components of that system fit together (albeit loosely), changes in one part affecting many of the others, the whole being more than the sum of its parts. This holistic systems orientation means that functions and dysfunctions become part of any complete analysis. There are many functions served by sociocultural systems, such as maintaining order, distributing goods and services, and providing meaning to human life—but the principal function is to exploit the environment to provide sustenance for human life itself.

- *Societies are sociocultural systems whose principal function is to allow human beings to regulate the flow of food and other energy from the natural environment.*

- *The primary mechanisms by which sociocultural systems regulate this flow of energy are through technology, the division of labor, and social practices of production and reproduction. These mechanisms are called the infrastructure.*

This is a definitional point, but an important one. The interrelationships between production and reproduction have played a vital role for those social scientists working in the tradition of Malthus and Spencer and at least a secondary role in the other major perspectives. For example, Marx dealt with the "forces of production" (or technology and work patterns) as the foundation for his "relations of production" (or economy). Durkheim focused on the consequent division of labor due to technological and population growth. Weber rooted his rationalization process in an "increasingly sophisticated technique of fashioning external life." Productive and reproductive forces play a significant causal role in cultural materialism and exert a potent integrating force on the rest of the sociocultural system. The reproduction component of the infrastructure is not a simple variable of population growth and decline. Reproduction includes all social practices and technologies employed for expanding, limiting, or maintaining population size. Such practices would include mating patterns, contraception, infanticide, and abortion. In addition, such demographic factors as disease patterns, age mortality rates, age and sex ratios, and other factors that affect population size and composition are also included in this category.

Production activities consist of social behaviors focused on exploiting food and other forms of energy and raw materials from the natural environment. The amount and type of resources that can be harvested depend on subsistence technology (such as hunting and gathering, horticulture, agrarian, and industrial) and resulting work patterns. The amount and type of resources needed depend highly on population size, composition, and consumption levels.

Societies can be remarkably stable over time; those societies that successfully strike a balance between reproduction and the energy they consume from their resource base are exceptionally stable. In such societies, the hold of tradition has been solid; tradition has been a great conservative force throughout history. However, recent increases in production and population have essentially broken this hold of tradition, and sociocultural change is now very much the norm.

Both positive and preventive checks are needed to limit population size to what can be supported by the environmental-production relationship. Before modern birth control techniques were developed, the mix strongly favored positive checks such as infanticide or body trauma abortion. Under these conditions, there are severe psychological and biological costs to limiting population growth; individuals are therefore susceptible to the lure of technological innovations that allow more children to live. With the advent of birth control, preventive checks have become more widespread. However, positive checks—abortion, infanticide, and high infant mortality rates, particularly among the poor and uneducated—still play a significant role in keeping population numbers in line.

- *The structure of human societies consists of all human groups and organizations within a sociocultural system. These social organizations regulate labor and allocate social goods and services.*

The social structural components of human societies arise from the necessity of maintaining the orderly allocation of goods and services among individuals and groups that make up the sociocultural system. While all human groups and organizations exist on a continuum, the primary/secondary dichotomy is a convenient label that encompasses all human organizations responsible for allocating and distributing goods and services within a society. A primary group typically consists of a few individuals with an enduring personal relationship; examples include a family, a circle of close friends, or a small religious cult. These groups regulate production, reproduction, exchange, and consumption within domestic settings. Secondary groups or organizations tend to be more impersonal; members interact without emotional commitment to one another. These organizations are coordinated through bureaucracies. They perform many functions, such as regulating production, reproduction, socialization, education, and enforcing social discipline within and between sociocultural systems. Examples include governments, political parties, the military, corporations, educational institutions, foundations, service and welfare organizations, and professional and labor organizations.

- *The superstructure consists of the symbolic aspects of sociocultural systems, the cultural knowledge base, values, beliefs, norms, and ideologies of society.*

This symbolic world is the evolutionary result of language acquisition and is essentially a shared perception of reality in which the community exists. In this symbolic world, the individual becomes more than a simple biological entity but a social being. Although the superstructure exists within the mind of individuals, it is the product of consensus, and this consensus changes as the forms of human interaction change. The superstructure can again be divided into two parts: the cultural superstructure, which consists of shared cultural activities and products as a fund of oral and written knowledge and lore, aesthetic standards, and sports. On the other hand, the mental superstructure consists of Weber's four primary motivators of human action: *zweckrational* or rational action concerning a goal; *wertrational* or rational action concerning a value; affective or emotional action; and traditional action, which is dictated by custom or habit. In addition to adapting Weber's typology within the mental superstructure, we will also adapt his rationalization hypothesis. Increasing bureaucratization causes a shift in the typical mix of human motivations; *zweckrational* dominates modern behavior.

- *The "primacy of the infrastructure" refers to the fact that production and reproduction (the infrastructure of sociocultural systems) strongly affect the organizational structure of the society, which in turn strongly affects the ideas and ideologies of society (the superstructure).*

The infrastructure is given such importance because it is through production and reproduction practices that society adapts to its environment by modifying the amount and type of resources needed for survival (i.e., through the infrastructure that society survives). Since these practices are essential for life itself, all widespread structural and superstructural patterns must conform or be compatible with these infrastructural practices. Infrastructures of societies—population and production variables—put powerful constraints on the range of widespread social institutions, ideas, and ideologies of sociocultural systems.

- *Sociocultural systems evolve in response to changes in their natural environment or from contact with other societies.*

Changes in the natural environment occur through natural means (climate change, volcanic eruption, and the like) or because of human activities impacting the environment (population growth, depletion of critical resources, desertification, or deforestation, for example). Contact with other societies is the most common source of innovations in sociocultural evolution. Such contact is one reason the process is so rapid compared with biological evolution.

- *Sociocultural systems evolve by adapting the mental and behavioral activities of individual men and women who respond to cost-benefit options.*

These adaptations result from everyday decisions individuals make about reproduction, work, and standard of living.

- *The intensification process refers to applying ever more rationalized technology and labor techniques to regulate production and population.*

Marvin Harris asserts, "Anthropologists have long recognized that in broadest perspective cultural evolution has had three main characteristics: escalating energy budgets, increased productivity, and accelerating population growth" (1979, p. 67). By escalating energy budgets, Harris refers to the fact that humans, like all other life on earth, must invest energy in the food-gathering process to obtain energy from their environment. The amount of energy social systems invests in wresting a livelihood from the environment—human, animal, and mechanical energy—has grown significantly through time. Hunting and gathering societies expend only a fraction of the energy in exploiting energy from the environment to survive than do slash-and-burn farming villages, which in turn, expend only a fraction of the energy than irrigation states and so on up to the massive hyper-industrial societies of today (p. 67). Throughout sociocultural evolution, this expansion in energy budgets has been accompanied by a parallel increase in human productivity and population, dramatically affecting the rest of the sociocultural system.

However, the remarkable exponential growth of the infrastructure through time may obscure a more fundamental characteristic of infrastructural intensification. Increasing production and population growth are the long-term outcomes of intensifying social infrastructures. However, population growth only sometimes occurs with production increases. The modern demographic transition—the changing nature of the relationship of population growth to production—means that simple growth is not a universal characteristic of intensification. The modern demographic transition is the latest population plateau in the historical record.

However, another characteristic of infrastructural intensification is universal, a process apparent from the transition from hunting and gathering to horticulture to the intensification of hyper-industrial infrastructures today. Over time, there has been a tendency for infrastructural practices to rationalize. There has been an increasing application of rationality (observation, logic, and, more recently, science) to manipulating the environment to offset depletion and provide more significant amounts and varieties of energy than ever. This same rationalizing process is seen in regulating population—from medical control of disease, fertility, and mortality, to birth control technologies, to the population control programs of nation-states and international organizations. This rationalization of the societal infrastructures is done at the expense of population regulation based on tradition, values, and emotions.

- *The intensification/rationalization of the infrastructure is due to several factors: a) changes in the natural environment due to society's actions such as depletion and pollution, or those due to natural environmental change; b) contact with other societies; c) stimulation by the economic and political self-interests of elite individuals, groups, or organizations within the structure; and d) stimulation by ideologies within the sociocultural system itself.*

Weber ([1927] 2003), the supposed idealist, best illustrates the intensification principle in his analysis of the Industrial Revolution in England. He defined the Industrial Revolution as the "mechanization and rationalization of work" (p. 303). He asserts that England gained much technical knowledge of the textile industry through contact with other societies, particularly Italy's early cotton manufacturing. It is from this technological base that England develops the industry. Historically, Weber then traces the development of the cotton industry in 18th century England as being the first establishment of the factory system "which determined the character of the evolution of capitalism" (p. 302). He details the limitations of technology on the development of the textile industry. However, Cartwright overcame these limitations with the invention of the power loom in 1785, "one of the first inventors who combined technology with science and handled the problems of the former in terms of theoretical considerations" (pp. 303-304). His application of science is a major development as Weber ascribes Cartwright's invention directly to rationalizing the means of production rather than an invention by tinkers and dreamers. Using observation and reason to achieve the desired end applied to the mode of production becomes a great intensifier of the general evolutionary process. Weber goes on to marry rationalization to capitalism, asserting that capitalism bears primary responsibility for rationalization's modern character.

At this point, Weber turns to purely material-environmental relationships to explain the evolution of the modern factory. He writes that until the 18th century, England's primary fuel source was wood.

> Everywhere the destruction of the forests brought the industrial development to a standstill at a certain point. Smelting [of iron] was only released from its attachment to organic materials of the plant world by the application of coal […] In the face of the further development [in the use of iron] arose two difficult problems. These were set, on the one hand, by the danger of deforestation and, on the other, by the perpetual inroads of water in the mines […] The solution of the [first] problem was reached through the coking of coal, which was discovered in 1735, and the use of coke in blast furnace operation, which was undertaken in 1740 […] The threat to mining was removed by the invention of the steam engine. The steam engine was developed as a way of pumping water out of the mines, and by the end of the 18th century coal was being produced in quantities necessary for modern industry (pp. 305-305).

As the coal shafts had to be dug deeper, the steam engine was first invented to pump water out of the mines; then, it was adapted to haul the coal up the shafts, ventilate the mines, and transport the coal to markets. "Each of these called the other forth" (Landis, 1969, p. 95). Soon, the engine was used to intensify production (and thus profits) in a host of other industries, spreading from England to other industrializing societies throughout the world.

According to Weber, the switch from a resource base primarily based on wood for energy and raw materials to one based on coal and iron had three significant consequences. First, by developing the technologies to exploit fossil fuels and iron, England freed itself from traditional constraints of animal power and plant growth (Weber [1927] 2003, p. 305). The second consequence, Weber points out, was to reduce the need for human labor in the production process. In almost Marxist terms, he adds: "Not altogether, it is true, for it goes without saying that labor was indispensable for the tending of machines. But the mechanizing process has always and everywhere been introduced to the definite end of releasing labor; every invention signifies the extensive displacement of hand workers by a relatively small manpower for machine supervision" (p. 306). The third consequence, Weber writes, is the systematic application of science to the production process, which frees production from the fetters of tradition (p. 306).

So, it is in classic materialist fashion that Weber first cites the intensification of production, leading to environmental depletions such as forests and readily available coal. These depletions called for technological solutions such as using coke in blast furnaces and the invention of the steam engine to pump water out of mines, as well as changes in the division of labor, which created the necessary material conditions for capital industrial development. He then further characterizes these developments as part of the rationalization process.

In social evolution, societies sometimes deplete their essential resources. When this happens, societies collapse. However, suppose society has accumulated the technical knowledge to shift to a new mode of production. In that case, the shift is from a readily accessible source using existing technology (wood, for example) to a less accessible source (such as coal). Each succeeding energy source is more difficult to exploit. Each takes more general knowledge, capital, technology, and technical skill to tap—from coal to oil to nuclear fission to nuclear fusion.

Similarly, as we use up energy within a particular resource base, we must exploit less accessible sources (such as oil platforms on the North Sea, miles deep in the Gulf of Mexico, or drilling in the Arctic). Alternatively, use increasingly sophisticated technologies to tap into the remaining reserves (such as horizontal drilling, shale oil, or fracking). New energy (such as nuclear fission or fusion) and raw material sources (such as plastics) take more sophisticated and complex technologies to exploit.

The intensification of production has also significantly increased productivity. Although people must work harder to exploit each succeeding resource base, each new resource base represents a richer energy source, allowing more food and other products to be produced. The increased wealth caused by intensification is often used to support more children in pre-industrial societies. With industrialization, the development of modern birth control techniques, and the consequent devaluation of children, the relationship between growth in production and population has been broken—at least as far as natural population growth. However, hyper-industrial societies attract many immigrants drawn to the promise of the economic opportunity afforded by wealth and labor shortages in the host countries.

Not all these factors deserve equal weight. Material factors—environmental, production, and reproduction—are hypothesized to be the strongest, for these factors are central to the system's overall survival. Then structural factors need to be considered, which either promote or dampen infrastructural trends and are based on either ownership or control of productive forces. Finally, one needs to consider ideological factors (some of which are propaganda and other manipulation techniques at the behest of elite interests) that motivate human action.

- *An intensifying infrastructure causes the growth of secondary organizations at the expense of primary groups.*

The growth of secondary organizations—governments, military, corporations, and educational institutions—is called bureaucratization; it applies logic and reason to human organization. This bureaucratization is directly attributable to the greater need to coordinate and control more people and more complex production systems. Primary groups tend to dominate the structures of traditional societies; such societies are often organized around kinship ties and regulate their members through informal norms and folkways of the culture. On the other hand, secondary organizations tend to dominate the structures of more modern societies, gradually taking over the functions of primary groups throughout the evolutionary process.

This structural shift is due to the intensification of production and population growth. As many have noted, far more people can be sustained in each area through farming than can be supported through hunting and gathering. With the development of agriculture, an autocatalytic relationship between production and population is set in motion, stimulating the other. Before the development of agriculture, all human beings lived in small band-type societies, communal societies with little inequality, a system of reciprocity or sharing of food and resources, and little division of labor. While often ruled by a headman, such "rulers" were little more than the man with the most influence because of his hunting prowess or wisdom; he was little more than the first among equals. With population and production growth, social organization becomes more complex, and bureaucratic administration becomes the norm. Bureaucracy, of course, leads to oligarchy or rule of the organization by those at the top. In societies dominated by bureaucracy, enormous economic, political, and social power are vested in those who lead these organizations.

- *Following Marx, "The ideas of the ruling class are, in every age, the ruling ideas."*

Structural elites at the top of the dominant bureaucracies provide feedback on infrastructural change consistent with their material interests. The interests of the elite will weigh more heavily than that of non-elites. Structural interests can often be decisive in determining whether change is propagated throughout the system or whether it is extinguished. This feedback loop is part of the systemic character of sociocultural systems. Structural elites exist in all societies—though the basis for their dominance and the extent of their power is an empirical question. The fact that elites tend to promote ideas and ideologies consistent with their material interests has been amply demonstrated by sociologists reviewed in these pages and shared experience

- *The bureaucratization of the structure of sociocultural systems provides positive feedback to the infrastructure's intensification.*

The bureaucracies in the modern West that effectively promote intensification include both the state and capitalist organizations but can be conveniently combined into the "capitalist system." The capitalist system refers to privately held bureaucratic organizations which control the production and distribution of potentially profitable goods and services; this system exists within an international system of nation-states that assure the domestic and international conditions conducive to capital accumulation.

The capitalist system is an incredibly effective intensification mechanism because it stimulates tremendous productive forces within the infrastructure. Capital organization stimulates the productive drive of thousands. The system spurs thousands of men and women to innovate in their frantic search for goods and services that might potentially find a profitable market. The capitalist system also spurs the consumption drive of billions. Through advertising, our consuming lives are formed and shaped, old needs are satisfied in quantity and new "needs" are constantly being created and exploited. The capitalist system is a great "intensifier," a stimulus to people to increase their efforts in all production and consumption activities (Harris, 1971, p. 265). This feedback loop between the structure and the infrastructure is part of the systemic character of sociocultural systems.

- *The bureaucratization of the structure of sociocultural systems causes the rationalization of the superstructure, that is, the increasing dominance of observation, logic, and science in human affairs.*

Again, the capitalist system is an especially effective cause of rationalization in the superstructure as capitalist enterprises promote a single-minded focus in millions of individuals upon consumption, innovation, and economic growth. The nation-state controls tax policy, military expenditure, welfare, education, trade policies, and military expansion and shares the interest in both production and consumption with capitalist enterprises. The rise of the modern nation-state in the 19th and 20th centuries has greatly enlarged bureaucratic organizations, with their drive toward the efficient attainment of organizational goals, often at the expense of tradition, values, and emotions. The growth of capitalism and the nation-state, and their enlargement and centralization, profoundly impacts human character and personality.

For example, with advanced industrialization, children lose much of their economic value—they are no longer used in the production process. With the rise of the state (and increasing longevity), they no longer provide adequate social security in the parent's old age. With the lengthening of education and the increasing costs of raising a child, children are becoming much more of a financial liability. With monopoly capitalism, consumer values begin to predominate. These changes have finally broken the links between production and population in hyper-industrial societies. Smaller families have become the norm; income increases are used to accumulate possessions and comforts rather than children among the upper classes. (As Betty J. Miner often said, "You can have nice things, or you can have children." This lament was a commentary on the fact that children in advanced industrial societies are costly to raise to the age of 18, and thus one must forgo many nice things, as well as the fact that children often break nice things. Betty J. had nine children.)

As the scope and strength of primary groups have declined, their influence on human character and values has also declined. This decline has necessarily impacted tradition, values, and emotions—the foundation of primary groups—thereby loosening the bonds that tie the individual to society and creating the structural and superstructural condition for widespread anomie. Weber's four motivators of human action—values, emotions, traditions, and goal-oriented rational behavior—define our very humanity. Infrastructural and structural change consistently promote and instill goal-oriented rational behavior over behaviors guided by values, traditions, and emotions. Such a society promotes alienation—cutting off the individual from the self, her fellow humans, and a part of her humanity.

Individuals successfully internalize society's norms and values through the social bonds of love and commitment to small groups like the family. Such internalization of these values is necessary for the individual to "rise above" their more egoistic drives and desires.

- *The rationalization of superstructure promotes the structure's bureaucratization and the intensification/rationalization of the infrastructure.*

This feedback loop is part of the systemic character of sociocultural systems and has been fully explored by the many sociologists who have followed Weber on this issue. Superstructural feedback often determines the speed and character of sociocultural stability and change. Feedback from the "cultural superstructure" can also be critical, mainly if a society exploits its environment to the point of "relative" depletion (that is, the cost of raw materials becomes prohibitive). If a sociocultural system does not have the cultural knowledge base to switch to innovative technologies to exploit a new (and less accessible) resource base, that system will collapse.

- *Sociocultural evolution is based on altering existing technologies, structures, behavior patterns, and knowledge.*

One of the distinguishing characteristics of both biological and social evolution is the cumulative nature of change (Lenski, 2005, pp. 39-40). "Cumulative change," according to Lenski, "is a distinctive kind of change associated with systems composed of multiple, interrelated parts. Within these systems, some parts change while others remain unchanged. Thus, cumulative change is a process that combines elements of continuity with elements of change; many parts of the system are preserved for extended periods while new parts are added, and other parts are either replaced or transformed (4). Earlier adaptations are "absorbed and incorporated" into newer biological or social systems, thus greatly influencing later adaptations. Just as an animal's past evolutionary history and its relation to the current environment is essential in understanding that animal's adaptation to that environment, a society's history or heritage is significant in understanding societal stability and change (p. 188). Therefore, the force of historical experience plays a significant role in shaping social institutions and thought. The cumulative nature of sociocultural evolution is primarily responsible for the greater complexity.

- *Societies that have grown in population size and technology have also grown in complexity, trade, and military power. This size and complexity have allowed them to prevail in conflicts over territory, resources, and trade with societies that have maintained more traditional sociocultural patterns.*

There is a selection process in the world system that favors larger, more powerful societies at the expense of smaller, less powerful ones. As previously stated, sociocultural change is a cumulative process, which is the primary factor in the growth of the complexity and size of societies throughout human history (Lenski, Lenski, and Nolan, 1991, p. 8). However, to fully appreciate the process of sociocultural evolution, you must recognize that it includes both continuity and change (pp. 65-66). Most societies have experienced little change throughout their history (p. 46). However, societies have gotten more extensive in the global system, developed more sophisticated methods of exploiting their environments, and developed a more complex division of labor (Lenski, 2005, p. 31). This paradox has created confusion among supporters and critics of social evolutionary theory. Lenski rhetorically asks, can the global system of societies change so radically, particularly in the last 10,000 years when individual societies appear so resistant to change? The answer is that social evolution exists on two levels, and these two levels—individual societies and the global system of societies—follow divergent evolutionary paths (p. 32).

At the global system level, there has been a dramatic reduction in the number of societies in the last 10,000 years due to a process that Lenski identifies as "inter-societal selection." Societies that have grown in size and technology have also grown in complexity and military power, allowing them to prevail in conflict over territory and other resources with societies that have maintained more traditional sociocultural patterns (1991, p. 47). Successful adaptations are spread through social contact and military and economic conquest. Societies that adopted innovations that increased productive capacity, population growth, structural complexity, and military power have survived to transmit their culture and institutional patterns (1991, p. 63). At the individual level, societies respond to changes in their natural and social environments, which, combined with their distinct histories, produce innovative adaptations, some of which get passed on to other societies within the global system and become part of the inter-societal selection process. Sociocultural evolution, therefore, operates on two distinct levels, within individual societies and the world system of societies. The two processes combined determine "…which societies and which cultures survive, and which become extinct, and the role that each of the survivors plays within the world system" (1991, p. 66).

Diamond (1997) echoes this insight in his popular book *Guns, Germs, and Steel*. With population growth, he maintains, wars begin to change their character. During the hunting and gathering era, where population densities were low, conflict between groups often meant that the defeated group would merely move to a new range further removed from the victors. With non-intensive food production and consequent moderate population level, there is no place for the defeated to move; in horticultural societies with little surplus, there is slight advantage in keeping the defeated as enslaved people or in forcing the defeated area to pay tribute. "Hence the victors have no use for survivors of a defeated tribe unless to take the women in marriage. The defeated men are killed, and the victors may occupy their territory (p. 291). With intensified food production and high population densities, as with states that produce a surplus of food and have a developed division of labor, the defeated can be enslaved, or the defeated society can be forced to pay tribute to the conquerors.

Because food production was far more advanced on the Eurasian continent, there was great competition, diffusion, and amalgamation among the states that evolved. These states were far larger in population, more sophisticated in terms of technology, and more centralized politically than the New World tribes, chiefdoms, and early states, and the Pacific Islands, Africa, and Australia. Moreover, Diamond contends that this set the stage for the extremes in wealth, military power, and political influence we see today in the world system.

A Research Strategy

The research strategy that Harris advocates is to begin all analysis of sociocultural phenomenon with the infrastructure, that is, population, production, and environmental relationships. The reason for giving the infrastructure such priority rests with the fact that it is through population and production that societies manipulate the environment and regulate the amount and type of energy needed to sustain human life. "Infrastructure, in other words, is the principal interface between culture and nature, the boundary across which the ecological, chemical, and physical restraints to which human action is subject interact with the principal sociocultural practices aimed at overcoming or modifying those restraints." Harris continues,

> Since the aim of science is the discovery of the maximum amount of order in its field of inquiry, priority for theory building logically settles upon those sectors under the greatest direct restraints from the givens of nature. To endow the mental superstructure [ideas and ideologies] with strategic priority, as the cultural idealists advocate, is a bad bet. Nature is indifferent to whether God is a loving father or a bloodthirsty cannibal. But nature is not indifferent to whether the fallow period in a swidden [slash and burn] field is one year or ten. We know that powerful restraints exist on the infrastructural level; hence it is a good bet that these restraints are passed on to the structural and superstructural components (Harris, 1979, p. 57).

The researcher should examine structural variables only when all infrastructural causes have been explored. She examines the superstructure when these have been exhausted, exploring the web of direct, indirect, and feedback effects. It is emphatically not the case that structures and superstructures are merely passive effects along for the ride, instead "they often act as stimulants that energize and mobilize people and resources on behalf of particular kinds of sociocultural change. *They do so successfully, however, only to the extent that they feed back to and are compatible with evolving infrastructural conditions*" (Harris 1998, pp. 147-148, emphasis added).

As sociocultural systems evolve, the typical character, beliefs, attitudes, and motivations of the men and women interacting within these systems also evolve, further contributing to

388

sociocultural change. Demonstrating and describing relationships among the parts and the whole of sociocultural systems and the impact of these systems on individual behavior is the stuff of sociology.

Bibliography

NOTE: In the case of dual dates, the first date refers to the original edition, regardless of the language in which the work was written.

Alpert, Harry. 1939. *Emile Durkheim and His Sociology.* New York: Columbia University Press

Antliff, A. (2001). *Anarchist Modernism: Art, Politics, and the First American Avant-Garde.* Chicago: The University of Chicago Press.

Aron, Raymond. 1970. *Main Currents in Sociological Thought* (Vol. I & II). New York: Anchor Books.

Arnowitz, Stanley. 2012. *Taking it Big: C. Wright Mills and the Making of Political Intellectuals.* New York: Columbia University Press

Berry, Wendell. 1977. *The Unsettling of America.* San Francisco: Sierra Club.

Boserup, Ester. 1965. *The Conditions of Agricultural Growth.* New York: Aldine Publishing Company.

Boserup, Ester. 1970. *Woman's Role in Economic Development.* London: George Allen & Unwin.

Braverman, Harry. (1974) 1998. *Labor and Monopoly Capital: The Degradation of Work in the Twentieth Century.* New York: Monthly Review Press.

Carneiro, Robert L. 2003. *Evolutionism in Cultural Anthropology.* Boulder: Westview Press.

Cohen, Mark. 1977. *The Food Crisis in Prehistory: Over Population and the Origins of Agriculture.* New Haven, CT: Yale University Press.

Collins, Randall. 1980. "Weber's Last Theory of Capitalism: A Systematization." *American Sociological Review , 45,* 925-942.

Collins, Randall, and Michael Makowsky. 1998. *The Discovery of Society* (4th ed.). New York: Random House.

Coser, Lewis. (1971) 1977. *Masters of Sociological Thought* (2nd ed.). New York: Harcourt Brace Jovanovich, Inc.

Dandeneau, Steven, and Robin Dodsworth. 2007. "Being (George Ritzer) and Nothingness: An Interview." *The American Sociologist , 37* (4), 84-92.

Darwin, Charles. (1876) 1958. *Autobiography.* (N. Barlow, Ed.) London: Collins.

Diamond, Jared. 1997. *Guns, Germs, and Steel: The Fates of Human Societies.* New York: WW Norton & Company.

Durkheim, Emile. 1956. *Education and Sociology.* (S. Fox, Trans.) New York: The Free Press.

Durkheim, Emile. (1925) 1961. *Moral Education: A Study in the Theory and Application of the Sociology of Education.* (E. Wilson, and H. Schnurer, Trans.) New York: The Free Press.

Durkheim, Emile. 1953. *Sociology and Philosophy.* New York: The Free Press.

Durkheim, Emile. (1897) 1951. *Suicide: A Study in Sociology.* (J. Spaulding, and G. Simpson, Trans.) New York: The Free Press.

Durkheim, Emile. (1893) 1960. *The Division of Labor in Society.* (G. Simpson, Trans.) New York: The Free Press.

Durkheim, Emile. (1912) 1954. *The Elementary Forms of Religious Life.* (J. Swain, Trans.) New York: The Free Press.

Durkheim, Emile. (18950 1950. *The Rules of Sociological Method.* (S. A. Solovay, and J. Mueller, Trans.) New York: The Free Press.

Elias, Norbert. (1968) 2000. Postscript. In N. Elias, *The Civilizing Process* (pp. 449-483). Malden: Blackwell Publishing.

Elias, Norbert. (1939) 2000. *The Civilizing Process.* (E. Dunning, J. Goudsblom, S. Mennel, Eds., and E. Jephcott, Trans.) Malden: Blackwell Publishing.

Elias, Norbert. 1998. *The Norbert Elias Reader.* (J. Goudsblom, S. Mennell, Eds., E. Jephcott, R. van Krieken, J. Goudsblom, and S. Mennel, Trans.) Malden: Blackwell Publishing.

Elias, Norbert. (1970) 1978. *What is Sociology?* New York: Columbia University.

Elwell, Frank W. 1992. *The Evolution of the Future.* West Port: Praeger.

Elwell, Frank W. 1999. *Industrializing America: Understanding Contemporary Society Through Classical Sociological Analysis.* West Port: Praeger.

Elwell, Frank W. 2006. *Macrosociology: Four Modern Theorists.* Boulder: Paradigm Publishers.

Elwell, Frank W. 2013. *Sociocultural Systems: Principles of Structure and Change.* Canada: Athabasca University Press.

Engels, Friedrich. 1883. *Eulogy for Marx* (March 22). Retrieved March 22, 2008, from 1883: The Death of Karl Marx: http://www.marxists.org/archive/marx/works/1883/death/dersoz1.htm

Engels, Friedrich. 1890. Letter to J. Bloch in Königsberg
https://www.marxists.org/archive/marx/works/1890/letters/90_09_21.htm

Foster, John Bellamy. 2007. About Foster. (F. Elwell, Interviewer)

Foster, John Bellamy. 2002. *Ecology Against Capitalism.* New York: Monthly Review Press.

Foster, John Bellamy. 1998. Introduction to the 1998 Edition of Monopoly Capital. In H. Braverman, *Labor and Monopoly Capital: The Degradation of Work in the Twentieth Century* (pp. ix-xxiv). New York: Monthly Review Press.

Foster, John Bellamy. 2000. *Marx's Ecology: Materialism and Nature.* New York: Monthly Review Press.

Foster, John Bellamy. 2006. *Naked Imperialism: The U.S. Pursuit of Global Dominance.* New York: Monthly Review Press.

Foster, John Bellamy. 1999. *The Vulnerable Planet.* New York: Monthly Review Press.

Freund, Julien. 1968. *The Sociology of Max Weber.* New York: Vintage Books.

Gerth, Hans H., and C. Wright Mills. (1946) 1958. *From Max Weber: Essays in Sociology.* New York: Galaxy Books.

Gerth, Hans H., & Mills, C. Wright Mills 1953. *Character and Social Structure: The Psychology of Social Institutions.* New York: Harcourt, Brace & World, Inc.

Goudsblom, Johan, and Stephen Mennell. 1998. Idea and Individual. In N. Elias, J. Goudsblom, and S. Mennell (Eds.), *The Norbert Elias Reader* (pp. 5-7). Malden: Blackwell Publishing.

Harris, Marvin. 1968. *The Rise of Anthropological Theory.* New York: Crowell.

Harris, Marvin. 1971. *Culture, Man, and Nature: An Introduction to General Anthropology.* New York: Thomas Y. Crowell Company.

Harris, Marvin. 1974. *Cows, Pigs, Wars and Witches: The Riddles of Culture.* New York: Vintage Books.

Harris, Marvin. 1977. *Cannibals and Kings: The Origins of Cultures.* New York: Vintage Books.

Harris, Marvin. 1979. *Cultural Materialism: The Struggle for a Science of Culturre.* New York: Random House.

Harris, Marvin. 1981. *America Now: The Anthropology of a Changing Culture.* New York: Simon and Schuster.

Harris, Marvin. 1989. *Our Kind: Who We Are, Where We Came From, and Where We Are Going.* New York: HarperCollins.

Harris, Marvin. 1998. *Theories of Culture in Postmodern Times.* Walnut Creek: AltaMira Press.

Hirsch, J. (2003). *Portrait of America: A Cultural History of the Federal Writers' Project.* Chapel Hill: The University of North Carolina Press.

Horowitz, Irving L. 1983. *C. Wright Mills: An American Utopian.* New York: Free Press.

Johnson, Chalmers. 2004. Blowback: The Costs and Consequences of American Empire. New York: Holt.

Kuhn, Thomas. (1962) 1996. *The Structure of Scientific Revolutions* (3rd ed.). Chicago: University of Chicago Press.

Landis, David S. 1969. *The Unbound Prometheus: Technological Change and Industrial Development in Western Europe from 1750 to the Present.* London: Cambridge University Press.

Lenski, Gerhard. 1966. *Power and Privilege: A Theory of Social Stratification.* New York: Random House.

Lenski, Gerhard. 2005. *Ecological-Evolutionary Theory: Principles and Applications.* Colorado: Paradigm.

Lenski, Gerhard. 2003. About Lenski. (F. Elwell, Interviewer)

Lenski, Gerhard, and Jean Lenski. 1987. *Human Societies: An Introduction to Macrosociology (5th edition)*. New York: McGraw-Hill Book Company.

Lenski, Gerhard, Jean Lenski and Patrick Nolan 1991. *Human Societies: An Introduction to Macrosociology (7th edition)*. New York: McGraw-Hill Book Company.

Livingston, Michael G. 2000. *Harry Braverman: Marxist Activist and Theorist*. Retrieved (September 29). July 11, 2007, from Marxist History: http://www.marxists.org/history/etol/newspape/amersocialist/harry_bravermn .htm

Malthus, T. Robert. (1798) 2001. An Essay on the Principle of Population. In F. W. Elwell, *A Commentary on Malthus' 1798 Essay on the Principle of Population as Social Theory* (pp. 127-294). Lewiston: Mellen Press.

Marx, Karl. (1847) 1920. *The Poverty of Philosophy*. Translated by H. Quelch. Chicago: Charles H. Kerr and Company.

Marx, Karl. (1859) 1904. A Contribution to the Critique of Political Economy. Translated by M. L. Stone. Originally published as *Kritik der politischen Ökonomie*. Chicago: Charles H. Kerr and Company.

Marx, Karl. (1867) 1915. *Capital: A Critique of Political Economy*. Vol. 1, *The Process of Production of Capital*. Edited by Frederick Engels. Translated by Samuel Moore and Edward Aveling. Reprint, Chicago: Charles H. Kerr and Company. Originally published as *Das Kapital: Kritik der politischen Ökonomie,* vol. 1.

Marx, Karl. (1875) 2008. *Critique of the Gotha Program*. Reprint, Maryland: Wildside Press.

Marx, Karl. (1891) 1902. *Wage Labor and Capital*. Translated by Harriet E. Lathrop, M.D. New York: New York Labor News Company.

Marx, Karl. 1964. *Selected Writings in Sociology and Social Philosophy*. (T. Bottomore, Trans.) London: McGraw-Hill.

Marx, Karl. 1964b. *Early Writings*. Edited and Translated by T. B. Bottomore. New York: McGraw-Hill.

Marx, Karl, and Friedrich Engels. (1846) 1994. *The German Ideology, Part 1*. Edited by Lawrence H. Simon. Indianapolis: Hackett Publishing Company, Inc.

Marx, Karl, and Friedrich Engels. (1848) 1954. *The Communist Manifesto*. Edited and translated by Friedrich Engels. Reprint, Chicago: Henry Regnery Company. Originally published as *Manifest der Kommunistischen Partei*.

Marx, Karl, and Friedrich Engels. (1962). *Selected Works, 2 Vols*. Moscow: Foreign Language Publishing House.

McNeil, William. H. 1993. *A History of the Human Community*. New Jersey: Prentice Hall.

Mennel, Stephan. 2007. *A Biographical Sketch of Norbert Elias (1897-1990)*. Retrieved June 1, 2007, from The Norbert Elias Foundation: http://www.norberteliasfoundation.nl/index_NE.htm

Merton, Robert K. (1948) 1968. *Social Theory and Social Structure*. New York: The Free Press.

Merton, Robert K. (1994) 1996. "A Life of Learning." In R. K. Merton, & P. Sztompka (Ed.), *On Social Structure and Science* (pp. 339-359). Chicago: The University of Chicago Press.

Merton, Robert K. 1996. *On Social Structure and Science*. (P. Sztompka, Ed.) Chicago: The University of Chicago Press.

Mestrovic, Stjepan G. (1988) 1993. *Emile Durkheim and the Reformation of Sociology*. Boston: Rowman & Littlefiedl Publishers.

Mestrovic, Stjepan G. 1993. *The Barbarian Temperment: Toward a Postmodern Critical Theory*. New York: Routledge.

Mestrovic, Stjepan G. 1994. *The Balkanization of the West: The Confluence of Postmodernism and Postcommunism*. New York: Routledge.

Mestrovic, Stjepan G. 1997. *Postemotional Society*. London: Sage Publications.

Michels, Robert. 1915. *Political Parties: A Sociological Study of the Oligarchical Tendencies of Modern Democracy*. (P. Eden, and P. Cedar, Trans.) New York: The Free Press.

Mills, C. Wright. (1951) 1973. *White Collar: The American Middle Classes*. New York: Oxford University Press.

Mills, C. Wright. (1956) 1970. *The Power Elite*. New York: Oxford University Press.

Mills, C. Wright. 1958. *The Causes of World War Three*. London: Secker and Warburg.

Mills, C. Wright. (1959) 1976. *The Sociological Imagination*. New York: Oxford University Press.

Mills, C. Wright. 1960. *Listen Yankee: The Revolution in Cuba.* New York: Ballantine Books.

Mills, C. Wright. 2000. *C. Wright Mills: Letters and Autobiographical Writings.* (Kate Mills, & Pamela Mills, eds.) Berkeley: University of California Press.

Nisbet, Robert. (1953) 1970. "Preface" to *The Quest for Community: a Study in the Ethics of Order and Freedom* (pp. xxi-xxxv). San Francisco: ICS Press.

Nisbet, Robert. (1953) 1990. *The Quest for Community: a Study in the Ethics of Order and Freedom* (pp. xxi-xxxv). San Francisco: ICS Press.

Nisbet, Robert. 1975. *Twilight of Authority.* New York: Oxford University Press.

Nisbet, Robert. 1988. *The Present Age.* New York: Harper & Row, Publishers.

Parsons, Talcott. 1937. *The Structure of Social Action.* New York: The Free Press of Glencoe.

Perrin, Robert G. 1999. "Robert Alexander Nisbet." *The Proceedings of the American Philosophical Society. 143, No. 4*, pp. 695-710. New York: American Philosophical Society.

Petersen, William. 1990. "Malthus, the Reactionary Reformer." *American Scholar, 59* (2), 275-283.

Postman, Andrew. 2003. "Eulogy for Neil Postman." (October 8). New York.

Postman, Neil. (1982) 1994. *The Disappearance of Childhood.* New York: Random House.

Postman, Neil. 1985. *Amusing Ourselves to Death: Public Discourse in the Age of Show Business.* New York: Viking Penguin Inc.

Postman, Neil. 1992. *Technopoly: The Surrender of Culture to Technology.* New York: Alfred A. Knopf.

Postman, Neil. 1995. *The End of Education: Redefining the Value of School.* New York: Random House, Inc.

Ritzer, George. 1975. *Sociology: A Multiple Paradigm Science.* Boston: Allyn and Bacon, Inc.

Ritzer, George. 1993. *The McDonaldization of Society.* Newbury Park: Pine Forge Press.

Ritzer, George. 1995. *Expressing America: A Critique of the Global Credit Card Society.* Thousand Oaks: Pine Forge Press.

Ritzer, George. 2004. *The Globalization of Nothing.* Thousand Oaks: Pine Forge Press.

Ritzer, George. 2005. *Enchanting a Disenchanted World: Revolutionizing the Means of Consumption* (2nd ed.). Thousand Oaks: Pine Forge Press.

Ritzer, George. 2007. "About Ritzer." (F. Elwell, Interviewer. August 25).

Ritzer, George. (n.d.). *George Ritzer Home Page.* Retrieved August 20, 2007, from University of Maryland: http://www.bsos.umd.edu/socy/ritzer/

Rosen, Jay. 2003. *Neil Postman: A Civilized Man in a Century of Barbarism.* Retrieved July 2, 2007, from Salon.com: http://dir.salon.com/story/tech/ feature/2003/10/10/postman/index_np.html

Rubenstein, Richard L. 1975. *The Cunning of History: The Holocaust and the American Future.* New York: Harper and Row.

Salerno, Roger A. 2004. *Beyond the Enlightenment: Lives and Thoughts of Social Theorists.* West Port: Praeger.

Sanderson, Stephen K. 1990. *Social Evolutionism: A Critical History.* Oxford: Basil Blackwell.

Sanderson, Stephen K. 1999. *Social Transformations: A General Theory of Historical Development.* Lanham: Rowman & Littlefield Publishers, Inc.

Sanderson, Stephen K. 2007. *Evolutionism and Its Critics: Deconstructing and Reconstructing an Evolutionary Interpretation of Human Society.* Boulder: Paradigm Publishers.

Sanderson, Stephen K. 2007. "About Sanderson." (F. Elwell, Interviewer June 20.)

Sanderson, Stephen K., & Alderson, A. S. 2005. *World Societies: The Evolution of Human Social Life.* Boston: Pearson Education, Inc.

Seidenberg, R. (1932/1994). I Refuse to Serve. In R. F. Sayre, *American Lives: An Anthology of Autobiographical Writing* (pp. 504-514). Madison, Wisconsin: The University of Wisconsin Press.

Seidenberg, R. (1950). *Post-Historic Man: An Inquiry.* Chapel Hill: The University of North Carolina Press.

Seidenberg, R. (1961). *Anatomy of the Future.* Chapel Hill: The University of North Carolina Press.

Shirer, William L. 1960. *The Rise and fall of the Third Reich: A History of Nazi Germany* (Vol. I and II). New York: Simon and Schuster.

Short, RV. 1998. "Malthus, A Prophet Without Honour, (Thomas Robert Malthus, author of Essay on the Principle of Population)." *The Lancet*, 1676.

Smith, Adam. (1776/2000). *An Inquiry into the Nature and Causes of the Wealth of Nations*. Retrieved March 19, 2008, from The Library of Economics and Liberty: http://www.econlib.org/LIBRARY/Smith/smWN.html

Strate, Lance. 2003. "Post(modern)man, or Neil Postman as a Postmodernist. " Retrieved July 1, 2007, from Neil Postman Online: http://web.archive.org/ web/20031203084041/http://jonathandruy.com/nptribute/51-2-strate.pdf

Traxel, D. (1980). *An American Saga: The Life and Times of Rockwell Kent*. New York: Harper & Row, Publishers.

Wang, Randy. 1995. *Udana 86-87: A Parable*. Retrieved March 20, 2008, from The Blind Men and the Elephant: http://www.cs.princeton. edu/~rywang/Berkeley /258/parable.html

Wallace, Alfred R. 1905. *My Life*. London: Chapman and Hall.

Wallerstein, Immanuel. 1974. *The Modern World-System: Capitalist Agriculture and the Origins of the European World-Economy in the Sixteenth Century*. New York: Academic Press.

Wallerstein, Immanuel. 1980. *The Modern World-System II: Mercantilism and the Consolidation of the European World-Economy, 1600-1750*. New York: Academic Press.

Wallerstein, Immanuel. 1989. *The Modern World-System III: The Second Era of Great Expasnion of the Capitalist World-Economy, 1730-1840*. New York: Academic Press.

Wallerstein, Immanuel. 1998. *Utopistics: or, Historical Choices for the Twentyfirst Century*. New York: WW Norton.

Wallerstein, Immanuel. 1999. *The End of the World as We Know It*. Minneapolis: University of Minnesota Press.

Wallerstein, Immanuel. 2000. *The Essential Wallerstein*. New York: The new Press.

Wallerstein, Immanuel. 2003. *The Decline of American Power*. New York: The New Press.

Weber, Max. (1903-1917) 1949. *The Methodology of the Social Sciences.* (E. Shils, H. Finch, Eds., E. Shills, and H. Finch, Trans.) New York: Free Press.

Weber, Max. (1904) 1958. *The Protestant Ethic and the Spirit of Capitalism.* (T. Parsons, Trans.) New York: The Citadel Press.

Weber, Max. (1921) 1968. *Economy and Society.* (G. Roth, C. Wittich, Eds., G. Roth, and C. Wittich, Trans.) New York: Bedminster Press.

Weber, M. (1925) 1954. *Max Weber on Law in Economy and Society.* (E. Shils, and M. Rheinstein, Trans.) New York: Simon and Schuster.

Weber, Max. (1927) 2003. *General Economic History.* (F. Knight, Trans.) Mineola, New York: Dover Publications, Inc.

Weber, Max. (1962). *Basic Concepts in Sociology by Max Weber.* (H. Secher, Ed., and H. Secher, Trans.) New York: The Citadel Press.

Weber, Max. (1946) 1958. Essays in Sociology. In M. Weber, H. Gerth, and C. W. Mills (Eds.), *From Max Weber.* New York: Oxford University Press.

Whitehead, Alfred North (1931) 1963. *Adventures in Ideas.* New York: Simon & Schuster Inc.

Winch, Donald. 1987. *Malthus.* Oxford: Oxford University Press.

Made in United States
North Haven, CT
14 August 2025

71656001R00220